The Peasant Family
and Rural Development
in the Yangzi Delta,
1350–1988

PHILIP C. C. HUANG

The Peasant Family and Rural Development in the Yangzi Delta, 1350–1988

STANFORD UNIVERSITY PRESS
Stanford, California
1990

Stanford University Press
Stanford, California
© 1990 by the Board of Trustees of the
Leland Stanford Junior University

Printed in the United States of America

Published with the assistance of the
National Endowment for the Humanities

CIP data appear at the end of the book

Preface

The documentary materials for this book were collected mainly in 1977, at the same time as for my earlier North China book, and field research was carried out mainly between 1983 and 1985, as part of a larger collaborative project on Huayang township (near Shanghai), funded by the National Endowment for the Humanities and sponsored by the Committee for Scholarly Communication with the People's Republic of China, of the U.S. National Academy of Sciences. A final field visit was made in 1988.

My first debt is to the 1930s and 1940s ethnographers—Fei Xiaotong, Hayashi Megumi, and researchers of the South Manchurian Railway Company (Mantetsu)—who did the detailed studies of eight delta villages. They have shown me the up-close reality of delta peasant life as no conventional historical documents can. One of the surveys, of the Huayangqiao villages in Songjiang county, near Shanghai, formed the starting baseline for my own field research.

The ethnographic method I adopted was patterned closely after the Mantetsu researchers' study of customary practices in six villages of North China, undertaken at the same time as the study of the delta villages. Their method is particularly well-suited to a research environment involving short periods of access: intensive interviews with two to four selected informants at one time, concentrating on selected topics, but ready at all times to follow out in detail any surprises that emerge. Concrete questions in search of concrete answers is of the essence in such research.

A word should be said about the special research environment of present-day China. To go beyond the standard briefings by the political cadres, I have found especially helpful the testimonies of peasants, who are usually little concerned with ideology. Technical cadres, who have no particular stake in the current political line, are another important source, and statisticians, bound by the highly centralized requirements of the State Statistical Bureau for consistency and accuracy, provide their own check on the policy line. The informants and the topics of the 101 half-day interviews, which form the backbone for the post-1949 half of the book, are listed in the References.

My second great debt is to my fellow American researchers on the Huayang project. Joseph Esherick, who concentrated on collective action and industry, Linda Grove on the town, and Elizabeth Perry on politics, were constant sources of inspiration and support throughout our research. Although they worked mainly in the commune seat and I the village, and although I have not drawn on the empirical material they gathered (except for one section of Chapter 12 on rural industry), I owe more to them than can be enumerated here.

Lü Zuoxie, the leader of the Chinese team of the project from Nanjing University, and Lu Aogen, the head of the Foreign Affairs Office of Songjiang county, made all the local arrangements for the research. Needless to say, nothing could have been accomplished without them. Luo Lun was a member of the team during the first summer of the research, until his health prevented him from continuing. Yan Xuexi and Chen Zhongping, who worked respectively mainly on industry with Esherick and on the town with Grove, were the other members of the Chinese team. To all of them I owe much in the way of ideas and information. In Huayangqiao, my greatest debt is to Mr. He Yonglong, former party branch secretary and brigade head—he knows more about the subject than I could ever hope to.

Our research team planned originally to publish a collection of interviews and source materials along the lines of the Niida Noboru–edited set based on the Mantetsu's study of six North China villages (KC). The tapes of the interview and verbatim transcripts of them, the selections intended for inclusion in the collection, originals of the tables, and detailed household-by-household surveys and questionnaires are all in the possession of Professor Lü at Nanjing University. Time and a change in the publishing environment in China might yet permit those materials to be published for the use of other researchers.

For the pre-twentieth century part of the book, the Yangzi delta affords exceptionally rich documentation in standard historical sources, especially local gazetteers and agricultural treatises. Those have permitted a more precise reconstruction of long-term rural change than I was able to do for the North China plain. Of the enormous body of secondary scholarship on the delta region, I have learned the most from the works of Wu Chengming and Xu Xinwu, whose respective works on commerce and handicrafts shaped importantly my view of how the delta peasants adapted to the big socioeconomic changes of the region.

In this book as in the North China study, I have adhered to a preference for telling the larger story of structural change with a spotlight on the most basic information about the lives and choices of common people. I have also remained partial to a research procedure that proceeds from empirical reality to theory and back to reality, rather than the reverse. Where I have departed from my earlier approach is in crossing the great 1949 divide to follow the changes down to the 1980s, and in the interregional comparisons between the Yangzi delta and the North China plain; my hope is that each of the two halves helps to illuminate the other.

I have benefited much from working with my graduate students. The dissertations of Lynda Bell, Kathy Walker, and Honming Yip, and research papers by Cheng Hong, Li Rongchang, and Lu Hanchao are cited at relevant places in the text. Others, whose work is not cited, also contributed through our seminar discussions, which always helped to sharpen my own thinking. Ben Elman and Francesca Bray provided helpful suggestions on portions of the manuscript. Joseph Esherick, Kathryn Bernhardt, Myron Cohen, and Ernest Young gave me tough yet constructive comments that reshaped the manuscript substantially. Kathryn, especially, cheerfully helped me through several rewrites of parts of the final manuscript, as well as extended discussions of some of the knottiest issues. The printed text has benefited greatly from the work of Barbara Mnookin, who has shown me again what a difference expert copyediting can make for a book.

Finally, readers from outside Chinese studies should note that 1 standard *mu* equals ⅙ of an acre (or ¹⁄₁₅ of a hectare), 1 standard catty equals 1.1 pounds (or 0.5 kilogram), and 1 standard *shi* equals roughly 160 catties.

Los Angeles, California   P.H.
August 1989

Contents

Appendixes

References

Tables

APPENDIXES

Maps

The Peasant Family
and Rural Development
in the Yangzi Delta,
1350–1988

CHAPTER I

Introduction

Peasant farming for subsistence-level returns persisted in China's advanced Yangzi delta area through six centuries of vigorous commercialization and urban development between 1350 and 1950, and three decades of collectivization and agricultural modernization between 1950 and 1980. Only in the 1980s did transformative development begin to come to the delta countryside, to result in substantial margins above subsistence in peasant incomes. The focus of this book is on the hows and whys of the persistence of the peasant condition of subsistence farming in the delta, and the hows and whys of its recent change. My emphasis is on the livelihood of peasants, not the gross output of the whole economy or the average per capita income of the entire population. The spotlight is on socially and spatially specific development and nondevelopment, and what that story tells about Chinese history as a whole and social science theories on peasant societies and economies in general.

THE CLASSICAL VIEW: SMITH AND MARX

Adam Smith (1723–90) and Karl Marx (1818–83), despite their obvious differences, shared the belief that commercialization would transform the peasant economy.* For Smith, free competition in the market, joined with the individual's search for enrichment, would bring a division of labor, accumulation, and innovation, and, with them, capitalist development. For Marx, similarly, the rise of a commodity economy would usher in the age of capital.

Marx further equated peasant farming with "petty" production,

---

*Smith did not use the term "peasant economy," to be sure, but there is no question that he saw precapitalist agriculture as stagnant and backward, in large measure because of government-imposed constraints on free trade (Smith 1976 [1775–76], esp. 1: 401–19; 2: 182–209).

and capitalism with large-scale wage labor–based production. The development of a commodity economy would be accompanied by capitalistic "relations of production" between those who owned the means of production and their proletarian workers. If Smith did not pay nearly the same amount of attention to the social relations of capitalist production, he shared the same assumption to a considerable degree: the division of labor and specialization would open the way to capital "improvements" and economies of scale (Smith 1976 [1775–76], 1: esp. 7–16.)*

Smith and Marx, of course, based their shared assumptions largely on the English experience. There was, after all, the empirical example of England's enclosure movement and the eighteenth-century agricultural revolution in which peasant farms gave way with commercialization to large-scale wage labor–based capitalist farms. Thus reinforced, these assumptions came in time to hold the force of a paradigm, considered almost too obviously true to require any discussion or comment.

The same assumptions reigned supreme even in revolutionary Russia and China. Lenin drew directly from Marx to argue for the interlinked development in prerevolutionary Russia of a commodity economy and the peasants' social differentiation into capitalistic kulak farmers and rural proletarians. In Russia no less than in England, from Lenin's point of view, peasant economy could only be a stagnant and precommercial economy, and commercialization could only be accompanied by capitalist development and capitalistic social stratification (Lenin 1956 [1907]). His successor, Stalin, saw "socialist" collectivization as a way to avoid the social ills of capitalism and still modernize the peasant economy. The collective ownership of the means of production would overcome the problems of capitalist stratification, and collectivized agriculture would transform peasant petty production into efficient, large-scale farming.

Mao Zedong was to adopt the same formulation of the problem and the same choice. Socialist collectivization was seen as the only possible alternative to market-driven capitalist development. No serious consideration was given to the possibility that there might be other paths to rural development besides capitalism and socialism. Nor, by the same token, that subsistence farming might persist despite commercialization or collectivization (Mao 1955a,b).

---

*Though Smith did observe that small proprietors would make highly industrious farmers (p. 441), his point was not that small-scale farming would be more productive than large-scale, but that proprietary farming would enjoy superior incentives to tenant ("farmer") farming (p. 418).

Historical studies in Maoist China were dominated by the classical model outlined above. "Feudal economy" was equated with precommercial "natural economy," and capitalist economy with commercialized large-scale production. The distinctive Chinese twist to the model was the notion of "incipient capitalism." On this analysis, the "sprouting of capitalism" had begun in China at about the same time as in early modern England and Europe, and but for the disruptive intrusion of Western imperialism, China would have followed the capitalist path of development. In this way, Chinese history was fitted into the Stalinist five-modes-of-production formula, by which all societies are bound to move through the primitive, slave, feudal, capitalist, and socialist stage. At the same time, Western imperialism was condemned for its destructive impact on China. (The alternative suggestion, that Western imperialism brought capitalist development to China, was unacceptable to most Chinese patriots.)

Under the broad theoretical rubric above, the first generation of postrevolutionary scholars of China's agrarian history focused, first of all, on commercial development during the Ming and Qing. Powerful studies were undertaken to identify and quantify the major commodities traded, with the spotlight on those goods that were traded across long distances, or between countryside and town, as part of an integrated "national market," thought to be characteristic of capitalist development. The results of those researches, begun in the 1950s, finally began to appear in print in the 1980s.[*]

Other scholars of the first postrevolutionary generation searched for the rise of the capitalist relations of wage labor predicted by the classical model. In the official ideology of the 1950s and 1960s, production relations were considered the determinative half in Marx's original pair of factors ("production relations" and "productive forces") shaping human history. If "feudal" relations between landlords and tenants could be shown to have given way to capitalist relations between employer and wage worker, it was thought, that would constitute a prima facie case for the coming of capitalist development. From this analytical frame, much empirical evidence was marshaled on the coming of wage labor–based production in the Ming and Qing (Zhongguo renmin daxue 1967; Nanjing daxue 1980).[†]

[*]Wu Chengming 1985 is the outstanding study on the development of a commodity economy in the Qing.
[†]Li Wenzhi et al. 1983 is the crowning achievement in scholarship on the spread of rural wage-labor relations.

In the reformist 1980s, the spotlight shifted to developments in the "productive forces," reflecting a new ideological emphasis on productive forces, not production relations, as the determinant of historical development. A new generation of scholars began looking for evidence of expanding productivity alongside commercialization. In the widespread disillusionment with collective agriculture, they turned back to what they considered the only other alternative: markets and capitalism. Proof that agricultural development occurred alongside commercialization in the Ming and Qing would argue for a renewal of the approach in present-day China. The outstanding representative of this new academic tendency has even argued that the overall economic development of the Yangzi delta in the Qing exceeded that of "early modern" England (Li Bozhong 1985a,b, 1984).

The new Chinese scholarship on economic development in Qing China has found echoes in American scholarship. One line of thought gaining increasing influence among neo-Smithian American scholars maintains that the changes accompanying the expansion of markets in the Qing period should be seen as "early modern" development, similar to what happened in England and Western Europe during the 1500–1800 period. This view would incorporate China into a universal modernization model, and have Qing history taught as China's "early modern" history.*

There is much to commend in the incipient capitalism scholarship. To my mind, it has succeeded in demonstrating beyond question the degree to which the Yangzi delta was commercialized during the period 1350–1850, in a process centering around what I term in this book "the cotton revolution." It has also documented the considerable changes in the social relations of production during the Qing. The substantial rise of wage labor–based production in both countryside and town, agriculture and industry, in Qing China is now beyond question as well.

But the new scholarship has failed to document improved productivity or income per unit labor. Despite the vigorous commercialization of the Ming and Qing, small-scale family farming near subsistence levels persisted down to the eve of the Revolution. As I have

*Not yet fully articulated in print at the time of this writing, the "early modern" view of Qing China is implicit in a number of works, most notably Rowe 1984. Where this line of thinking parts company with the new scholarship in China is on the issue of imperialism. The "early modern" view leads easily to the position that imperialism stimulated further commercialization and development (Faure 1989; Rawski 1989). Such an apologetic view is of course unacceptable to most patriotic Chinese scholars.

shown elsewhere, the managerial farms that emerged with commercialization on the North China plain between the 1700s and 1930s resembled capitalist enterprises only in their use of wage labor: they clearly failed to generate any real advances in labor productivity, whether through economies of scale, increased capital use, or technological improvement (Huang 1985). In the Yangzi delta, too, subsistence farming persisted with no significant improvement in labor productivity. Indeed, by the twentieth century, small-peasant farming at subsistence levels there had driven out wage labor–based large-scale farming, which had been quite prevalent until the late Ming.

The simple fact is, the predictions abstracted from the English experience by Smith and Marx did not happen in China—or, for that matter, in most of the rest of the Third World. Family farming at subsistence levels not only persisted through the vigorous commercialization that came with the age of imperialism and the formation of an integrated "world economy"; it is still very much alive in many parts of the world. Even in continental Europe, especially France, small-scale peasant farming persisted much longer than in England (Brenner 1982).

What we need to do is to separate out commercialization from transformative development. The delta record shows that peasant economy can persist despite very high levels of commercialization. Or conversely, that peasant production can sustain a very high level of market growth. The classical assumption that commercialization inevitably brings capitalist development is simply wrong.

TWO MODERN VIEWS: CHAYANOV AND SCHULTZ

Two major schools of thought on peasant economy today are represented by A. V. Chayanov (1888–1939) and Theodore Schultz (b. 1902). Both depart from Smith and Marx by acknowledging the persistence of the peasant economy in the face of the modern market economy. The question is how and why. And if commercialization alone fails to work transformative change, then how is the peasant economy to be transformed?

Contrary to both Marx/Lenin and Smith, Chayanov maintained that peasants would continue to behave differently from capitalists even within the context of a commercialized national economy. The peasant family farm, he pointed out, differs from a capitalist enterprise in two major respects: it relies on its own labor, rather than hired labor, and it produces mainly to satisfy the family's own consumption needs, rather than to maximize profits on the market.

This kind of a production unit cannot be expected to exhibit the same market behavior as a profit-maximizing capitalist enterprise. It is unable to compute the costs of wages against returns, for it hires no labor; it is unable to weigh unit production costs against returns, for its inputs, the family's entire year's labor plus capital inputs, and its output, the year's total harvest, are nondivisible lumps. Its search for optimization takes the form of an equilibrium at the margins between the satisfaction of consumption needs and the drudgery of labor, not between profits and costs.* For this reason, Chayanov insisted that the "peasant economy" forms a distinctive system, obeying its own logic and principles (Chayanov 1986 [1925]: esp. 1–28, 70–89).

Such an economy undergoes cyclical "demographic differentiation," rather than the social differentiation leading to capitalism that Lenin envisioned. In evidence, Chayanov pointed to Russia's peasant economy, where in his view social differentiation resulted not from the peasantry's stratification into kulaks and rural proletarians as commercialization proceeded, but from the changing laborer/consumer ratio in the family cycle. A young couple without children enjoys the most favorable ratio until it bears nonworking, consuming children. When the children come of age and enter into production, a new cycle begins (ibid., chap. 1).

The way to transform Russia's peasant economy, Chayanov believed, was neither Stalinist collectivization nor capitalist free-market production. Instead, the peasants should voluntarily band together in small cooperatives, which would at once overcome the problems of peasant petty production and avoid the bureaucratic encumbrances of large-scale collective agriculture, along with the social stratification and monopolistic tendencies of capitalism (Shanin 1986: 7–9).

Chayanov was silenced by force under Stalinist rule (Shanin 1986; Solomon 1977), and his legacy might have died with him, were it not for the gigantic fact of the persistence of the peasant economy in much of the Third World to this very day. The carriers of the Chayanovian tradition, at first, were mainly anthropologists studying obscure corners of the preindustrial world. "Substantivists," as

---

*Chayanov dubbed the resulting level of intensity in family labor use the "measure of self-exploitation of peasant labor" (p. 72), a rather unfortunate choice of words that has given rise to much misunderstanding: the word "exploitation" has led Marxists and non-Marxists alike to associate the concept somehow with the notion of the "extraction" of the "surplus value" of labor, the classical Marxist meaning of "exploitation." Chayanov himself intended no such meaning (pp. 72–89). It simply makes no sense in any case to speak of a family extracting the surplus value of its own labor.

they came to be known in the anthropological discipline (Dalton 1969), pointed out that the peasant economy simply did not operate by the assumptions of the modern market economy. In the United States, this tradition came to be represented by the works of Karl Polanyi (Polanyi et al. 1957) and, more recently, Teodor Shanin (1972) and James Scott (1976). Their theme is the difference between the peasant economy and the capitalist market economy.*

Although Adam Smith himself saw the peasant economy as pre-commercial, there has always been among his followers the contra-dictory impulse to claim universal applicability for classical eco-nomics, as well suited to peasant economies as to developed market economies. The pervasive commercialization of peasant economies in the Third World during the twentieth century has helped to en-courage this impulse. At the same time, the American experience, in which the family farm remained the major social form through the commercialization and mechanization of agriculture, came to serve as an alternative model to the classical English experience. Its ex-ample has led many to forecast a "green revolution" for the Third World peasant economies with the coming of modern farm inputs and increased market exchange.

Nobel Laureate Theodore Schultz has lent systematic theoretical support to this vision. His contention is simple enough: a competi-tive market operates in peasant economies no less than in capitalist economies. Factor markets operate so well that "there are com-paratively few significant inefficiencies in the allocation of the fac-tors of production" (Schultz 1964: 37). In the labor market, for ex-ample, "each laborer who wishes and who is capable of doing some useful work is employed" (p. 40). Moreover, "there are, as a rule, no significant inequalities in the rate of return to investment among the factors of production employed in traditional agriculture" (p. 72).

Peasants in these economies are no less "rational," in short, than capitalist entrepreneurs. They will respond to market incentives and opportunities to maximize their profit and optimize their use of re-sources. Stagnation in traditional agriculture, therefore, results not from the lack of peasant enterprise and industry, or of a free and competitive market economy, but from diminishing marginal re-turns to traditional investments. The peasant producer ceases to in-vest only when it no longer pays to do so.

*In China, ideas similar to Chayanov's notions are embodied in the theory of "small-peasant economy" (*xiaonong jingji*). For Xu Xinwu (1981a,b), the key to the peasant economy is the unity of farming and industry in the peasant household, where "the men farm and the women weave." This unity accounts for the great tenac-ity and resistance to commercialization and capitalist change.

What is needed to transform the traditional economy is modern inputs at reasonable cost. Once modern technological factors can be made available at a price that would make their adoption profitable, peasant producers can be expected to adopt them with little hesitation, for they are, in the final analysis, profit maximizers no less than capitalist man. It follows, then, that the way to transform traditional agriculture is not to tamper with the peasant family form of production organization and the free-market system, as the socialist countries have done, but rather to ensure the availability of modern factors of production at reasonable cost (ibid., esp. chap. 8). In this way, Schultz retains the core of Adam Smith's original vision of the transformative powers of the market, while taking into account the persistence of peasant farming.

This Schultzian view of peasant economy gained considerable influence in the reformist China of the 1980s. Marketized peasant family farming came to be seen in some quarters of the leadership as the social basis for economic development. The ideological emphasis shifted from the supposed backwardness of family farming to the enterprising achievements of profit-seeking peasants stimulated by market incentives. Much propaganda surrounded the so-called "ten thousand yuan households" of the reformed countryside. Members of the State Council's Center for Rural Development even argued that increased agricultural productivity from the restoration of marketized family farming was the cutting edge for the development of China's national economy in the post-Mao era (Fazhan yanjiusuo 1985: 1–22; Fazhan yanjiusuo zonghe ketizu 1987; Zhongguo nongcun fazhan wenti yanjiuzu 1985–86). Theodore Schultz himself was an honored guest of China's top leaders (*Renmin ribao*, May 17, 1988). The prescriptive model differs from Adam Smith's in picturing the peasant farm and not the capitalist farm as the basic social unit for transformative rural development, but it remains the same as the classical model because it attributes the dynamic for rural transformation to market incentives above all else.

BEYOND SCHULTZ AND CHAYANOV

Both Schultz and Chayanov, of course, did what theorists normally do: isolate and simplify selected variables in order to highlight logical connections not otherwise apparent. Their contributions consist in clarifying the kinds of relationships outlined above. But it would be misguided for anyone to try to argue that China's reality corresponds completely to either theoretical model. We know, for example, that in the period 1350–1950 a fairly developed labor market took shape in the Yangzi delta, such that about one-third of the peasant households hired out to some extent, while a third hired in some labor. It would be counterfactual to project onto late imperial China Chayanov's abstract model of peasant households producing entirely with their own labor. At the same time, even in the twentieth century, the delta's labor market was limited largely to day-labor. There was hardly any market for long-term labor, or for women and child laborers, even though they had long since come to be involved greatly in rural production. It would be equally counterfactual to imagine for the Yangzi delta Schultz's perfect factor market encompassing all available labor. The fact that cruder followers of Schultz, just as of Chayanov, have insisted on equating empirical reality with what had been for the masters themselves mainly convenient abstractions for the purpose of clarifying certain theoretical relationships has given rise to much unnecessary debate between the two "schools." The actual situation in the delta was a mixture of the two, in which both sets of logic obtained.

But it is not enough to say just that the delta's peasant economy contained elements of both models; we need to understand the hows and whys of the historical *process* of commercialization itself. On this question, neither Schultz nor Chayanov can be of much help. Schultz takes as a given a perfectly competitive factors market in a peasant economy; he has nothing to say about the development of such a market. Chayanov, similarly, pictures the peasant economy and the capitalist market economy essentially as separate entities; he does not consider the possibility of commercialization generated from within the peasant economy itself and the effects this might have on peasant production.

The easiest answer to the question is to picture a transition from Chayanov's model to Schultz's: the peasant farm producing to meet household consumption needs gives way with commercialization to the enterprising farmer producing for profit on the market. The problem with such a picture, however, is that it takes us back to the classical model, with its simple promise of a peasant economy leading to a capitalist market economy. It would, in fact, be essentially the same as Marx's original scheme of "simple commodity production." While useful descriptively for its spotlighting of small-peasant commercial production and, by extension, petty nickel-and-dime transactions, that scheme makes the mistake of assuming that small-peasant commodity production must give way with increased commercialization to capitalist commodity production (Marx 1967

[1867], 1: esp. 71–83; Mandel 1968, 1: 65–68). The historical record, however, is that simple commodity production persisted and became ever more elaborate in the delta during the Ming and Qing without giving way to a capitalist economy. It even made a dramatic comeback in China in the 1980s, after three decades of collectivized agriculture and rigid control of rural commerce.

Where this book departs from all previous analyses is in the thesis that commercialization in the delta's rural economy was driven not by Schultz's logic but by Chayanov's, even though Chayanov himself had intended his analysis to apply mainly to the precommercial family farm. Chayanov had pointed out how a family farm might behave differently from a capitalist enterprise when placed under population pressure: a capitalist farm will stop putting in labor when its marginal returns drop below the market wage, for that would mean a negative return. A peasant family farm, on the other hand, will continue to put in labor so long as household consumption needs are not met, even if the marginal returns to that labor sink well below prevailing market wages (Chayanov 1986 [1925]: 113–17). This behavior, I suggest, can be understood and illustrated in different ways. The peasant family might continue to put in labor even when its actual marginal returns are very low simply because the family has no concept of marginal returns to marginal labor input, since it sees its labor input and harvest for the year as essentially a nondivisible lump. Subsistence pressures from undersized farms can drive such labor input to very high levels until, logically, its marginal product approaches zero. Or, if a peasant family has more labor than its farm needs under optimal conditions, and if that labor is unable (or unwilling) to find alternative employment in an already oversupplied labor market, it would be perfectly "rational" for the family to put this "surplus" household labor to work for very low returns, since such labor has little or no "opportunity cost." Finally, even without population pressure, the peasant family might work for returns lower than the equivalent of market wages for the simple reason that the incentive for working on one's own farm is different from that of working for another as hired labor. Contemporary America abounds in examples of the small mom-and-pop business that survives and thrives by the use of family labor of lower cost than hired labor.

In North China, as I showed in my earlier study (Huang 1985: esp. 8–9), peasant families generally tolerated lower marginal returns than did managerial farms relying on hired labor. The managerial farm using hired labor could adjust its labor supply to optimal levels.

The family farm, however, could not hire and fire labor at will, and had to live with labor in excess of what was optimal. Such relative surplus labor,* when it was unable or unwilling to find an outlet in off-farm employment, often worked for very low marginal returns in order to meet household consumption needs. That kind of labor was what sustained much of the commercialization of the North China peasant economy during the Qing. In the Yangzi delta, as will be seen, a similar kind of logic was at work, in which peasant households responded to pressures on the land by resorting to ever greater use of auxiliary household labor for low returns.

We have long known that population increase and commercialization were the two big changes in the Ming-Qing delta countryside, but the influence of the classical model of Smith and Marx has directed our attention away from searching out the interconnections between the two, even though they were contemporary with one another. We have treated them as separate and independent processes, looking only for transformative changes in connection with commercialization, and subsistence pressures in connection with population increase. We have not thought to look to population increase to understand commercialization, and commercialization to understand population increase. My suggestion is that those two processes were in fact intimately connected. Population increase, acting through the distinctive properties of the peasant family farm, was what drove commercialization in the Ming-Qing Yangzi delta, even as it was itself made possible by commercialization.

GROWTH WITHOUT DEVELOPMENT

Before considering further the dynamic behind the process of commercialization in the delta, we need to distinguish three patterns of agrarian economic change: first, simple *intensification*, in which output or output value expands at the same rate as labor input; second, *involution*, in which the total output expands, but at the cost of diminished marginal returns per workday; and third, *development*, in which output expands faster than labor input, to result in increased marginal output per workday. Put differently, with intensification labor productivity remains constant, with involution it diminishes at the margins, and with development it expands.

Agricultural intensification is driven by population increase (Boserup 1965), but at a given level of technology, population pressure

---

*To be distinguished from absolute surplus labor, of zero value, against which Schultz argued (1964: chap. 4) so vehemently.

will sooner or later lead to diminished marginal returns for further labor intensification, or what I, following Clifford Geertz (1963), term involution.* The degree to which a peasant economy will involute depends very much on the relative balance between its population and available resources. Intense population pressure, relative to resources, can lead to increasing quantities of surplus labor and intense subsistence pressures, the conditions under which extreme involution can take place. In contrast to intensification and involution, development generally occurs with not just increased population pressure, but an efficient division of labor, increased capital inputs per unit labor, or technological advance.

In the Euro-American experience, agrarian change in the early modern and modern periods was generally accompanied by expansion in both absolute output and output per unit labor. Therefore it has not seemed so important to distinguish what might be termed simple "growth," with expanding output, from "development," with improved labor productivity. For China, however, the distinction is crucial, graphically demonstrated by the experience of the first three decades after the Revolution, during which total agricultural output expanded threefold, but labor productivity and per capita income improved little, if at all.

This book will show that the postrevolutionary pattern was in fact a telescoped version of the same pattern in the six centuries preceding the Revolution, during which agricultural output expanded enough to keep pace with dramatic population growth, but chiefly by intensification, and involution.† Productivity and income per labor day either stagnated, as in intensification, or shrank, as in involution.

Involution must be distinguished from modern economic development, for it does not lead to transformative change for the countryside. Small-peasant production at subsistence levels persists, becoming ever more elaborated with commercialization, intensified cropping, and household industry. As this pattern of change advances,

---

*My usage of the term "involution" differs from Geertz's in several respects. Geertz speaks of diminished marginal returns with involution, but not of "involutionary growth" and "involutionary commercialization," which are central to my analysis. Geertz identifies "agricultural involution" only with wet-rice production; I do not. Also, I believe Geertz is mistaken to portray wet-rice yields as almost infinitely inflatable with further labor input. Delta rice yields topped out by the Song, until the introduction of modern inputs. Subsequent involution took the form mainly of the switch to more-labor-intensive commercial crops, rather than further intensification of rice.

†Perkins 1969 is the authoritative study of agricultural intensification in the Ming and Qing.

INTRODUCTION 13

peasant production, far from giving way to large-scale production, actually comes to obstruct the development of wage labor–based production by virtue of its ability to sustain labor input at returns that are below market wages. And far from giving way to labor-saving capitalized production, it actually obstructs development in that direction by pushing change in the direction of lower-cost labor intensification and involution.

It should be clear that involutionary change as outlined here can permit real, though limited, expansions in annual household incomes from the fuller employment of household labor, or what I term *involutionary growth*, something not noted in Clifford Geertz's original notion of "agricultural involution." Agricultural labor everywhere is normally seasonal labor and way underemployed by the standards of eight-hour, year-round urban employment. Added employment for diminished returns per workday at the margins can still increase the household's total annual income. This is similar to the *growth without development* that characterized the collectivized decades: though cash payments per labor day remained little changed, household annual incomes expanded because of the massive entrance of women into remunerated farmwork and the added number of days worked per year by the farmworkers.

I believe the distinction between growth *without* development and growth *with* development is a critically important one for comprehending the persistent poverty and underdevelopment of the Chinese countryside.* The modernization of agriculture as we know it in the developed countries consists above all in improved productivity and incomes per workday. That is what has allowed a relatively tiny group of farmers to feed an entire population. It is also what has freed agriculturalists from production at the barest margins of subsistence. In the terms of this book, those changes form the core of the meaning of "rural development."

INVOLUTIONARY COMMERCIALIZATION

Involutionary growth in the Yangzi delta during the Ming and Qing did not take the form simply of further labor intensification in rice cultivation. Rice yields in the delta, it turns out, were not indefi-

*This is not to say that no examples can be found of development, where returns per workday expanded. I will have occasion to refer to a number of such instances. But given the long-term population/resource squeeze in the delta, growth with development almost always gave way to involutionary growth, when most gains in productivity were eaten up by continual expansions in the agricultural labor force.

nitely inflatable in the manner suggested by Clifford Geertz's notion of "agricultural involution." They had already reached something of a plateau by the southern Song and early Ming. There was little or no expansion thereafter until the introduction of modern inputs after 1950. Here mounting population pressure on the land had to find different outlets.

What happened was an increasing switch to more-labor-intensive commercial crops, especially cotton and mulberries (for silk). We have not in the past understood properly the nature of this switch. I will show that those cash crops were produced by a greater use of labor for higher total values of output per unit land but lower average returns per labor day. The growth of commercialized "sideline" household handicrafts based on those commercial crops was a part of this process. The sideline activities generally brought lower returns per workday than "mainline" farming. They were pursued to some extent by adult males in their spare time, but to a far greater extent by women, children, and the elderly, for whose labor there was little or no market outlet.

One of the consequences of a high level of *involutionary commercialization* sustained by *the familization of rural production* was that family farming outcompeted wage labor–based managerial agriculture, for the simple reason that managerial enterprises had to rely mainly on adult male labor paid at prevailing market wages. A family farm that used spare-time and auxiliary household labor at net returns well below the prevailing market wages could sustain much higher levels of labor intensification, and hence higher gross returns from the farm, as well as higher prices (or "rent") for the land. It was a pattern Chayanov hinted at when he analyzed the competitive coexistence of family and capitalist farms (Chayanov 1986 [1925]: 115–17, 235–37; see also Huang 1985).

The same logic applied to the handicraft industries. The crucial difference between the delta's handicraft industry and the cottage industries in early modern England and Western Europe that became a springboard to later industrialization* is that its returns to labor remained so abysmally low that it could never provide a full source of subsistence. Handicraft industry remained interlocked with family farming, relying on the household's spare-time and unmarketable la-

---

*Much debate surrounds the subject of "protoindustrialization" (Mendels 1972, Medick 1976, Levine 1977, Kriedte et al. 1981, Ogilvie 1985). Multiple patterns have been demonstrated, including instances where the cottage industries were involutionary rather than precursors to later industrialization. I refer here to the latter pattern.

bor to form a crutch for and not an alternative to subsistence farming (Huang 1985: 193–95).

The coexistence of the family and marketized sectors, with their distinct and yet interpenetrating logics, produced a partly marketized economy that cannot be understood simply in terms of a perfectly competitive factors market of the Schultzian type. The duality, as will be seen, extended beyond labor to the commodities, land, and credit markets.

INTERNATIONAL CAPITALISM AND RURAL INVOLUTION

Involutionary commercialization continued in the delta even under the impact of international capitalism. The increased production of cotton and silkworms to supply the new foreign and Chinese mills, as well as the increased handweaving of cotton cloth made possible by machine-spun yarn, drew on unemployed and underemployed peasant family labor in the same way as they had earlier, during the Ming and Qing. The further familization of rural production provided peasant households with increased employment, to be sure, but at diminished marginal returns per workday, again in the same way as before. Like the earlier commercialization, the accelerated commercialization that accompanied international capitalism brought not transformative change but further involution of the peasant economy.

This is not to suggest that the rural economy was not affected by imperialism and the development of urban capitalism in China, as some advocates of the "dual economy" thesis would have it (e.g., Hou 1963; Murphey 1977). On the contrary, the rural cotton economy was fundamentally reshaped by the breaking apart of the old family production unit that grew its own cotton, spun its own yarn, and wove its own cloth. Now most cotton peasants sold their raw cotton to the urban mills and bought machine-spun yarn to do their weaving. A change of this order in something as basic as the cotton economy left virtually no peasant household untouched. It is not a question of the countryside remaining unchanged. It is simply that the rural economy continued down the path of familization and involuted production, even as it was fundamentally restructured.

This fact has been obscured in part by the emotional and political concerns that still inform much of the scholarship on imperialism. Scholars have felt impelled to either emphasize the stimulative effects of international capitalism in order to apologize for imperialism or emphasize its disruptive effects in order to condemn imperialism. But it has also been obscured, probably in even greater part, by the assumptions based on the classical English experience. In China, this book will suggest, industrialization and urban development did not go hand in hand with transformative rural change, as the classical model predicts. Indeed, the ever-widening gap between town and countryside in the modern era became one of the rallying cries of the Revolution. To comprehend the empirical reality of the changes in the Chinese economy under international capitalism, we are going to need to think in terms of a paradoxical coincidence of urban development with rural involution.

COLLECTIVIST INVOLUTION

Involutionary growth was to persist even under collectivization and the partial modernization of agriculture. Since the postrevolutionary state imposed strict controls on commerce, agricultural intensification and involution no longer took the form of commercialization. But it was involutionary change nonetheless. Collective organization, it turned out, shared with family production the basic organizational characteristic of tolerance for surplus labor: it would not, could not, "fire" its surplus labor the way a capitalist enterprise using wage labor could. The problem was exacerbated by a state policy that rigidly limited off-farm employment. The state, in any case, had almost a built-in interest in perpetuating involution, which maximizes yields per unit land and hence the amount that can be procured by the state, regardless of the severely diminished marginal returns per workday.

The introduction of modern inputs was not to alter this fundamental picture, for the incremental gains in productivity were eaten up by the diminished marginal productivities that came with the tremendous expansion of the labor force, first by the full mobilization of women workers and later by the coming of age of the baby-boom generation. At the end of the three decades of collectivization and agricultural modernization, the majority of Chinese peasants continued to live close to the margins of bare subsistence, still nowhere near the living standard we associate with modern development.

This fact of collectivist involution has been obscured, once again, by the presuppositions of the classical model. The new revolutionary leadership in China had assumed, with Stalin, that large-scale "socialist" farming would generate transformative development while avoiding the social inequities of capitalism. Mao assumed, with Marx and Lenin, that free-market capitalist development would inevitably be accompanied by social stratification, and that small-scale family farming could only be backward and precapitalist. The only alternative was the "socialist transformation" of the country-side. The power of this ideological vision was so strong, and the collectivist reorganization so dramatic, that our attention has been diverted from the fundamental fact of the persistence of the peasant condition of subsistence farming.

THE REFORMS

In the reformist China of the 1980s, I will suggest, the rural change of the greatest long-term import was the de-involution in crop production that came with the diversification of the rural economy, and not the turn to marketized farming in crop production, as is commonly assumed. That assumption is hardly peculiar to those who decry socialism in all its facets. In fact, the disillusionment with collective agriculture in China led reformers to fall back on the classical model's market alternative. Collectivist agriculture, they argued, sapped the creative and entrepreneurial energies of the peasants. Family farming with market incentives would release those creative energies and power through transformative change, best represented by the "ten thousand yuan households."

This official version of things struck ready chords in the American press and scholarship. Marketized family farming instantly called to mind America's own experience in agricultural modernization. And there was something irresistibly alluring in the thought that, after three decades of "Maoist" radical revolution, the Chinese Communists finally saw the superiority of the capitalist way over the socialist route of planned collectivist agriculture. Some scholars, still under the influence of the classical model, looked for evidence of differentiation between capitalistic rich peasants and rural proletarians alongside marketization. Many cast the issue in the black-and-white terms of socialism versus capitalism.

The actual record of reform in the Yangzi delta tells a very different story: crop yields failed to advance with the introduction of the household responsibility system in farming in the 1980s, and few peasants grew rich along the lines predicted by the classical model and official propaganda. To put it bluntly, marketized farming in the 1980s did no better in crop production than it did in the six centuries between 1350 and 1950, or than collective agriculture did in the preceding three decades.

The crucial development in the delta, I will show, came not from the "private" crop production and petty commerce that were given so much press, but rather from rural industry and new sidelines. It was rural industrialization and sideline development that finally contrived to lower the number of laborers sharing in a relatively fixed crop-production pie and reverse the centuries-old pattern of involution. The really important issue for the Yangzi delta countryside, in other words, was not—and is not—between marketized family farming and planned collectivist agriculture, or capitalism and socialism, but rather between involution and development.

In looking across the entire historical span from 1350, I hope to make clear that the delta's record runs counter to many of our common assumptions. Some of us have assumed that commercialization would transform the peasant economy, but the record shows that the transformative potential of commercialization could be overpowered by involution. Others have assumed that small-scale peasant production must give way to large-scale farms, but the record shows that this impulse could be submerged by the full elaboration of the small involuted family farm. Some have looked to collective agriculture as the way to transform the peasant economy, but the record shows that involuted subsistence farming could persist despite collectivization. Some, finally, place their hopes on the rise of a rural bourgeoisie with market growth, but the record shows that the truly transformative development is rather de-involution in farming through rural industrialization and sidelines development, mostly under collective units. The fact is that neither capitalism nor socialism in the classical visions of Smith and Marx, or even the later insights of Chayanov and Schultz, quite scratched where it really itched. The delta countryside needed, and is giving shape to, a path of development that does not conform to any of the predictions. To grasp the roots of the delta's historical rural underdevelopment and recent rural development, we are going to have to set aside most of our old assumptions.

I

TO 1949

CHAPTER 2

The Yangzi Delta Ecosystem

To focus mainly on the Yangzi delta—the course I have adopted—
has both advantages and disadvantages. The narrower focus permits
sustained attention to one region as an integrated entity and to the
interrelationships among different dimensions. Central to this book
is the presumption of the interdependence of natural environment,
social-economic structure, and human agency. Each aspect, it will
be shown, interacted with the other parts of the entire "system." It
is in this sense that I use the term ecosystem here. The disadvantage
of such an approach, of course, is that no single region can adequately represent the full complexity of China. To overcome the
limitations of a narrow regional focus, I will make frequent comparative references to the North China plain, the subject of my last
book (Huang 1985).

THE DELTA AREA

Bordered by the New Tongyang Canal in the north and Hangzhou
Bay in the south, the Yangzi delta is bowl-shaped, sloping toward the
Taihu (Lake Tai). An alternative reference to the Yangzi delta, in
fact, is the Taihu Basin, a term that conveys the outlines of the topography of the region. The area under study falls mainly in the
northern half of this basin, or the area encompassed by present-
day Suzhou district (*diqu*) and Shanghai municipality. Suzhou district roughly equals Qing Suzhou prefecture, plus Wuxi county (and
Jingui in the Qing), Jiangyin county (both under Changzhou prefecture in the Qing), and Taicang county (under Taicang department in
the Qing).* Shanghai municipality roughly equals Qing Songjiang

---

*It incorporates, counterclockwise from south to north, the counties of Wujiang,
Kunshan (and Xinyang in the Qing), Taicang, Changshu (and Zhaowen in the Qing),
the new (since 1961) county of Shazhou (part Jiangyin, part Changshu in the Qing and
the Republic), Jiangyin, Wuxi, and Wuxian (and Yuanhe and Changzhou [to be distinguished from Changzhou prefecture] in the Qing).

prefecture, plus most of Taicang department (except for Taicang county).* I shall have occasion to refer also to Nantong district (roughly Qing Tongzhou, minus Jingjiang county, but including Haimen Ting), as well as to Jiaxing district (Jiaxing and Huzhou prefectures in the Qing), in Zhejiang province. Map 1 shows the current administrative boundaries. Map 2 gives the Qing prefectural lines and locates the eight villages of the study: Touzongmiao, Xiaodingxiang, Yanjiashang, Yaojing, Dingjiacun, Sunjiaxiang, Kaixiangong, and Huayangqiao.[†]

Within the area under study, the land slopes from north to south and east to west. It is lowest toward the center of the basin, which lies less than 3 meters above sea level, lower than the high-tide mark. As Map 3 shows, the area southeast of Lake Tai is the lowest of all, as low as 1.7 meters in Wujiang county. Fields in these zones require built-up embankments. Away from the center, the ground rises to 3–5 meters, making for better drainage and drier soil (Jiangsu nongye dili 1979: 166).

Map 4 shows the general cropping pattern in the region in the 1930s. Cotton, a dry crop, was grown mainly on the high-lying ground of the outer basin. The proportion of cultivated land under cotton rises to more than 60 percent there, as against less than 20 percent on the low ground. With rice, the reverse was true, for wet-rice requires the flooding of fields at transplant time and was best grown on low-lying land with easy access to water. The proportion of the cultivated area under rice was lowest in the ridge-like belt (see below and Map 5) just west of Shanghai city (vicinity of the county seats of Taicang, Jiading, Shanghai, and Fengxian), because of difficult access to water.[‡] In the lowest-lying area to the east of Lake Tai,

---

*It includes, counterclockwise from the south, the counties of Jinshan, Fengxian, Nanhui, Shanghai, Chuansha, Baoshan, Jiading, Qingpu, and Songjiang (Huating and Louxian in the Qing), plus the island of Chongming.

†Huayangqiao actually comprises four natural villages: Xue Family Village (Xuejiada), He Family Village (Hejiada), Xubushanqiao, and Xilihangbang; the last is made up of Gao Family Hamlet (Gaojiada), Lu Family Hamlet (Lujiada), and the Lu Family's South Hamlet (Nanda). For convenience, I refer to the whole cluster as "Huayangqiao," though the residents do not themselves speak of it as such—and do not even have a name for the whole. The translated English names will be used for easy recall. During the collectivized years, Xuejiada and Hejiada made up a single production team, called Xuejiada, which will be referred to as such, to distinguish it from the two separate villages.

‡Zhongguo shiye zhi: Jiangsu sheng, 1933, 2: 2-5, improves on Zhang Xinyi's (1930a) cultivated acreage data by unifying the different mu measures of the individual counties, but uses his rice acreage data without modification. To use the Zhongguo shiye zhi cultivated acreage data for computing the proportion of land planted in rice would only skew the data further.

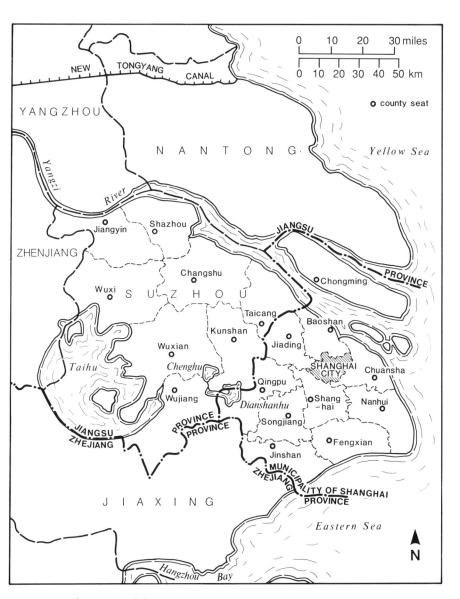

Map 1. The Yangzi delta in 1980

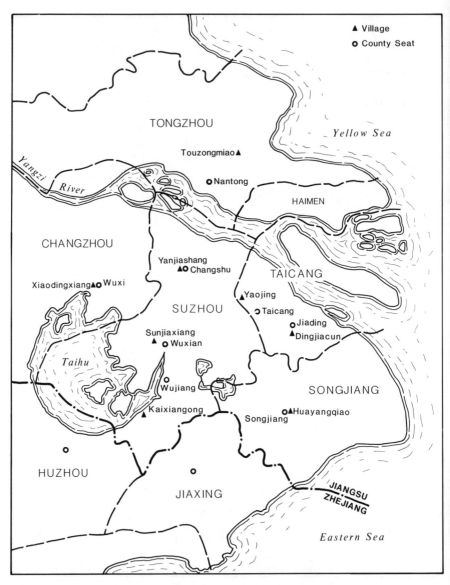

Map 2. The Yangzi delta in 1820 and the eight villages of the study

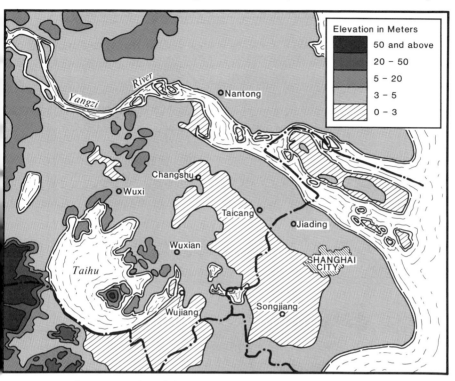

Map 3. The topography of the Yangzi delta

rice was grown with mulberries, planted on the built-up embankments to help retain the soil. This, along with Jiaxing district to the
south, was the country's traditional sericulture center. Farther away
from the lake, in Kunshan, Songjiang, and Qingpu, where there was
ready access to irrigation, but no necessity for embankments held
firm by mulberries, the proportion of rice grown was the highest,
usually more than 60 percent. The eight villages referred to in this
book are readily classifiable according to these different ecological zones.

HISTORICAL GEOGRAPHY

Two geographical forces shaped the topography of the delta: the interaction between the Yangzi River and the ocean tides, which built
up the basin's ridge-like periphery; and the inundation and sinking
of parts of the central land mass some time in the eighth–twelfth
centuries.

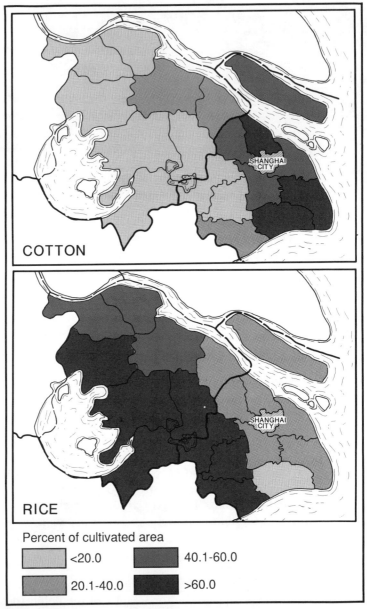

COTTON

RICE

Percent of cultivated area

<20.0   40.1-60.0

20.1-40.0   >60.0

SHANGHAI CITY

Map 4. Rice and cotton cultivation in the Yangzi delta, 1930. Based on data from Zhang Xinyi 1930a. The rice figures include glutinous rice, which accounted for 50.5% of the cultivated acreage in Wuxian, exceeding the 36.3% under regular long- and short-grain rice.

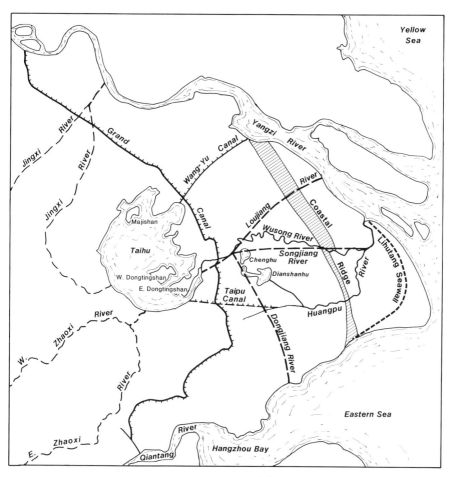

Map 5. Historical geography of the Yangzi delta

It was long thought that the delta was formed during the past several millennia by the steady extension of the sand spit from the Yangzi River eastward into the sea. Ding Wenjiang (1887–1936) was the first to suggest that silt deposits from the river extended the land mass at a rate of a mile every 69 years (1 km every 43 years; Tan Qixiang 1973). Shanghai municipality would have attained its present width of 100+ kilometers, then, over a period some 4,000 years, assuming a uniform rate of extension.

But historical geographers in postrevolutionary China have demonstrated that the river's sand spit could not have extended eastward at anything so simple as the regular rate that Ding proposed. That rate supposed a uniform amount of silt deposited by the river. In fact, the river's silt content is dependent on the rate of soil erosion in the Yangzi valley. The extension of the land surface is also subject to the action of ocean tides, which wash away portions of the shore and cause the formation of an underwater sandbar. Above ground, a ridge forms (Chen Jiyu 1957).

Combining clues from the present land mass with documentary sources, climatological research, and archaeological excavations, Tan Qixiang and other historical geographers in China have been able to put together the following account of the formation of the land surface of Shanghai municipality:

1. In the 4,000-odd years before the fourth century A.D., the Yangzi valley was well forested, and the river carried relatively little silt. That was also a fairly warm period, with average annual temperatures two to three degrees (Celsius) higher than today. The result was a relatively high sea level that slowed the extension of the land. In those four millennia, the land surface of present-day Shanghai municipality extended a mere kilometer every 500–3,000 years. The ridge formed during that period extended southeastward from the Yangzi north of Taicang to Fengxian (see Map 5).*

2. Subsequent deforestation increased the Yangzi's silt content. The building of the old Hanhaitang seawall in the beginning of the eighth century, and then of the Lihutang seawall in 1172, checked the action of ocean tides and accelerated the extension of the land surface inside the seawalls. A cold period, with temperatures two to four degrees below contemporary averages, lowered the sea level and accelerated the extension. Some 30 kilometers were added in the nine centuries between 300 and 1200 A.D. This too is relatively high ground, forming what some contemporary geographers term the "dish-edge high ground" (dieyuan gaodi) of Shanghai municipality.

3. The centuries since have seen a total extension of merely a few kilometers to something over 10 at the widest points, also of relatively high-lying land, beyond the Lihutang seawall. The reasons for this slow rate are not entirely clear. The temperatures and sea level have been relatively low, and the river's silt content high. What is different is the absence of a seawall to break the ocean tide and also, it appears, the southward shift of the Yangzi's main channel, with a consequent erosion of the sand spit (Tan Qixiang 1973, 1982; Ma Zhenglin 1981: 210–11; Shanghai nongye dili 1978: 9).

*Measuring 8 km at its widest points to the north of the Wusong River (the old course of the Songjiang River), and as little as 1.5 km south of the river.

Whatever the exact reasons for the slowdown in the final period, it is clear that the Yangzi delta, far from being formed by the single and uniform buildup of silt deposits, was shaped through the complex interaction of multiple variables, both natural and man-made. The old theory had also suggested a relatively simple process for the formation of the Taihu basin as a whole. The sand spit to the south of the Yangzi, the theory went, eventually joined up with one north of the Qiantang River and turned what is now the Lake Tai area into a lagoon. Continual buildup of the lagoon bottom over the centuries carved up the body of water, eventually producing the delta plain as we find it today, studded by lakes and crisscrossed by rivers (*Jiangsu dili* 1980: 28; Ma Zhenglin 1981: 210).

Here again recent research has overthrown the old theory. Numerous archaeological finds have been made at lake-bottom sites uncovered during drought years and in the course of land reclamation, proving that some of the land surfaces are more than 15,000 years old. Neolithic remains have been found, for example, in the center of Lake Tai between the Majishan and the Western Dongtingshan. During a drought in 1955, Neolithic "stamped pottery" was found near the southeastern shore, in Wujiang county; and the remains of a stone street more than 20 meters long were found near the Wu county shore. East of the lake, at the northwestern shore of the Chenghu (Lake Cheng), land reclamation uncovered massive quantities of artifacts dating from the Neolithic period down to the Han and Song (Fudan daxue 1981: 187, 191; Wei Songshan 1979: 59).*

Archaeological and documentary evidence of various kinds have together forged the following new hypothesis. Lake Tai was not formed until the middle of the Recent Epoch, when the mouth of the Jingxi River (flowing northeastward into the Yangzi) silted up, causing the Jingxi to change course eastward (see Map 5) and intersect with the Zhaoxi. East of the lake, the Wusong River divided, forming the so-called "three rivers" (*sanjiang*), the Loujiang (present-day Liuhe, flowing into the Yangzi), the Wusong (flowing into the sea) and the Dongjiang (flowing into Hangzhou Bay), which together drained Lake Tai. The basin remained almost all land surface until the three rivers began to silt up (*Jiangsu dili* 1980: 28–29). The Dongjiang was the first to do so, probably by the eighth century.

*This site did not yield any artifacts from the Six Dynasties, Sui, or Tang era—a mystery as yet unsolved by historical geographers (Fudan daxue 1981: 188). One theory holds that floods were rampant through the period, and much of the surface was under water (Wei Songshan 1979: 61).

Poor drainage was the cause of the sinking in the central basin during the eighth–twelfth centuries.*

Archaeological evidence (such as that from Lake Cheng) demonstrates conclusively that the process was one of abrupt inundation rather than gradual erosion. Some 250 meters beyond the dike of the reclaimed area of the Chefang commune, for example, there is an area of more than ten mu covered by large stones, still largely intact, and distinctly visible in drought years. It could not have been submerged by the gradual action of lashing waves. Since Lake Cheng is not mentioned in late-eleventh-century sources, but is referred to in 1165–73 sources, the sinking probably occurred between those two periods. The name of the lake itself, *cheng*, is a homonym in local dialect with the word "sink," *chen* (Fudan daxue 1981: 188). A multitude of lakes were created by such inundations. In the years following, the new lakes contracted from silting and reclamation, only to be periodically expanded by flooding and erosion. The contraction of the lakes is shown by archaeological evidence from the eastern part of Lake Tai.† The evidence for their expansion we saw above: the relics of submerged areas that had formerly been land.

This pattern of repeated expansions and contractions might explain the confusion in historical sources between the terms *weitian* and *yutian*. Weitian (lit. "enclosed fields") should strictly speaking refer to reclaimed lake- or riverfront land (polders); yutian (lit., "embanked fields") refers to fields surrounded by built-up embankments on low-lying land. In its broadest meaning, yutian refers to an entire system, including both the fields and the drainage and irrigation ditches that crisscross them.‡ Yet historical sources use the two terms interchangeably, causing much confusion over separate and distinct phenomena. One possible explanation for that confusion, I would suggest, is that reclaimed lakefront land could easily turn into just another embanked field as the lake got pushed farther back. At the same time, embanked fields could easily revert to lakefront reclaimed land after an inundation. In any event, it is important in our analysis to separate the two conceptually. The two could work

---

*By one theory, the sinking was due principally to geological action (Wei Songshan 1979: 60); another holds that it was mainly a result of flooding. The issue is unresolved (Fudan daxue 1981: 188).

†The town of Songling in Wujiang county, for example, had been an islet in Song times; contemporary poetry records the spectacular view it afforded. But by the Qing, the area to the south had been filled in by silting and reclamation. The Eastern Dongtingshan, similarly, only became a peninsula in the nineteenth century. The entire eastern part of Lake Tai, in fact, is in danger of silting up completely, a point that will be discussed in some detail later (Fudan daxue 1981: 191–92; Wei Songshan 1979: 64).

‡Miu Qiyu (1982: 20) makes the useful distinction between the two.

against each other: excessive reclamation of lakefront land (weitian) affected the lake's water-holding capacity and could thus endanger the entire embanked-fields (yutian) system.

In time, the delta's distinctive topography forged a regional economic system embracing both its peripheries and its center. The high-lying outer areas grew mainly cotton in the Qing, and supplied both raw cotton and cloth to the low-lying areas of the central basin. The center developed an interdependent system of dry and wet agriculture, of wet-rice in the middle of the fields and mulberries for sericulture on the embankments. Income from silk went to pay for the cloth imports. In between the two areas, neither so low as to require embankments nor so high as to make irrigation difficult, the land was planted almost exclusively in rice. This area supplied the other two with surplus grain to pay for the cotton and cloth.

Such an ecosystem contrasts sharply with the dry-farmed North China plain. As I have detailed elsewhere (Huang 1985: chap. 3), the river systems there do not lend themselves to irrigation. Before the Herculean postrevolutionary efforts to restructure the natural environment, the total water flow per unit area was only one-sixth to one-eighth that in the Yangzi delta. Moreover, in the spring growing season, after the long, dry fall and winter, most rivers were too low for irrigation. By best estimates, only 7 percent of the total cultivated area in Hebei and 3 percent in Shandong were irrigated before the Revolution, and almost all of that by wells. Dry crops like sorghum and millet, and, after the eighteenth century, maize, predominated.

THE WUYUE MODEL

The basic structure of the embanked-fields system of the Yangzi delta was completed under the tenth-century Wuyue state (907–82). A relatively small regional state, it was not encumbered by the concern of later governments for the transport of tribute grain up the Grand Canal or by centrifugal administrative divisions. Though later writers may have romanticized the record to some extent, it seems clear that the Wuyue was exceptionally vigorous in its efforts at water control. Rivers were dredged and dikes maintained, by a standing water-control "army" (Liaoqian jun) ten thousand strong. For arterial drainage, the Wuyue relied on the Loujiang and Wusong rivers. The third of the old "three rivers"—the Dongjiang—had silted up by this time, but the state was able to develop the Xiaoguanpu River as a replacement and to maintain drainage southeastward into Hangzhou Bay (Miu Qiyu 1982).

Around this arterial system, the state developed and maintained a canal system summed up in the expression, "a vertical canal (*zongpu*) every five or seven *li* [1.0 li = 0.5 km], a horizontal canal (*hengtang*) every seven or ten *li*." The largest of these canals were 20–30 feet deep and 200–300 feet wide. Embankments were kept high and wide, and an elaborate network of sluice gates was maintained to control the flow of water for irrigation and transport (Miu Qiyu 1982). A century later, the Song hydrologist Jia Dan (1067) found 265 canals still operating and traces of 132 others.

The drainage system of the time worked so well that contemporary official sources recorded only four serious occurrences of waterlogging during the 98 years that the Yangzi delta region was under Wuyue control (880–978). The Wuyue state's extraordinary record led later hydrologists to look to the period as the golden age of water control in the basin.

DECLINE AFTER THE WUYUE STATE

A system like the Wuyue state's requires vigorous human effort to maintain. The arterial rivers must be dredged periodically, lest they silt up completely, and so must the tributaries and man-made canals and ditches. And the dikes along the rivers and the embankments around the fields must periodically be shored up. The complexities of the task are suggested by the six-level administrative classification developed in postrevolutionary China: "grade one" for the basin's arterial rivers, under central government management; two, multi-county regional rivers, under the provincial government; three, channels connecting grade one and two rivers, under the joint administration of the central and local governments; four, multi-commune (township) rivers within a single county, under the county; five, multi-brigade (administrative village) rivers within a single commune, under the commune; and six, tributaries of the grade five rivers, usually under brigades and teams (natural villages and hamlets; *Jiangsu nongye dili* 1979: 170–71). Dikes and embankments can be similarly classified, their construction and maintenance differentiated according to the level of administration. All parts of the system must be maintained for water to be effectively drained and brought down to the fields for irrigation. It is a daunting task even under the best of circumstances. And the circumstances were not of the best for the Wuyue's successors.

The pressures on maintaining the system were greatly aggravated by the mounting population pressure on the delta after the fall of the

Wuyue. Massive migrations southward accompanied the shift of the Song dynasty capital from Kaifeng in the North to Hangzhou in the southern half of the delta. By Ming times, cultivated area per capita had declined to about 3.5 *mu*, and by the Qing, it had dropped to just 2.5 mu (Appendix B; a standard, or *shi mu*, = 0.1647 acre = 0.0667 ha). With the land/population squeeze came deforestation at the upper reaches of the rivers flowing into Lake Tai, which aggravated the silting problem. Reclamation of the silted areas of the lake, rivers, and canals, in turn, reduced the carrying capacity of the catch-basin and its drainage channels.

The result was long-term decline. Table 2.1 shows the incidence and frequency of waterlogging and drought (of a scale serious enough to be recorded in the official records and gazetteers in the Taihu basin during the millennium 901–1900). The two serve as good indicators of the state of water control in the delta. Neither waterlogging nor drought is simply the result of the vagaries of climate; both are intimately linked to the degree of effectiveness of water control. When rivers and canals flow smoothly and with sufficient water, an area's tolerance for drought, as well as for rain, is greatly increased. When rivers and canals silt up, the threshold of tolerance for both drop. As can be readily seen, the long-term trend in the basin was

TABLE 2.1

Waterlogging and Drought in the Taihu Basin, 901–1900

Period	Waterlogging		Drought	
	Incidence	Frequency (years)	Incidence	Frequency (years)
901–1000	6	16.7	3	33.3
1001–1100	16	6.3	8	12.5
1101–1200	31	3.2	24	4.2
1201–1300	29	3.5	10	10.0
1301–1400	47	2.1	17	6.0
901–1400	129	3.8	62	7.7
1401–1500	48	2.1	19	5.3
1501–1600	57	1.8	38	2.6
1601–1700	56	1.8	50	2.0
1701–1800	48	2.1	39	2.5
1801–1900	48	2.1	28	3.6
1401–1900	257	1.9	174	2.9
901–1900	386	2.5	236	4.2

SOURCE: *Jiangsu sheng jin liangqian nian . . . .* 1976.
NOTE: Major floods on the order of the 1931 flood (which caused severe damage to crops in 24 counties in the basin) occurred 20 times between 1401 and 1900, in 1454, 1481, 1509, 1510, 1522, 1561, 1587, 1608, 1624, 1651, 1670, 1680, 1708, 1724, 1732, 1781, 1804, 1823, 1833, and 1849, or every 25 years on average.

toward more occurrences of both: six instances of waterlogging and three of drought in the tenth century, compared with no fewer than 48 instances of waterlogging and 39 of drought in the eighteenth century. Put another way: in the first five centuries after 900, water-logging occurred once in 3.8 years, and drought once in 7.7; in the five centuries after 1400, the frequency increased respectively to once in 1.9 and 2.9 years.

The Arterial System

The arterial system declined inexorably from the Song on. The Wusong, long the principal drainage channel, silted up ever more rapidly after the 1140s. Natural silting action was aggravated by the short-sightedness of the state: to ensure the smooth shipment of tribute grain on the Grand Canal, the government extended it by building the Wujiang dike from the Wusong to Pingwang at the southeastern tip of Lake Tai. Despite a project undertaken at about the same time to straighten out the middle stretches of the Wusong (between Baihejiang and Panlonghui), the smooth flow of water into the river from its source in the lake was blocked, accelerating the silting up of the lower reaches. More and more of the river water turned northward to flow into the old Loujiang (reconstructed into the Zhihe canal in 1055). In 1175, the government undertook a major project to dredge the lower reaches, but to no lasting avail. Fi-nally, in 1403, the Ming state simply blocked off the Wusong at its intersection with the Loujiang and directed the water north. The (present-day) Liuhe then became the main drainage river for the basin. By the end of the eighteenth century, the Liuhe likewise silted up, and the Huangpu, originally just a southward tributary of the Wusong, later joined to Dianshan Lake in the Ming, became the main drainage channel (see Map 5; Wei Songshan 1979: 63).

The inability of successive dynasties to reverse or arrest the silt-ing up of the basin's rivers explains the increasing frequency of wa-terlogging and drought. Government efforts tended to be patchwork responses to major crises rather than fundamental solutions. Major dredging efforts tended to follow giant floods, occurring at roughly 25-year intervals.*

---

*Jiangsu sheng jin liangqian nian . . . 1976. In addition to all the relevant passages from 93 gazetteers, this remarkable 450+ page compilation contains materials from numerous miscellaneous sources, including 20th-century newspapers, and the results of county investigations undertaken in the early 1950s. See also Xu Jinzhi 1981. Hamashima 1982: 98–105 lists water-control projects undertaken between 1404 and 1644.

The arterial problem has yet to be resolved. The Huangpu is no longer the main drainage channel for Lake Tai, because the badly silted-up part of the lake lets too little water escape eastward (Fudan daxue 1981). A project in the early 1950s to join the lake's southeastern corner with the Huangpu via a canal—the Tai(hu)-(Huang)pu, running through Jiangsu and Zhejiang provinces to Shanghai municipality—fell through. Jiangsu province apparently dug its section, but thereafter cooperation among the provincial and municipal governments broke down. Zhejiang and Shanghai both abandoned the work, concerned that a project whose benefits to them were not so immediate as to Jiangsu would raise the water level within their own jurisdictions. Jiangsu province then dug another canal from the northern end of the lake to the Yangzi. This Wang(-Ting)-Yu(-shan) canal then became the principal drainage channel for the lake (Fudan daxue 1981: 193–94), but by the late 1970s it was clear that it needed to be enlarged (*Jiangsu nongye dili* 1979: 168).

Tan Qixiang (the leading authority on the basin's historical geography) advocates the completion of the abandoned Taipu canal to provide better eastward drainage (possibly turning southward through Jinshan county into Hangzhou Bay, rather than further loading the Huangpu); the redigging of the long-disappeared Dongjiang to drain southward into Hangzhou Bay; and the preservation of all the basin's lakefront land against reclamation to provide auxiliary drainage. All this must be done, he says, if the abrupt inundations of the eighth–twelfth centuries are not to be repeated (Fudan daxue 1981: 194; see also *Jiangsu nongye dili* 1979: 168–69). In the mid-1980s there was much talk among local water-control officials of a centrally coordinated effort to seek a fundamental and lasting solution. Whether such an effort will come to anything depends on the ability to overcome the divisions in interests of the various local bureaucracies involved.

Local Water Control

For the kind of large-scale arterial projects discussed above, the early Ming state used corvée labor enforced through the *lijia* household registration system and the extraeconomic powers that resident landlords wielded over their "serfs" and tenants. With increased commercialization and the movement of landlords into towns and cities, however, the state had to turn to new forms of labor mobilization. The new absentee landlords had little interest in organizing water-control projects and lacked the wherewithal to mobilize labor for them in any case. By the late Ming, the state had developed a three-

sided program to fill the gap. It imposed a labor tax based on landownership (*zhaotian paiyi;* Hamashima 1982). Then, because many
of the absentee landlords were gentry who were exempt from corvée
labor, and hence from the tax on their land, it tried to limit gentry
privilege (*youmian xianzhi*). And finally, it required corvée-exempt
landlords to pay for the board of tenants who worked on water projects (*yeshi dianli*).

But we should not make the mistake of projecting modern government back to earlier times. Imperial water control, like imperial
administration, generally stopped at the county level; subcounty-
level communes and brigades are new additions of the postrevolutionary government. I have shown elsewhere, with evidence from
the nineteenth-century Baodi county government archive, just how
limited the Qing state's tax collection apparatus was: its lowest tax
collection agent was a quasi-official figure who was nominated by
the local and village powers and who had to oversee singlehandedly
an average of 20 villages (Huang 1985: chap. 13). And as Ping-ti Ho
(1985) has shown, the Ming-Qing state's success in measuring and
registering land for tax purposes was a far cry from its claims, which
in fact lay well beyond the capacity of the bureaucratic apparatus of
the time. A vigorous county government of the late imperial period
might have managed canal and dike systems at its own level, but the
state's reach would not have extended all the way down to the village level. Even today, commune- and brigade-level water control is
considered outside of the purview of the formal "state" (*guojia*) administration and mainly the concern of the collective units.

Hamashima (1982) suggests that, in the early Ming, responsibility
for local waterworks fell on the resident landlords (in what was
called the *tiantou zhi* or "field-heads system"), declared principles
notwithstanding. It was the landlords with fields immediately adjacent to the dikes and small canals who could be relied on to undertake routine maintenance on them. For them, the payoff was control
over the access to water, to river mud for fertilizer, to fishing in the
streams, and the like.

The precise role that village communities played in water control
is not clear. Morita (1967) maintains that when the "field-heads system" collapsed with the urbanization of the landlords, peasant col-
lectivities (*kyōdōtai*) emerged to fill the gap. His scenario is based
mainly on Fei Xiaotong's 1936 field study of Kaixiangong village, in
Wujiang county, at the heart of the Taihu basin. Here the land lies
below the high-tide water level, and villagers were faced with the
threat of frequent waterlogging. Placed collectively at risk, the members of a group of embanked fields (a *jin,* in local terminology, which

was a subdivision of a larger group of embanked fields called a *yu*) developed cooperative ways to drain their waterlogged fields. In one such grouping of 336 mu, for example, a bronze brace was beaten to signal the need for emergency work, and all participants had to respond within 30 minutes or pay a stiff fine. All households were required, for every six mu farmed, to furnish one worker to operate the fifteen water pumps. The burden of managing each of the three-man pump teams was rotated among the group's members, as was the burden of overall management of all fifteen. The appointment of a new manager was marked yearly by a feast (Fei 1939: 172–73).

I believe Morita has exaggerated the extent to which collective effort characterized the delta peasants' water-control activities. In Kaixiangong, Fei's study makes clear, collective drainage in times of flood and severe waterlogging was the only form of organized community water control. These were emergency situations in which all members of the community were placed equally at risk, and the community was thus able to mobilize itself for collective action. But the routine maintenance of dikes and embankments or the dredging of canals and ditches was much harder to coordinate, because members of the community were affected differently. If part of a dike or embankment caved in, for example, the impact was on only the households whose fields were adjacent to it. Those same households were of course also in the best position to maintain the waterway, and it would have been difficult to get more distant households to take on the work. The same kind of logic applied to the dredging of local canals and ditches. A slow-flowing stream with little water could provide sufficient irrigation water for the adjacent parcels, though not for those farther inside the dish-shaped yu. The peasants' sense of urgency about such chores was thus different depending on the location of their fields within the embankments. Indeed, as we shall see, by the mid-1980s, just a few years after the agricultural decollectivization of the Yangzi delta, the coordination of such chores had once again become a major problem, and as in an earlier day, the responsibility had perforce fallen on the affected households.

Beyond the level of the natural village, at what would be the commune/township level today, the problems of water management were compounded, not just for routine maintenance, but even for responses to emergencies. There one could not count either on the voluntary organization of a group of villages whose residents did not know one another or on the reach of the state so far below the county level of administration.

The Qing state tried to fill the gap with artificial supravillage units like the *qu* or *tu*. But these faced nearly insurmountable problems of management. Why should a member of the unit whose own fields were not threatened exert himself on behalf of a neighboring group of embanked fields? Indeed, Governor Zhou Kongjiao pointed to this problem as early as 1608 (*Songjiangfu zhi* 1817, 11: 6a,b). The heads of these units, moreover, were generally unsalaried quasi-officials, without ready access to the coercive apparatus of the county government, and by the late Ming, most were themselves just small cultivators who lacked the clout to impose their will on their fellow peasants (Hamashima 1982: 90–97).

The Guomindang's artificial subcounty *baojia* system of the 1930s worked no better. The collective drainage organization in Kaixiangong clearly had nothing to do with the artificial state-imposed bao-jia system, which was largely a shell with little substance (Fei 1939: 8, 109–11). In the Republican period, as in the Qing, there continued to be a large gap between large water-control projects managed by the state and village-level responses to emergencies.

What actually obtained was a haphazard system in which the lowest levels were left to fend for themselves until a situation degenerated into a disaster. When disaster struck at the village level, the problem could be met by collective community organization, as in Kaixiangong, and a disaster at the county level or above could be dealt with by the state. But any problem that fell between those two levels easily went unattended. Ideally, but rarely, a capable government official might draw on preexisting community organizations to coordinate multi-community action. Hamashima (1982: 13–14) documents such an instance in the fifteenth century, when Zhou Chen (1381–1453), an exceptionally able state official, used public grain to recruit peasants for such work. Or, enlightened local elites might provide the leadership to coordinate multi-village action, perhaps under the encouragement of the state. More often, things were allowed to deteriorate until the disaster reached a scale that the bureaucracy could no longer ignore. In this haphazard system we find another of the roots for the centuries-long degeneration of water control in the delta.

STATE, ELITE, AND PEASANT IN THE
DELTA ECOSYSTEM

As pressures on the ecosystem mounted, divisions of interest among state, elite, and peasant were unavoidable. As the eastern shores of Lake Tai silted up, for example, local people were drawn to reclaim the marshes to grow reeds, to use as fish ponds, or to enclose as fields, further contracting the lake's water-holding capacity and adversely affecting water drainage in times of overflow. In 1763, at the request of Governor Zhuang Yougong of Jiangsu province, further reclamation was prohibited, and any new plots removed. But this was a patchwork response by the state, which could not arrest the long-term drying up of the eastern Taihu, as has been seen (*Wuxian zhi* 1933, 42: 29a; *Songjiang fu zhi* 1817, 11: 41b).

Another example, one of the best-documented cases, involved Dianshanhu (Lake Dianshan). The conflict here was chiefly between the local peasants, with periodic help from the state, and the powerful local elites. Unlike nearby Lake Cheng, Lake Dianshan was not a major arterial drainage path, and because it was given to drying up at the edges, reclamation was easily accomplished. Powerful local families, since they possessed the necessary capital and labor, dominated the reclamation efforts. As Circuit Supervisor Zhao Lin explained in "On Water Control" (ca. 1200), "In the last few decades, powerful local families have been the main people reclaiming lake-front land. In times of drought, they monopolize the upper reaches [of the irrigation canals], so that others around the lake have no way to irrigate; in times of flood, there is no place for the water to drain to." As a result, he said, hundreds of thousands of mu of peasant land around the lake had gone uncultivated. During the early years of the Chunxi reign (1174–89), the state had dug the Shanmenliu, a stream some 5,000–mu long, to open up "the throat" north of the lake and ameliorate the situation (*Songjiang fu zhi* 1817, 10: 7b). But shortly thereafter, powerful local families moved in and built a dike "several *li*" long just south of the "throat," reclaiming large areas at the northern edge of the lake, and once more plugged up the drainage. In 1186, the Zhexi Supervisor Luo Dian had reopened the drainage path, and flooded areas were once again salvaged for the peasants (ibid., 11a,b), only to have powerful families soon encroach again. A century later, local officials repeatedly complained of the same old problems (ibid., 14b–16a). In 1298, the Yuan state attempted to prevent further reclamation by setting boundaries for the lake and established an office to enforce them, but to little avail (*Gusu zhi* 1506, 12: 14a–b, 2: 9a). Over the years 1295–1307, Cao Xuanwei, whose father had served as a county magistrate, was able to reclaim "several tens of thousands of *mu*," which he then leased out to tenants, thereby becoming one of the richest men in the area (*Qinchuan sanzhi buji xubian* 1835, 8: 7a–b). After that, little could be done to overcome the perennial waterlogging.

There were other kinds of problems and divisions. Absentee landlords and their tenants were not equally concerned about water control, and questions unavoidably arose about who should have to shoulder the burden; this was the background to the late Ming policy of requiring the landowner to provide the board, and the tenant the labor. Another kind of split was noted by the compiler of an eighteenth–century Wuxi gazetteer. In some of Wuxi's higher areas, when drought struck, wealthier peasants who farmed near the water source could still get water by using several dozen *jiegao* pumps (pivotlike, with a heavy weight suspended at one end and a bucket at the other), while the poor, lacking such resources, saw their crops fail. The same compiler also noted the conflict of interest between residents in different parts of the county: the cultivators on the lowlands feared rain; those on higher ground wished for lots of rain to ensure their water source (*Xi Jin shi xiaolu* 1752, 1: 4b–5a).

Given so wide a divergence of interests, long-term ecological degeneration was almost unavoidable, only periodically slowed by vigorous state effort. When the state functioned as it was supposed to do, it could intervene to protect the peasants' interest against the abuses of the powerful, as the above examples show. It also filled indispensable managerial functions in crisis situations, organizing large-scale projects in ways that local societies could rarely do on their own. But more often the bureaucracy's role as manager and protector was merely symbolic, without real substance, as the Dianshan example also shows. Worse, the state might take self-serving actions that worked to the detriment of water control for local society, as happened in the 1140s, when it sacrificed the Wusong for the sake of the Grand Canal.

By comparison with North China, what stands out about water control in the Yangzi delta was the frequent three-way interaction among state, elite, and peasant. In North China, waterworks involved chiefly either the Yellow River dikes, a task of building and maintenance manageable only by the state, or diminutive small wells belonging to individual households (Huang 1985: chap. 3). There were few water-control projects of the scale of the Yangzi delta's, too small for the state to reach, yet too big for individual households or villages to undertake. Those were the projects that in the Yangzi delta drew the elite, the peasant, and the state into necessarily complex and changing interrelationships of a sort that did not exist in North China.

TWO CONTRASTING ECOSYSTEMS

We are now ready to examine how the natural environment of the Yangzi delta gave rise to a different social and economic structure, and even different patterns of political action, from those of the North China plain. A fundamental difference was that between the irrigated agriculture of the delta and the dry farming of North China. In terms of cultivated acreage per capita, the Yangzi delta was more densely populated than the North China plain: a mere 2.10 mu per farm person on the eve of the Revolution, compared to 4.21 for Hebei and 3.70 for Shandong in the 1930s (Huadong junzheng weiyuanhui 1952: 5–6; Tudiweiyuanhui 1937: 23).* But the comparative figures are misleading, for the delta had a longer frost-free season and hence a substantially higher cropping index: 159.0, compared with Hebei's 122.6 and Shandong's 143.7.† If we adjust for the differential cropping frequencies and compare instead sown acreage per farm person, the gap narrows to 3.34 (sown) mu per farm person in the delta, compared with 5.16 in Hebei and 5.32 in Shandong, or a ratio of about 100 to 157. This difference is more than offset by the higher yields of irrigated agriculture: an average rice yield of 400 catties (unhusked) per mu in the Yangzi delta, compared with 175 catties for maize in Hebei and Shandong, and 160–70 for millet and sorghum, or a difference of more than 229 to 100.‡ Considering only these crops, the ratio of the delta's per capita grain output to North China's works out to 146 to 100. If we further take into account the different grain-cropping regimes (rice, followed by wheat in the double-cropped areas of the delta, and sorghum/maize/millet, followed by wheat in year one, then spring-sown soybeans, followed by a fallow winter in year two in North China), the gap would be greater still.

Higher per capita agricultural output, plus abundant water trans-

*The figure for Jiangsu province as a whole is 3.80, according to Tudiweiyuanhui 1937: 23, but that lumps the Yangzi delta in with the ecologically very different northern half, including the area on the other side of the Huai River. The figure cited here, based on a survey of 875,460 households in 973 *xiang* in 25 southern Jiangsu counties, is the more accurate one for our purposes.

†The delta figure is based on data in Zhang Xinyi (1930a: 33–42) for the 17 counties of Shanghai municipality and Suzhou district. The Tudiweiyuanhui (1937: 19) figure for Jiangsu province as a whole, 167.1, seems high, since so much of the zone between the lowlands of the central basin and the high-lying outer rim was essentially monocropped under rice. There was relatively little winter wheat, because wheat, a dry crop, did not grow well in the soggy rice fields.

‡Yield figures are from Perkins 1969: 275, 277, 278–79. The rice figure is for Jiangsu province as a whole. (Of the three sets of figures given by Perkins, I have opted for the originals of Ta-chung Liu and Kung-chia Yeh). Zhang Xinyi's (1930a: 33) data for the 17 counties work out to 283 catties (unhusked) per mu, which is too low, and the Tudiweiyuanhui's (1937: 20) 56 *dou* (5.6 *shi*) for Jiangsu province is simply too high. The maize yield is the average of Perkins's figures for Hebei and Shandong; and the millet and sorghum figures are from his national averages. They are consistent with village yield data compiled by the Mantetsu investigators (see Huang 1985).

port, made for a much more highly commercialized peasant economy in the Yangzi delta. The seventeen-county area of main concern had 27.1 percent of its cultivated acreage under cotton in the 1930s, compared with 10 percent in Hebei and 6 percent in Shandong (Zhang Xinyi 1930a: 34–35; Huang 1985: 128). Within the delta region, the proportion under cotton was highest in present-day Shanghai municipality—45.6 percent—and the cotton handicraft home industry there was correspondingly the most highly developed. These two factors added up to a substantially higher per capita income in the Yangzi delta countryside than on the North China plain.

Higher per capita agricultural output also explains the delta's different landholding system. A large surplus above subsistence made investments in land by absentee landlords more attractive, and the more highly commercialized economy made the accumulation of capital for those investments more feasible. Together, these factors produced a higher degree of concentration of landownership in the Yangzi delta than in North China.* Rented land in North China represented about 18 percent of the total cultivated area, against about 42 percent in our Yangzi delta counties (Huang 1985: 82; Huadong junzheng weiyuanhui 1952: 6–7). Even if we take into account the higher incidence of wage labor–based managerial agriculture in North China (about 10 percent of the cultivated area in the 1930s, compared with an insignificant amount in the Yangzi delta; Huang 1985: chap. 4; Chap. 4, below), landownership was clearly more concentrated in the Yangzi delta than in North China.

The difference in landownership made for very great differences in the interrelationships among state, elite, and peasant in the two regions. In North China, most peasants were owner-cultivators who were taxed directly by the state. In the Yangzi delta, the majority rented the subsoil (an important distinction, which we will come to in due course) and were taxed only indirectly via rent paid to the subsoil landlord, because, after the tax reforms of the second quarter of the eighteenth century, when the labor tax (ding) was merged into the land tax (di) (tanding rudi), the state levied taxes only on owners of the subsoil, typically absentee landlords from the late Ming on. Thus, in land relations as in water control, the peasant dealt with the state chiefly through the elites, not directly, as he did in the North.

---

*Arrigo (1986) argues convincingly that any measure of landownership concentration must take into account not only rented land, but also land farmed with hired labor. Using Buck's (1937b) data, she demonstrates a correlation between the degree of concentration and the amount of surplus above subsistence produced.

As a result, the peasant communities in the two regions came to have very different structures (as will be seen in more detail later). In North China, communities of peasant cultivators developed organized leadership to cope with the demands of the state. Villages had informal "councils" of leaders (*huishou*), who were responsible for tax collection and, by extension, oversaw other village affairs as well (Huang 1985: 237–44). In the delta, where there was no comparable stimulus for the formation of village government, community structures revolved mainly around kinship ties.

Peasant collective action accordingly chose different targets in the two regions. It most frequently took the form of community tax resistance against the state in North China, and of rent resistance against absentee landlords in the delta. That, at least, was the general pattern until after the Taipings, when the state was compelled to take a more active role in mediating the relationship between landlord and tenant in the Yangzi delta. County governments then took to meeting annually with the biggest landholders to decide on rent rates for the year, with the result that aggrieved peasants directed their protests not just against the landlords but also against the state (Bernhardt 1986).

Overall, however, the Yangzi delta evinced greater social stability than the North China plain. In part this was because of its higher income floor. Fewer peasants, as will be seen, slid down the social-economic ladder to become landless agricultural laborers or to drop out of the bottom of village society. It was also much more ecologically stable: a mere 20 major floods in the 500 years between 1401 and 1900, as opposed to almost annual flooding on the North China plain (the Yellow River burst its dikes 1,593 times in recorded history; Huang 1985: 59). In North China, low-yield, disaster-prone dry farming combined with high population density to lay the basis for severe scarcity and chronic instability (Huang 1985: chap. 3). The large pool of landless agricultural laborers and "floating poor," uprooted from their villages, produced a higher degree of trans-village social integration at the bottom of society. It was no accident that the North China plain was the breeding ground for the Boxer uprising (Esherick 1987) and the setting for the dramatic spread of the Communist movement. The Yangzi delta countryside, by contrast, not only exerted a conservative influence on the Taipings, but was also much more resistant to Communist organizing than the North China plain. Here in fact the rural revolution was largely enacted from above only after military victory.

CHAPTER 3

Commercialization and Family Production

The classical view of Smith and Marx takes for granted the waning of peasant family production with vigorous commercialization. The historical record of the delta in the Ming and Qing, however, demonstrates just the opposite. What occurred was not the erosion of the peasant family production unit, but a fuller elaboration and strengthening of it. The added labor required for the new cotton economy and the expanded silk economy came above all from the auxiliary labor of the peasant households. In the process, women and children came to take on an increasing share of the household's productive activities, to result in what I call the *familization* of rural production. Commercialization, far from undermining peasant family production, both promoted and was undergirded by it.

COTTON AND CLOTH

Cotton lies at the heart of the story of commercialization in the Ming–Qing Yangzi delta. In 1350, no one in China wore cotton cloth; by 1850, almost every peasant did. The dramatic spread of cotton, replacing hemp, affected every household and powered a host of related changes. Its story dwarfs those of all other crops and industries in importance for this period.

Cotton enjoys a number of advantages over hemp. It is a higher yielding and more easily processed plant than hemp, and the finished product is more comfortable and warmer.* Once cotton spinning and weaving were introduced (by Huang Daopo in the late thirteenth century into Wunijing, south of present-day Shanghai city, near the Huangpu River; *Chongxiu Fengxian xian zhi* 1878, 19: 3a),

---

*The fibers of the hemp plant are short and require a rather elaborate process of twisting together (*ji*) to join the ends and, for stronger fabrics, of twisting two threads into one (*jianian*) (Li Zailun 1982). Ramie continued to be favored by the upper classes for use in the luxury fabric known as "summer cloth" (*xiabu*) because of its coolness (ibid.).

cultivation of the plant spread rapidly. Hemp came to be used only for coarse products like sacking, rope, fish nets, and funeral attire. At first, cotton was grown mainly in the higher parts of Songjiang prefecture and Taicang department, especially along the coastal ridge (see Map 5), where irrigation for rice was difficult, and the saline soil was inhospitable to most other crops. By the early seventeenth century, according to the local gazetteer, only one-tenth of Jiading's cultivated area was under rice; all the rest was planted in cotton and beans (*Jiading xian zhi* 1605, 7: 3a). Later, with the silting up of the Dutai and Wunijing rivers in the 1660s, irrigation became difficult in Shanghai county, so that almost all the land was shifted from rice to cotton and beans (*Songjiang fu xuzhi* 1883, 7: 34b–35a). From the ridge, cultivation first spread east toward the sea and then west toward the lower-lying heart of the Tai basin. In the 1620s, by Xu Guangqi's estimate (1956 [1639]: 703), "of the nearly two million *mu*" of Songjiang prefecture's cultivated land, "more than half are under cotton, which should be in excess of one million *mu*." If Xu is anywhere near the mark, an even higher or at least equal proportion of the cultivated land was under cotton in that period than in the 1930s (42.4 percent in Songjiang, 50.0 percent in Taicang; Zhang Xinyi 1930a: 28, 35–36).

Expanding cotton cultivation, in turn, triggered a booming handicraft spinning and weaving industry, which extended even to neighboring Changshu county (in Suzhou) and Wuxi county (in Changzhou), neither a major cotton grower itself. By the seventeenth century, as Ye Mengzhu's detailed treatise on the Yangzi delta economy observes (1935 [ca. 1693], 7: 5a–6b), the Shanghai county area was exporting thick *biaobu* cloth via the Grand Canal to North China, and the thinner *zhongji* up the Yangzi River to Jiangxi and Hunan-Hubei, thence to Guangdong and Guangxi (see also Xu Guangqi 1956 [1639]: 708). Exports to North China declined in the eighteenth century, for Zhili and Shandong had by then developed their own spinning and weaving industries (Huang 1985: 118–20), but a new market developed in the Northeast as more and more settlers poured into Fengtian prefecture. On the eve of the Opium War, according to the estimates of Xu Xinwu (n.d.), Songjiang prefecture was exporting perhaps 15,000,000 bolts (*pi*) of cloth a year to the Northeast and Beijing, 10,000,000 to Guangdong, and 1,000,000 to Fujian.* In addition, about 10,000,000 bolts a year passed through

*The pi varied from place to place, but a standard bolt of native cloth in Shanghai after the late 19th century was 1.4 feet wide by 23.3 feet long and weighed 1.32 standard catties. This is the size bolt discussed here (Wu Chengming 1985: 389).

neighboring Changshu, and 3,000,000 through Wuxi, the second- and third-most-important cloth-trading centers of the delta. In all, the delta exported perhaps 40,000,000 bolts a year in the 1830s (Wu Chengming 1985: 278–79).*

It took about seven workdays to produce a bolt of cloth: 2 days for the fluffing and sizing of the cotton, 3.6 to 4 for the spinning, and 1 for the weaving (Wu Chengming 1985: 389–90). Exports of 40,000,000 bolts of cloth would thus have required about 280,000,000 workdays to produce, or about 117 workdays per household (based on a population of some 2,400,000 households in 1816; Appendix B).

In 1860, on the eve of the intrusion of international capitalism into China, about 45 percent of all peasant households nationwide engaged in cloth weaving (and most of these, 80 percent, grew their own cotton). In Songjiang prefecture, the country's leading cotton handicrafts center, where virtually all peasant households wove, the average household produced 66.3 bolts of cloth a year, but kept only 8.4 bolts for its own consumption (Xu Xinwu n.d.).† The high degree of the delta countryside's commercialization is simply beyond dispute.

MULBERRIES AND SILK

Just as cotton and cotton cloth were central to economic growth in Songjiang prefecture and Taicang department, so mulberries and silk were central to growth in Suzhou prefecture. Concentrated in the areas east and south of the lake, especially the counties of Wuxian and Wujiang in Suzhou, and the northern Zhejiang prefectures of Huzhou, Jiaxing, and Hangzhou, the silk industry expanded greatly in the Ming and Qing, powered by and itself powering the general commercialization and urbanization of the time. As the merchant classes expanded, the well-to-do among them, along with other rich urbanites, not just the members of the official classes and the degree-holding gentry, took to wearing silk. The industry responded by producing more durable and cheaper goods to suit the new consumers and supply the enlarged market for silk products (Wu Chengming 1985: 95–99).

*This would have required more than 50,000,000 catties of ginned cotton, or the yield from 1,700,000 mu of land (at an average yield of about 30 catties per mu; Zhang Xinyi 1930a: 36), out of a total cultivated area of about 16,000,000 mu.

†To arrive at these figures, Xu and his associates made careful estimates of per capita cloth consumption and of the proportion of households engaged in weaving based on interviews, then factored in population changes, consumption levels, domestic production, and foreign imports. The per household figure of 8.4 bolts assumes 5 household members, or 1.68 bolts a year per person.

In the process, silk weaving became a specialized activity almost completely separated from peasant farming. Even by the late Ming, much of the weaving was done by hired workers employed in workshops in the towns. Documentation on the subject is limited, but a 1601 report on a riot by silk workers in Suzhou city spoke of several thousands of dyers and a comparable number of weavers (who would lose their source of livelihood when these industries in the city shut down; Wu Chengming 1985: 156). By the eighteenth century, there were at least 20,000 silk looms in the Suzhou area (plus another 20,000 around Hangzhou, and 40,000 around Nanjing; ibid., p. 370). The three official Imperial Silk Manufactories (Zhizaoju), in the cities of Suzhou, Hangzhou, and Nanjing, accounted for only a small share of the production: 1,836 looms and 7,055 artisans in 1745 (ibid., p. 368). A century later, in 1840, just 10 percent or so of all domestically produced silk fabric was still woven by peasant cottage industry (ibid., p. 325).*

Mulberry cultivation, silkworm raising, and silk reeling, however, remained exclusively peasant household activities. Those three activities were combined within the peasant family production unit in the same way as cotton growing, cotton spinning, and cotton weaving were. Only in modern times, with improved cocoon preservation methods, did silk reeling come to be separated from peasant household production and undertaken in filatures.

GRAIN

Cotton and mulberry cultivation both helped to power the further commercialization of grain. Before the Ming and Qing, Suzhou and Changzhou prefectures were grain-surplus areas. The Yangzi delta was long the principal source of the capital's tribute grain. As the Song saying, still current in the mid-Ming, had it: "When the crops ripen in Suzhou and Changzhou, all under heaven are well supplied."† Increased mulberry cultivation and the dramatic spread of cotton cultivation, however, turned the region into a grain-short one that had to be supplied by grain imports from other regions. By the end of the Ming, the earlier saying about Suzhou and Changzhou began to give way to a new one: "When the crops ripen in Hunan and

---

*The majority of the urban workshops, to judge by 20th-century evidence, would have been small operations employing just a handful of workers. In Suzhou city in 1913, the average establishment had 1.5 looms and 7.7 employees; Wu Chengming 1985: 377.

†A more commonly quoted version makes it Suzhou and Huzhou (Wu Chengming 1985: 89).

Hubei, all under heaven are well supplied." In the eighteenth century, the delta got most of its rice imports via the Yangzi River from
Sichuan, Hunan, Anhui, and Jiangxi. By Wu Chengming's estimate
(1985: 274–75), about 15,000,000 shi of rice were shipped down to
the Yangzi delta and Zhejiang province each year, enough to feed a
population of 4,000,000–5,000,000. This was supplemented by other
grains from the Northeast, via coastal shipping. By the 1830s, more
than 10,000,000 shi of wheat and soybeans entered Shanghai this
way (ibid., p. 273).

URBANIZATION

Silk, cotton, and market rice powered a dramatic growth of towns
and cities in the Yangzi delta in the Ming and Qing. Suzhou city, the
country's principal silk-weaving and cotton cloth–processing center, became the largest metropolis in China (until its decline after
the middle of the nineteenth century). More telling still was the rise
and development of large towns linked to the marketing of cloth,
silk, and grain. This process is charted statistically in Appendix C.
Table C.1, based on a partial count of towns (zhen*), market-towns
(shi), and markets (cunji) in present-day Shanghai municipality by
their first appearance in a gazetteer, gives a rough indication of the
scale of urbanization in that part of the delta during successive reign
periods. Fully 362 new towns emerged in the Qing, and by far the
greatest share of those for which the basis of town formation can be
identified—28 of 69—emerged around the commercialized cotton
economy (Table C.2).†

The sheer number of new towns founded in the Ming and Qing
tells us that the urban population must have increased faster than
the general population. Skinner estimates that 7.4 percent of the
population of the "lower Yangzi region" lived in towns of 2,000 or
more in 1843, a substantially higher proportion than the 4.2 percent
of townsmen in the less-commercialized "North China region,"

---

*The zhen was originally a military unit, rendered by Charles Hucker (1985) as a
"Defense Command" or a "Garrison." By Ming and Qing times, however, large market towns (shi) were given the administrative status of zhen—hence its contemporary meaning of a town (Liu Shiji 1978e).

†Wang Wenchu (1983: 114) lists 38 zhen in Songjiang prefecture, plus Jiading and
Baoshan counties, by the specialty cloth for which they were known. Liu Shiji (1978a:
34–36) gives 48 for Songjiang and Changzhou prefectures and Taicang department.
For Suzhou prefecture, Liu shows four connected with silk weaving and the silk trade.
He lists nineteen others in the delta areas of Zhejiang province: six in Hangzhou pre-
fecture, five in Huzhou prefecture, and eight in Jiaxing prefecture (p. 32).

though still modest compared with the 27.5 percent (for towns of 5,000 or more) in England in 1801 (Skinner 1977: 229; Wrigley 1985: 682, table 2).

PEASANT FAMILY PRODUCTION

What happened to peasant family production in the midst of all these changes? To answer that question, we need to turn to the cropping records, which are for the peasants what written documents are for the elites.

North China

I begin with North China, for the changes there, also powered chiefly by a commercialized cotton economy, can be drawn in sharper relief than in the delta, a region that began at a much higher point of agricultural intensification at the start of the Ming. In part the North China plain's lag was due to the dry-farming agrarian regime; but it was also due to the massive depopulation that occurred in the Mongol campaigns against the Jin in the 1210s, campaigns that left Hebei and Shandong provinces with a combined total population of only about 7,000,000 at the start of the Ming (Huang 1985: 114). We also have richer twentieth-century field-research materials about the cultivation practices of various crops for North China.

The major crops of the North China plain were spiked millet, grown since Han times (Hsü 1980: 83–84), and sorghum, cultivated after the fourteenth century. Because of sorghum's distinctive tolerance for water, it became the main crop on easily waterlogged land. An agricultural treatise of 1596 (Li Shizhen's *Bencao gangmu*) observed that the crop was by then widely grown in the North (Amano 1962: 31–32). In the twentieth century, it was the main spring crop in the lower Yellow River valley, prompting Buck (1937a) to term this the "winter wheat–kaoliang [sorghum] area."

Neither sorghum nor millet required much labor. Sorghum needed only an average of 6.4 days per mu in the 1930s, and millet 6.9 days (Buck 1937a: 314). The Mantetsu field investigators reported that even then women and children did very little in sorghum and millet farming. For these crops, plowing and pulverizing the soil, planting, cultivating, and harvesting were all relatively heavy work. Sometimes boys helped weed the millet fields, and children helped pluck the lower leaves of the sorghum. Otherwise, men did almost all the work as far as these two crops were concerned (Kita Shina 1943: 60–61; KC, 1: 236; KC, 3: 129–32).

Only the growing of other crops brought women and children to do more work in the fields. A winter crop of wheat or barley put pressures on farm labor in May–June, when the winter crops had to be harvested at the same time that the spring-planted crops required cultivating. Women and children therefore generally helped with the harvesting, especially of barley, which was relatively light work. They also helped in the threshing, winnowing, and milling of the grain (KC, 3: 130–31; Kita Shina 1943: 65; KC, 5: 451–52). Such multiple cropping, of winter wheat after millet, might have been practiced already in Han times. By the sixth century, the method of rotating and growing three crops in two years—millet + winter wheat + soybeans + fallow—was already well known, as documented in the agricultural treatise Qimin yaoshu. It was to become the dominant cropping system on the plain down to the twentieth century (Zhongguo nongye yichan yanjiushi 1984, 1: 253–54; Hsü 1980: 111).

The system was modified somewhat with the introduction of maize. Found in Shandong already in the Ming (Amano 1962: 53–56), the New World crop spread steadily on the North China plain during the Qing, replacing sorghum where land was least susceptible to waterlogging. (The massive cultivation of maize in easily waterlogged areas came only after systematic efforts to control the problem in the 1960s. In the irrigated regions of China, its spread was limited mainly to mountainous and hilly areas with difficult access to water.) By the eve of the Revolution, maize had come to occupy 8–10 percent of the cultivated acreage on the plain (Perkins 1969: 236, 251; Zhongyang remin zhengfu nongyebu 1950: 53). Where it was interplanted with winter wheat, it might have raised the intensity of farm labor, but in general it did not require significantly more labor than sorghum or millet.

Labor input did increase when sweet potatoes came to be grown in place of conventional foodgrains. Though hateful to the peasants as a staple, sweet potatoes had the advantage of very high yields per unit area, able to sustain more people than conventional foodgrains. First grown in Shandong in 1749 as an emergency measure under famine conditions, sweet potatoes occupied about 3.5 percent of the cultivated area in Hebei-Shandong by the twentieth century (Huang 1985: 116). In the 1930s, the crop required an average of eleven days of labor per mu, substantially more than millet, sorghum, or maize. Though cultivable under the harshest of soil and climatic conditions, sweet potatoes are highly responsive to increased inputs of labor, water, and fertilizer. In the late 1930s, the peasant growers of

Tiaoshanying village, in central Hebei, an area with highly developed well irrigation, put in 28.3 days of labor per mu, compared with an average of only 5.1 days for dry-farmed foodgrains. Here children and women often stood watch over the irrigation ditches, while two or three men worked the waterwheel that pumped water from the wells. Further, in August the tendrils of the crop had to be moved, which was relatively light work, and women helped with this. Sometimes they also helped with the harvesting, generally done in groups of four to five men and women (Kita Shina 1943: 61).

Near towns and cities, commercialized vegetable farming engaged the entire household. In Tiaoshanying, one mu of vegetable garden required 93.9 days of labor, a good part of which was furnished by the women and children. In transplanting cabbage, for example, a team of eight people generally worked together, with four pulling the shoots, transporting the water, planting, and watering, two transporting the shoots, and two digging the holes for planting. Women and children helped in this work, as well as in harvesting (Kita Shina 1943: 61, 87).

But it was commercialized cotton cultivation, above all, that most brought auxiliary household labor into production. First grown on the plain in the sixteenth century, cotton occupied about 8 percent of the cultivated area of Hebei and Shandong by the 1930s, concentrated especially in central and southern Hebei and northwest Shandong (Huang 1985: 126–28). Cotton required substantially more labor than the dry-farmed foodgrains: an average of 11.6 days per mu in this area (Buck 1937b: 316). Moreover, cotton differs from the other crops in its harvesting work, which though relatively light extends over a much longer period, generally lasting about six weeks from late September to early November, as against two weeks for most other crops. Buck (p. 320) estimated that harvesting accounted for 34 percent of the labor put into cotton, much higher than the 13 percent for sorghum, maize and millet, 16 percent for wheat, and 10 percent for rice. The cotton harvest came at the same time as the harvesting of sorghum, millet, and maize, as well as the planting of winter wheat, all relatively heavy work. The result was a division of labor by gender: cotton picking came to be principally women's work. Children were often mobilized too, since they could strip this relatively short plant more easily than an adult (*Songjiang fu zhi* 1817, 6: 10a-10b). Men who did not have to harvest other crops on their own farms generally hired out as harvesters for additional income (KC, 3: 129–32; Huang 1985: 143).

With cotton cultivation, of course, came handicraft spinning and weaving. In most cotton-growing villages, women and girls spun their own yarn and wove their own cloth, at least for meeting the needs of home consumption. In places with good access to transportation, along the river systems of central and southern Hebei and the Grand Canal in northwest Shandong, a commercialized handicraft industry developed. By the eighteenth century, North China, still reliant on imports of cotton cloth from the delta 100 years earlier, was not only able to meet its own needs, but was exporting cloth as far as the Northeast and Korea (Huang 1985: 118–20). The female members of the household generally did the bulk of the work.

The overall trend, then, was toward the increased familization of rural production, which is directly counter to what the "natural economy" model tells us to expect: instead of decreasing the involvement of women and other family members in production, agricultural commercialization increased it. The production unit summed up in the expression, "the men farm and the women weave," which is conventionally used almost as an alternative designation for a pre-commercial peasant economy, was actually elaborated and strengthened by commercialization.

The Yangzi Delta

A parallel process occurred in the Yangzi delta, to end in an even greater elaboration of the family production unit. In the middle zone of the delta plain, where transplanted wet-rice had been grown at least since the Song, Japanese field investigators of the 1930s and 1940s reported relatively little farmwork being done by women and children. Apart from helping to pull shoots at transplanting time, their participation was limited mainly to helping with the threshing, and sometimes also operating the pumps or weeding and raking. The pattern only changed if a shortage of male labor developed, usually because of hiring out among the poorer peasants. In the single-cropped and relatively labor-abundant Huayangqiao villages, rich and middle peasant women did almost no work in the fields (MT, Shanghai 1940: 158).

Rice was hardly double-cropped at all in the delta until after the Revolution. Early-ripening rice was widely known even in the eleventh century. In 1011, for example, the Zhengzong Emperor ordered that large quantities of early-ripening (long-grain) champa seeds be supplied to the delta from Fujian. But it was used mainly for its drought-resistant qualities, as an emergency crop in a famine (*Wuxing zhanggu ji* 1560, 13: 4b–5a). The local people always preferred the short-grain variety to long-grain champa, and the crop remained restricted to areas without ready access to irrigation (*Huzhou fu zhi* 1874, 32: 2b–3b). Its use as the first of two rice crops came only in the 1960s under vigorous state sponsorship.

Increased demand for labor in foodgrain cultivation in the delta came not with a second crop of rice, then, but with the planting of winter wheat, which spread with the massive southward migrations at the end of the Northern Song. In the 1130s, during the early years of the Southern Song, wheat prices even rose to two times those of rice, giving a powerful stimulus to wheat cultivation. At the same time, since most tenants paid rent only on the fall harvest, a spring crop was an added bonus entirely one's own, especially critical for tiding over farm families in the months before the autumn harvest (Fan Shuzhi 1983). The spread of winter wheat was limited only by soil conditions. A dry crop that does not do well in the soggy soil of rice fields, wheat was grown mainly on high-lying ground (*Wujiang xian zhi* 1747, 38: 5a; *Wuxian zhi* 1933, 52: 7b–8a; *Xi jin shi xiaolu* 1752, 1: 5b). But in areas where land pressure was most extreme, as, for example, in parts of Huzhou and Jiaxing in the nineteenth century, peasants apparently built up rice fields to grow winter wheat after they harvested their rice, then lowered them again for rice (*Huzhou fu zhi* 1874, 32: 4a; *Jiaxing fu zhi* 1878, 32: 14b). Where the second cropping followed cotton rather than rice, barley was preferred because it had a shorter growing season than wheat (*Jiading xian xuzhi* 1930, 5: 15b). In the delta, as in North China, wheat and barley cultivation raised labor demands and propelled the greater involvement of auxiliary household labor in agricultural production.

As we have seen, cotton spread both east and west from the coastal ridge during the Ming, to occupy perhaps more than 50 percent of the cultivated area by the seventeenth century. As a result, women and children were drawn deeply into agricultural production. Where cotton was the dominant crop, as in the high-lying periphery of the basin, both men and women were involved in its cultivation: this was the case in both Fengxian and Nanhui (H-III-30; *Nanhui xian zhi* 1879, 20: 3a). Where it was grafted onto a dominant rice regime, it sometimes came to be principally women's work, as in Huayang-qiao (H-III-10). Rice was generally harvested during the middle third of October, overlapping with the early weeks of the cotton harvest. Women and children did the cotton harvesting to relieve the pressures resulting from this kind of agricultural intensification (MT, Shanghai 1940: 88, 94).

The cottage industry in cotton grew at an astounding pace. Already in the Zhengde period (1506–21), Songjiang prefecture's cloth was said to "clothe the entire empire." By 1860, as noted earlier, almost every peasant household produced cloth, and by the estimate of Xu Xinwu (n.d.), seven-eighths of their product was for the market, not for home consumption. So here, as in North China, the family production unit was elaborated and strengthened, not eroded, with the commercialization of agriculture in the Ming–Qing period.

Parallel developments occurred in sericulture. When combined with the double-cropping of rice and winter wheat, sericulture required the participation of family labor. For one thing, mulberry cultivation raised the farm labor requirement to 32.3 days per mu. In addition, the spring silkworms require very intense labor during their 28-day feeding period. During the first three "sleeps" of the worms, the work of feeding mulberry leaves to the worms and of keeping the straw trays clean is relatively light: one person could easily watch over the one "sheet" of eggs that the average household kept. But in the fourth and fifth stages, the breeding trays are heavy with worms weighing 30 to 40 catties, and the frequency of the feeding goes up, with a single sheet of worms consuming about 200 catties of leaves a day.*

In many places, women bore the main burden of this intense work. As the 1874 Huzhou prefectural gazetteer puts it:

> The women work especially hard. During the silkworm feeding period, . . . they must get up six or seven times a night. Mulberry leaves with morning dew are especially good for the silkworms; the women therefore pick the leaves early in the morning, with no time to comb their hair or wash their faces. The leaves cannot stand fog; on cloudy days, therefore, they pick the leaves at night. The leaves cannot stand sand and dust . . . or heat. . . . They must be spread evenly on the straw trays. . . . As for the men, they are faced with the start of the busy farmwork season and cannot attend much to the silkworms. Thus, from beginning to end, the women account for 90 percent of the work. (Huzhou fu zhi 1874, 30: 2a–2b)

Until the introduction of the modern filature, almost all silkworm cocoons were reeled into raw silk by the individual peasant households, usually the women. In this respect, silk was very much like cotton. But silk weaving required higher capitalization and was early detached from the family farm. Typically, peasants sold their raw silk to merchants (sihang), who transported it to the major towns and cities for processing. Nevertheless, in combining mul-

*Details about silkworm feeding come from interviews at Kaixiangong village in 1985 (H-III-36, 37).

berry growing, silkworm rearing, and silk reeling, the peasant family farm worked on the same principle as the cotton-growing, yarn-spinning, and cloth-weaving household.

VARIATIONS BY CLASS AND GENDER

Within the broad patterns outlined in the preceding section, there were of course variations, even within the same locality and village. My own oral-history work in Huayangqiao shows that there was substantial variation by social-economic status. Work associated with rice cultivation, for example, ranged across a continuum from the lightest to the heaviest. At one end were such tasks as threshing and husking, pulling up shoots from the seedbeds (*bayang*), and weeding, and at the other, planting, harrowing, transporting fertilizer and the harvested paddy, and the like. Almost all the peasant women helped with threshing and husking, work that did not really take them away from the house. Except for this, the Xue women of Xue Family Village, who belonged to the richest households, did not do any farmwork. They almost never went into the fields, and the households hired help even for the very light work of pulling the shoots. At the other end of the spectrum were He Huihua and Guo Zhuying of the South Hamlet, who had married into Huayangqiao from villages where women did much more farmwork. After marriage, they continued to do all kinds of work in the fields, even planting, a job that in these villages was considered to require the greatest skill and was usually the sole prerogative of men. Though the other poor peasant women did not plant, they did middle-range tasks like raking, driving the oxen for the water pumps, and even harrowing, in addition to the ligher chores of shoot-pulling and weeding. In general, poorer peasant women tended to do more farmwork because their men usually hired out in the busy season. Middle- and rich-peasant women did comparatively little, both because they did not have to and because they tended to imitate elite values and ideals to a greater degree (H-III-15).

Planting is the best example of the influence of elite mores on peasant economic behavior. In Huayangqiao, an entire ethos surrounded this work. It was the highest-paid task of the whole production cycle: one peck of rice (*dou*, ca. 16 catties) for one day's work, compared with one-half peck for tasks like weeding and harrowing and one-third for the "women's task" of pulling up the paddy shoots. Employers vied for the best planters, usually contracting with them well ahead of time, at New Year's. The employer was expected to provide generous board for the planters: the usual fare called for six big pieces of pork of two-three ounces each a day, plus fish, chicken, and wine. Women were assumed to be incapable of doing anything requiring so much skill. He and Guo had both learned to plant in their natal villages, where the same fictions associated with planting did not exist (H-I-16; H-III-15).

After the Revolution, the irrationality of this assumption was rather quickly demonstrated. Women, fully mobilized for planting under a piecework system based on the number of mu planted, regularly outperformed the men.* Today, in these very same villages, planting is in fact seen as "women's work." One woman pointed out that, in planting single-cropped rice, the men sometimes limited their contribution to transporting the heavy shoots. The rub was that one of their loads usually lasted for half a day of planting, and they would have little else to do while the women slaved away (H-III-16).

That a fiction could be so completely and irrationally maintained attests to the power of custom and ideology. In this case, I think that the association of planting with men might have been linked to the custom of footbinding, which made sloshing around in the flooded fields a rather messy business. Wu Xiaomei of Xubushanqiao, for example, said she never did any farmwork for which she had to take off her shoes, which ruled out not only planting but also weeding whenever the fields were wet (H-I-15).

But these prejudices, if they existed, could be overcome when there was an economic imperative for women's participation in farmwork, as for example in the areas that grew cotton. In some places, cotton cultivation even came to be known as strictly women's work. Silkworm growing, silk reeling, and cotton spinning and weaving, of course, were approved women's work. Variations across different village social strata and from one village to the next, and one area to another, should not obscure the broad and basic trend outlined earlier: with the coming of commercialized cropping and the development of handicraft industries came the demand for the involvement of women and children in production, and hence the fuller elaboration of the family work unit that combined farming with home industry.

*The women's superiority was quantified and recorded in production team account books. The local peasants contend the women's more supple waists give them greater stamina than men in the task of planting.

THE NORTH CHINA PLAIN VS. THE YANGZI DELTA

For all their similar tendencies toward the familization of production, there were important differences of degree between the North China plain and the Yangzi delta. Buck's regional field survey data show a sharp contrast in the extent of women's involvement in farmwork: in the "Yangzi Rice-Wheat" area, they did 19.1 percent of all farmwork (and children 7.6 percent), but 8.5 percent (and 4.7 percent) in the North, a better than two-to-one difference (Buck 1937b: 305). Irrigation, greater commercialization, and greater development of home industry all made for a higher degree of familization in the Yangzi delta.

As the preceding sections make clear, it will not do to simplify the picture into a matter of North China women and children doing no production and Yangzi delta women and children doing a lot, or to think of the difference between the two regions as merely one of dry farming versus riziculture. Each region in fact shows a continuum from little to great involvement. The two continuums overlapped, as in the development of cotton cultivation and cotton textiles, but the delta extended much farther toward full familization, exemplified by the highly commercialized cotton-weaving household of Songjiang and silkworm-raising, silk-reeling household of Suzhou (and Jiaxing and Huzhou).

The synchronic spatial differences should not obscure the more fundamental diachronic trends evidenced in both regions. Even Buck's data, disaggregated to the county level, tell of the temporal trends. For example, in Zhengding county in central Hebei, known since the late Ming as a major cotton-growing center, women did 17.3 percent of the farmwork, a much higher proportion than the average for North China. In the delta, the figure was 24.1 percent for the traditional sericulture area of Jiaxing, and an extraordinary 37.3 percent in the new sericulture area of Wuxi (Buck 1937b: 305). In both regions, clearly, commercialization and agricultural intensification brought the increased familization of production.

CHAPTER 4

Commercialization
and Managerial Agriculture

The classical view of Marx and Smith is that commercialization will be accompanied by the rise of larger-scale production based on wage labor. "Incipient capitalism" scholars in China especially have expended much effort on searching out the evidence for this development. The Ming-Qing record of the Yangzi delta, however, shows that commercialization brought not the rise of wage labor–based managerial agriculture, but its demise. This is the more surprising because in North China, commercialization was indeed associated to some degree with the spread of managerial agriculture (Huang 1985). By the logic of that story, the much more highly commercialized Yangzi delta should have witnessed an expansion of managerial agriculture. This chapter begins with the empirical evidence and then looks into the question of why the delta took a different turn.

MANAGERIAL AGRICULTURE IN THE DELTA

The Twentieth Century

The truth on managerial agriculture in the Yangzi delta has been obscured by the nature of the available statistical data. The twentieth-century provincial data for Hebei and Shandong accurately reflect the conditions on the North China plain. But the data on Jiangsu province are highly misleading, scrambling up as they do two very different geographical regions: one dry-farmed and highly disaster-prone, north of the Huai, really a part of the North China plain; the other under wet-rice and relatively more stable.* Indeed, to look only at the totals is to see a picture in the 1930s not too different from the North China plain: 1.31 percent of all farms larger

---

*Geographers further subdivide the area south of the Huai into the Lixia River area, the Yangzi River area, the Taihu area, and the coastal belt (*Jiangsu dili* 1980: 116–20). For our purposes, the larger distinction will suffice.

than 100 mu, compared with Hebei's 1.71 percent (Tudiweiyuanhui 1937: 26); 12.1 percent of all farmwork done by hired labor, compared with Hebei's 23.4 percent (Buck 1937b: 305); and 8.8 percent of the population employed as agricultural laborers, compared with Hebei's 11.6 percent (Chen Zhengmo 1935: 58).

But ethnographic surveys of individual villages tell a very different story. In the Hebei–northwest Shandong case, they confirm the picture drawn by the aggregated provincial data: Mantetsu surveys of 33 villages suggest that managerial agriculture accounted for an average of about 9–10 percent of the total cultivated area, and that year- or long-term laborers accounted for 12.5 percent of all village households and for five-eighths of all farmwork done by hired labor (the rest being done by day-laborers; Huang 1985: 80–81). But in our eight delta villages, there was not a single farm that met the definition of a managerial farm used here (i.e., a farm relying mainly on hired labor, usually employing three or more laborers). As Table 4.1 shows, four of the eight had no farms that employed year-laborers at all; the others had rich peasant farms employing one or two year-laborers, but no larger-scale farms using principally hired labor. The year-laborer households represented only 2.9 percent of the four villages' combined total; in none did the proportion reach 5 percent.

Buck's county data allow a glimpse at the real situation in the Yangzi delta: of the total farmwork, only a negligible amount in Changshu, 5.3 percent in Wuxi, and 4.5 percent in Kunshan was done by hired labor, far below the Jiangsu provincial average of 12.1 percent (Buck 1937b: 305). Our best disaggregated source is the systematic survey of southern Jiangsu conducted in 1949 by the Land Reform Committee of the East China Commission for Military Administration (Huadong junzheng weiyuanhui 1952). Twenty-two townships, administrative villages, and natural villages in eight delta counties were surveyed, including one of just 62 households and one as large as 2,687 households. Table 4.2 gives the average percentage for the eight counties, weighting each county equally without regard to the number of households surveyed. This corrects for a disproportionate emphasis on Wuxi, which accounted for 42 percent of the total of 65,812 people surveyed. The county had very few agricultural laborers (28 identified households and 143 people among those surveyed), because of the wide availability of sideline and off-farm employment. The result, an average of 3.8 percent for agricultural-laborer households, seems to me a good working figure for the incidence of long-term agricultural wage labor in the delta.

TABLE 4.1
Agricultural Laborers in Eight Yangzi Delta Villages, 1939–40

Village	Total households	Year-laborer households		Day-laborer households	
		Number	Percent	Number	Percent
Touzongmiao, Nantong	94	3	3.2%	33	35.1%
Xiaodingxiang,[a] Wuxi	80	0	0	20	25.0
Yanjiashang, Changshu	55	0	0	6	10.9
Yaojing, Taicang	52	1	1.9	22	42.3
Dingjiacun, Jiading	53	0	0	14	26.4
Sunjiaxiang, Wuxian	209	4	1.9	15	7.2
Kaixiangong, Wujiang	360	17	4.7	—	—
Huayangqiao, Songjiang	63	0	0	28	44.4

SOURCES: Touzongmiao: MT, Shanhai 1941b; Xiaodingxiang: ibid., 1941a; Yanjiashang: ibid., 1939b; Yaojing: ibid., 1939c; Dingjiacun: ibid., 1939a; Sunjiaxiang: Hayashi Megumi 1943; Kaixiangong: Fei Hsiao-tung (Fei Xiaotong) 1939; Huayangqiao: MT, Shanhai 1940.
[a] Includes the adjacent hamlets.

Considered in conjunction with the ethnographic evidence, what these figures show is that, in contrast to the North China plain, managerial agriculture was virtually nonexistent in the Yangzi delta in the 1930s. Only relatively small rich-peasant farms (in which the peasant-owner himself worked in the fields, with the help of an equivalent amount or less of hired labor) used hired labor.* Those accounted for the 3.8 percent or so of hired-laborer households. Landowners who did not farm their land themselves (a group that accounted for 42 percent of the cultivated area [Huadong junzheng weiyuanhui 1952: 6–7]; as against about 18 percent in North China) almost invariably chose to lease land to small tenants instead of managing their farms with hired labor.

The Ming-Qing Period

Wage labor–based rich peasant and managerial agriculture was probably less widespread in the delta in the 1930s than in the Ming, when the cotton economy began to develop and the silk economy to expand. Wage labor had spread enough in the rice-and-sericulture

*On the intricacies of the definitions of rich, middle, and poor peasant and managerial farmer, see Huang 1985: 69–70.

TABLE 4.2

Agricultural Laborers in Twenty-Two Yangzi Delta Townships and Villages, 1949

Township/ village	Popu- lation	House- holds	Agricultural laborers			
			Households		Population	
			Number	Percent	Number	Percent
Qingpu county				*8.0%*		*4.4%*
Chengbei xiang	4,425	991	46	4.6	106	2.4
Chelu cun,						
Xuejian xiang	237	62	7	11.3	15	6.3
Jiangyin county				*3.1%*		*2.6%*
#1 Xinmin cun,						
Changjing zhen	559	130	6	4.6	20	3.6
Xinmin et al.,						
Dunan xiang	2,956	718	22	3.1	64	2.2
Wukong xiang	8,210	1,814	30	1.7	158	1.9
Wuxi county				*0.4%*		*0.5%*
#3 bao, Xuedian						
zhen	1,090	—	0	0	0	0
Yanqiao xiang	1,889	—	0	0	0	0
#10 bao, Beiyan						
zhen	1,607	—	—	—	6	0.4
#3 bao, Yuqi						
zhen	951	—	0	0	0	0
#9 bao, Beiyan						
zhen	1,507	—	—	—	14	0.9
Fangqian xiang	3,872	773	9	1.2	35	0.9
#8 bao, Zhouxin						
zhen	1,052	—	0	0	0	0
#5 bao, Xindu						
zhen	1,382	—	—	—	10	0.7
Yunlin xiang	12,514	2,687	15	0.6	57	0.5
Cunqian cun,						
Yanqiao xiang	1,476	302	4	1.3	21	1.4
Jiading county,						
Tangxi xiang	2,669	581	7	1.2	10	0.4
Wujin county,						
Meigang xiang	3,303	726	23	3.2	73	2.2
Songjiang county,						
Xinnong xiang	3,430	808	49	6.1	138	4.0
Kunshan county				*2.9%*		*1.0%*
Taiping xiang	2,540	524	14	2.7	22	0.9
Xiaoyu xiang	2,375	546	17	3.1	25	1.1
Wuxian county				*5.1%*		*3.0%*
Baoan xiang	7,004	1,575	65	4.1	171	2.4
Hejin cun, Yanli						
xiang	764	168	10	6.0	27	3.5
Combined average				*3.8%*		*2.3%*

SOURCE: Huadong junzheng weiyuanhui 1952: 13, 29, 30, 62–64, 81, 107, 116, 128, 134, 142, 153, 158, 165, 173.

economy of Wujiang county by the late fifteenth century to prompt this remark in the local gazetteer: "The propertyless peasants who hire out as farmworkers in the rich families are called *changgong* (long-term workers). Those who borrow grain to eat in advance, and then work for a month or two in the busy seasons are called *duangong* (short-term laborers)" (*Wujiang zhi* 1488, 6: 225). Not much later, the Suzhou gazetteer noted another term for the "propertyless who hire out": *manggong*, or "workers of the busy seasons" (*Gusu zhi* 1506, 13: 6b). Similar references were made to Huzhou and Jiaxing prefectures during the Jiajing period (1522–66). The Xiushui county (present-day Jiaxing) gazetteer of the Wanli period (1573–1620) likewise observed: "The fourth to the seventh month . . . are busy months, and the rich peasants hire labor to farm, either long-term laborers or short-term laborers" (cited in Li Wenzhi et al. 1983: 56–57). The same kind of phenomenon occurred in the cotton economy, documented, for example, by the Songjiang prefectural gazetteer of 1512 (ibid., p. 56).

The other side of the process was the rise of the farmers who employed this labor. Wu Kuan (Minister of Rites during the Xiaozong reign, 1488–1505) noted that there were several thousand diligent "upper peasants" (*shangnong*) in the delta region (Zhu Zongchou 1981: 575). In Wujiang county, reclaimed lakeshore land provided the opportunity for cultivators to make good. Zhu Guozhen (a *jinshi* degree holder of the Wanli period, 1573–1620) noted that within a 20-li area of his residence, two households had accumulated "10,000 pieces of gold" from scratch in this way. In Changshu, the effective irrigation of high-lying land along the river helped enrich a certain Gui family. Elsewhere in Changshu, the Tan brothers made good by combining agriculture with fish ponds. In the southern half of the delta, in Gui'an county in Huzhou, finally, a certain Mao Gen developed a lucrative large farm growing "hundreds of thousands" of mulberry trees (Fu Yiling 1963: 61–67).

The spread of wage labor and the rise of such well-to-do managerial farmers, we might speculate, were associated with the effects of the early stages of increased agricultural commercialization in the region. Commercialized farming meant, on the one hand, greater risks because of the greater investments involved, especially in fertilizer; a failed cash crop was more devastating than a failed subsistence crop. More peasant households, therefore, slid down the socioeconomic ladder to become agricultural laborers. But commercialization also meant greater opportunities for profitable farming, hence the emergence of "rich" farmers.

The regressive tax policies of the Ming, before the coming of the "Single Whip" reforms of the 1520s–60s, also encouraged managerial agriculture. As Gu Yanwu (1613–82) observed in some detail, in the Yangzi delta the Ming taxed "official land" (*guantian*) at rates close to rents, from 0.4 up to 1.0 shi of rice per mu, but put a far lower rate on "private land" (*mintian*), usually 0.05 shi per mu. Official land, from estates dislocated during the wars of dynastic transition, loomed especially large in the Yangzi delta, accounting for fully 85 percent of all land in Songjiang prefecture and for 63 percent in Suzhou prefecture in 1502. Small peasants cultivating the official land were burdened with much higher taxes than wealthy families. Powerful families, moreover, were able to have their lands classified as private land, even when it was actually official land. Another source of abuse was the corvée, a tax levied on the individual taxpayer. Gentry families were exempt from these personal taxes, and the wealthy commoner landlords sometimes arrogated to themselves similar privileges. But the only way for the small peasants to escape the heavy tax burden was to run away, and many did so. In 1432, for example, when Suzhou Prefect Kuang Zhong offered immunity to any runaways who returned, fully 36,670 households responded. Gu Yanwu estimated that in areas of very heavy taxes, more than half the peasants fled. Under these conditions, powerful and wealthy families had both the opportunity and the labor supply to set up managerial estates (Gu Yanwu 1662, 4: 43–44, 1962 [1695], 10: 234–42; Liang Fangzhong 1980: 351; Chen Hengli 1963: 207–25).

But contrary to what the "incipient capitalism" scholars have suggested, this did not signal a period of ever-expanding managerial agriculture in the Yangzi delta. In fact, it soon topped out—its difficulties recorded in the seventeenth-century *Shenshi nongshu* (Mr. Shen's agricultural treatise) and other texts—and began to give way to small farming, so that by the twentieth century there was virtually no managerial agriculture to speak of.

ROOTS OF THE DECLINE OF MANAGERIAL AGRICULTURE

The reasons for the demise of managerial agriculture in the delta can be gleaned from *Mr. Shen's Agricultural Treatise* (ca. 1640), which documents in considerable detail farming on the low-lying land around Gui'an county (present-day Wuxing county), Huzhou prefecture. The agrarian system there was typical of the yutian areas: rice was grown inside embanked fields, and mulberries on the embankments. The local sericulture economy, it is clear, was already highly familized by this time. Shen notes at considerable length how hiring labor to raise silkworms simply did not pay. Even with an optimal crop, the margin of return over costs, not counting labor, was a mere 0.2 tael per basket (*kuang*) of silkworms (at this time, a shi of rice cost around 1.25 taels). For a family that relied on its own labor and successfully raised the usual ten kuang, the activity paid. But if one had to hire labor, or if the brood were less than full, silkworm raising did not pay. It was an activity that was viable only if done by the auxiliary labor of low opportunity cost in peasant families (*Shenshi nongshu* 1936: 16).

But familized production had the paradoxical effect of pushing up the cost of male labor. Since the low-paying work was absorbed by women and children whose labor was of little opportunity cost, the men could work mainly in the heavier and better-paying kinds of farmwork. Shen (ibid., pp. 13–14) recorded the relatively high cost of that labor:

> The hired people now are arrogant and lazy as a matter of common practice. They can only be motivated by wine and food, and are much different from a hundred years ago. . . . The old custom called for one day of meat and two days of vegetables in the summer and fall; nowadays we should alternate them from one day to the next. If the work is heavy and difficult, we should provide meat every day. . . . The old custom called for one ladle of wine for three people, whether in the busy or the off-season; now we should provide one ladle per worker for heavy work, and half a ladle for medium-grade work.

The increased cost of wage labor that Shen complains of can be ascribed in part to the Single Whip tax reforms, which closed the source for the cheap runaway labor of the fifteenth and early sixteenth centuries. But that does not explain why the wages were strikingly higher than those prevailing in North China. On the plain, hired laborers typically got meat and wine only at the "feasts" marking the start and close of the year's work, and never as regular fare. If they received "fine grain" of wheat flour at noon, rather than "coarse grain" of millet, maize, or sorghum, that was considered classy fare (Huang 1985: 198–99). Effectively, the Yangzi delta worker enjoyed the equivalent of North China's seasonal feasts every other day. As Table 4.3 shows, the difference extended to the cash wage paid by employers, so that the total combined wage of day-laborers and year-laborers in the 1930s was typically about 50 percent higher in the delta than in Hebei–northwest Shandong.

TABLE 4.3
Agricultural Laborer Wages in Hebei–Northwest Shandong
and the Yangzi Delta, 1929–33

(Yuan)

County	Day-laborer				Year-laborer			
	Cash wage	Board	Other	Total	Cash wage	Board	Other	Total
Hebei–N.W.								
Shandong	*0.25*	*0.21*		*0.46*	*42.5*	*39.6*	*2.8*	*84.9*
Changli	0.30	0.20		0.50	60.0	30.0	2.0	90.0
Zhengding	0.32	0.30		0.62	33.3	40.0	0.8	74.1
Jiaohe	0.28	0.22		0.50	44.0	36.0	1.3	81.3
Nangong	0.18	0.20		0.38	37.7	40.0	2.7	80.4
Xushui	0.22	0.18		0.40	52.0	48.0	3.1	103.1
Cangxian	0.22	0.25		0.47	37.0	30.0	1.7	68.7
Qingxian	0.43	0.24		0.67	41.7	45.3	3.3	90.3
Tongxian	0.35	0.25		0.60	60.0	55.0	10.0	125.0
Enxian	0.08	0.19		0.27	37.7	37.3	2.8	77.8
Huimin	0.19	0.14		0.33	40.3	43.3	1.0	84.7
Tangyi	0.21	0.16		0.37	23.5	30.5	2.7	56.7
Yangzi								
delta	*0.32*	*0.40*	*0.01*	*0.73*	*49.5*	*65.2*	*6.3*	*121.0*
Changshu	0.20	0.30	0.02	0.52	36.0	49.0	4.0	89.0
Kunshan	0.38	0.25		0.63	72.0	72.0	3.6	147.6
Wuxi	0.33	0.72	0.01	1.06	60.0	50.0	7.5	117.5
Wujin	0.35	0.35	0.02	0.72	30.0	90.0	10.0	130.0

SOURCE: Buck 1937a: 328.

NOTE: The wage data in Chen Zhengmo 1935, grouped by provinces, have the same problems as the author's data on agricultural laborers. Wages differed greatly between northern and
southern Jiangsu, as they did between northwestern and eastern Shandong. Buck's data, broken
down by counties, are more accurate for our purposes.

Part of the explanation, of course, was the generally higher standard of living and more abundant employment opportunities afforded by the delta's relatively highly commercialized and urbanized
economy; equally important, however, was the two-tiered structure
of labor in the farm economy, where the women and children absorbed the lower-paying work. From eighteenth-century reports of
homicides in the Board of Punishment archives, Wei Jinyu has
culled 70 cases in which more than one family member hired out.
His data show that even at that time there was little market for the
labor of women. Indeed, their work was not considered worth the
cost of board, so that husband-and-wife teams were generally paid
less than a single laborer: in Henan, for example, a couple averaged
2,775 copper *cash* a year, a male laborer 3,564 *cash*. The laborer who
hired out with his wife was in effect charged part of his wife's board
(Li Wenzhi et al. 1983: 407, 413–17).

By the twentieth century, there was a limited market for female and child labor in Huayang. Male day-laborers were paid one peck (*dou*, 0.1 shi) of rice for one day's work in transplanting or two days' work in other tasks; women got one peck for three days' shoot-pulling. As long-term laborers, children were paid 0.5 shi of rice a year at age twelve (Chinese *sui*),* 1.0 shi at thirteen, and 1.5 shi at fourteen and fifteen, compared with 4.0 shi for adult males. Children also cost the employer substantially less in board: Lu Longshun recalls that as a child laborer, he had to eat in the kitchen after everyone else was finished, while the adult laborer ate with the family (H-I-1, 2).

But the market for female (and child) labor never developed up to the need for it, principally because so much social stigma was attached to the hiring out of women. It was bad enough for a man to have to hire out himself; for his wife or daughter to do so marked him as being at the bottom of the social ladder. In Huayangqiao in the 1930s and 1940s, not one woman or girl hired out; that was something done only by the very poor from other places. For this reason, though women accounted for 19.1 percent of all farmwork done in Buck's "Yangzi rice-wheat area" in the 1930s, they represented only 6.3 percent of the total hired labor (Buck 1937b: 305). It would have been difficult for an employer to hire women for low-paid farm tasks.

In the course of its development, California's agribusiness solved the problem by the use of cheap migrant labor, first Chinese, then Japanese (and dust-bowl refugees), and now Mexican. As a host of researchers, from Carey McWilliams to Cletus Daniel, have pointed out, the ready supply of migrant labor permits agribusiness to compete with family farms using auxiliary household labor of low opportunity cost, and goes a long way to explain its strength (and the weakness of family farming) in the state (Chan Sucheng 1986: 272–301).

In Mr. Shen's Huzhou of the seventeenth century, managerial farms were already squeezed by labor costs relative to returns. According to his detailed account, one hired adult male year-laborer, with the help of (adult male) day-laborers during the busy seasons, could farm eight mu of paddy and four mu of mulberries. On the rice paddy, Shen tells us, production costs and day-laborer wages ate up the receipts from the spring harvest (usually of winter wheat, which followed the fall crop of rice). The farmer reaped just the fall rice crop, worth about 22 taels. The year-laborer cost him 3.0 taels in cash and 6.5 taels in board. On top of this, he paid out 1.0 tael in

*Counting from two (sui) at the first New Year's after birth.

travel expenses, 0.3 tael for farm-implement repair, and 1.2 taels for fuel and wine, bringing the total to 12 taels. The employer thus net- ted at best ten taels from his eight mu of paddy: about what he would get if he just leased out the land.

As for the mulberries, Shen provides no more than the ambiguous notation that "from managing four mu of [mulberry] dry fields, the value is four taels" (*Shenshi nongshu* 1936: 15). Chen Hengli (1963: 79–89) interprets this passage to mean that the production cost for four mu of mulberries was four taels, and estimates that the leaves would have fetched about 36 taels, or nine times the production costs. This leads Chen to very high estimates of the net income from mulberry cultivation and, in turn, to his conclusion that there was a dynamic managerial agriculture and "incipient capitalist" develop- ment at this time.

I believe Chen's interpretation is mistaken, for it simply does not square with the rest of Shen's text. The sentence following the one on mulberries reads: "Eight *mu* of rice fields, deducting rent pay- ments, nets eight *shi* of good quality rice, which is worth ten taels." The preceding sentence almost certainly parallels this one, and the four-tael figure should refer to net income. Otherwise, Shen would be contradicting his own theme in the essay: that farm management did not pay. He writes: "In the western part [of our county], all the land is leased out, and [the owners] enjoy their profits in leisure. . . . But in our area, the leasing out of land is not the practice, and those who own land have no choice but to farm-manage it. To farm it, they have no choice but to hire year-laborers. They work hard all year round—not by choice, but because they have no choice" (*Shenshi nongshu* 1936: 15). Shen himself owned land in both areas. True to his own observations, he leased out more land than he farm-managed (Chen Hengli 1963: 2).

Further confirmation for my interpretation can be found in Zhang Lüxiang's sequel to *Mr. Shen's Agricultural Treatise* (1658). At the end of his text, Zhang appends an essay on plans that he had drawn up for the family of a deceased friend, who owned ten mu of land. Working the land with hired labor, Zhang advised, would not be viable, for it would reduce the net return to "the same as that from a stone field." Neither would leasing out the land, for "the rental in- come would merely be enough to meet tax payments." The only thing that would work was for the family to farm the land itself. To that end, Zhang urged a diversified cropping portfolio: three mu of mulberries, three mu of beans, followed by winter wheat, two mu of bamboo, and two mu of fruit. Rice should be avoided, because it required too much labor. The mulberry leaves from three mu of mulberry trees would feed 20 kuang of silkworms and produce 30 catties of raw silk. A second crop of silkworms could be raised in the summer. In addition, the family should maintain a small fish pond, raise five or six sheep, and supplement its income with handicraft work by the women (the widow and her mother) at home. This way, the family would be able to support itself (Zhang Lüxiang 1983 [1658]: 177–78).

The operation that Zhang advocated for his friend's family was in fact quite similar to that described in Mr. Shen's Agricultural Treatise: three of ten mu (30 percent) under mulberries, compared with four of twelve mu (33.3 percent) in Shen's example. The difference is that Zhang's calculations explicitly included the income from sericulture. Clearly, mulberry cultivation, even when augmented with silkworm raising and silk reeling, hardly brought the kind of returns that Chen Hengli attributes to it. The area could not have had the kind of lucrative managerial agriculture Chen imagines.

In the centuries after Mr. Shen's Agricultural Treatise, managerial agriculture in the delta, far from being in the process of long-term linear development, as the "incipient capitalism" scholars suggest, actually declined. Indeed, Li Wenzhi's own data based on an extensive study of gazetteers confirm this suggestion: the areas that saw the dynamic spread of wage labor in the Qing were mainly those that commercialized later than the delta, like Shandong and Hunan-Hubei. Virtually all of Li's extensive gazetteer citations for the late Ming period come from the Yangzi delta, as opposed to only three of sixteen for the Qing (Li Wenzhi et al. 1983: 56–57, 59–61). The same pattern holds for the Board of Punishment homicide cases cited by Li. As Table 4.4 shows, despite a definite increase in the incidence of homicides involving long-term laborers for China as a whole, there was no dramatic increase for Jiangsu and Zhejiang, as there was for Zhili and Shandong.

Another agricultural treatise (Jiang Gao 1963 [1834]: 11a, b) spells out the arithmetic and logic for rice cultivation in the Songjiang region:

> In the past, the cost of hiring people for farmwork was still relatively light. But now wages have gone up, and food prices have risen. In the busy season, one laborer for a day costs two sheng of rice, half a catty of meat, 30 wen of pickled vegetables, tobacco, and wine, plus 50 wen in wages, or a total of 200 wen a day. One mu of land requires ten workdays, or 2,000 wen. Fertilizer costs another 2,000 wen. The peasant who self-farms or exchanges labor with others might be able to reduce

TABLE 4.4
Homicide Cases Involving Year-Laborers in Zhili, Shandong, Jiangsu,
Zhejiang, and All of China, 1721–1820

Period	Zhili	Shandong	Jiangsu	Zhejiang	China
1721–1740	3	3	3	0	19
1741–1760	5	4	2	2	37
1761–1780	7	3	5	3	43
1781–1800	6	10	2	1	48
1801–1820	7	11	2	3	107

SOURCE: Li Wenzhi et al. 1983: 64–65.

costs a bit, but still he must pay out 3,000+ *wen*. Now, in recent years the harvest from one *mu* in a good year, on the farm of a well-to-do peasant, has amounted to only just over two *shi*, of which one *shi* goes to pay rent, and one *shi* to pay for hired labor. There is little left over, not even enough to cover daily expenditures. Moreover, since the great flood in 1823, even a yield of two *shi* has been rare.*

In this example, wage and price increases and a decline in yields created a crisis situation even for the family farm using only day-labor. Tao Xu (1884: 17) provides an even more detailed accounting for a ten-mu rice- (plus winter wheat, interplanted with soybeans) farm in Suzhou in the late nineteenth century. The crops, including stalks and vegetable sidelines, had a gross value of 61,000 wen. Soybean-cake fertilizer (including 800 wen for farm equipment) cost 5,800 wen, and labor costs, including cash wages and board, totaled 33,200 wen, leaving a net income for a managerial operation of 22,000 wen. Since rents on the farm yielded 22,800 wen, the landowner could earn more from leasing out his land than from farming it himself with hired labor. By the same token, no one could afford to rent land to farm with hired labor.

MANAGERIAL AGRICULTURE IN NORTH CHINA

I have shown in detail elsewhere the history of managerial agriculture on the North China plain (Huang 1985: chaps. 4–10). It rose with the coming of commercialized agriculture, especially with the spread of cotton cultivation after 1500, and the increased returns from farming that accompanied such commercialization. Homicide records in the Qing Board of Punishment archives document the process of the social differentiation of the peasantry during the

*I am indebted to Li Bozhong for calling my attention to this treatise.

Qing: some small peasants made good through farming and came to
employ wage workers on their farms, while others slid down the socioeconomic ladder from the increased investments and risks involved in cash-cropping. By the third quarter of the eighteenth century, the process had gone far enough to alter fundamentally the
nature of wage labor in the North China countryside: earlier, the
employers had been mainly upper-class landowners, and the wage
workers mainly subcommoner "worker-serfs" (gugongren). By 1788,
the Qing court formally recognized the new social realities by redefining the legal status of agricultural workers—changing them
from the subcommoner category of serf-workers to the commoner
category of agricultural worker. The Board of Punishment noted, in
1760, that "the commoners in managing their farms, in planting and
harvesting, often need help, [and that] relatives and members of the
same status employ each other." The ruling in 1788 was that agricultural workers were generally men who were "hired by the peasant and tenant households to perform agricultural labor, . . . who
normally sit and eat with their employers, and address them as
equals, and are not differentiated from them as serfs are from masters." They should therefore be treated by the law as regular commoners (Huang 1985: 98).

With the penetration of the modern world economy into the
North China plain, agriculture was to commercialize further and
cotton was to come to account for perhaps 8 percent of the cultivated area in Hebei-Shandong. Managerial agriculture also developed further, so that by the 1930s, farms employing three wage-
workers or more (and usually larger than 100 mu in size) came to
account for 9–10 percent of the cultivated area.

Those farms thrived on the very cheap wage labor made available
by the presence of massive amounts of surplus labor in the family-
farm economy. Managerial and family farms alike relied principally
on male farm labor, since surplus male labor reinforced cultural
strictures against women's going outside the house to participate in
production. But the managerial farms enjoyed the advantage of being
able to adjust their labor supply to optimal levels required by the
farm, while the family farms were often burdened with surplus family labor that they could not "fire." More efficient use of labor,
coupled with the farmers' own participation in production, made for
higher returns than leasing out to tenant family farms: a difference
of 13–14 percent return on the price of the land (including the imputed value of the farmer's household labor), compared with about 5
percent (Huang 1985: 173).

Once the managerial farms reached a scale of 200 mu (and six-eight hired laborers) or more, however, they were faced with both economic and social-political constraints. The managerial mode of operation was viable only if the farmer himself participated in production and supervised the work of hired laborers. Given the high degree of fragmentation of land parcels, direct management by the farmer himself remained efficient only on the scale of a work team of three or four men. Larger numbers would have meant either much time wasted moving from parcel to parcel, if the workers were kept together, or difficulties in supervision, if the workers were split up into smaller groups. The cost of employing an overseer separated from production would have quickly eroded the advantage these farms enjoyed over the smaller family farms.

The existing rates of return on managerial agriculture could not easily be increased. It was already operating at a high level of intensification, within the constraints of the existing farm technologies and ecological environment. Further advances required large-scale investments in irrigation and drainage work, or qualitative technological changes such as the use of chemical fertilizer and mechanical power. Most managerial farms were not in a position to contemplate changes of such a scale. At the same time, the abundance of cheap labor acted as a powerful disincentive against labor-saving capitalization: the managerial farms did not even turn to the use of animal power beyond the minimum necessary for the natural environment of the area, much less mechanization. Returns from these farms thus remained pretty much fixed at the levels that already prevailed.

Within the existing socioeconomic system, commerce and usury brought higher returns than farming, and education to climb up the status ladder erected by the state also offered the possibility of very high returns. The few managerial farmers that could withstand the downward pressures of partible inheritance and reach a scale to be able to afford these alternative pursuits, usually those with 200 mu or more, therefore, tended to give up farm management. The result was that the most successful farmers often became landlords who combined land leasing with commerce, usury, and education for their offspring.

There was thus something of a stagnated equilibrium between managerial and family farming. The most successful family peasants became managerial farmers, only to slide back down into the small-peasant economy within a few generations. Or, they became landlords and in so doing returned their land back into the family-farm economy by leasing them out to small tenants. Though managerial agriculture stood out from the family-farm economy, it was also the major avenue for the reproduction of landlords and of small tenant farming. It was, in the end, but an appendage to the small peasant economy.

THE PARADOXICAL EFFECTS OF COMMERCIALIZATION

If managerial agriculture and commercialization were indeed positively associated in North China and yet negatively associated in the Yangzi delta, how are we to explain the paradox?

In Michang village (Fengrun county, northeastern Hebei), where managerial agriculture thrived in the twentieth century, actual wage costs for the managerial farms averaged a relatively low 27.4 percent of gross farm income.* At the same time, the relative weakness of the landlords kept rents on land newly placed under cotton relatively low—a mere 30.9 percent of gross income from the crop in 1937 (compared with an average of 53.7 percent in Hebei province as a whole and 49.8 percent in Shandong; Tudiweiyuanhui 1937: 43). In this village, low wages and low rents combined to power the development of managerial agriculture, which reached 17.7 percent of the cultivated area by 1937 (Huang 1985: 173, 186).

But elsewhere on the North China plain, in still more highly commercialized Sibeichai village in Luancheng county, which had been a major cotton-growing area since the early Qing, there was no managerial farming to speak of in the twentieth century. There landlordism was very much stronger, personified by an absentee landlord cum merchant-usurer named Wang Zanzhou, who owned outright 304.5 of the village's 2,054 mu and held pledged title to another 80 in 1941. Wang and his father had been able to institute a fixed-rent system pegged to an effective rate of more than 50 percent, a much higher return than any managerial farmer could hope to obtain. As a consequence, leasing landlordism simply snuffed out any possibility for the development of managerial farming (ibid., pp. 174–77).

These two rather extreme examples illustrate the paradoxical workings of commercialization on managerial agriculture. In Michang, the higher returns of cotton farming powered the rise of successful managerial farms; in Sibeichai, that same commercialization drew merchant capital to the land and tipped the local scales of

---

*At the time of Land Reform, the Communist Party used the general rule of thumb that wages on farms cultivated by hired labor ran around one-half, and production costs one-sixth, of gross farm income (Hinton 1966: 406–7).

power in favor of landlordism, which was then able to set rent rates high enough to block the development of managerial agriculture. Conditions in most of the cotton-growing areas of North China, of course, fell somewhere between these two extremes.

In the highly commercialized Yangzi delta, greater employment opportunities tipped the relative balance between wage and rent rates in favor of landlordism. By the figures of *Mr. Shen's Agriculture Treatise* for Huzhou in the 1640s, wages ate up more than half the income from eight mu of paddy. Thus a landowner would net less as a managerial farmer than as a landlord. Roughly the same ratio between the cost of wages and gross income applied to the rice + mulberry farm described in the sequel to Shen's work. Similar ratios obtained in rice farming with day-laborers in Songjiang in the 1830s and in rice farming with year-laborers in Suzhou in the 1880s.

Commercialization, then, could work both for and against managerial agriculture.* It could power higher net incomes after expenses and thereby foster the growth of managerial agriculture. Yet it could also contribute to higher rent and wage rates, which obstructed managerial agriculture.

FAMILY FARMING VS. MANAGERIAL FARMING

A clearer way to think about the development and nondevelopment of managerial farming is to focus on the relative strengths of family farming and managerial agriculture. Where family agriculture could sustain higher rates of net farm income than managerial farming, and hence higher land prices and rents, there would be little development of managerial agriculture. The reverse situation would allow for a more vigorous development of managerial agriculture.

Clearly, the differential strengths of family and managerial farming did not depend on the size of the farm; there were few economies of scale to be gained in the agricultural systems of either North

---

*The relationship between managerial agriculture and population pressure was similarly paradoxical. On the North China plain, too many people in search of too few jobs forced down wages, helping to foster the development of managerial agriculture. But that same population pressure also tended to push up rents, which favored landlordism instead of managerial farming. The dynamic was the reverse in the Yangzi delta. There lower population pressure on the land kept rent rates comparatively low, often substantially lower than 50 percent—an average of 34.7 percent of gross produce in Jiangsu province as a whole, and 35.3 percent in Zhejiang, according to the Guomindang Land Commission's surveys (Tudiweiyuanhui 1937: 43)—which should have favored managerial agriculture. Yet that same relative labor shortage helped create a wage level that was prohibitive for managerial agriculture. High population pressure, or its reverse, thus worked both for and against managerial agriculture.

China or the Yangzi delta. What mattered was the degree to which the strengths peculiar to the family work unit were articulated. Where rural production was highly familized, drawing on the auxiliary labor of women and the old and young, the family work unit easily outcompeted the wage labor–based managerial organization, for the simple reason that auxiliary family labor was much cheaper than hired labor.

From this point of view, it was the very low degree of familization of rural production on the North China plain that enabled managerial farms to outcompete family farms. Farmwork for dry-farmed food-grain crops, as has been seen, was done almost exclusively by men. Consequently, the competition between family and managerial farms was chiefly a competition between family adult male labor and hired adult male labor. In that competition, the managerial farms enjoyed the advantage of being able to adjust their labor supply to an optimal level consistent with the demands of the farm, while the family farms using family labor could not.*

The effects of the familization of rural production vis-à-vis managerial agriculture can also be seen in terms of relative wages. Familization helped to sustain higher wages for the adult male work force in the Yangzi delta. A highly developed market for female and child labor would probably have forced down the wages of the adult males. But that development was precluded both by cultural strictures against women hiring out and by the strength of the family production unit, especially in household sideline production.

To the extent that commercialization was associated with a more intensive use of family labor, it might be seen as negatively associated, after a certain point, with managerial agriculture. But to spotlight only commercialization, without attention to the crucial mediating factor of differential labor use in the two types of farms, is to miss the real explanatory dynamic behind the contrasting agricultural histories of the two regions.

CONTRASTING PATTERNS OF SOCIAL STRATIFICATION

The contrasting agricultural histories of the two regions are paralleled by contrasting stories of social change. In North China's Zhili (Hebei) province, as I have shown elsewhere (Huang 1985: 85–105), there were three important trends in the Qing: (1) the decline of

---

*In the cotton-growing areas of North China, to be sure, production was more highly familized. But that familization never quite reached the scale of the Yangzi delta's.

state-granted estates (which were especially prominent in this capital province) accompanying the urbanization of the Manchu aristocracy and the collapse of serfdom; (2) the gradual decline of gentry-owned managerial estates as the gentry elite became increasingly urbanized; and (3) the social stratification of the peasantry into upwardly mobile managerial farmers and commoner landlords, on the one hand, and downwardly mobile tenants and laborers on the other. The combined result of these three trends was an agrarian social structure on the plain in 1800 very different from that in 1644. At the start of the Qing, aristocrats and gentry towered above commoners in the countryside, and such commoner tenants and laborers as existed worked not for other commoners but for that elite. Production relations entailed differences not only in class, but also in legal status. An offense by a tenant, wage worker, or serf against a landowner was subject to the severest punishment; in the reverse case, the landowner generally went unpunished or was subject only to very light punishment. Thus, for example, an employer-master who beat his worker-serf without causing permanent injury was not legally liable at all, whereas a worker-serf who dared lift his hand against his master could get three years at hard labor plus 100 strokes with a heavy stick. By the end of the eighteenth century, however, production relations in agrarian North China were mainly confined to commoners: between the 10 percent or less of wage-workers and their commoner managerial-farmer or rich-peasant employers; between the 25 percent or less of tenants and their commoner or absentee landlords, and between the 35 percent or less of day-laborers and their peasant employers. Substantially the same configuration endured into the twentieth century.

In the Yangzi delta, (1) is not relevant because court-granted estates were restricted by and large to the capital province of Zhili, but (2) was paralleled, though the gentry elite probably moved to the towns and urban centers earlier and even more completely than in North China. An additional factor here was the infusion of urban monies into rural landownership because of the comparatively high returns it afforded. The incidence of tenancy was thus considerably higher: 42 percent of the cultivated acreage by the twentieth century, as has been seen. As for (3), since farming became sufficiently familized to swamp managerial farming during the Qing, the main trend within the villages of the Ming-Qing period was not social stratification, but rather the further elaboration of the peasant family production unit.

Such stratification as occurred in the Yangzi delta villages took chiefly the form of what I term in my North China book "partial differentiation," "the semiproletarianization of the peasantry," or "the formation of a poor peasant society and economy"—the division of the small peasants into a relatively well-to-do group and a relatively poor one whose members had to hire out part time. To judge by the ethnographic surveys of the delta area, possibly 30.7 percent of all peasants here hired out as day-laborers by the twentieth century (Appendix A), compared with 36.2 percent on the North China plain (Huang 1985: 80). For the rest, the main social distinction in the delta countryside was between tenant villagers and urban absentee landlords.

These considerations, however, take us quite far from the main concern of this chapter: to demonstrate and explain the paradoxical demise of managerial agriculture in the relatively developed and highly commercialized Yangzi delta. The key to understanding that apparent paradox lies in the family production unit. In the end, small-peasant family production simply eliminated managerial agriculture from the delta. That was how the peasant family farm remained the dominant social form there even after centuries of vigorous commercialization, contrary to the classical assumptions of Smith and Marx.

CHAPTER 5

Commercialization and
Involutionary Growth

What of the third part of Smith's and Marx's classical view of peasant economy—that commercialization will see an increase in labor
productivity? In this chapter, I shall suggest that the Ming-Qing period did see substantial growth in the delta's rural economy, in the
sense of an absolute increase in the levels of output and output
value. There was even some growth if we take as our unit of analysis
the annual income of the entire household. But close examination
will show that this growth was attained at the cost of declining returns per workday. Growth in annual household income came not so
much from increased returns per workday as from the fuller employment of household labor: of the women, children, and elderly who
had been at best partially employed in production, and of the adult
male(s) during his spare time. It was *growth without development*,
or *involutionary growth*, a pattern that would be repeated on a
much more massive scale and in telescoped time in the postrevolutionary years.

  I do not want to suggest that labor productivity cannot advance in
preindustrial agriculture. Quite the contrary. The modern world has
in my opinion no exclusive claim to economic development, as is
sometimes assumed. Looking at the broad sweep of Chinese history,
several major examples of agricultural development come immediately to mind: the invention and spread of iron implements in the
Warring States and Han periods (which might be termed "the an-
cient agricultural revolution," occurring mainly in the Wei and
Yellow River valleys of North China), the perfecting and spread of
transplanted wet-rice in the Yangzi delta in the Tang and Song
(which might be termed "the medieval agricultural revolution")*,

---

*A "revolution" that is mistakenly associated with champa rice by some (Elvin
1973: 121–24). In fact, champa rice was used mainly as an emergency crop under famine conditions because of its drought-resistant qualities. Its use as the first of two rice
crops came only in the 1960s under vigorous state sponsorship.

and major infrastructural breakthroughs such as the building and systemizing of the delta's grid-like irrigation and drainage system in the tenth-century Wuyue state, discussed in Chapter 2. Though the case cannot be made for lack of data, it seems to me more than plausible that productivity and per-workday income in agriculture increased with those marked technological advances.

The Yangzi delta, however, was already a highly developed and very densely populated economy by the early Ming. Wet-rice and sericultural production was already highly advanced, and winter wheat was grown as a second crop after rice in areas hospitable to such a regime. Population had reached 4,700,000, and cultivated acreage per capita was down to no more than three–five mu (Appendix B). There was little room for increased frequency of cropping, so that further agricultural intensification generally meant switching to more-labor-intensive cash crops. This was a much harder baseline from which to advance than the Wei River valley of the Warring States and early Han periods, or the Yangzi delta in the Tang, Wuyue, and Song.

Scholars who have argued for development in the delta's rural economy during the Ming-Qing period point mainly to the expansion of sericulture, the coming of cotton and cotton handicrafts, and the increased use of beancake fertilizer. Let us consider the implications of each for its returns to peasant labor.

SILK

Sericulture

Wherever mulberries were cultivated beyond the embankments of the rice fields or the open spaces near houses, they entered into direct competition with wet-rice. In terms of gross income per unit land, sericulture clearly enjoyed a considerable edge over rice. According to Zhang Lüxiang's sequel to Shen's agricultural treatise (1983 [1658]: 101), a mu of mulberries fed anywhere from two to ten+ kuang of silkworms, with an implied average of seven or eight, and when silk prices were high and rice prices low, a single basket of silkworms could produce as much gross income as one mu of rice. So in normal times, we might infer, the gross income from one mu of mulberries was several times that from rice.

Such evidence has prompted Fan Shuzhi (1983) and Li Bozhong (1985a) (as well as Liu Shiji in Taiwan: 1978a,b,c) to argue that the spread of sericulture at the expense of rice meant agricultural development. But the evidence outlined above in fact has only to do with gross income per unit land; it says nothing about returns per unit labor. To consider the latter, we need to take into account labor input and production costs, and to differentiate between returns per workday, as opposed to returns per work-year, and between income per worker, as opposed to income per household.

Li Bozhong's own figures (1985a) show that the per-mu labor input for cultivating mulberries and rearing the silkworms was 93 days, compared with 11.5 days for rice. This ratio of 8.1 : 1 is at least twice the "several times" by which gross incomes from sericulture normally exceeded those from rice.* So if we think in terms of gross income per workday rather than per mu, sericulture actually fell well short of rice, except when relative prices favored sericulture to an unusual degree. (That was to happen in the second half of the nineteenth century when, under the stimulation of foreign markets, prices moved decisively in favor of silk and led to a massive displacement of rice in a new sericulture zone centered on Wuxi county.)

Turning to net income per workday after production expenses, we find that the gap narrows a bit, but not enough to tip the balance in favor of sericulture. By Li's figures, each mu under sericulture required 5.5 times the capital input of rice (two times as much for fertilizer; an equivalent expenditure for fuel, to warm the rooms for the silkworms; and higher expenses for silkworm eggs than for rice seed). This is substantially lower than the differential in number of workdays put in. Capital input per workday, therefore, was lower for sericulture than for rice, by a ratio of perhaps 8 : 5 (Li Bozhong 1985a: 9–10). But this is not enough to offset the differential in gross income per workday. Net income per workday was on balance still generally lower from sericulture than from rice. This remained true even under the inflated silk prices of the twentieth century.

But the fact of lower returns per workday in sericulture does not exclude the possibility of increased yearly, as opposed to daily, labor income, and increased household, as opposed to individual worker, income. A peasant could suffer reduced returns per workday but attain greater returns in the year by fuller employment. Thus, the change from a rice-only cropping pattern to rice and sericulture could mean the difference between, say, 150 days of work a year and 300 days, thereby more than offsetting the diminished per-workday income in sericulture. It could also mean productive employment for unemployed members of the household; their labor might account, for example, for half or more of the 93 days of work required

---

*There is of course much guesswork in such figures, but, as we shall see, 20th-century survey data suggest that this ratio is plausible.

for sericulture in Li Bozhong's computations. The net result, then, would be increased net income per household per year even though average net income per workday declined.

Under these conditions, sericulture became irresistible in areas under severe land pressure. It was an undesirable activity only in those areas where labor, including household auxiliary labor, was truly a scarce resource that had to be computed in terms of value per working hour per person—the normal situation in a modern urban society, but exceptional in a peasant society. Labor markets were not nearly so well developed in this peasant society, most certainly not for women, children, and the elderly, or for the spare time of adult males. Theirs was labor of little opportunity cost, and theirs was the main labor source for the intensification and involution that sericulture entailed.

Silk Handicrafts

Mulberry cultivation and silkworm raising were generally accompanied by home-reeling, a relatively non-capital-intensive handicraft industry. Peasant households could easily afford the simple equipment required for silk reeling. And until the coming of new drying technologies in the late nineteenth century, reeling almost had to be done by the grower, since cocoons had to be reeled within seven days of their formation, before the moths emerged.

Silk weaving, by contrast, was relatively capital-intensive, requiring a fairly complex loom operated by at least two or three skilled workers. Moreover, as a high-priced luxury item consumed by the upper classes, silks brought a relatively high return. These characteristics ensured the separation of silk weaving from peasant households and its development as an almost exclusively urban activity.

This activity, as we have seen, triggered the growth of urban wage labor–based workshops in the Ming and Qing (Wu Chengming 1985: 157–58, 382, sums up the available evidence for the period; see also Xu Xinwu 1981a: 89). But we must not exaggerate the extent of "incipient capitalist" development in the rise of this industry. The historical record makes clear that most of the weavers were small-scale operators, often artisan households and their apprentices. As late as 1913, the average shop in Suzhou had only 1.5 looms and 7.7 workers. Before the advent of steam heating for the cocoons and mechanical spinning and weaving, there were few economies of scale available to the silk weaver. By the mid-sixteenth century, even the imperial silk manufactories, which had employed thousands of workers in the early Ming, had begun to procure their goods from dispersed small producers (*jihu*). From the start of the Qing, the manufactories relied wholly on licensing small workshops.

Responsibility for coordinating the many steps involved in silk production fell to putting-out merchants, a group that emerged in the eighteenth century and came to dominate the entire industry by the late nineteenth. Called *zhangfang*, the putting-out merchant purchased the raw material from silk companies (*sihang*), arranged for the spinning and dyeing, and then "put out" the weaving to small producers. In 1913, Suzhou city had 57 zhangfang, who between them controlled 1,000 small weaving shops, with a total of 1,524 looms and 7,681 workers (Wu Chengming 1985: 143–59, 376–82). These putting-out merchants are usually cited as examples of "incipient capitalists," but this system seems to me only to underscore the dispersed and labor-intensive character of the production process, even in this most highly capitalized sector of the handicraft industries of the Ming and Qing.

From the standpoint of peasant production, reeling was the important activity. Unlike weaving, it remained within the peasant household, tied inextricably to household farming. The reasons for that bonding of household farming with silk reeling will become clearer in our discussion of cotton handicrafts below.

COTTON

Cultivation

In unirrigated areas and in the coastal areas with saline soil inhospitable to other crops, the turn to cotton clearly brought substantial development. In the words of a certain Tao Zongyi, who lived in Songjiang during the middle of the fourteenth century: "Fifty *li* east of Songjiang city is the area called Wunijing. Here the land is hard and infertile, and cannot furnish sufficient food for the people. They sought a way to maintain themselves and turned to cultivating it [cotton]." And then, having mastered the skills of spinning and weaving introduced in the late thirteenth century, the local peasants "attained affluence in their lives" (*Qinchuan sanzhi buji xubian* 1835, 7: 8a). Cotton cultivation and cotton handicrafts, it seems, raised the living standard from below subsistence to "affluence." For an area like this, the coming of cotton represented a dramatic agricultural advance, a productivity breakthrough that, if depicted graphically, would be plotted as a step upward rather than a gradually inclining curve.

In other ecologically harsh areas of the delta, though, cotton merely furnished a livelihood—nothing that could be characterized as prosperity. The Jiading county gazetteer describes the situation there in 1583:

> Jiading county borders the sea on three sides; the land is high and infertile, and sandy underneath. It is difficult either to store water or to irrigate with waterwheels. Although there are rice fields registered here, in actual fact only cotton is grown. When water gathers, [the crops] get soaked. When drought comes, [the crops] wither. There are also frequent typhoons. Out of ten years, there are nine with poor harvests. The little people depend entirely on the cotton market. Whether night or day, or hot or cold, they labor at their weaving without stop. (*Jiading xian zhi* 1605, 7: 1a–b)

In relatively stable areas with better access to irrigation, cotton often had to compete with high-yielding wet-rice for acreage. The question of relative returns from cotton cultivation then becomes a complex one, just as in the case of mulberry cultivation. Past research has often assumed that cotton, a cash crop, must have commanded higher returns than a foodgrain like rice (Liu Shiji 1978a; Fan Shuzhi 1983). But this assumption ignores the fact that rice was also a highly commercialized crop. Tables 5.1 and 5.2 show rice and cotton prices in Shanghai county in the seventeenth century. As might be expected, rice prices show considerable seasonal fluctuation, reaching their nadir in the months after the fall harvest and peaking in the spring hungry season. But the price did not vary

TABLE 5.1

Rice Prices in Shanghai County, 1632–82

Year	Season or month	Taels per shi	Year	Season or month	Taels per shi
1632	summer	1.0	1659	3	2.0
1642	spring	5.0	1661	10	1.5
1647	—	4.0		11	2.0
1650	2	1.0	1662	1	2.1
	9	2.5	1669	—	0.7
1651	2	3.0	1670	6	1.3
	3	3.5		10	0.9
	4	4.0	1680	summer	2.0
	6	4.9	1682	5	0.85
1652	summer	4.0		winter	0.9
1657	11	0.8			

SOURCE: Ye Mengzhu 1935 [ca. 1693], 7: 1a–3a.
NOTE: All prices are for polished white rice.

TABLE 5.2
Cotton Prices in Shanghai County, 1621–84

Year	Season or month	Taels per dan	Year	Season or month	Taels per dan
1621–27	—	1.6–1.7	1670	fall	1.7–2.5
1628–35	—	4.0–5.0		10	3.0+
1644–45	—	0.5–0.6		end 10	4.0
1649	—	3.4–3.5	1671	11	3.0
1650	9	5.0	1674	—	1.9[a]
1651	3	9.0	1677	summer	2.6–3.0[a]
1657	3	2.5	1679	fall	1.5–1.6
1659	3	4.5	1680	summer	3.0
1661	winter	2.0	1681	summer	3.5–3.6
1662	1	3.0	1682	5	4.1[a]
	7	2.0	1684	fall	1.3–1.4[a]

SOURCE: Same as Table 5.1, pp. 5a–5b.
[a] Top grade cotton.

much over time. The opposite is true of cotton: there is no discernible seasonal pattern, but the price could rise and fall steeply in a matter of years. The two price movements appear largely unconnected, if only because each crop was affected by rather different sets of climatic factors. The year 1650, for example, saw the second-highest cotton price of the century, but unexceptional rice prices; 1670 saw a sharp rise in cotton and falling rice prices.

Under the circumstances, the peasant's decision between cotton and rice would have been very much shaped by their relative prices. In Taicang in the period 1628–44, according to the department gazetteer, "60–70 percent of the land is suited for rice, but it has all been given up for cotton" (cited in Liu Shiji 1978a: 31). Here, returns were clearly higher from cotton than from rice during the period. Yet we learn that in Shanghai county just 20 years later, in the 1660s, net returns from rice exceeded those from cotton. Rice had been given up only because the irrigation rivers and canals had silted up: "The Dutai and the Wunijing have become shallow and are no longer adequate for irrigating the rice fields. The rice fields in Shanghai [county] are therefore all growing cotton and beans." As a result, Shanghai had to rely on nearby Huating (Songjiang) county for its rice. The same thing, the gazetteer noted, was happening in the southeast of Huating. In a few decades, the entire region east of Jinshan would suffer the same fate as Shanghai. These developments "[had] meant a 30 percent decline in the riches of the region" (*Song-jiang fu xuzhi* 1883, 7: 34b–35a).

If it is true that returns from the two crops differed only to the extent that relative price movements favored one or the other, then returns per workday were likely lower for cotton than for rice. According to the fragmentary data of Buck (1937b: 314–17), each mu of cotton in the "Yangzi rice-wheat region" required an average labor input in the 1930s of 21.0 days, compared with 10.5 for rice. Assuming that Buck's averages are reasonably close to the mark, cotton clearly brought a lower per-workday return than rice.

Cotton Handicrafts

The relative profitability of the two crops, of course, cannot be considered apart from what cotton offered in the way of expanded opportunities for household sideline employment and production. On average, each mu of cotton yielded 30 catties, enough for about 22.7 bolts of cloth.* Producing that amount of cloth took fully 159 days. Rice could not furnish anywhere near that much employment. To take 1940s Huayangqiao as an example, each mu of rice supplied about 800 catties of straw, sufficient to produce 560 catties of straw rope in eight workdays (H-III-16). As cultivated acreage in the delta shrank from the three–five mu per capita in 1393 to about one–two mu in 1816 (Table B.2), the added employment furnished by cotton could not help being one of the major considerations that helped to power its spread.

This is not to say, however, that returns per workday from cotton home industry exceeded those from cultivating rice. By the early eighteenth century, certainly, returns for cotton handicrafts had sunk to abysmally low levels. A cotton spinner could produce an average of five ounces of yarn a day, from about five ounces of ginned cotton or fifteen of unginned. In the eighteenth and early nineteenth centuries, returns from such work generally ran around 30 percent to 50 percent of the worth of the raw cotton (Fang Xing 1987: 88; see also Wu Chengming 1985: 389–90). A spinner's earnings for a day's work, in other words, were worth 5.0 to 7.5 ounces of unginned cotton. In the period 1690–1740, when rice and cotton prices held fairly steady, each catty of unginned cotton was worth two times its weight in rice (Fang Xing 1987: 91–92). A spinner's daily earnings thus amounted to ten to fifteen ounces of rice, which by present-day

---

*Each bolt weighs 1.32 catties. About 4 percent of the ginned cotton is wasted in fluffing, and the weight added in weaving is about 5 percent (Xu n.d.). I have not tried to take account of the 1 percent difference here.

rations—44 catties (63 unhusked) per month for adult female peasant laborers and 47 catties (67 unhusked) for males in Huayangqiao, Songjiang county—was only enough to sustain a pre-teen child. It is not surprising, therefore, that spinning was done almost entirely by children and the elderly, seldom even by adult women. An adult male laborer could not, would not, work for that kind of return.

For the peasant household deciding to use its auxiliary and spare-time labor for home industry, wage rates in the labor market were of little relevance; they applied chiefly to adult men, and then only seasonally. Nor would the household calculate in the expense of food as a labor cost, since those household members had to be supported in any case. The only relevant consideration was the gross return minus production costs for raw materials and tools. The peasant household under subsistence pressures will put in such labor so long as total returns exceed production costs, even if the added work entails great drudgery and abysmally low returns.

An enterprise using hired adult male labor simply could not compete against a household production unit like this. Even if the enterprise could hire women and children, overcoming cultural and logistical constraints, it would still suffer the disadvantage of having to provide their board, once they were divorced from their family farms. Those costs generally ran about as high as wage costs, and sometimes higher. Under these conditions, only those heavily capitalized parts of rural industry beyond the reach of the individual peasant household were able to develop larger-scale production based on hired labor. Industries that were non-capital-intensive and used tools that individual peasant households could afford were invariably dominated by small-scale household production.

Cotton spinning is the example par excellence of this type of rural industry. The simple one-spindle spinning wheel was widely available, and something that even the poorest households could afford. Used by household labor of little or no cost, it held on with tremendous tenacity throughout the centuries of expansion in the cotton economy. A three-spindle, foot-pedaled wheel, though used in Songjiang prefecture by the eighteenth century, never made much headway there and remained unknown elsewhere. That complex and more taxing wheel required the use of adult labor in its prime, and only outproduced the simple wheel by about 50–100 percent (Xu Xinwu 1981a: 90–91), a differential in productivity that was simply not sufficient to justify forsaking the household's low-cost auxiliary labor. Consequently, as late as the turn of the twentieth century, the hand-turned, single-spindle wheel still predominated even in Songjiang, effectively snuffing out technological innovation until the introduction of the mechanical spinning wheel.

Though cloth weaving was relatively more capital-intensive than spinning, a simple loom was still affordable by all but the poorest of peasant households. With it, a weaver could generally produce one bolt of cloth a day. In the decades of stable prices (before inflation set in after the 1730s), a bolt of cloth was worth 0.2 to 0.3 silver tael (Fang Xing 1987: 92, 94). With contemporary rice prices running around 0.06 tael a catty, this translated into gross earnings of 3.3 to 5.0 catties of rice a day. Deducting the cost of three catties of unginned cotton (ca. 0.013 tael) or one catty of yarn (0.02 tael), the weaver would net just about twice as much grain as he needed for his own consumption.

At that level of return, weaving was a tolerable activity for an adult male worker and certainly desirable for an adult female. But it provided no more than a barely adequate subsistence, with virtually no possibility for enrichment. As Xu Xinwu (1981a: especially 88–89) has shown, we do not have one documented instance of a cotton cloth weaver who made good—who went on to found a larger-scale workshop, engage in commerce, or acquire a large farm.

The urban weaver was at a competitive disadvantage vis-à-vis a peasant household that grew its own cotton, did its own spinning with auxiliary household labor, and lived on its own crops. That is why most cloth weaving continued to be done in peasant households down to modern times. Not one large-scale, wage labor–based cotton weaving workshop emerged in the Ming and Qing. The oft-cited example of Foshan in Guangdong province (based on the account of an early-nineteenth-century foreign traveler), where there were supposedly some 2,500 workshops employing an average of 20 workers, turns out to be an exaggerated report about silk rather than cotton weaving. There is no other documentation of any cotton-weaving workshops of that scale before the Opium War. Urban weaving was limited to the small workshops of relatively poor artisans, sometimes with a few apprentices, but never large enough for specialization and the division of labor (Xu Xinwu 1981a: 62–64).

INVOLUTIONARY RURAL INDUSTRIALIZATION

What is truly striking about the growth of handicraft industry in the Ming-Qing period is the extent to which it remained inextricably tied to peasant farming. Throughout these centuries, cotton spinning and weaving and silk reeling continued to be done almost entirely by peasant households. They were, from the start, a means of supplementing household incomes that were declining from contractions in the size of farms. As an expanding population pressed incomes in both sectors downward, the bond between them only became stronger. Each came to rely on the other to furnish complete subsistence. Thus was forged the peasant household's reliance on these twin crutches of its livelihood.

Neither farming nor home industry generated much in the way of surplus, typically yielding only enough between them for the necessities of subsistence and rent or tax payments. Neither offered much potential for accumulation and capitalization. Both remained chiefly a way to sustain the household's basic livelihood. The evidence on this can fill an entire chapter and has been cited by a score of writers. Let me give just a few examples to illustrate the major patterns.

In ecologically unstable areas like Jiading county, returns from farming had already become so low by the seventeenth century that cotton handicrafts were the mainstay of the household's subsistence: "[The peasants'] rent and tax, clothing and food, implements, social expenditures, and child rearing and funeral expenses all come from this [weaving]" (*Jiading xian zhi* 1605, 6: 36b). In the eighteenth century in nearby Baoshan county, whose saline soil was unsuited to other crops, "the people near the seashore place especially great value on cotton; they depend on it for their clothing and food, and their tax payments" (cited in Liu Shiji 1978a: 31).

In the fertile and relatively stable core areas, the problem was land scarcity and farms too small to maintain a family for a full year: "After paying taxes or rent, the harvest from the field is exhausted before the year ends; [the peasants'] clothing and food depend entirely on this [cotton handicrafts]" (quoted in Fang Xing 1987: 80). Even in fertile, stable, and relatively prosperous Wuxi county in the mid-eighteenth century, the local gazetteer tells us:

> The peasants here get only three winter months' of food from their rice fields. After they pay off their rent, they hull the rest of the rice, put it in a bin, and turn it over to the pawnshop to redeem their clothing. In the early spring, the entire household spins and weaves in order to exchange cloth for rice, because the family no longer has any grain left. By the busy fifth month, they take their winter clothing and pawn it for rice. . . . In the fall, whenever it rains, the sound of the shuttle of the loom again fills all the villages, and [the peasants] carry their cloth to trade for rice to eat. It is in this way that the peasants of our county, even in times of poor harvests, manage to eke out a living so long as the cotton ripens in other places. (*Xi Jin shi xiaolu* 1752, 1: 6b–7b)

The same applied to silk reeling. Gu Yanwu (1613–82) puts it best:

> Here the harvests from the rice fields are enough for only eight months
> of food for the people. The remaining months as a rule are supplied by
> exchanging [silk] for rice. Taxes and family needs alike are dependent
> on silkworms. . . . All loans and contracts wait for the conclusion of
> sericulture for payment. Even for the winter taxes, they [the peasants]
> generally dare not sell rice to meet the payments, for fear that rice
> prices might rise. Instead, they usually pawn their rice for silver [to
> meet the tax payment], and then redeem the rice with interest after the
> silk work is done. (Gu 1662, 84)*

In Wujiang county in the eighteenth century, "Once the [peas-
ants'] children pass the age of ten, they labor from morning to night
in order to fill their stomachs" (*Wujiang xian zhi* 1747, 38: 7b). In
Wuxian, "Once the girls come of age they learn to raise silkworms"
(*Guangfu zhi* 1900, "Fengsu": 18). But the sericulture peasants
themselves could never afford to wear the silk fabrics: "Though the
silk of Hu [zhou prefecture] has spread throughout the empire, the
peasants of Hu have not one thread on their bodies" (*Wuxing beizhi*
1621–27, 26).

This kind of rural industrial growth, like the agricultural growth
examined earlier, was involutionary both socially and economically.
It was socially involutionary because it did not lead to a new social
organization of production but simply elaborated the existing one. It
was economically involutionary because it was usually not accompanied by an increase in workday income.

SOYBEAN-CAKE FERTILIZER

It remains for us to consider, finally, the third of the factors held
to have prompted the growth of productivity in the Ming and Qing:
the increased use of fertilizer, especially soybean cake for rice
cultivation.

To begin with, data on rice yields are limited and ambiguous. Wu
Chengming has gathered all the figures to be had on Songjiang and
Suzhou prefectures for the Song, Ming, and Qing. As can be seen in
Table 5.3, longitudinal data for a single locale are hard to come by.
Wu (1985: 190–91) tries on the basis of these data to argue that unit-
area yields were higher in the Qing than in the Ming, as does Wu

---

*Gu is referring specifically to Chongde county in Jiaxing prefecture (Zhejiang), in
the southern half of the delta, but the observations apply well to the Suzhou sericulture areas, which were yutian areas just like Jiaxing.

TABLE 5.3
Rice Yields in Suzhou and Songjiang Prefectures, 1023–1850

Period	Locale	Shi per mu (husked rice)
1023–1063	Suzhou	2–3
1425	Kunshan county (Suzhou)	2
1506–1521	Shanghai county (Songjiang)	1.5–3+
Late Ming	Suzhou and Songjiang	1+–3–
1662–1722	Suzhou and Songjiang	1.5–3–
	Shanghai county	1.5–2
	Wujiang county (Suzhou)	2
1796–1820	Suzhou	2–3
1821–1850	Suzhou[a]	3

SOURCE: Wu Chengming 1985: 40–41, 190–91. Perkins (1969) groups rice-yield data by province for all of Jiangsu. Because of the wide divergencies between northern Jiangsu and the Yangzi delta area, Perkins's (1969) province-wide data are not useful for my purposes here.
[a] "High-grade land."

Hui (1985: 168–70, 177, 194). But the argument, though plausible, is simply not justified by the skimpy and ambiguous data. Indeed, if anything, the figures suggest that rice yields had already reached something of a plateau in the Song; thereafter, they simply hovered in the range of one–three shi per mu.

Li Bozhong acknowledges that there was no significant increase in the Yangzi delta's wet-rice yields during the Ming and Qing, and that per-mu labor input for rice remained essentially at the mid-Tang level, but he also insists that there was a substantial increase in the use of fertilizer in the Ming and Qing (1984: 25–28). Though Li overstates the case for the Ming, I do agree with him on the Qing.* By all evidence, soybean-cake fertilizer did come to be used widely by the delta peasants from the eighteenth century on. Its spread was in all likelihood linked to the massive importation of soybeans from the Northeast into Shanghai after the ban on coastal shipping was lifted in 1685. By Bao Shichen's time (1775–1855), more than 10,000,000 shi of "wheat and soybeans" reportedly were exported annually from Fengtian to the delta.†

Whether yields in wet-rice increased in the Qing under these con-

*Li maintains that the use of soybean-cake fertilizer dated back to the late Ming. But the sources he cites (1985: 27–28) actually refer variously to hemp or ramie-seed cakes (*madoubing*), cotton-seed cakes (*mianbing*), rape oil–seed cakes (*caibing*), and a certain (now extinct) *meidoubing*. On the last, see Chen Hengli and Wang Da 1983: 110.

†According to Adachi 1978, some 3,500 *shachuan* boats plied the coast between the Northeast and Shanghai, each capable of carrying 1,500–3,000 shi and of making three or four trips a year.

ditions remains unclear. The available data, as has been seen, suggest that they did not—at least to any great degree. Li Bozhong (1984: 34–36) imputes the problem to diminishing marginal returns to fertilizer inputs, so that ever-greater amounts were needed to attain the same yields. An alternative explanation—that more fertilizer was required to maintain the same level of yields with increased frequency of cropping—seems less plausible; Wu Hui (1985: 171, 180) estimates that cropping frequency increased little between the Ming and the Qing, when grain fields had a multiple index of 132 percent—with perhaps 5 percent under beans and 7 percent under wheat as winter crops.

THE STRUCTURE OF THE COMMODITY ECONOMY

The commercial economy that arose in the Ming and Qing reflected directly the involutionary nature of the changes outlined above. Marketed goods continued to be produced chiefly by small peasants—in the manner suggested by the classical Marxist notion of "petty commodities production." And much of the trade consisted of nickel-and-dime transactions among peasants, small peddlers, and merchants.

Thanks to the work of Wu Chengming and his associates, we can now be relatively clear about the volume and kinds of "commodities" traded in those centuries. Nationwide, the exchange of cotton cloth for grain accounted for two-thirds (69.9 percent) of the total volume of trade on the eve of the Opium War (Table 5.4). Peasant

TABLE 5.4
Volume of Trade in China, ca. 1840
(millions of taels)

Commodity	Value	Percent	Net import (+) or export (−)
Grain	138.833	39.71%	—
Cotton	10.859	3.11	+3.025
Cotton cloth	94.553	27.04	+0.802
Silk	10.220	2.92	−2.252
Silk fabric	14.550	4.16	—
Tea	27.082	7.75	−11.261
Salt	53.529	15.31	—
TOTAL	349.626	100.00%	—

SOURCE: Wu Chengming 1985: 284 (and for his procedures), 319–29.
    NOTE: The figures exclude goods exchanged on local markets and the share of grain, cotton, etc., sold to meet tax payments.

households that wove traded their surplus cloth to make up for their grain shortage, and peasant households that grew chiefly grain traded their surpluses for the cotton cloth to make their clothing. Wu Chengming excludes from his definition of "commodities" items traded locally: for example, the grain peasant producers sold in local markets that was destined for consumption by nearby peasants (as opposed to that destined for urban consumers or long distance trade). Wu also excludes the share of grain, cloth, silk, tea, and salt that was sold to meet tax payments. We will return to this question in Chapter 6, when we look at Wu's scheme against twentieth-century field research on what peasants actually sold and bought. But for the purposes of this discussion, his scheme will do fine; adding the marketed grain that he excludes would only make its share of the total "commodity" trade that much larger. The basic points about the structure of commerce would still hold: the trade in the Yangzi delta consisted primarily of an exchange between peasants of surplus grain for surplus cloth, and vice versa.

There was little two-way exchange of goods between town and country of the sort that Adam Smith depicted in his observations based on the experience of early modern England. Silk and silk products, which accounted for 7.1 percent of the total commodity trade nationwide by Wu's estimates, were produced by peasants (though fabricated in the towns and cities) but consumed almost entirely by urbanites.

This commercial economy was predicated on a system of production in which peasant households absorbed the ever-diminishing marginal returns by resorting more and more to household auxiliary labor of low opportunity cost. Few made good from production for the market; little capitalization of production took place; and household incomes remained low, as did the scope of the rural market for other than subsistence products. This was the commercialization of small-peasant production and subsistence, not of incipient capitalist enterprise.

In such trade, merchants undertook only to aid in the circulation of goods. Their profits came from transporting rice from grain-surplus to grain-short areas, and cotton goods from weaving to nonweaving areas. There was no incentive for them to enter into the production process themselves, since under existing technologies they could not hope to compete against the more cost-effective peasant household. Production in the delta's cities and towns was therefore limited mainly to those activities that were beyond the capability of the individual peasant household. That ruled out cotton spinning, silk reeling, and, to a large extent, also cotton weaving—the big three, in other words, of the handicraft industries of the time.

Urbanization, it is true, did go well beyond the merely administrative city—which Max Weber had equated with the imperial Chinese city (Rowe 1984: 1–14)—owing mainly to the kind of commerce outlined above. But the rise of cities and towns in the Ming-Qing had little to do with production: they never became production centers for urban manufactures targeted at peasant consumers. What little production there was—the fabrication of silk, the processing of high-quality cotton cloth, and the like—was for the consumption of urbanites. The movement of goods between countryside and town was almost entirely unidirectional. The countryside furnished the urban elites with silk and cloth, and rent and tax grain, but received little in return.

CHAPTER 6

Peasants and Markets

From what we have seen so far, it is clear that the neoclassicists' market-economy model does not come close to describing the historical reality in the Yangzi delta. In this chapter, I turn to the empirical data on the commodities and factors markets of the delta in twentieth-century ethnographic surveys to make some preliminary suggestions about the structure and workings of its rural markets. As we shall see, while the classical Marxist category of "petty commodities production" is useful descriptively, it is the substantivist tradition originating with Chayanov that furnishes the seeds for understanding the logic of that commercial economy. This tradition directs our attention to peasant strategies for survival more than to those for gain. In the hands of Karl Polanyi and James Scott, this tradition also emphasizes the importance of the social milieu in shaping trade in precapitalist economies. Kinship, reciprocity, gifts, morality, and the like play major roles, in contradistinction to the simple workings of supply and demand in capitalist "price-making markets" (Polanyi et al. 1957: especially chap. 13; Scott 1976).

PEASANT MARKETING IN THE TWENTIETH CENTURY

Table 6.1 shows the main categories of goods sold by peasant households in six Yangzi delta and North China villages in the late 1930s. As is readily apparent, crops—primarily grain and cotton—constituted by far the largest percentage of goods sold: an average of 65.6 percent for the four villages for which we have complete data. Those items, combined with sideline products, chiefly cotton yarn and cloth in the cotton-growing villages and straw products in rice-growing Huayangqiao, accounted for 82.1 percent of all the goods sold.

This total is consistent with the structure of the commodity economy outlined by Wu Chengming in his pathbreaking study. Wu, as

TABLE 6.1

Main Commodities Sold by Peasants in Six North China
and Yangzi Delta Villages, 1936–39

(household averages)

Village	Crops		Farm animals		Sidelines		Total (yuan)
	Yuan	Percent	Yuan	Percent	Yuan	Percent	
North China, 1936[a]							
Michang (Fengrun)	139.9	74.8%	9.9	5.3%	37.2	19.9%	187.0
Dabeiguan (Pinggu)	23.8	51.9	18.5	40.3	3.6	7.8	45.9
Qianlianggezhuang (Changli)	22.4	60.5	4.9	13.2	9.7	26.2	37.0
Yangzi delta, 1939[b]							
Touzongmiao (Nantong)	28.0	?	?	?	60.1	?	—
Xiaodingxiang (Wuxi)	45.7[c]	?	?	?	12.7	?	—
Huayangqiao (Songjiang)	287.0	74.7	50.8	13.2	46.3	12.1	384.1
Average		65.5%		18.0%		16.5%	

SOURCES: Michang: MT, Kitō 1937b; Dabeiguan: ibid. 1937a; Qianlianggezhuang: ibid. 1937c; Touzongmiao: MT, Shanhai 1941b; Xiaodingxiang: ibid. 1941a; Huayangqiao: ibid. 1940.
[a] Average for all households in the village.
[b] Average for sampling of 12 to 20 households in the village.
[c] Includes cocoon sales.

has been seen (Table 5.4), suggests that the exchange of foodgrains for cotton and cotton cloth accounted for 69.9 percent of all "commodity trade" in China on the eve of the Opium War. The survey data, of course, differ from Wu's in their exclusive focus on peasants and in their inclusion of the localized trade that is excluded from Wu's somewhat idiosyncratic definition of commodities. By Wu's conception, only those goods belonging to an integrated national market signal the coming of "incipient capitalism" and justify the usage "commodities." If we remove Wu's particular ideological preoccupation (see below) and think of commodities more generally as marketed goods, it becomes clear that goods restricted to localized markets figured prominently in peasant marketing. Farm animals, especially, made up a major part of what peasant households marketed, averaging in these villages 18.0 percent of the value of all goods sold. They were particularly important in a village like Dabeiguan, which grew mostly millet and maize and possessed more ample feed (from the husks and chaff of the grain) for farm animals.

The records on what the peasants of these villages bought with

TABLE 6.2
Commodities Purchased by Peasants in Three North China Villages, 1936
(averages for all households)

Commodity	Michang Yuan	Michang Percent	Dabeiguan Yuan	Dabeiguan Percent	Qianliangge-zhuang Yuan	Qianliangge-zhuang Percent	Average (percent)
Agricultural							
Foodgrain	28.47	39.9%	9.11	41.5%	59.10	65.0%	48.8%
Meat	3.75	5.3	1.28	5.8	2.63	2.9	4.7
Vegetables	?	—	?	—	?	—	—
Fruit	?	—	?	—	?	—	—
SUBTOTAL	32.22	45.2%	10.39	47.3%	61.73	67.9%	53.5%
Cotton	0.26	0.4	0.06	0.3	0.23	0.3	0.3
Tea	?		?		?		
Sugar	0.24	0.3	0.07	0.3	0.20	0.2	0.3
Leaf tobacco	?	—	?	—	?	—	—
SUBTOTAL	0.50	0.7%	0.13	0.6%	0.43	0.5%	0.6%
Traditional processed							
Salt	3.89	5.4	3.87	[17.6][a]	4.94	5.4	[9.5][a]
Wine	1.90	2.7	0.43	2.0	0.58	0.6	1.8
Soy sauce	?	—	?	—	?	—	—
Edible oils	2.80	3.9	0.05	0.2	1.25	1.4	1.8
Straw hats	?	—	?	—	?	—	—
SUBTOTAL	8.59	12.0%	4.35	19.8%	6.77	7.4%	13.1%
Industrial							
Wheat flour[b]	4.05	5.7	1.45	6.6	0.73	0.8	4.4
Yarn	?	—	?	—	?	—	—
Cloth	7.20	10.1	1.09	5.0	2.27	2.5	5.8
Clothing	0.26	0.4	?	—	?	—	0.1
Kerosene	2.68	3.7	1.48	6.8	2.44	2.7	4.4
Matches[c]	2.97	4.2	0.84	3.8	2.60	2.9	3.6
SUBTOTAL	17.16	24.1%	4.86	22.2%	8.04	8.9%	18.3%
Other	12.79	18.0	2.22	10.1	13.90	15.3	14.5
TOTAL	71.26	100.0%	21.95	100.0%	90.87	100.0%	100.0%

SOURCE: See Table 6.1.
[a] Questionable figure.
[b] American wheat flour.
[c] Includes other lighting and fuel expense.

the cash they got for their goods underscore the same points. As Tables 6.2–6.4 show, foodgrain and cotton goods were clearly central to peasant marketing, accounting for an average of 31.0 percent and 6.8 percent, respectively, of all goods purchased in the six Yangzi delta villages, and 48.8 percent and 6.2 percent of those in North China.* Meat (chiefly pork) was also important, though with a significant

*The cotton-goods figure is the combined average of cotton, yarn, cotton cloth, and clothing.

TABLE 6.3

Commodities Purchased by Peasants in Three Yangzi Delta Villages, 1938

(averages for sample of households)

Commodity	Yanjiashang (Changshu) Yuan	Percent	Yaojing (Taicang) Yuan	Percent	Dingjiacun (Jiading) Yuan	Percent	Average (percent)
Agricultural							
Foodgrain	11.33	19.9%	25.92	28.2%	32.92	30.7%	26.3%
Meat, fish, poultry	2.88	5.1	11.42	12.4	20.50	19.2	12.2
Vegetables	4.89	8.6	4.08	4.4	6.35	5.9	6.3
SUBTOTAL	19.10	33.6%	41.42	45.0%	59.77	55.8%	44.8%
Cotton	2.15	3.8	0.38	0.4	?	—	1.4
Tea	4.65	8.2	1.53	1.7	?	—	3.3
Sugar	1.62	2.9	3.43	3.7	4.00	3.7	3.4
Leaf tobacco	1.42	2.5	4.91	5.3	7.52	7.0	4.9
SUBTOTAL	9.84	17.4%	10.25	11.1%	11.52	10.7%	13.0%
Traditional processed							
Salt	2.92	5.1	9.17	10.0	5.39	5.0	6.7
Wine	6.92	12.2	0.24	0.3	1.92	1.8	4.8
Soy sauce, edible oils	4.19	7.4	9.83	10.7	4.87	4.6	7.6
Straw hats	0.89	1.6	0.62	0.7	?	—	0.8
SUBTOTAL	14.92	26.3%	19.86	21.7%	12.18	11.4%	19.9%
Industrial							
Yarn	?	—	?	—	?	—	—
Cloth, clothing	4.85	8.5	2.28	2.5	7.78	7.3	6.1
Kerosene	2.06	3.6	3.50	3.8	4.61	4.3	3.9
Matches	1.15	2.0	3.44	3.8	?	—	1.9
SUBTOTAL	8.06	14.1	9.22	10.1	12.39	11.6	11.9
Other	4.86	8.6	11.15	12.1	11.27	10.5	10.4
TOTAL	56.78	100.0%	91.90	100.0%	107.13	100.0%	100.0%

SOURCES: Yanjiashang: MT, Shanhai 1939b; Yaojing: ibid. 1939c; Dingjiacun: ibid. 1939a.

difference between the Yangzi delta and the North China villages, a result of their differential standards of living. Meat (and fish and poultry) accounted for 11.7 percent of all purchases in the delta, against just 4.7 percent in the North.

Salt was another major item: 6.1 percent in the Yangzi delta and 5.4 percent in North China. Tea was important in the delta, accounting for 2.2 percent of the purchases, but so insignificant in the North that the investigators did not count it (again reflecting the differential in the standards of living). These data lend credence to Wu's choices for the major items of China's commodities trade in the 1840s.

Other important purchases in the delta, not on Wu's list, were

Peasants and Markets 97

TABLE 6.4
Commodities Purchased by Peasants in Three Yangzi Delta Villages, 1939
(averages for sample of households)

Commodity	Touzongmiao Yuan	Touzongmiao Percent	Xiaodingxiang Yuan	Xiaodingxiang Percent	Huayangqiao Yuan	Huayangqiao Percent	Average (percent)
Agricultural							
Foodgrain	61.09	48.7%	43.24	41.1%	24.83	17.0%	35.6%
Meat, fish,							
poultry	6.44	5.1	8.14	7.7	29.87	20.4	11.1
Vegetables	8.89	7.1	3.55	3.4	6.04	4.1	4.9
SUBTOTAL	76.42	60.9%	54.93	52.2%	60.74	41.5%	51.6%
Cotton	?		0.45	0.4	1.25	0.9	0.4
Tea	2.16	1.7	0.21	0.2	1.65	1.1	1.0
Sugar	2.63	2.1	2.95	2.8	5.23	3.6	2.8
Leaf tobacco	5.61	4.5	2.75	2.6	6.67	4.5	3.9
SUBTOTAL	10.40	8.3%	6.36	6.0%	14.80	10.1%	8.1%
Traditional							
processed							
Salt	6.19	4.9	6.55	6.2	7.42	5.1	5.4
Wine	3.42	2.7	3.95	3.8	11.03	7.5	4.7
Soy sauce	0.36	0.3	3.18	3.0	11.83	8.1	3.8
Edible oils	6.42	5.1	11.35	10.8	16.28	11.1	9.0
Straw hats	?		0.47	0.5	0.43	0.3	0.3
SUBTOTAL	16.39	13.0%	25.50	24.3%	46.99	32.1%	23.2%
Industrial							
Yarn	?		?		1.58	1.1	0.4
Cloth	5.63	4.5	3.61	3.4	4.18	2.8	3.6
Clothing	2.62	2.1	3.01	2.9	1.42	1.0	2.0
Kerosene	4.72	3.8	5.00	4.8	8.30	5.7	4.7
Matches	1.81	1.4	1.27	1.2	1.72	1.2	1.2
SUBTOTAL	14.78	11.8%	12.89	12.3%	17.20	11.8%	11.9%
Other	7.50	6.0%	5.49	5.2%	6.61	4.5%	5.2
TOTAL	125.49	100.0%	105.17	100.0%	146.34	100.0%	100.0%

SOURCES: See Table 6.1.

sugar, leaf tobacco, wine, soy sauce, and edible oils. Their total share was 22.5 percent, compared with only 3.9 percent in the less well-off North. Assuming that household consumption levels did not vary too greatly over time, these and other purchases of agricultural and traditional-processed items, most of which had been available for centuries, demonstrate the long-standing patterns of peasant marketing in the two regions.

Where the twentieth-century survey data show clear departures from older patterns is in the new category of "industrial products." By the 1930s, it is clear, machine-spun yarn, matches, and kerosene were widely used by Chinese peasants. Even machine-woven cloth had spread to a considerable extent (as discussed below). Together

these four new products accounted for an average of 11.9 percent
of the peasants' purchases in the Yangzi delta, and 13.8 percent in
North China.

Of all the new industrial items, the cotton products wrought especially profound changes. Xu Xinwu (n.d.) presents comparative data
for 1860 and 1936. He and his associates estimate that 45 percent of
all peasant households wove cloth in 1860, 80 percent of them from
their own cotton and yarn. Virtually all of the cloth consumed in
China (96.8 percent) was handwoven, of which nearly half (46.1 percent) was home-supplied. By 1936, the proportion of weaving households had declined to 30 percent of all peasant households, peasant
handwoven cloth to 38.8 percent of all cloth consumed, and home-
supplied cloth to a still-lower 28.7 percent. By then, even those who
wove their own cloth had come to rely greatly on machine-spun
yarn, which by now accounted for 75.9 percent of all yarn used in
village handwoven cloth (compared with a mere 0.6 percent in 1860).
With these changes came a much more thorough commercialization
of the cotton economy: the proportion of home-supplied cotton fell
from 69.4 percent of total cotton consumption in 1860 to a mere
10.9 percent; and fully 87.1 percent of all the cotton grown in China
entered the market. Thus was the old peasant household's trinity of
cotton cultivation, yarn spinning, and cloth weaving broken up.

The 1930s ethnographic data confirm Xu's macroscopic computations: as Table 6.5 shows, the cotton-growing villages in our sample
sold an average of 85.4 percent of their cotton crop. In villages that
grew little or no cotton, like Xiaodingxiang and Huayangqiao in the
Yangzi delta and Qianlianggezhuang in North China, households relied heavily on purchased cotton products to meet their consumption needs (Table 6.6).

Such a high degree of commercialization of the cotton economy
could not but affect other crops. Michang in North China and Yaojing, Dingjiacun, and Touzongmiao in the Yangzi delta all had over
30 percent of their cultivated area under cotton (Table 6.5). That
kind of concentration on a cash crop compelled a high reliance on
purchased foodgrain for household consumption. The four villages
spent an average of 36.9 percent of all cash purchases on consumption grain (Tables 6.2–6.4). The "fine grains" (xiliang, like rice and
wheat, as opposed to cheaper "coarse grains," culiang, like sorghum
and maize) were especially highly commercialized. Huayangqiao village, which grew rice almost exclusively, marketed a whopping 43.1
percent of its rice crop (Table 6.5).

Although these data qualify Wu Chengming's analysis in impor-

TABLE 6.5

Major Crops in Nine North China and Yangzi Delta Villages, 1936–39

Village	Foodgrain			Cash crop		
	Crop	Percent of sown area	Percent sold	Crop	Percent of sown area	Percent sold
North China, 1936						
Michang	Sorghum	44%	8.4%	Cotton	31%	93.4%
	Maize	15	2.3			
Dabeiguan	Millet	36	11.6	Cotton	11	69.5
	Sorghum	20	3.0			
	Maize	10	2.3			
Qianlianggezhuang	Sorghum	38	2.7	Fruit	28	81.6
				Peanuts	7	84.4
Yangzi delta, 1938–39						
Yanjiashang[a]	(1) Rice	100	18.6			
	(2) Wheat	83	5.3			
Yaojing[a]	(1) Rice	60	?	Cotton	34	?
	(2) Wheat	82	?			
Dingjiacun[a]	(1) Rice	33	[8.8]	Cotton	50	92.2
	(2) Wheat	22	[69.3]	Broad beans	42	78.6
Touzongmiao[b]	(1)			Cotton	39	86.4
				Soybeans	49	94.1
	(2) Barley	73	?			
	Wheat	12	?			
Xiaodingxiang[b]	(1) Rice	76	0	Mulberries	23	6.6[c]
	(2) Wheat	58	?	Broad beans	11	?
Huayangqiao[b]	(1) Rice	95	43.1			
	(2) —	—	—	Alfalfa	92	0

SOURCES: See Tables 6.1, 6.3.

NOTE: (1) signifies spring-planted crops, (2) fall-planted ones. Percentages for multi-cropped Yangzi delta villages refer to each cropping. The three North China villages, all in northeastern Hebei, were single-cropped. Bracketed numbers are based on incomplete data.

[a] 1938
[b] 1939
[c] Combined total of spring and fall harvests. All but 242 of the 19,260-*jin* (catty) spring crop was kept for the household's silkworms; 17.8% of the fall crop was sold.

tant ways, it is abundantly clear that even as late as the 1930s, grain and cotton products remained central to the peasants' involvement with the market—a fact consistent with what we would expect, given the enormous role that sheer survival played in this economy.

LOCAL, NATIONAL, AND INTERNATIONAL MARKETS

It is useful to classify the goods peasants bought and sold by the spatial scope of the markets involved. In the pre-refrigeration and traditional transport economy of rural China, perishable goods like meat, vegetables, and fruit were clearly limited to a marketing area that

TABLE 6.6

Cloth Consumption in Six North China and Yangzi Delta Villages, 1936

Item	Square yard	Percent	Square yard	Percent	Square yard	Percent
NORTH CHINA, 1936						
	Michang		Dabeiguan		Qianliangge-zhuang	
Purchased						
Ready-made						
cloth	2.13	27.6%	0.33	9.5%	0.70	35.2%
Raw cotton	0.22	2.8	0.05	1.5	0.22	11.0
Yarn	?		?		?	
Self-supplied						
Cotton	5.37	69.6	3.08	89.0	1.07	53.8
TOTAL	7.72	100.0%	3.46	100.0%	1.99	100.0%
YANGZI DELTA						
	Touzongmiao		Xiaodingxiang[a]		Huayangqiao	
Purchased						
Ready-made						
cloth	1.71	32.9%	0.34	22.1%	0.55	10.1%
Raw cotton	?		0.36	23.4	2.07	38.1
Yarn	?		0.84	54.5	0.81	14.9
Self-supplied						
Cotton	3.41	65.6	0	—	2.00	36.9
Cloth	0.08	1.5	0	—	0	—
TOTAL	5.20	100.0%	1.54	100.0%	5.43	100.0%

SOURCES: See Table 6.1.

NOTE: All figures are per capita averages. Square-yard figures for purchased and self-supplied cotton are computed by equating 1 jin (catty) of ginned cotton with 2.7 square yards of "native cloth" (tubu). This equivalence is based on the formula used in Xu Xinwu n.d.:

ginned cotton − 4% = wadding/yarn
yarn + 5% = cloth by weight
1.25 huiguan jin of cloth = 1.32 shi jin =
1.0 pi = 3.6337 sq. yds. of cloth

For self-supplied cotton, I have deducted 25% from the total for the estimated use for wadding. The amounts of purchased cotton and cloth are based on total cash expenditures, converted at the year's local prices.

[a] The Xiaodingxiang survey gives no price data for 1939, only for "before the war" and "now," 1940. The figures are based on the Touzongmiao price data. The unusually low per capita figure might be explained by the inappropriateness of the Touzongmiao data or by curtailed consumption in the face of inflation in cloth prices.

did not extend beyond a few days' travel from the point of origination. More durable goods like grain and cotton had a much longer reach and were not confined to the local markets. Thus was Yangzi delta rice shipped to North China in the Qing, North China cotton to the Yangzi delta, Northeast China wheat and soybeans to the Yangzi delta, and so on. Those goods belonged to a market of national scope. With the forced "opening" of China to international capitalism, almost all of these goods (except salt) became further linked to commodity markets of international scope. Chinese cotton was exported to Japan, tea to England, North America, and Russia, silk to France and the United States, soybeans to the United States and Australia, and so on, while English and Japanese yarn, and Javanese, Filipino, and European sugar, and so on, increasingly entered the rural Chinese markets.

Dwight Perkins (1969: 136–37) has usefully distinguished between long- and short-distance trade, pointing out that transport costs precluded the long-distance circulation of all but a few relatively high-priced commodities, especially luxury items like tea and silk. He estimates that of the 30–40 percent of the total farm output marketed, 7–8 percent entered long-distance trade, until that trade more than doubled in the twentieth century.

Though Perkins mentions the role of cotton goods in long-distance trade several times, we are left with the impression that long-distance trade consisted chiefly of the one-way flow of luxury goods from the countryside to the urban upper classes (Perkins 1969: chap. 6). But as we saw in Chapter 5, Wu Chengming has now added a crucial clarification to Perkins's study: the small-peasant exchange of grain for cotton goods and vice versa, which Perkins largely overlooked, actually played a central role in the commercial economy of Qing China, accounting for more than two-thirds of the total "commodity trade" (Table 5.4).

To grasp fully the import of Wu's finding is to do away once and for all with the old notions of "economic dualism" that long held sway among China historians. On this view, the modern world economy's impact on China was restricted mainly to the treaty ports, leaving the rural economy largely untouched (Chi-ming Hou 1963; Murphey 1977). Wu Chengming's findings remind us of the great impact that twentieth-century changes in the structure of China's cotton economy had on peasant lives. After all, every peasant household was directly involved either as producer-seller-consumer or as purchaser-consumer of cotton goods. For China's cotton economy to become internationalized was for every peasant household to become linked with the world market. This is a theme to which we will return in the next chapter, when we examine the effects of imperialism on China's peasant economy. A clear notion of the hierarchy and change in the spatial scope of goods will be essential to that analysis.

THE SOCIAL CONTENT OF PEASANT MARKETING

To complete the picture of peasant marketing, we need to examine the social context in which it was conducted, along the lines urged by the substantivists. If we focus specifically on the delta, it becomes clear that peasants principally marketed their grain and cotton in three ways and for three purposes:

1. To make rent payments to the landlord, usually absentee, in either money or kind. If a money payment was required, the tenant sold his grain or cotton, then paid the rent. If his payment was in kind, most of it would be sold later by the landlord. In either case, rent crops generally found their way into the market. We might call this kind of marketing *extraction-driven commercialization*.

2. To cover immediate production (excluding rent but including tax) and subsistence expenses. Often peasants sold grain immediately after the harvest to meet outstanding debts, only to repurchase grain later at higher prices to meet consumption needs, a double transaction that Wu Chengming calls *fanxiaoliang*. We might call this kind of marketing *survival-driven commercialization*.

3. To sell for gain the surplus after rent payments, taxes, production expenses, and consumption needs had been met. Some peasants even hoarded their crops to await seasonal price upswings in order to maximize their profit. We might call this kind of marketing *enterprise-driven commercialization*.

On the North China plain, with its low incidence of tenancy (ca. 18 percent of the cultivated area), agricultural commercialization was largely survival- and enterprise-driven, and involved chiefly cotton and wheat. At one end of the social-economic spectrum were poor-peasant farms that had less land than was required for the household's own subsistence foodgrain consumption. Those farms had little choice but to turn to cotton for the possibility of greater returns in any one year, even though the risks involved were often greater and the long-term returns sometimes lower. This was because cotton required more investment in fertilizer and labor, hence correspondingly greater risks from natural disaster or adverse price movements. Most of these farms also sold their winter wheat crop for cash and repurchased lower priced coarse grains for home consumption. At the other end of the spectrum were the large, labor-employing managerial farms, which generally turned to cotton as a part of a diversified cropping portfolio, in order to maximize their profits. In between the two types of farms were a continuum of family farms ranging from those preoccupied mainly with survival to those commanding a substantial surplus that could be sold for gain (Huang 1985: chaps. 4–11).

In the Yangzi delta, by contrast, extraction-driven commercialization—of landlord-merchants selling the foodgrain they received as rent—was the predominant form of agricultural commercialization. Here perhaps 45 percent of the cultivated land was rented, and in the highly commercialized areas, the figure rose to close to 100 percent. In our eight-village sample, the average was 65 percent.

Consider the case of the Huayangqiao villages. In 1939, of the total cultivated area, 88 percent of the subsoil (on which more below) was rented, all but four mu of it from absentee landlords (MT, Shanghai 1940: table 6), and almost all this land (95 percent) was under rice. The annual rent on the rice land was quoted in two rates, one nominal (*xuzu*) and one actual (*shizu*). The nominal rate for a mu of good land, the peasants say, was usually 1.2 "old" or "big" shi (200 catties, as opposed to the 160-catty "market" or standard shi) of husked rice, and 1.0 shi for land of average quality—or 240 catties and 200 catties, respectively. The actual rent was generally 70 percent of the nominal rent (sometimes as high as 80 percent), or 168 catties for good land, and 140 catties for the average. The usual yield was 320 catties (2 standard shi) of rice; the best yields reached 480 catties (H-I-1, H-III-2). Typically, then, a rent payment took 43.8 percent of the yield. In 1939, Huayangqiao peasants sold 458.0 shi out of a total rice output of 1,061.9 shi (43.1 percent). Most of this went for rent payments (MT, Shanghai 1940: tables 1, 11).

Most Huayangqiao peasants sold their rice to one of the seven rice dealers (*mihang*) in Huayang town and paid their rent in cash. In 1939, only three paid in kind (MT, Shanghai 1940: table 6). (In the later years of the war, when prices ran out of control, these villages simply divorced themselves from the unstable monetized economy and used rice as the standard unit of value.) Whether paid in kind or in cash, the rents entered circulation via the rice dealers and formed the backbone of the area's market economy. The seven rice dealers were the town's biggest merchants. They annually sold an estimated total of 70,000 shi before the Japanese occupation, 20 percent of which was consumed locally and the rest shipped to Shanghai (ibid., p. 182). The entire town economy revolved around this trade.

Beyond rent payments, Huayangqiao peasants marketed their rice principally for survival. A few were well-to-do enough to sell off surpluses for gain. By the time the Japanese researchers studied Huayangqiao, the war had greatly inflated the selling price of rice. In 1939–40, a standard shi fetched an average price of 22 yuan, with a low of 17 yuan at harvest time and a high of 36 yuan the following spring. All the peasants who could afford to do so "hoarded" their grain for as long as they could to sell at the spring highs. Lu Guantong, who was sufficiently well off to lease out four mu of land and hire twelve days of labor to help his family of three farm eight mu of land, behaved like a true profit-maximizing entrepreneur: he sold four shi of his twelve-shi harvest in November–December to meet rent payments and expenses for the New Year holidays, kept four shi for his household's consumption, and sold the other four, one shi at a time staggered over a four-month period. He got 28 yuan a shi in January, 33.6 yuan in February and March, and 36 yuan in April, the highest price obtained by anyone in Huayangqiao on the 1939 crop. Xue Jinfa, for another example, sold his family's surplus of two shi in February for 31 yuan apiece. In all, six of the 63 households in this village cluster were able to hold back 73 shi of rice until after New Year's. This was the marketing of enterprise.

The other villagers all sold to meet household expenses and debts. Thirty-nine of them completed their sales before New Year's. Of those, 26 were forced to purchase rice later at a higher price. Yang Ji's household of three, for example, which farmed only three mu and hired out 40 days to augment its farm income, sold four shi of its 4.9-shi harvest immediately, for an average price of 22 yuan. The household then bought rice little by little at steadily rising prices into the following spring. In the end, it repurchased all the rice it had sold, plus another 0.6 shi. Yang's household and the other 25 households like it sold anywhere from two to twelve shi of rice; most purchased from 0.5 to 2.0 shi at higher prices the following winter and spring (MT, Shanhai 1940: tables 1, 9, 11).

Peasants undertaking such sales bore a very different relationship to the market than those engaged in entrepreneurial marketing. Consider the different implications for each in a rising market like Huayangqiao's: the entrepreneurial producer selling his surplus after meeting household consumption needs gained from the higher prices, getting a higher cash income from his sales. The subsistence producer who sold to meet survival needs before New Year's, however, did not stand to profit, and those who had to buy rice later in the year at higher prices were in effect borrowing against their consumption at interest. This kind of market involvement should not be mistaken for entrepreneurial marketing, nor should such peasant behavior be mistaken for profit-maximizing rationality. Theirs was the rationality of survival, not of profit maximization.

THE PETTY-TRADE MARKET

The composition of commodities traded and the social context of peasant marketing, then, show that the Marxist notion of "petty commodity production" has considerable descriptive validity for the delta: the items that accounted for the bulk of the rural trade, grain and cloth, were produced on a small scale, by peasant farms and by peasant household handicrafts. Where this trading system parted company from the classical Marxist scheme is that it was not transitional to capitalist commodities exchange, as Marx assumed. We saw in the preceding chapter how the pattern of commercialization in the Ming and Qing was involutionary rather than transformative. Petty trade does not necessarily develop into capitalist trade. Small-scale peasant commodity production does not necessarily give way to large-scale capitalist production. The twentieth-century field data show, in fact, how very tenacious petty trade was (and in the reformist China of the 1980s, as will be seen, the rural petty-trade market returned with a vengeance). Machine-spun yarn did break apart the old unified combination of cotton growing, yarn spinning, and cloth weaving. But it did not alter the fundamental fact that subsistence goods like grain and cotton/yarn/cloth continued to occupy the bulk of total peasant trade. Moreover, except for yarn, these goods continued to be produced mainly by small peasant producers.

This trade, of course, also differs from the two-way rural-urban trade of which Adam Smith made so much. For Smith, the exchange between urban manufactures and rural "rude" products played a fundamental role in powering transformative economic development. The trade of the Yangzi delta in the Qing, however, clearly consisted of only a minimum of rural-urban exchange. Peasants purchased mainly subsistence goods produced by other peasants. They purchased little in the way of urban manufactures outside of small quantities of subsidiary necessities. Even in the twentieth century, the inroads made by urban manufactures remained very limited: to yarn or cloth, matches, and kerosene.

The social story underlying peasant involvement in this petty-trade market tells not so much of mutually beneficial rural-urban exchange, as envisioned by Smith, as of extraction and of the harsh struggle for survival. Part of the trade consisted of a unidirectional flow of surplus from countryside to town, mainly in the form of rent payments, with nothing in return, and another large part, of peasant exchange for subsistence. Only a small share of the trade fits the Smithian image of entrepreneurial trade for gain.

THE LAND MARKET

The land market in the delta likewise differed fundamentally from the perfectly competitive factor market postulated by Smith and the neoclassical economists. Land purchases and sales were subject to elaborate and severe constraints right down to the eve of the Revolution. No one should imagine a market of perfect competition, subject only to the laws of supply and demand.

The Qing, it is true, did see an increasing transfer of land, but in fact this usually involved multiple and convoluted stages of alienation, not an outright sale. Rather than selling their land, households in need, from sickness or death, poor harvest or the marriage of an offspring, would usually offer it up for *dian* (pledge) or *huomai* (conditional or revocable sale) in return for a large percentage of its value. Sometimes the household would find itself unable to redeem the land at the end of the agreed-on period—a not too surprising result, since by the usual arrangement, the household continued to cultivate the land and pay the standard land rent to the pledge-holder, effectively halving its income from the pledged parcel. Already struggling at the margins of subsistence, the household often found itself faced with the necessity of having to sell the land outright. In practice, as time went on, the pledge-holder could gain full title by paying the balance between the original consideration and the land's actual value, in a procedure called *zhaotie*.

This practice, however, contravened Qing law, which in any case adopted an ambiguous stance toward such conditional transactions. Though the law legitimized the arrangements by attempting to regularize the taxing of them, it also still held to the old moral vision that landownership was in theory inalienable, so that where a land transaction was specified as revocable, the code in effect gave the pledge-maker indefinite rights of redemption. Even if the agreement did not specify that the sale was revocable, the pledge-maker still had 30 years within which to redeem the land. Only if the original contract stated specifically that the sale was an irrevocable one (*juemai*) could the land be lost without any right of redemption (*Da Qing lüli huitong xinsuan*, [8]: 987–88). Even the Republican Civil Code, its Western sources of inspiration notwithstanding, provided

for extended rights of redemption: conditional sales could remain re-
vokable for as long as 30 years. For arrangements of under fifteen
years, the law specifically forbade making the sale irrevocable when
the pledge-maker failed to redeem the land (*The Republican Civil
Code* 1930: 233).

The inconsistency between the law's provisions and the actual
practice of buying and selling land led to frequent lawsuits, in which
the original owner would try to exercise his right to redeem his land
long after the pledge-holder had purchased outright title to the land
through the customary practice of *zhaotie*.* It was to prevent such
disputes that the Republican code provided that a pledge-maker had
to redeem his land within two years of the expiration of the term of
the original agreement (ibid., p. 235).

In the Yangzi delta, a two-tiered form of landownership evolved
that at once accommodated the old principles and the new practice.
Land was conceived as consisting of both subsoil and topsoil, and the
property rights in the subsoil came to be traded more and more
freely, in response both to the wish of urban elites to invest in land,[†]
and the need of impoverished peasants to sell it. In Huayang by the
twentieth century, a nearly freely competitive market in subsoil
rights had come into being: they could be sold almost like stocks
and bonds, without any regard to who owned the topsoil and who
actually used the land. Most of the time, the villagers were not even
aware of the transactions. Yet even then topsoil ownership, never acknowledged by law but decisive in terms of actual land use, continued to be subject to the old constraints of convoluted alienation
and the first right of purchase by kin and neighbors.

The difference was most graphically illustrated in the differential
ownership and turnover patterns between subsoil and topsoil in
Huayangqiao. Subsoil rights were so frequently bought and sold that
by 1940, fully 479 of the 549 mu of subsoil in these villages were
owned by 80 outsiders, mostly in small parcels. Topsoil ownership,
by contrast, showed extraordinary stability over time: the villagers
could recall only two such sales (MT, Shanghai 1940: tables 5 and 6).
It was topsoil ownership that carried the traditional constraints—of
extended rights of redemption in any conditional sale, and of the
customary prior right of purchase by kin and neighbors in an out-

*Feinerman 1989 discusses this phenomenon; my preliminary survey of court
records of the Qing and Republican periods suggests that there were large numbers of
such cases.
†Beattie 1979 analyzes well the late imperial gentry's motivation for acquiring land.

right sale. They were practices that had their roots partly in the tradition that the family, not the individual, was the property-holding unit, and partly in the practical considerations of field access by those farming adjacent plots (Huang 1985: 260).

The two sides to this story are the spread of land buying and selling, a part of the larger trend of commercialization considered in this book, and the persistence of ideological and social constraints that ran counter to the logic of the modern market and warn us against any simple projecting of the capitalist market system onto this economy.

THE CREDIT MARKET

The rural credit market of the delta likewise remained far from a perfectly competitive money market even after the six centuries of vigorous commercialization during the Qing. Delta peasants, it is clear, functioned in multiple credit "markets." Their most immediate source of credit, and the most used down to the twentieth century, was kin and neighbors or friends within their own village or in an affinally connected one. These "informal" loans, in kind or in cash, often carried no interest or lower interest than the "market" rates, and were based on "good feeling" (ganqing), connections (guanxi), and reciprocity.*

An extension of this source was the credit society made up of kin, friends, and neighbors. A villager in need would get together a group of people close to him for help. In return for a ceremonial banquet (as in Sibeichai village in the 1930s, for example; KC, III: 356) or for a modest amount of interest (4.3 percent in Kaixiangong village; Fei 1939: 272), he gained the use of their pooled funds. He was allowed to repay the amount in increments over a period of years. These intracommunity loans were based on very different principles from those we associate with the modern-day capital or money market: the key element was reciprocity for mutual benefit, not the investment logic of costs and returns (Fei 1939: 264–72; H-I-14).

Above this village system was the credit market that we usually associate with the word "usury." Wealthy merchants, landlords, or professional moneylenders in town would extend credit to the villagers on the goods they purchased (see, for example, KC, II: 194) or

*The fact that reality fell short of the "moral economy" ideal is shown by the very large share of credit-related disputes among the 300,000-odd homicide cases in the Qing Board of Punishment archives.

lend them small amounts of money or goods. In the case of large amounts, the peasant often had to put up his land as security (Huang 1985: 176–77). Interest rates on these loans seldom operated by the law of supply and demand. Peasant borrowing from usurers was generally for emergency or survival purposes and defies the logic of simple calculations of costs and returns. Moreover, custom and law played a strong role in governing interest rates in the rural usury market: the usual range was 2–3 percent a month, and the legal maximum 3 percent during the Ming and Qing (Dai Yanhui 1966: 334).

Farther removed from villagers were the pawnshops, generally found only in larger towns and county seats. Loans on pawned goods generally involved higher effective interest rates than conventional usury, ranging generally between 2 percent and 4 percent a month (Pan 1985: chap. 5). Finally, there was the conditional sale of land. This can be seen as the most drastic form of peasant borrowing, for instead of just putting up his land as security, the peasant yielded title to it. Though ostensibly only for a limited term, with a right to redemption, these pledging arrangements, as we have seen, were often preludes to the outright sale of the land.

Almost all loans, whether from kin and neighbors, the usurer, the pawnshop, or the pledge-holder, had to do with emergencies and survival and not with productive investment. The usual calculations associated with a capitalist loan, governed by supply and demand in the credit market, and by the prospect of returns measured against costs, do not apply. The peasant (or anyone for that matter) borrowing for survival can be made to tolerate interest rates that no capitalist enterprise could or would bear.

Peasant borrowing for productive investment was rare and at best amounted to a small part of total peasant borrowing in the above forms. Mostly this involved merchant-supplied fertilizer and usually, in the twentieth century, for export-related crops like mulberries for silk cocoons in Wuxi and to a lesser extent, highly commercialized grain crops. In Huayangqiao, for example, merchants advanced soybean-cake fertilizer in return for a lien on the peasant's rice crop. But what might have begun as a form of credit for productive investments quickly got sucked up into the general population/resource squeeze of the delta. By the twentieth century, peasants who had to purchase beancake on credit paid an effective interest rate of 20 percent a month for the five-month period between the application of the fertilizer and the harvest. Entrepreneurial borrowing had given way to survival borrowing, and merchant credit blended into loan-sharking.

At the highest level of the credit market stood the "native banks" (*qianzhuang*), and by the twentieth century, modern banks as well, both generally found only in the larger urban centers. These establishments operated closest to the logic of the modern market, though the native banks, at least, were still subject to the influence of the lower levels of the credit market. Tied to the rural usury market based on borrowing for survival rather than for profitable investment, most of them expected higher interest rates than the modern banks shaped mainly by the urban and international credit markets. In any case, banks (whether native or modern) were far removed from the immediate world of the peasants and affected their lives only indirectly.

THE LABOR MARKET

The nearest thing to a freely competitive market in the countryside was the market for short-term day-labor, as Li Rongchang (1989) points out. Here reality approached the model: almost any man who wished to hire out could, and almost anyone who could pay could hire someone. Typically, in the busy seasons would-be workers gathered before sunrise around a known local spot, perhaps a big tree or a temple. The hiring was generally completed before the crack of dawn. Some of the people would be known to each other, and the savvy employers would vie for the best workers. Contracts were generally made for just the day and never for more than a few days (Huang 1985: 198–99). On the North China plain, about 36 percent of all peasant households had at least one male who hired out for an average of 40–50 days a year as a day-laborer (ibid., pp. 80–81). In the Yangzi delta, the figure was somewhat lower, perhaps 31 percent (Chap. 4).

But this market still fell far short of the neoclassical ideal. It was, first of all, a seasonal market, in full operation only during the busy period of planting and harvesting. Moreover, it was a very localized market, since most day-laborers were small peasants who had to remain within walking distance of their homes. The temporal as well as spatial extent of the market, in other words, was severely constrained.

When we move away from the day-labor market, connections figure more and more. No long-term agricultural laborer could obtain a job without some introduction or the services of a middleman. On the North China plain, 10 percent of peasant households had a member who hired out as a year-laborer (Huang 1985: 81), compared with the much lower 3.8 percent in the Yangzi delta (Chap. 4). In addition to agricultural wage labor, some peasants had access to employment in town (as in Huayang), in the cities (e.g., Shajing village peasants in Beijing), or on the Northeast frontier (e.g., Houjiaying peasants; Huang 1985: 215). These jobs typically also required connections. That is why we generally find the workers in urban jobs or on the frontier bunched together by village of origin or by kinship. These were not freely competitive positions open to anyone wishing to hire out.*

Most important so far as the delta is concerned is the point I have emphasized in the preceding chapters: that a substantial part of the productive labor force—especially women—remained outside of the labor market. Cultural constraints against women venturing outside the home, plus the logistical difficulties of managing female labor that came with those constraints, kept the market for their labor from developing any further. As we have seen, this had the paradoxical effect of sustaining artificially high wages for the relatively few male adults who did sell their labor and encouraging the persistence of the small-peasant economy. The result, as we know, was the effective elimination of managerial farms from the delta countryside. It is a phenomenon that flies in the face of the premise of Schultz's neoclassical model, in which all workers are integrated into a single, perfectly competitive market.

MARKETS AND DEVELOPMENT

In short, while the neoclassical model is useful for calling our attention to the formation of product and factor markets in the Yangzi delta during the Ming and Qing, it will not do for us to imagine perfectly competitive markets as postulated in that model. Most of the goods traded by peasants were subsistence goods of the Marxist "petty commodities" variety. And the land market continued to be governed in good measure by principles of inalienability, the credit market by reciprocity and survival, and the long-term labor market by social connections. The gap between the market opportunities for and the supply of productive female and child labor, finally, tells of underemployment and labor surplus in the countryside.

Once again, we need to separate out commercialization from eco-

*See Li Rongchang (1989) for a full argument and detailed documentation of the differences between the day-labor and the longer-term labor market, and between the local and the "external" labor market. The Mantetsu six-village survey (KC, I–V) provides considerable detail for the North China plain.

nomic development, contrary to the classical assumptions of Marx and Smith. The fact is that the product as well as factor markets of the delta in the late imperial and Republican periods indicate not transformative development but involution: peasant marketing consisted chiefly of the exchange of subsistence necessities with little two-way trade between town and country; peasant households marketed more for rent payments and survival needs than for enterprise; and peasants borrowed more for emergencies and survival than for productive investment. This kind of near-subsistence economy could nonetheless sustain a very high level of commercialization, as has been seen. But that commercialization brought little in the way of accumulation and productive investment. It had more to do with extraction and survival than with the coming of economic development or "incipient capitalism." The markets of such an economy should not be confused with the kind of commercialization that was accompanied by the rise of capitalist production in which producers (whether family farmers or enterprises) generated a surplus and accumulated for productive investment. The association between market development and capitalization in the early modern and modern West was in fact coincidental and even anomalous; it should not be projected as the norm onto all forms of commercialization in all times for all parts of the world.

Wu Chengming's conception of commodities seems to me to err precisely in assuming a necessary association between market growth and economic development. For Wu, as for so many of the incipient capitalism school, the concern is to demonstrate that imperial China was on its way to capitalism and therefore fits the Stalinist five-modes-of-production formula. While other incipient capitalism scholars had been concerned with demonstrating the "sprouts of capitalism" in "production relations" (e.g., wage labor), Wu's concern is to demonstrate those sprouts in market development. The formation of a nationally integrated market, supposedly, is sufficient to prove China's incipient capitalism.

In point of fact, however, the production of goods for a nationally integrated market could be locked into a non-capitalizing mode, and production for localized markets might actually engender capitalization. The production of cotton goods in the Qing, as has been seen, remained tied to the small peasants' primitive spindles and looms and depended almost entirely on their low-cost household labor. Even though the goods did indeed belong to a nationally integrated market, such production led to little or no capital accumulation. By contrast, animal raising could provide opportunities for capital accumulation, even though the trade was strictly localized (and as such excluded by Wu from the commodities category). Take Zhang Chonglou of Dabeiguan village, for example. One of three managerial farmers (who cultivated more than 100 mu with hired labor), Zhang employed a highly successful strategy of mixing crop raising with hog raising. In 1936, he raised 22 pigs, which brought him 141 yuan of the total 535 yuan he had in cash income that year. Thanks to this activity, Zhang had managed to expand his farm operation, acquiring 65 mu of new land in the 23 years between 1913 and 1936. He farm-managed his holdings with hired labor in a productive organization that bore a strong resemblance to a capitalist enterprise (Huang 1985: 73).

Zhang's case underscores the problems with Wu's conception of commodities. True, hogs were limited by and large to the local market. Yet if they promoted capital accumulation, surely they were more significant from the standpoint of the development of "capitalist sprouts" than non-capitalizing cotton handicraft production. My own preference is to consider trade from the standpoint of its social context and its potential for capital accumulation and economic development, rather than simply from the standpoint of whether or not it belonged to a national market. Wu Chengming's wish to equate "commodities" traded for their "exchange value" in a nationally integrated market with incipient capitalism, and goods traded locally for "use value" with "precapitalism," thus seems to me to put the emphasis on a secondary rather than a primary condition of capitalist development. Whether producing for a local, national, or international market, the crucial question is whether the production unit met the central criterion in Marx's original conception of capitalism: of units of enterprise bent on the accumulation of capital for its own sake.

We might think in terms of a hierarchy of development-generating potential in the varieties of commercialization outlined above. Peasant production on the model of enterprise-driven commercialization clearly held the highest potential for rationalization, capitalization, and increased labor productivity. Similarly, peasant or farmer purchase of land for the purpose of expanding an agricultural operation, rather than merchant or landlord investment in land for long-term security, and peasant borrowing for the purpose of productive investment, rather than for household emergencies, approximate the capitalistic accumulative ideal. These come the closest to what we commonly associate with capitalistic or early modern economic development. It is to those kinds of marketing activities that we should look for signs of incipient capitalism. Peasant market production for subsistence and peasant borrowing for household crises held little promise for capital accumulation and development in and of themselves. Where the intensification of production expanded the absolute levels of output, they tended to do so through the mobilization of hitherto underemployed or unemployed labor, generally for diminished returns per workday, and not through the capitalization of production. It will not do to assume that all forms of commercialization and all kinds of markets were necessarily associated with capitalism or economic development. The commercialization of the Ming-Qing and Republican delta countryside was mainly involutionary rather than transformative.

CHAPTER 7

Imperialism,
Urban Development,
and Rural Involution

Whether imperialism had a beneficial or deleterious effect on China is a much and often passionately debated question, at least on this side of the Pacific. We have had, at one pole, the argument that imperialism was the agent for the spread of modern civilization. Mark Elvin (1973: 315) has put it the most bluntly of all: "It was the historic mission of the modern West to ease and then break the high-level equilibrium trap in China." In this view, imperialism offered China's long-stagnant economy the opportunities of international markets, modern technology, and capitalist development. If Chinese peasants did not attain modernity, it was not because of imperialism but rather in spite of it. At the opposite pole are the arguments of "semicolonialism" and "dependency." Imperialism, far from bringing economic development, caused underdevelopment. It triggered massive rural pauperization by breaking apart the traditional "natural economy," with its combination of agriculture and household industry. True, it stimulated the development of capitalism in China. But it also reduced the Chinese bourgeoisie to a condition of dependency and nipped in the bud the "sprouts of capitalism" that had sprung up before its coming (Mao Zedong 1972 [1939]). It imposed on rural life the vagaries of the capitalist market system, subjecting the countryside to a widening, scissorlike gap in the terms of rural-urban trade and the whiplash effects of capitalism's boom and bust cycles (Zhang Youyi 1957: vol. 3). Imperialism, finally, was exploitative, taking advantage of rural China's cheap labor and raw materials and extracting the surplus it produced. In so doing, it created and perpetuated the underdevelopment of the agrarian economy (Frank 1967, 1978).

For a time, "economic dualism" lent a new twist to this quarrel: the effects of imperialism were not so much beneficial or deleterious as insufficient; they were largely limited to the treaty ports. What emerged in China with the coming of the West was an economic structure comprising two distinct systems, each going its separate and independent way. Low-cost traditional products continued to serve the countryside and the rural markets; higher cost machine products were restricted mainly to the cities. Imperialism brought neither development nor underdevelopment; its modernizing effects never really penetrated the countryside (Hou 1963; Murphey 1977).

The economic dualism thesis has since been largely discredited by the mounting evidence on rural commercialization, not only in the twentieth century, but already in the Ming and Qing, long before the intrusion of imperialism (Wu Chengming 1985; Huang 1985). Given what we now know about the structure of the cotton economy during the Qing and its changes in the twentieth century, for example, we can simply no longer insist on the separation of the rural and urban economies. On the other hand, as will be seen below, economic dualism is useful on the descriptive if not the analytical level: for distinguishing urban change from rural change and suggesting the possibility of simultaneous urban development and rural underdevelopment.

After economic dualism came Immanuel Wallerstein's (1974, 1979) theory of the "world capitalist system." This thesis has the virtue of objectifying the issue of imperialism, treating it as a systemic matter and removing it from charges and countercharges of evil individuals or national governments. In that model, capitalism came to China as part of a worldwide phenomenon that began in early modern Europe and expanded to encompass the entire world.

For an accurate grasp of the effects of imperialism in China, as I see it, we need first to move beyond ideologically motivated arguments of whatever stripe. Some scholars, to be sure, will continue to argue for one set of effects to the exclusion of the other. What I want to suggest in this chapter is that both sides have much to commend them; we need to acknowledge the reality of both the development and the underdevelopment that resulted from imperialism. That international capitalism and the world market stimulated major sectors of the Chinese economy is beyond question. But it is no less certain that they caused considerable dislocation and depression.

Still, it is not enough merely to say that imperialism encouraged both development and underdevelopment. We need a systemic analysis capable of explaining those paradoxical phenomena. Specifically, we need to answer three questions. What precisely were the areas of development and underdevelopment? What was the structure of the new economic system that emerged in China under imperialism? How might that structure explain the concurrence of development and underdevelopment?

If we are to answer these questions, it is clear that we must separate out urban change from rural change. Part of our difficulties with this subject stems from the fact that we intuitively think of development as a single phenomenon involving mutually reinforcing urban and rural change. That was the assumption in the classical model of Smith and Marx. But the fact of continuing peasant poverty in the face of the rise of modern metropolises should suggest to us the possibility of the conjoining of urban development with rural underdevelopment.

This chapter will show that, in the urban sector, the effects of imperialism were on balance stimulative. To be sure, imperialism caused dislocation in some areas of the urban economies. Its competitive advantage vis-à-vis indigenous capital also obstructed the development of some Chinese industries. But there can be no mistaking the overall process of urban development that was set in motion in the delta by imperialism: the rise of new industries and of modern cities large and small. In the rural sector, however, the ultimate effect, despite some major changes in the economic and commercial structure, was not transformative development, but the further involution of peasant production.

This suggestion that there was a basic difference between town and country must not be mistaken for an espousal of the old economic dualism model. It will not do to posit, as that model does, that imperialism left the countryside unaffected. This chapter will show that imperialism profoundly changed the rural economy and marketing system. I also want to explicitly reject here the implications of that model, the suggestion that imperialism will cause development when and where it penetrates. What actually happened in the delta was that imperialism forged a new economic system in which urban industrial development was interlocked with rural involution through merchant middlemen.

To grasp accurately the nature of the changes that occurred in the delta countryside, we will need to call on several of the themes of the preceding chapters: to distinguish commercialization from development, and agricultural intensification and involution from development. It will not do to equate, as Smith and Marx did, commercialization with development, and urban development with rural development.

THE RISE AND DECLINE OF YANGZI DELTA TOWNS

One index of urban development in the delta is the rise of new towns. Appendix Table C.3 pulls together the available gazetteer information on small-town formation and change in the Shanghai area between 1862 and 1911. In all, we have information for 107 of the 457 towns named in the gazetteers of the Shanghai region over that period: 40 of the 107 were new towns, and the other 67 had experienced enough change for the gazetteer compilers to have taken note of it.

Industrialization, which advanced at substantial rates, was clearly one major dynamic of change.* Eight of the 40 new towns arose around new factories, including cotton textile mills, cotton-towel factories, and the new Jiangnan arsenal. And three of the 28 old towns that prospered did so for the same reason. The rise of the Shanghai metropolis itself was another major dynamic. Six of the new towns were suburbs, and one of the old ones thrived under its influence.

Few would quarrel with either as a factor in development, or with other obvious ones like the coming of railroads (accounting for the rise of two new towns and increased prosperity for one) and the steamship (which powered the rise of three transport nexuses, two of them totally new). But other factors are less obvious. For example, the widespread availability of machine-spun yarn pushed cotton cloth weaving into new areas, and stimulated the rise of eight new towns and the growth of three old ones. The increased commercialization of raw cotton also had its effect: three new towns emerged around the expanded cotton trade, and five old towns gained new prosperity from it.

Another not-so-obvious factor was the turn to sericulture in the Shanghai area. Mulberry cultivation and silkworm raising had been limited largely to the low-lying yutian parts of the central basin until after the middle of the nineteenth century, when international demand raised the returns on silk and encouraged an entirely new sericulture zone extending along the high-lying belt from Wuxi to Taicang to Nanhui. One new town and six old ones profited from this expansion.

Finally, some localities adapted to changing conditions by developing new handicraft industries. Chuansha county became a center of handicraft lacing; five of its existing towns thrived with the introduction of this industry, and three new ones sprang up around it.

*There are no reliable estimates of the rate of industrial development in 19th- and 20th-century China. Fan Baichuan (1983: 20) estimates a 14–15 percent annual growth rate in total capital of Chinese capitalist enterprises between 1900 and 1911. Wang Yuru (1987) estimates that the value of industrial output grew 4 percent a year between 1920 and 1936, or a near doubling of the value over the period.

(Handicraft towel weaving, responsible for the rise of another of its new towns, Batuan, was also a new industry.)

At the apex of the new urban development stood three major cities, Shanghai, Wuxi, and Nantong. Shanghai, of course, became China's leading industrial and commercial city, and Wuxi did not lag far behind it. By 1933, Wuxi had jumped into third place, after Shanghai and Guangzhou, ahead even of Tianjin in industrial output (Yan Zhongping et al. 1955: 106). Wuxi's industrial labor force of 62,760 was second only to Shanghai's in size, and the value-added in industry was already three times that in agriculture (MT, Shanghai 1941a: 9–10). In 1913, the delta's third major industrial center, Nantong, ranked third in the nation in the number of mill spindles, well above Tianjin and Qingdao at the time (Yan Zhongping et al. 1955: 107–8). Indeed, we already see in the early decades of the twentieth century the beginnings of the delta's three economic regions, each centering around one of these cities.

Changes like these, however, must not blind us to the shock effects of international capitalism. Fourteen of the 67 old towns declined as the production of handicraft cloth fell to machine products. All of us have long been aware of the substantial body of anecdotal evidence on this phenomenon in contemporary accounts (see, for example, those in Zhang Youyi 1957, 3: 482–522). The Appendix C data provide a clearer sense of its dimensions. By 1911, 22 towns had died out for all practical purposes, the gazetteer compilers noting either that markets were no longer held in them or simply that they no longer existed. Unhappily, the causes are not specified, and we will have to wait for future research to clarify just why and how these towns disappeared. But it seems clear that if more than half of the existing towns declined or disappeared so soon after the intrusion of international capitalism, its depressive effects cannot be overlooked. On balance, though, the overall urban pattern was unmistakably one of development and modernization.

COTTON CULTIVATION AND COTTON INDUSTRIES

Imperialism had an enormous effect on the delta's cotton economy. True, cultivation did not expand as it did in North China (where the twentieth century saw a threefold increase; Huang 1985: 125–28), for the simple reason that cotton was in competition with high-yielding wet-rice, not low-yielding dry-farmed foodgrains. When cotton did displace rice, it was a result of unusual circumstances. In Huating county, for example, cotton began displacing rice in the

1870s not because of its higher returns but because the Taiping wars impoverished many peasants, so that they were unable to purchase the oxen and farm implements necessary for rice (*Chongxiu Huating xian zhi* 1878, 23: 4b–5a).

In some areas, cotton gave way to sericulture because of the growth of export demand for silk. The process is documented for parts of Nanhui county after the Taipings (*Nanhui xian zhi* 1879, 22: 35a). In Huating in the 1870s, mulberry cultivation and silkworm raising apparently brought twice the return of cotton growing, spinning, and weaving (*Chongxiu Huating xian zhi* 1878, 23: 4b–5a). But sericulture, even with export demand, could never reach the dimensions of cotton and the cloth that by now all peasants wore. It made only limited inroads against cotton cultivation.

In fact, cotton acreage may not have increased at all in the late nineteenth and twentieth centuries. Perkins (1969: 261) estimates a plausible 11,800,000 mu under cotton in Jiangsu province in 1914–18, and a little changed 12,600,000 mu in 1931–37. Nevertheless, the breakup of the three-way combination of cotton cultivation, spinning, and weaving profoundly changed the delta peasants' lives. Gazetteers of the time abound in references to this phenomenon. The Nanhui county gazetteer of 1929 notes, for example:

> Earning income from yarn and cloth began in Yuan times. The women of the poor households depended on it for a living. In the last thirty years, however, textile mills have sprung up all over Shanghai. The yarn they produce is white and smooth, far superior to the handspun yarn. Earnings from yarn spinning have thus disappeared entirely. [Machine-woven] "foreign cloth" has flourished. It is wider and cheaper than handwoven cloth. Earnings from [handwoven] "native cloth" have thus also gradually disappeared. (*Nanhui xian xu zhi* 1929, 18: 3a–b)

Modern textiles did not wipe out all the old handicraft industries, of course. Traditional handicrafts managed to hold on in some places, especially in Shanghai and Fengxian (Xia Lingen 1984). In several areas, hand weaving even thrived from the expanded supply of yarn, as we have seen. Others, like Jiangyin county, developed an "improved handwoven cloth" (*gailiang tubu*) by adopting the new iron-geared loom (*Jiangyin xian xuzhi* 1921, 11: 14a–15a). The towel-weaving industry that grew up in Jiading and Chuansha counties after the 1900s depended in part on low-cost female labor in the peasant household (*Jiading xian xuzhi* 1930, 5: 49a), and 50–60 percent of Nanhui county's new sock-weaving industry was centered in the peasant household. These three counties also developed a viable home lace-work industry (Xia Lingen 1984).

Nevertheless, fourteen of the 39 towns in Shanghai municipality that disappeared or declined after 1861 were explicitly said to have done so because of the decline in native cloth. Even the decline of Suzhou city, the traditional center for processing handwoven cloth, and the rise of Shanghai, the center of the modern mills, were linked to this process in an important way.

The decline of Suzhou and the rise of Shanghai, of course, tell also about a larger realignment in the commercial structure of the delta. The old commercial network centered around the Grand Canal shrank in importance after the 1850s with the change in the course of the Yellow River and the silting up of the canal north of Linqing (Huang 1985: 55). There was a concomitant rise in coastal shipping after the opening of Shanghai to foreign trade in 1842, and the coming of the steamship soon after allowed the commercial traffic in heavy goods to travel up the Yangzi from Shanghai. Under the impact of these successive blows, Suzhou city ceded position to Shanghai as the country's leading commercial and industrial center.

The increased trading of cotton, yarn, and cloth that came with the breakup of unified family production formed the backbone of the delta's new commercial structure. By 1936, the proportion of raw cotton entering the market in China had jumped from 30 percent in 1860 to 87 percent (Xu Xinwu n.d.). Three of the new delta towns in Table C.3 owed their existence to the trade in cotton, and five old ones prospered by it. Machine-produced yarn and cloth came to replace grain and handspun cloth as the leading commodities in the Chinese economy. This increased commercialization of the cotton economy was the driving force behind the fortyfold increase in "commodity trade" after the Opium War estimated by Wu Chengming (1984).

SERICULTURE

The other big change in the delta countryside was the spread of sericulture along the high-lying belt from Jiangyin to Fengxian with the growing world demand for silk. Hit with a severe disease in its silkworm crop in 1854, the French silk industry turned to China for its supply of raw silk, and quickly found that because of the cheap labor in China, the imports cost less than the domestic product. What followed was something of an international division of labor, with China occupying the more labor-intensive parts of the production process, and France the more capital-intensive. In the twentieth century, the United States joined France to become a major purchaser of

Chinese raw silk, accounting for 30–40 percent of Chinese exports from Shanghai by the late 1910s and 1920s.* Raw silk exports from China increased from the 9,000 or so piculs (*haiguan dan*, which equals 120.96 catties, or 133.33 pounds) in the 1830s to more than 140,000 piculs by the late 1920s. (See Lillian Li 1981: 74–76, 82–85, for data on silk exports; comparative data on early-nineteenth-century silk fabrics are not available.)

The spread of sericulture for export was aided by the disruptions of the Taiping wars, which wiped the agricultural slate clean in some areas, making it easier to turn to new crops. In other areas, migrations from the old sericulture areas brought the necessary technical know-how. Local governments also actively encouraged sericulture as part of their postbellum efforts for economic recovery. In Jiangyin, cultivation began under official encouragement in the Tongzhi period (1862–74), reaching 100,000 mu by 1921 (*Jiangyin xian xuzhi* 1921, 11: 8a). In Wuxi, where the prospect of relatively high returns stimulated the planting of mulberries on resettled land (*Wuxi Jingui xian zhi* 1881, 31: 1b), cultivation reached a peak of 360,000+ mu in 1927, about 30 percent of the county's total cultivated acreage (Zhang Youyi 1957, 3: 626; see also MT, Shanhai 1941a: 9–10). In Taicang in the early 1870s, the local magistrate established a sericulture bureau, purchased seeds, and ordered the people to grow mulberries. In the next decade, some hundred thousand seedlings were planted (*Taicang zhou zhi* 1919, 3: 22b). In Nanhui, migrants from Zhexi [Huzhou] and Jiangning [Nanjing] brought the necessary skills to the area, while officials, once again, encouraged mulberry cultivation (*Nanhui xian xuzhi* 1929, 20: 9a). The same thing happened along the southern periphery of the Shanghai area, in Fengxian (*Chongxiu Fengxian xian zhi* 1878, 19: 2b). The entire process is summed up in the Songjiang prefectural gazetteer:

> There was never any sericulture in this area until the end of the Daoguang period [1821–50], when some rural people south of the Huangpu River began to plant mulberries and raise silkworms. . . . Then came the disruptions of war and the migration of Zhexi and Jiangning people into the area east of the Huangpu River. The people then took it up much more. The officials, furthermore, encouraged it. (*Songjiang fu xuzhi* 1883, 5: 5b)

---

*But Chinese silk was not able to capture the major part of the market supplied by the dynamic new filature industry in the United States, which used power looms and preferred the more standardized Japanese silk. The U.S. industry eventually came to rely on Japan for 90 percent of its raw silk.

RICE

The late nineteenth and twentieth centuries, finally, saw a fundamental restructuring of the rice economy of the delta. Rice was of
course already highly commercialized in the Qing. The major part of
the large quantities exported north along the Grand Canal was official tribute, but the government's rice carriers were permitted to
transport private stocks along with the tribute. Wu Chengming
(1985: 272) estimates that 5,000,000 shi of official rice and 1,000,000
of private commercial rice were being transported along the Grand
Canal around 1840. In addition, an indeterminate amount of delta
rice was shipped south to Fujian by sea (pp. 275–76). Not a grain surplus area itself, the delta had to rely on imports from other regions,
especially from Hunan and Sichuan, and secondarily from nearby
Anhui and Jiangxi—a total of about 15,000,000 shi. The delta also
imported soybeans and wheat from the Northeast via the coastal
route to Shanghai—about 10,000,000 shi—as has been seen. To pay
for these imports, it exported perhaps 40,000,000 bolts (pi) of cloth
to the North and Northeast, Guangdong (and thence to southeast
Asia), and Fujian (pp. 277–79). Here was the basic structure of long-
distance trade in the Qing: the exchange of cotton cloth for grain,
centering mainly around the Yangzi delta.*

Expanded cash-cropping and urbanization brought basic changes
to this structure. Wu Chengming (1984) estimates that by 1936 the
proportion of grain entering the "commodities" market had increased from about 10 percent in 1840 to just under 30 percent. The
rice market in the delta became highly integrated, centered in the
Shanghai metropolis and integrally tied to the world commodities
market.

INVOLUTIONARY GROWTH

Virtually no delta village was left untouched by the coming of imperialism. Our eight delta villages can be readily identified with the
broad patterns of change outlined above. Both Kaixiangong in Wujiang county, a traditional sericulture village, dating back to the
Ming and earlier, and Xiaodingxiang in Wuxi, which took to mulberry cultivation and silkworm raising only after the Taiping wars,
were now subject to the impact of market swings in the international

---

*By Wu's estimate, 25,000,000+ of the 30,000,000 shi of grain involved in long-
distance trade were destined for the delta (pp. 272–77).

silk trade. Yaojing in Taicang and Dingjiacun in Jiading, both traditional cotton-growing villages on the high-lying periphery of the
basin, and Touzongmiao in Nantong, which had taken to the new
handicraft textile industry that swept the county with the advent
of machine-spun yarn, were profoundly affected by the separation
of yarn spinning from cotton cultivation and cloth weaving. Yanjiashang in Changhsu, Sunjiaxiang in Wuxian, and Huayangqiao in
Songjiang, finally, remained rice-growing villages, but at a much
higher degree of commercialization than before.

Crop Production

As we have seen, accelerated commercialization was not necessarily accompanied by rural development in the sense of expanded
returns or productivity per workday. To take cotton cultivation first,
with cotton acreage's threefold increase on the North China plain in
the twentieth century under the combined stimuli of the world
commodities market and a rapidly developing indigenous textile industry, and with cotton bringing higher gross returns than grain, it is
easy to infer that the region must have experienced genuine rural development. But we saw that measuring development in terms of unit
area totally distorts the picture.

Cotton cultivation inarguably brought increased returns per unit
land on the North China plain, as shown in Table 7.1. In Michang
village, gross income from one mu of cotton in 1937 was 251 percent
that from sorghum, and 140 percent that from maize. Even with the
much higher expense for fertilizer, cotton still brought much higher
net returns (excluding the value of labor) than any of the other crops:
203 percent as much as sorghum, and 128 percent as much as maize.
Where land was scarce, these possibilities made cotton irresistible.*

But when we look at returns per workday, it becomes clear that
cotton did no better than maize. In Michang in 1937, one workday
on a cotton field brought a net income after production expenses of
1.04 yuan, compared with 1.18 for maize. The turn from maize in

* Although cotton had a relatively long growing season that, in North China, effectively precluded a second winter crop such as wheat on the same field, its cultivation
usually did not rule out growing winter wheat on much the same scale as before. This
is because the time constraints in the fall (the harvesting of the spring crops and the
planting of winter wheat had to be done within the space of six weeks) set limits on
the degree of double-cropping that could be done. Before the collectivization of labor
in the 1950s and the coming of tractor plowing in the 1960s, only a relatively small
proportion of the cultivated area on the plain could be placed under winter wheat: 7.7
percent in northeastern Hebei, 21.5 percent in central Hebei, and 36.1 percent in
southern Hebei in 1949 (Zhongyang renmin zhengfu 1950: 53).

TABLE 7.1
Income Per Unit Area and Per Unit Labor for Cotton, Sorghum, Maize,
and Wheat/Barley in Michang Village, 1937

Crop	Gross income (yuan per mu)	Fertilizer cost[a] (yuan per mu)	Workdays (per mu)	Net income (yuan) Per mu[b]	Net income (yuan) Per workday
Cotton	18.34	4.60	13.20	13.74	1.04
Sorghum	7.32	0.54	7.20	6.78	0.94
Maize	13.12	2.41	9.10	10.71	1.18
Wheat/barley[c]	5.37	?	7.80	?	0.69

SOURCES: MT, Hokushi Jimukyoku chōsabu 1938–41, 1: tables 3, 33, 34, 37, 42, 46.
NOTE: All income figures, except wheat, include the imputed value of subsidiary produce such as straw and chaff.
[a]Includes the imputed value of home-supplied fertilizer.
[b]Does not take account of other expenses (e.g., seed, farm implements), which were relatively minor. The cost of fertilizer was the main difference among the crops.
[c]From 1936 data (MT, Kitō 1937a), adjusted for 1937 price increases, and computed at the relative proportions of acreage under the two crops in 1936.

favor of cotton, therefore, provided increased employment per unit land but not increased income per workday. Had there been a shortage of labor and not of land, there would not have been any incentive to take up cotton cultivation. What pushed the expansion of cotton cultivation was the scarcity of land and the abundance of labor. Those conditions compelled the plain peasants to intensify cultivation at the cost of diminished marginal returns per workday. As in the Ming and Qing, this was commercialization accompanied by involution rather than genuine development.

If farm sizes had remained the same, even if marginal returns to labor shrank, peasant household incomes would have expanded by increments equivalent to the returns from the added employment. But farm sizes generally shrank over the long term under mounting population pressure: from something over fifteen mu per capita in Hebei–northwest Shandong in the early Ming to three mu in the twentieth century (Huang 1985: 116). What actually happened to peasant household incomes was thus the result not just of one change or the other, but of the combined working of two tendencies. Ultimately, it was the relative balance between expansion of income per unit area as a result of commercialization and contraction in farm size as a result of population pressure that determined the impact on household incomes. Where the former outbalanced the latter, the absolute levels of peasant incomes increased; the reverse meant declining incomes despite commercialization. Most often, the two trends operated in a complex relationship, depending on the particular stratum of the peasantry and the relative movements of prices.

Involutionary growth is evident also in the dramatic spread of tobacco cultivation in Shandong in the twentieth century. In Weixian, Shandong, one mu of "American seed tobacco" brought (at 1934 prices) 2.7 times the gross income of sorghum and 3.1 times that of wheat. But the production costs for tobacco, not counting labor, were considerably higher: 5.1 times those of sorghum and 2.6 times those of wheat. Labor requirements were also very much higher: 70 days per mu for tobacco, against fourteen for sorghum and six for wheat. So again we find that tobacco brought a higher net income (not counting labor expenses) per unit land than foodgrains, but a lower return per workday: 0.44 yuan a day for tobacco, at 1934 prices, compared with 0.95 for sorghum, and 1.40 yuan for wheat. The same pattern held at two other major tobacco areas, Fengyang in Anhui and Xiangcheng in Henan (Chen Han-seng 1939: 9, 56, 62, 73).

Hon-ming Yip (1988) has looked at this subject in more detail, with the aid of two Japanese surveys of four tobacco-growing villages and a survey of 24 tobacco-farming households by the Agricultural Department of the Presbyterian Mission (undertaken with the advice of John Lossing Buck). The mission study painstakingly recorded labor expenditures for each of the multiple stages of tobacco cultivation. The data show that tobacco cultivation drew heavily on auxiliary family labor for harvesting and the sorting, bunching, and flue-curing of the leaves (the last step alone required five days and four nights). The two Japanese surveys likewise detailed the income and expenses involved in tobacco cultivation. Yip's study leaves no doubt that, in terms of returns per workday, tobacco cultivation brought in far less than the prevailing wages for hired agricultural labor, even as it expanded the total income per unit land.

The same patterns of involutionary growth marked sericulture even in the most developed areas of the countryside of the Yangzi delta. In Xiaodingxiang outside Wuxi, the heart of the new sericulture area, sericultural work entailed sharply diminished marginal returns per workday. Rice followed by winter wheat required 34 days of labor per mu, compared with 80 days for growing mulberries and feeding two broods of silkworms. The gross income from the sale of the cocoons was higher than from the rice plus wheat, of course, as Lynda Bell (1985: 122–24) has shown: 15.96 yuan per mu, compared with 12.75 yuan per mu in 1939. And so was the net income after production costs, not counting labor: 11.96 yuan compared with

9.25 yuan. But in terms of net income per workday, cocoons brought less than rice plus wheat: 0.15 yuan versus 0.27 yuan.* This reflected in part the fuller employment of subsidiary labor of low opportunity cost in the peasant household—what I have called the familization of peasant production. If farm sizes remained unchanged, we should see expanded income to the household as a whole but at diminished returns per workday. The women and children were the ones who absorbed the reduced rewards to labor.

Rural Industry

The same pattern of involution obtained in the new peasant household handicraft industries. Expansion in sericulture did not lead to much in the way of new peasant industry. Indeed, peasant families now generally went only as far as the cocoon stage in production, abandoning the craft of reeling because the export market demanded silk of uniform standard. Merchants bought up the cocoons, dried them, and sold them to the new filatures in the cities (Bell 1985). Mechanized weaving, which was still more capital-intensive, was the preserve mainly of factories in the United States, as has been seen. Such new rural industries as arose did so chiefly in connection with cotton.

The best example is Nantong county, where as Kathy Walker (1986) shows, the heart of the local industrial development began in 1899, with the founding of the Number One Dasheng Mill by a gentry-official, Zhang Jian. His operations were based on the extraordinary combination of cotton produced by cheap labor on small peasant farms, machine spinning in the new mills, and handicraft weaving done, once more, by cheap labor in peasant households.

What the new handweaving industry meant for peasant households can be seen through the example of Touzongmiao village adja-

---

*Bell's figures are 0.23 yuan net income per workday for sericulture and 0.27 for rice + wheat. I believe her figure for sericulture is too high, and results from an underestimate of the work required: a total of 52 days, with 13 days for mulberries, 22 days for the spring brood of silkworms, and 17 days for the fall brood (1985: 122–24; cf. Bell 1988). The figure for mulberry growing is based on the Mantetsu surveys, in which only the time spent on weeding and fertilizing was counted, with no provision for the tasks of pruning branches and scissoring off the mulberry leaves (MT, Shanghai 1941a: 42–43). Based on the Kaixiangong villagers' estimate of ten workday equivalents (*gong*) for these tasks for each of the spring and fall crops (H-III-36), I add here seventeen days to Bell's thirteen for mulberry growing, which is still lower than Buck's 32.7 (Buck 1937b: 302). As for silkworm raising, Bell counts only the feeding period, whereras labor is required during the entire growing cycle, 29 days for the spring brood and 21 for the fall brood (MT, Shanghai 1941a: 55, 61). The total labor requirement for growing mulberries and feeding two broods of silkworms is therefore 80 days. Bell's conclusion, however, is the same as mine in substance.

cent to the county seat. Most of the work was done in the off-season, from November to April, and was performed by both men and women, young and old. There is no question that weaving opened the door for a fuller employment of farm labor. But in employing chiefly slack-season and auxiliary household labor of very low opportunity cost, weaving tended to remain a low-paying activity. In Touzongmiao's case, weavers earned less than agricultural laborers. The average adult, the villagers said, could weave one *fan* of cloth in an eight-hour day.* In 1939, the yarn for this would have cost the household 1.71 yuan, and the cloth would sell for 2.13 yuan; the net return to labor was thus 0.42 yuan, not counting board (MT, Shanghai 1941b: table 11; see also pp. 121–23). Day-labor wages that year averaged 0.38 yuan for heavy work, and 0.26 yuan per day for lighter work (ibid., table 9), and the workers got their board as well, which generally equaled or exceeded the amount of the cash wage. This gap reflected in part the difference between the earning power of adult male labor in its prime and that of female labor.

Given the vast supply of labor of low opportunity cost on the farms, change tended to move in the direction of increased labor input rather than capitalization to improve labor productivity. In Touzongmiao, as the Japanese field investigators reported, the weavers still used the old-fashioned wooden foot-pedaled loom, which they could buy for just 7–20 yuan. There was not a single improved iron-geared loom (*tielunji*) in the village, even though that loom had become widely available by the 1920s. Nationwide, according to Xu Xinwu (n.d.), cloth produced by the iron-geared looms accounted for a mere 10 percent of all handwoven cloth in 1936.† Even though the iron-

---

*A *fan* is a local measure equaling 0.8 (old) chi (6 percent longer than the standard chi, which equals 13.13 inches) × 24 chi, and weighing 1.18 standard catties (*shijin*).

†Most of this output was in the counties of Weixian (Shandong), Gaoyang and Baodi (Hebei), and Jiangyin (Jiangsu). The peasants of Weixian, for example, produced the so-called "improved native cloth" with these looms. Unlike the Nantong cloth, this wider *gailiang tubu* was oriented chiefly to the urban market. Some 70,000 iron-geared looms were purchased in the county in the 1920s, most of them by relatively well-to-do peasants, and some 90,000 peasant weavers were active in the industry. Here the capitalization and modernization of rural industry did occur. Yet even this development was predicated on the use of spare-time peasant labor of low opportunity cost. As Hon-ming Yip (1988) demonstrates, the combination of iron-geared looms and peasant household labor was so successful that it effectively snuffed out any competition from larger-scale workshops. Though productivity was substantially higher under the workshop organization—two workers could produce the equivalent of three farm weavers—the cost of the workers' board and of the workplace itself made it uneconomical. In the whole of Weixian county, there were only three small hand-weaving workshops in the 1930s; they accounted for less than 1 percent of the county's cloth output.

geared loom improved labor productivity by about 400 percent (ibid.), it was slow to break down the resistance to capitalization posed by the wide availability of cheap labor.

Under these conditions, rural industrialization in the delta followed chiefly the pattern of growth without development. True, there was an expansion in the total value of farm output; there was even an expansion in the output per laborer per year because of fuller employment. But it is a mistake to assume that the change meant increased income per workday. Quite the contrary: the invigorated handicraft cloth-weaving industry furnished additional employment only at reduced income per day. It was a process similar to the familization and involution that occurred in earlier centuries, especially in sericulture, in which low-paying work came to be absorbed by household auxiliary labor, especially of women. That economic involution, in turn, acted as a counterincentive to labor-saving capitalization.

INVOLUTION AND AGRICULTURAL MODERNIZATION

This is not to say that there was no modernization at all in crop production and rural industry in the Yangzi delta. The example of the first three decades of postrevolutionary rural China, during which income per farm person stagnated side by side with vigorous agricultural modernization (tractor plowing, electrified pumping, chemical fertilizers, scientific seed selection, and the like) and urban development, should alert us to the fact that neither is precluded by involutionary growth.

Wuxi stands as a good example. Industrial development combined with agricultural commercialization brought more agricultural modernization to this county than to any other in China. Boats using electric pumps went up and down the network of rivers and canals to bring mechanized irrigation to the fields. By 1949, 960 of these boats were irrigating about 50 percent of the county's total acreage (Jiangsu sheng Zhongguo xiandaishi xuehui 1983: 10). Once such technology became available, it was irresistible to the villages, for one person manning a 20-horsepower motor could irrigate fully 50 mu of rice fields in a day, as against only 1.0–1.5 a day by two men using barrels, and just 2–3 mu by two men using traditional foot-pedaled waterwheel pumps. The differential in labor productivity was greater even than that in cotton spinning, a ratio of 50–100:1 (MT, Shanghai 1941a: 78). The other technological advance in Wuxi came from the adoption, after the late 1920s, of improved strains of silkworms. Developed by the rapidly growing science of agronomy in Japan, these new strains promised higher yields and lower risks in cocoon production (ibid., p. 48). With these two developments came a higher degree of commercialization: of sericulture, because of market demand and increased output, and of rice, because of the expanded cultivation of mulberries (30 percent of Wuxi's cultivated acreage at its height in 1927; Zhang Youyi 1957, 3: 626). Both fed the further modernization of agriculture.

However, even in the case of vigorously modernizing Wuxi, as has been seen, crop production and handicrafts continued down involutionary paths. The great abundance of cheap female and child labor powerfully shaped the nature of agrarian change. The new sericulture still yielded smaller marginal returns per workday than rice. And the ability of the Wuxi peasant economy to absorb such low-return activity paved the way for the international division of labor noted earlier. So even for Wuxi, it will not do to project on the countryside the predictions of the classical model: of mutually reinforcing and spiraling urban and rural development with commercialization.

I do not want to contend that genuine development could not have taken place in due course. Had off-farm employment in Wuxi continued to the point where even auxiliary household labor became scarce and incomes per workday in peasant crop and handicraft production rose, and had the resulting surplus been available for capitalizing investments in rural production, transformative change in peasant livelihood could probably have come to the Wuxi countryside, as it was to do in the 1980s. But that point was far from being reached in the 1930s, despite the impressive modernization of agriculture that was taking place.

NEW PATTERNS OF EXTRACTION

New inputs like fertilizers, improved seeds, or mechanized irrigation generally came to the delta countryside through merchant intermediaries, along with high rates of interest for credit in their purchase or use. The process can be illustrated with a variety of examples.

In Songjiang, soybean-cake fertilizer was already so widely used in rice cultivation and so highly commercialized by the eighteenth century that its price fluctuated violently. The Wujiang county gazetteer of 1747 noted, for example, that though beancake fertilizer had once been quite cheap, costing about as much as rice straw, the price had recently risen to the point where the poor were having a hard time (*Wujiang xian zhi* 1747, 38: 4a–4b). In the Xianfeng period (1851–61), the Nanxun town gazetteer noted, the rich could afford to use mostly beancake, but the poor had to rely entirely on pig and sheep manure (*Nanxun zhen zhi*, vol. 21, cited by Zhu Zongzhou 1981: 576). The Songjiang prefectural gazetteer of 1883, finally, noted that the poor peasants could not afford to purchase beancake fertilizer in cash, but had to do so on credit (*Songjiang fu xuzhi* 1883, vol. 5, cited by Adachi 1978: 362).

The coming of steamships drove the prices up so high that the use of beancake in the delta declined for a time. Where before beancake from the Northeast could only be shipped as far as Shanghai, it could now be sent to Amoy and Swatow, where it was in much demand for the more lucrative sugar-cane agriculture. Meanwhile, the alternative of an overland supply was shut off when *lijin* duties were slapped on the overland transport of goods. As a result, Shanghai became just a way-station for beancake shipment from the Northeast down to Fujian and Guandong (Adachi 1978). It was only in the first decades of the twentieth century, with the accelerated settlement of the Northeast, the coming of mechanized bean-oil extraction, and increased coastal shipping, that beancake began to spread in the delta again. The closing-off of the Northeast provinces from China proper after 1931 drove the price up again (*Wuxian zhi* 1933, 52: 7b), but even so, beancake fertilizer continued to be widely used down to the outbreak of the Sino-Japanese War in 1937.*

Beancake appears to have been used in much the same way in the twentieth century as it was during the Qing: in the third application of fertilizer for rice, after green fertilizer, usually alfalfa, and pig excrement, usually mixed with straw ash (*Songjiangfu xu zhi* 1883, 5: 2b–3a; see also Min Zongdian 1984: 48). It was still used this way in Huayangqiao in the 1930s (MT, Shanghai 1940: 102–8; H-I-1, 3). What was new in the twentieth century was not the fact or the method of beancake fertilizer use, but the extent of that use.

---

*Though chemical fertilizer came to the Yangzi delta in the 1920s, it made only limited inroads. Relatively fast-acting and not well suited for rice, it could only be used as chase fertilizer and had to be applied twice (MT, Shanghai 1940: 106–7). Moreover, the peasants claimed it "burned" the soil, a complaint that one still hears today (H-I-1, 3). Those who could afford to therefore continued to use organic fertilizer. On the eve of the Pacific War, only 700 bags (140,000 catties) of chemical fertilizer was sold in Huayang town, compared with 35,000 beancakes of 45–50 catties each (MT, Shanghai 1940: 106–7). With the drying-up of the supply of beancake during the war, the use of chemical fertilizer doubled (to about 1,500 bags a year; MT, Shanghai 1940: 106), but this was seen as something that could not be helped, not as desired "modernization." Even now, under state sponsorship of the use of chemical fertilizer, older peasants retain their distinct preference for beancake, insisting that it is superior in result and better for the soil over the long term (H-I-1, 3).

The effects of beancake fertilizer on peasant livelihood must be seen in conjunction with the new patterns of extraction that came with this increased use. In Huayangqiao, the seven rice merchants in the town of Huayang dominated the fertilizer business. They sold the beancake, most of it imported from the Northeast, in one of two ways: for cash up front or on credit. Sale on credit was generally made against a lien on the rice crop, which the merchant would acquire at its market price, minus the price of the fertilizer and 20 percent interest per month for each of the months between June/July, when the beancake was applied, and November/December, when the rice harvest would be delivered to the merchants. The peasants thus effectively paid about 100 percent interest for the five months' advance. As the elderly peasants interviewed in 1983 put it, if a person paid cash for beancake, he got four cakes for one shi of rice; if he took it on credit, he got only two cakes (H-I-1, 3). In all, 70 percent of the households in Huayangqiao purchased their beancake on credit, giving the merchants in town an enormous share of the increased output generated by the use of the fertilizer (MT, Shanhai 1940: 106–7).

A similar situation prevailed in tobacco cultivation in North China. With American seed tobacco came the need for both beancake fertilizer and coal to flue-cure the tobacco leaves. In the localities studied by Chen Han-seng (1939), the arrangements for purchasing beancake fertilizer were similar to those in Huayang, though at a lower interest rate; peasants got the fertilizer in July against a lien on the November crop, which the merchant would acquire for its market price, minus the price of the fertilizer and 4 percent interest a month. The same kind of arrangement applied to coal: an advance in September against the cured leaves, to be repaid in January, at an interest rate of 6–8 percent a month. Tobacco cultivation might have brought higher gross incomes to the peasants of Shandong, but these were reduced by new forms of extraction at the hands of the merchants. Hon-ming Yip (1988) documents how Tian Junchuan, the British American Tobacco Company's top Chinese aide in Shandong, amassed a fortune by dealing in beancake and coal loans to peasants.

The turn to improved silkworm eggs in delta sericulture from the 1920s on carried the same implications. Sure, the improved strains were better. But they were also more highly commercialized. In the Wuxi villages, during the late 1920s and early 1930s, peasants bought the eggs from dealers in one of several ways: by advance order with a prepayment or deposit, by advance order without any money down, and at the last minute. Each method of payment meant a differ-

ent price for the eggs. Most of the households (45 or 58) paid from
1.81 yuan to 2.60 yuan per sheet. One household managed to pay
only 1.01–1.20 yuan, but six had to pay a steep 2.81–3.00 yuan. It
was only after 1934, with the establishment of the government-
regulated supply of eggs (under the Commission for the Improvement of Sericulture; Canye gaijin weiyuanhui) that the abuses of
merchant middlemen were checked. But, as the Japanese investigators noted, they reappeared with the outbreak of the war (MT,
Shanghai 1941a: 50–51).

The same pattern obtained in the new mechanized irrigation system in Wuxi, where the pumping boats were owned not by the peasants themselves, but by merchants from the outside. Peasants paid
for the service at the rate of 1.50 yuan per mu before 1937. The contrast between externally controlled capital and peasant poverty was
especially sharp in the case of Yangmuqiao hamlet. There not one
household owned any kind of a water pump, not even of the animal-
or foot-powered type. Consequently, those whose fields were not adjacent to the canal not only had to pay for the modern boats; they
also had to rent a foot-pedaled pump (to move the water to their
fields) from a neighboring villager at a rate of 2.00 yuan for one night
and day (enough to irrigate two or three mu with two men pedaling;
MT, Shanghai 1941a: 78–80).

This kind of agricultural modernization should not be confused
with the neoclassical economists' picture of entrepreneurial farmers
accumulating capital and making rational investment decisions to
maximize profit and modernize agriculture. The fact is that technological change in delta agriculture in the twentieth century was
seldom generated at the initiative and under the ownership of the
producers. Investments by well-to-do peasants to improve production represent only a very small part of the story. In the main, the
new technology came at the cost of new forms of extraction by merchants, often at usurious rates. Those rates, like the rates charged on
simple money loans, were sustained by poor peasants forced by survival pressures to borrow at a price that no profit-oriented enterprise
would pay. Like the agricultural commercialization before it, modernization in the countryside was driven not by peasant enterprise,
but by peasant survival.

THE ROLE OF MERCHANTS

Merchants served as the crucial links between this involuting peasant economy and the developing urban capitalism. They acted variously as the agents for the purchase of agricultural raw materials and

cheap labor by capitalist industry, as the distributors of the products
of capitalist industry, as the conduits of new inputs and technology
from capitalist industry, and, sometimes, as investors in capitalist
industry.

The simplest illustration of the first role is the cotton merchants
in Shandong. Japanese mills in Qingdao (nine of the ten mills there)
completely dominated the cotton-textile industry in the province.
They maintained their own purchasing firms in the large towns situ-
ated on major transport routes, but everywhere else, down to the periodic markets of the villages, they relied on Chinese merchants to
buy their supplies. From the Japanese mills' point of view, the at-
traction of Shandong was twofold: cotton was cheaper than the domestic product, and so was labor, with wages running about one-
third those back home. In this simplest of interlinkages between the
two economies, merchants served only as purchasing agents to supply Japanese capitalist industry (Yip 1986).

The situation was more complicated in the sericulture industry in
Wuxi, where merchants entered into the production process at the
point of cocoon drying, both to procure the raw material and to ensure more uniform quality. By 1933, Wuxi was the largest cocoon-
purchasing center in the country, with 373 merchant-owned cocoon
hangs. From there the raw material went to new Chinese filatures,
first in Shanghai and later in Wuxi itself (Bell 1985). Chinese capital
took on the silk-reeling part of the production process, which was
relatively labor-intensive and required access to cheap labor. The
most capital-intensive part of the production remained in the hands
of the weaving factories abroad, especially in the United States.

In their role as purchasing agents for capitalist industry, merchants served as middlemen, profiting from commissions based on
the difference between the buying and selling price. From this point
of view, they were "exploiters," and the involuted peasant economy,
as has been seen, permitted the extraction of rates tantamount to
usury. To the extent that the merchants were acquiring raw materials
destined finally for foreign industry, they were also "compradores."
Nevertheless, there can be no denying the importance of their commercializing and/or modernizing role—in stimulating the spread of
cotton and sericulture and in modernizing the cotton ginning and
cocoon-drying processes through their investments.

In the merchants' second major linkage function, as distributors
for the goods of capitalist industry, the product involved was above
all cotton yarn. This was the big new business of the twentieth century. In Weixian in Shandong, the 24 large merchant houses came to

dominate the local economy. The business was so lucrative that these firms came to overshadow local native and modern banks as credit institutions for the county's 257 retail cloth stores and 25 dyeing workshops. Since these merchants dealt almost exclusively in Japanese produced yarn, they were unmistakably "compradore" in their function (Yip 1988). But they also entered into the production process in new ways. The yarn merchants of Weixian were the first to institute the putting-out system, in which peasants contracted for a certain amount of yarn on the promise of delivering a predetermined amount of woven cloth. This proved to be more profitable than employing weavers, for it took advantage of the surplus peasant household labor (ibid.).

In Nantong, merchants played a still larger role and contributed importantly to local development. They bought and distributed the yarn produced by the Dasheng mills, repurchased the peasant-woven cloth, and took it to the Northeast to sell. They also provided a substantial part of the capital for the Dasheng mills. In so doing, they provided the crucial linkages for a system of production that competed successfully against the Japanese textile industry, not only in the local market but also in the Northeast.

But, as Kathy Walker points out (1986), the capital of these merchant houses inevitably carried the imprint of merchant capital, which profited mainly from the circulation of capital in the exchange of goods, not from its investment in the production of goods. The local merchants' investment in Dasheng was based on the terms and expectations of circulating and usurious capital. They required that an 8 percent guaranteed dividend (*guanli*) be paid off the top, regardless of the rate of profit. When profits were high, as they were in the first two decades after 1900, the merchant creditors invariably opted for distribution to shareholders. So long as Dasheng was able to generate profits high enough to sustain these requirements, the firm thrived.

In the 1920s, however, Dasheng came face to face with difficulties that finally exposed its weaknesses. Cotton prices rose in response to heightened demand as the international textile industry recovered from the First World War, while the price of yarn sank under the resulting stiffer competition. Dasheng thus found itself pinched by declining profit margins. It could not overcome the supply problem. Earlier the company had derived much strength from a direct purchasing system, which grew naturally out of its direct control over land brought into cultivation by a massive reclamation program. But that purchasing system had collapsed when the merchant-

shareholders rammed through a policy that saw the company's reclaimed land sold as soon as it came into cultivation. In the end, the
company retained only 7 percent of the land it reclaimed. By the
1910s, the company could no longer supply its own needs and had to
purchase its cotton from merchant firms. A severely damaged cotton crop as a result of a major typhoon in 1920–21 put the finishing
touches on the failing company. In 1925, the native banks decided to
pull their capital out of the company. The company was then turned
over to a consortium of modern banks in Shanghai, which brought
in a new-style entrepreneur, Li Shengbo, to reorganize and consoli-
date the combine. Thus ended the marriage of convenience between
the gentry-industrialist Zhang Jian (who died not long after, in 1927)
and the merchant capital of Nantong (H-III-43, 45).

It would be pointless to deny the modernizing role that merchants
and merchant capital played in Nantong. But the very success of
Zhang Jian's Dasheng enterprise was predicated on involutionary,
low-cost peasant production, of cotton and of handwoven cloth,
with the unsurprising result that both cotton cultivation and cotton
weaving continued along traditional lines. The Dasheng combine
tried briefly to operate large-scale capitalist farms, but quickly gave
up in favor of the more economical tenant family farm. And there
was little push from it for the iron-geared looms that became widely
available from the 1920s on, since production by the old looms was
sufficiently economical to compete with foreign enterprises.

In all these different ways in which the peasant economy came to
be linked up with capitalist industry, the merchants played a dual
role. They aided in market development and the circulation of goods,
and also served sometimes as suppliers of new technology and even
of industrial capital. But we need to keep in sight also their extractive
role, as middlemen for goods as well as for capital and technology.

Had merchants gone on from their role as circulators of goods to
become industrialists, as envisaged in the classical model of Smith
and Marx (and as occurred to some extent in Nantong), history
would surely have emphasized their development-generating side
more than their extractive-involuting side. That they did not, that
their role remained largely restricted to that of intermediaries, has
brought on them perhaps undeservedly harsh judgment. From the
perspective of the involuting peasant economy, merchants appear
much more as extractors than as developers. This view was to form
the basis for the Revolution's deep-seated hostilities toward commerce—hostilities in which anti-imperialist sentiments were added
to Confucian as well as Marxist biases against merchants.

RURAL LIVING STANDARDS

What happened to the peasants' living standards in face of all the vigorous urban development and commercialization? By the standard estimates of rural incomes in the first decades of the twentieth century, at least, peasant incomes barely kept pace with population growth. Perkins (1969) suggests an annual growth rate of 1.0 percent in agricultural output between 1916 and 1933, and Yeh and Liu (1965) a lower 0.8 percent, against a 0.9 percent rate of population growth. But Rawski (1989) strongly disagrees with these past estimates. He thinks that a more appropriate figure for the annual increase in farm output during these decades is 1.5 percent, so that there would have been a net improvement in per capita output of 0.5 percent a year (pp. 280–85). In his view, such a gain would constitute proof of the development-generating capacities of a market economy and of imperialism. Rawski acknowledges that he has no direct evidence to support his argument. He resorts instead to a set of indirect data, of which the most provocative is the suggestion that cloth consumption per capita increased some 50 percent during these years (pp. 91, 289–91). If that happened, he argues, peasant standards of living must have improved.

I believe Rawski is correct in asserting that past scholars erred in their assumption that per capita cloth consumption remained constant. If we proceed instead from the output data on cotton and cotton textiles, taking into account exports and imports, it becomes obvious that domestic consumption expanded significantly. This is precisely the procedure that Xu Xinwu and his associates have followed for their quantitative estimates. In their judgment, based on decades of research and extensive on-site investigations, per capita cloth consumption went up about a third in the century between 1840 and 1936 (Table 7.2).

This increase can be attributed in the main to the fact that machine-woven cloth was less durable than the handwoven product. As Xu points out, two handwoven cloth outfits generally lasted a peasant three years, while two machine-woven coarse cloth outfits lasted only two. Moreover, handwoven cloth could be mended again and again (and its scraps used in the end for padding in cloth shoes), while machine cloth disintegrated quickly.* At a ratio of 2:3, the differential in durability alone would account for an increased total

*These facts are documented at length in Xu's monumental study *Jiangnan tubu shi* (History of Native Cloth in the Jiangnan; n.d.) I am grateful to Professor Xu for allowing me to see this section of the manuscript.

TABLE 7.2
Per Capita Cloth Consumption in China, 1840–1936

Category	1840	1860	1894	1913	1920	1936
Population (millions)	400	405	415	430	440	450
Annual per capita consumption (bolts)	1.50	1.53	1.65	1.80	1.90	2.00
Urban and nonfarm	1.80	1.84	1.98	2.16	2.28	2.40
Rural weaving households	1.65	1.68	1.82	1.98	2.09	2.20
Rural non-weaving households	1.35	1.37	1.47	1.62	1.70	1.84

SOURCE: Xu Xinwu, n.d.
NOTE: 1 bolt = 3.6337 sq. yds.

consumption of 28.4 percent (one-half of 56.84 percent, Xu's estimate of the proportion of machine-woven cloth in 1936).

Urbanization would account for another increment, since urbanites generally consumed more cloth than peasants: a difference of 123:100, by Xu's figures. And new cotton cultivators would account for another since, to judge by our field-survey data, the populations of cotton-growing villages consumed more cloth than those of non-cotton-growing villages. As we saw in Table 6.6, cotton-growing and cloth-weaving Michang in North China consumed nearly four times as much cotton as non-cotton-growing-weaving Qianlianggezhuang (7.72 square yards per capita vs. 1.99). The third North China village, Dabeiguan, grew some cotton (11 percent of the cropped area) and did some weaving. Its per capita consumption was about one-half Michang's. In the Yangzi delta, cotton-growing and cloth-weaving Touzongmiao and Huayangqiao (5.20 and 5.43 square yards per capita, respectively) consumed about three and a half times as much as Xiaodingxiang. These village-level data also cast some doubt on the rather high per capita figure of 9.0 square yards estimated by Rawski; I prefer Xu's lower estimates 5.45 square yards in 1840 and 7.27 in 1936.

For the rest, I find Rawski's evidence utterly unconvincing. He cites Buck's survey on changes in living standards within memory to buttress his suggestion that things were improving. But, as Rawski himself acknowledges (p. 288), the 442 farms in the sample were rich peasant farms, averaging 45 mu, and the survey was therefore strongly biased toward the upwardly mobile. Next, Rawski cites Buck's survey of employers on farmworker wages. That survey relied on impressionistic recall for wages going back thirty years and did not attempt to take into account price changes. Rawski converts those data to "real" wages by applying a price index derived from unusual Wujin county to all 100 counties—a very questionable procedure. He emerges in any case with highly ambiguous findings: of 100 counties, fully 40 showed declining or unchanged "real" wages (pp. 296–97). But Rawski manages to find national improvement by averaging out the figures. What we need is better quantitative evidence and closer qualitative analyses of differential changes. Finally, Rawski seeks support for his hypothesis in the wage data for the Shenxin textile mill in Shanghai and for the Kailuan coal mine in Hebei and the Zhongxing mine in Shandong (Rawski, 1989, tables 6.6, 6.8). Readers who take the time to examine the original data will find them both fragmentary (no data at all for daily wages in the 1920s on the Shanghai mill, and for only ten of the 50 years tabulated on the mines) and ambiguous (ups and downs in real wages that tell more about fluctuating grain prices than any long-term rise). If we are to accept Rawski's argument, we must not only disregard the crudeness and ambiguity of the data, but also accept an entire package of deductive arguments: the three industrial enterprises, he maintains, would have paid higher wages to their workers only if rising rural living standards had forced them to do so. The logic is that, given a perfectly competitive factor market for labor, wage data on these few enterprises are adequate to argue for national trends of improvement in rural living standards. But we know in fact that workers in given factories and industries tended to come from the same locations, generally recruited through the same kinship, community, or brokering ties. Upward or downward wage movements therefore reflect local supply and demand more than the national market. They might, of course, also have reflected changing labor-management relations, or a host of other incidental factors. To argue for national trends on the basis of such evidence seems to me a highly questionable procedure.

More persuasive to me is David Faure's (1989, 1985) conclusion that the living standards of delta peasants producing export commodities rose with the price rises in those commodities through the 1920s. In fact, their per capita farm income might well have increased until the sharp downward turn in prices in the 1930s. But even so, we must take into account the different social effects of commercialization: some peasants made good while others suffered from the increased risks associated with commercialized cropping.

For the 30 percent of the Huayangqiao households that could afford to purchase beancake fertilizer in cash, the increased commercialization of rice definitely offered new opportunities for enrichment; for the other 70 percent, there were few possibilities for profit, not least because of the usurious credit terms that pushed up their production costs. For both, the use of beancake raised the stakes considerably— a peasant who had invested in fertilizer stood to lose much more from a failed crop than before (MT, Shanhai 1940: 107).

We need also to consider the differential social effects of seasonal price changes, because only peasants with a surplus were really in a position to take advantage of them: only six of 63 households in Huayangqiao were in that happy position. Above all, we must consider the devastating impact of the world depression on peasants now producing for an international market.

Let us look briefly at the issue from the standpoint of the peasants. The sericulturalist's life was uncertain enough even without the vagaries of the world market. A grower could never tell when his silkworms might catch some disease and leave him with a greatly reduced brood. And he always had to balance delicate considerations of costs and benefits. Prices of mulberry leaves generally rose rapidly during the feeding season in April and May, as more and more leaves were needed for fattening the silkworms. In 1939 in Wuxi, for example, prices in late May were 275 percent higher than in early April (MT, Shanhai 1941a: 57–58). There was thus strong incentive to buy early. On the other hand, early purchases incurred great risks: a grower could easily find himself stuck with lots of high-priced leaves and no silkworms to feed them to. For this reason, most peasants tried to coordinate silkworm raising with mulberry growing, buying only as many sheets as they could feed on their own. This was true of 34 of the 58 grower households in Xiaodingxiang; the other 24 were dependent on the volatile mulberry market and did the best they could to balance costs and risks (ibid.).

With the internationalization of Chinese silk, these uncertainties were severely aggravated. In the localized or even national market of old, a certain mechanism had always worked to mitigate the effects of market swings. A bumper crop of silkworms, for example, would bring down the price of cocoons and silk and push up the price of mulberry leaves, and vice versa. The fortunes of the sericulture peasant would not swing too widely. But when silk prices fluctuated with international demand totally unconnected to local supply conditions, a poor crop could be aggravated by low prices, multiplying the devastating consequences on the grower. Or the reverse: a bumper crop joined with favorable prices to bring prosperity.

The negative effects of market dependency have been well described in Mao Dun's novella *Spring Silkworms* (1956). Its central figures are the four members of Old Tung Pao's household, who are dependent on silkworm raising for their subsistence. Mao Dun details the vicissitudes of sericulture: how the daughter-in-law warms the eggs against her breasts to incubate them, how the night-and-day work of feeding is accompanied by great agonizing and superstition about the diseases that might afflict the brood, and how, when at long last, the family reaps a bumper crop, it is only to find that the local filatures, for totally unknown and incomprehensible reasons, are not purchasing cocoons that season. The family had had to go into debt to buy mulberries to feed the worms in the final stages. With the market depressed, it finds itself unable even to pay off its debt, much less obtain a profit for its labors.

To be sure, the higher prices resulting from the international demand for silk brought a measure of increased prosperity to growers before the crash. But those improvements must be seen in conjunction with the bust that followed. Cocoon prices fell 50–70 percent between 1931 and 1932 (Yan Zhongping et al. 1955: 338; Zhang Youyi 1957, 3: 623). The result was a drastic drop in the acreage devoted to mulberries—from 251,000 mu in 1930 to 84,000 mu in 1932 in Wuxi county, from 124,000 mu to 54,000 mu in Jiangyin county—with devastating consequences for peasant households that had come to rely on sericulture for their livelihood (Zhang Youyi 1957, 3: 626; Huang 1985: 123). That was the downside of the world market for China's peasant economy.

Available price data suggest that cotton did not suffer anything like the same drastic decline as silk (Yan Zhongping et al. 1955: 337; Shanghai shehui kexueyuan jingji yanjiu suo, 1958: 229; Xu Daofu 1983: 203–10). The scattered anecdotal references to hardship among cotton cultivators in the early 1930s because of a drop in prices (Zhang Youyi 1957, 3: 631–34) may reflect the expectations of the reporters more than actual conditions. A clear notion of how Chinese cotton growers were affected by the world depression will have to await future studies and new materials. Here we might just speculate that a much larger and more stable domestic market probably cushioned them from the kinds of shocks that hit the sericulturalists. Cotton cloth, after all, was a necessity for virtually every Chinese peasant.

Finally, lest the conclusion be drawn that price swings in the world commodities market affected only certain pockets of export agriculture, let us look at what happened to the rice markets of the Yangzi delta. As Cheng Hong (1988) shows, rice prices in Shanghai city rose fairly steadily through the 1920s (except for a dip in 1927–28, when the Guomindang government secured control over the delta, opening rice-supply routes from Jiangxi and Hunan). They reached a peak of 20 yuan per shi in June 1930, only to drop precipitously, bottoming out in 1933 at eight yuan.

There is a simple explanation for the sharp decline in 1930–33: massive amounts of cheap rice imported from Saigon and Rangoon by British and American merchants. At the height of this process, in 1930, 5,500,000 shi were imported into Shanghai, accounting for fully 86 percent of all the rice consumed in the city. Low-priced foreign imports continued to flow in through 1934, but good harvests enabled domestic producers to keep the proportion of imports in check. The proportion declined to about 12 percent in 1931, and though it jumped back up to more than 40 percent in 1932, it fell to about 12 percent again in 1933. Together, low-priced imports and abundant domestic supplies drove prices down to their nadir in 1933.

The effects were not restricted to metropolitan Shanghai by any means. Prices from the points of origination and outlying market towns clearly moved in synch with the Shanghai market. They were lowest in a place like the town (zhen) of Zhujiajiao, a point of origination for the city's rice, somewhat higher at intermediate points like the Songjiang county seat, and highest at the terminal point of Shanghai.

Even with good harvests, a 50 percent drop in price could not but have caused severe hardship for the rice growers of the Shanghai area. In terms of the commodities peasants purchased (in the proportions recorded by the Mantetsu field researchers in Huayangqiao, Songjiang), rice lost 51 percent of its purchasing power between 1926 and 1933 (and even more if one measures from the peak prices of June 1930, when its purchasing power was 8 percent higher than in 1926). Contemporary investigations suggest that the costs of cultivation actually exceeded the returns from rice during these difficult years.

The effects of the depression aside, the issue that Rawski is raising with such fury against past scholarship seems to me to be of relatively little significance. Even if we were to grant that peasant incomes in some areas grew 0.5 percent a year from the late 1910s until the depression, growth on that scale would only underscore the point I have been making. Such advances as occurred in the Chinese countryside in these years were seldom of the developmental variety, with marked improvements in labor productivity or incomes per workday (on the order of 3–4 percent a year over sustained periods, as occurred in West Europe and America, for example). Most often, they were of the involuting variety, in which growth in the value of output came only at the cost of lower marginal returns per workday.

RURAL INVOLUTION AND URBAN DEVELOPMENT

Whether imperialism caused development or underdevelopment in China is not an either/or matter, as it turns out. In fact, it forged a new economic system in which urban development and rural involution came to be interlocked, each an interdependent side of a single phenomenon. Capital-rich urban industries depended on labor-abundant peasant households for cheaply produced raw materials like cotton and cocoons, and for the cheap processing of industrial goods like cotton yarn. In the process, while urban industry flourished and the structures of urban-rural trade were transformed, peasant production involuted, its low-priced labor forming part of the very basis for urban development.

This was the system that made possible the concurrence of urban industrial development with rural poverty. Development undeniably did occur in places like Wuxi city and Nantong, not to speak of Shanghai. But, contrary to the classical vision of Smith and Marx, this urban development was not part of a bottom-up development involving an agricultural revolution and rural industrialization side by side with the rise of urban factories. The story was not one of mutually reinforcing urban-rural development.

One result was a widening of the long-standing and already substantial gap between the levels of urban and rural levels of development. While portions of Shanghai city, and even of Wuxi and Nantong, took on all the appearances of developed modern cities, their surrounding countrysides saw the persistence of subsistence farming (with consequences for urban history that have yet to be explored). The gulf separating town and countryside was to widen still further after 1949, when forced-draft industrialization accelerated the development of urban China, while involutionary growth and state extraction ensured the persistence of poverty in rural China.

This concurrence and interlocking of urban development with rural involution is easily overlooked because of our almost intuitive association of commercialization with capitalization, and urban development with rural development. In analyzing twentieth-century China under imperialism, as in analyzing late imperial China, we need to break apart the presumed ironclad bond between the two processes.

CHAPTER 8

Two Kinds of
Village Communities

Irrigated agriculture, high tenancy, and extensive commercialization fashioned a very different kind of rural community in the Yangzi delta than in North China. This chapter takes an in-depth look at two richly documented villages, Huayangqiao and Shajing, to examine up close how those shaping factors influenced community social structure, political organization, and change.

Scholars have differed on the makeup of the basic social fabric of a Chinese village community. Chinese historians usually emphasize the role of kinship, equating the "natural village" (zirancun) in effect with the "descent group."* In my own recent study (Huang 1985: 233–40), I emphasized instead the importance of supra-kinship territorial bonds. This chapter will suggest that those differences in emphasis are mainly attributable to regional variations resulting from ecological differences. The Yangzi delta is the usual frame of reference of Chinese historians, whereas my concern was the North China plain.

Scholars have also differed over the state's role in community formation. At one pole is the picture of communities subject entirely to the will and control of the imperial state and the gentry elite (Wittfogel 1957; Hsiao 1960). At the other pole is the image of the "moral community" forged by "reciprocity" that was largely beyond the reach of the state until modern times (Scott 1976). This chapter will suggest that village communities were shaped powerfully by their interaction with the state: the differing land tenure patterns of the delta and North China produced very different relations with state power and, as a result, very different community organizations to cope with that power.

Village communities were also shaped by market relations. In the

---

*I follow the lead of Freedman 1966 and Ebrey and Watson 1986 in reserving the word "lineage" for those kin groups that held substantial corporate property.

classical view of Smith and Marx, commercialization would lead to the disintegration of peasant communities; peasants would give way to capitalists and proletarians, and insular-solidary precommercial villages to commercialized-atomized neighborhoods. By this classical logic, we would expect the relatively more commercialized Yangzi delta villages to be more fluid than those of the North China plain. The fact is, they had far greater stability and continuity. The hows and whys of that counterintuitive fact are a major concern of this chapter.

RESIDENTIAL PATTERNS

Shajing (Shunyi county, Hebei province) and Huayangqiao (Song-jiang county, Shanghai municipality), on which we have detailed empirical data from both wartime Japanese field research and my own oral-history research, are good illustrations of more general regional differences between North China and the Yangzi delta.* Though similar in size (63 households in Huayangqiao and 69 in Shajing), they differed sharply in residential patterns. Shajing was a nucleated settlement, with all its households congregated in the center of the village (KC, 1: appended map). The residences of Huayang-qiao, by contrast, were clustered into four "villages," or *da* in local parlance: Xue Family Village (Xuejiada), He Family Village (Hejiada), Xubushanqiao (The Bridge at Xubushan Village), and Xilihangbang (The Western Lihang River Village). (See Map 6.)

We do not have far to look for one of the reasons for this difference. Surrounded by waterways as most villages in the rice and rice-silk zones of the Yangzi delta were, the Huayangqiao houses were concentrated along the rivers or along the canals leading from them, for immediate access to water. This consideration alone imposed limits on the size of delta communities. North China villages were not bound by this particular ecological consideration. There was little irrigation, and wells supplied the water for daily household needs. In Shajing, as elsewhere, these were located strategically throughout the residential area.

---

*This is not of course to maintain that all delta and North China plain villages matched these two. Within the definition of the delta used in this book, there were many dry-farmed areas, especially in the high-lying periphery. In fact, the cotton-cropping villages in the delta were much akin to their Northern counterparts. Nevertheless, the ecological, commercial, and landownership patterns set out below were the predominant ones in the two regions. My concern here is the logical connection between those patterns and community structures.

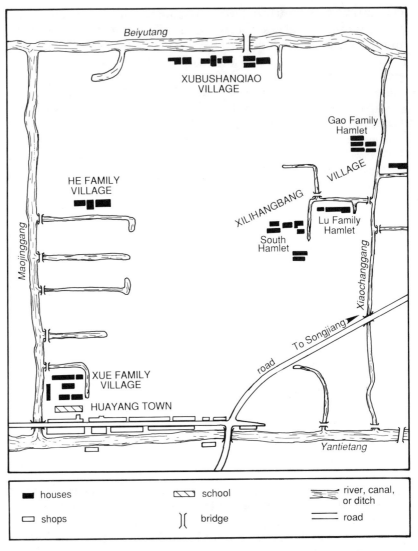

Map 6. Huayangqiao villages, Songjiang county, 1940. Source: MT, Shanghai 1940.

The size of descent groups and villages, of course, varied with the age of the community. The Huayangqiao villagers can only trace their origins back to the post-Taiping period, when the present settlements took shape. Ancestral gravesites were limited to four generations, and no household could reconstruct its genealogy beyond four generations (H-I-10–16).* The Zhangs of Shajing, by contrast, counted 60–70 graves for the Mantetsu investigators, and the Suns 40–50. The village had been formed in the early Ming by settlers from Hongdong county in Shanxi, though the families in the survey only dated back to the early Qing, when Hao Family village, as it was then known, was resettled (and renamed) after the devastations of the wars of dynastic transition (KC, 1: 67, 73; KC, 2: 59, 514).

A second major contrast between the two communities' residential patterns is the degree to which they reflected kinship ties. In Huayangqiao, the settlements were fundamentally agnatic (i.e. related by male descent). He Family Village was made up exclusively of Hes of the same patrilineal line—seven households in 1940. Xue Family Village had originally been made up entirely of Xues, five households in 1940. Two generations before the survey, a beggar surnamed Zhang had come to the village and became sufficiently accepted to settle down; there were four Zhang households in 1940. Despite the addition of this second, minor descent group, the village continued to be known as the Xue Family Village. The Zhangs were incorporated into that grouping by fictive kinship (H-I-14).

The central importance of these agnatic ties can be seen in the tendency for a village comprising more than one descent group to form separate hamlets (also called *da* locally) around each. Thus, Xilihangbang village was divided into Gao Family Hamlet (Gaojiada) in the north, Lu Family Hamlet (Lujiada) in the middle, and the South Hamlet (Nanda, also made up of Lus). The residents of these clusters evince a multi-layered sense of community identity, with the descent group at its core, identifying themselves only to outsiders by their village. In their own minds and those of their fellow villagers, they are from Hamlet X or Hamlet Y.

True, there was a certain sense of common identity among the Huayangqiao residents to the extent that the fictive kinship network encompassed all four villages. Almost everyone had a fictive kinship form of address for everyone else: *a-shu* (uncle), *a-jie* (elder sister), *a-ge* (elder brother), and so forth (H-I-20; H-II-26). But the community did not have a name, and by the 1930s and 1940s it had

---

*Three of the eight delta villages in this study were old ones that had not been severely affected by the Taipings and were substantially larger than Huayangqiao.

lost what little sense of shared identity it might once have derived from common religious organizations,* hence my difficulty in referring to it in any way other than the cumbersome "Huayangqiao cluster of villages," or, simply, Huayangqiao.

All this stood in sharp contrast to Shajing village. Common descent groups also tended to congregate there, to be sure. Most parents wanted their children to have houses contiguous to theirs, usually built as extensions of the original home. The Yangs, Dus, Lis, and Zhangs lived in such clusters. But those agnatic groupings did not represent separated communities. The villagers identified themselves unequivocally as members of Shajing village, never of a subentity such as the Li Family Hamlet or Yang Family Hamlet, as they did in Huayangqiao.

SOCIAL REFERENTS

The contrast between the supra-agnatic community and the descent-group community was particularly marked in the social domain. In Shajing, custom called for village-wide participation in weddings and funerals. "Doing it big" (daban) in weddings set the standard for what ought to be: enough tables at the banquet to invite all the households in the village for the "two eights," or eight bowls of meat dishes and eight plates of vegetables. Economic constraints forced some households to lower the standard to just "doing it modestly" (xiaoban), which meant inviting only members of the descent group and cutting the number of meat dishes to four. The poorest families were reduced to "not doing it" (buban): inviting only their immediate relations and serving only eight dishes, with no meat, just noodles (Huang 1985: 258).

The supra-agnatic community was also reinforced by a strong custom of village-wide cooperation. In Shajing, for example, the entire community customarily turned out to build a new house. On the first day, when the foundation was laid, 30 men helped; and 70 to 80 pitched in on the second, when the walls and the roof were built. The owner of the house, for his part, was expected to feed the helpers, the standard being "coarse at the two ends, fine in the middle" (liangtou cu, zhongjian xi), or coarse grains for the morning and evening meals, and fine grain at midday (Huang 1985: 220).

*Fei 1939: 99–106 details the structure and role of religious organizations in Kaixiangong village in the delta before the coming of the depression, and Duara 1988 examines the secularization of Shajing and other North China plain communities in the twentieth century.

In Huayangqiao, the descent group alone defined the peasants' social referents. In funerals for the male head of household and weddings for the male descendants, the social circle was sometimes extended to include the hamlet or village built around the descent group, but never to include all four villages, even though this meant only 63 households, fewer than in Shajing village. At Yang Tusheng's funeral in 1932, for example, no one from He Family Village, Xue Family Village, or Xilihangbang was invited. At Xue Baoren's wedding in 1931, similarly, all the residents of the Xue Family Village were invited, but no one else except affinal kin from outside. The two descent groups in Xilihangbang generally went their separate ways in social events: the Gaos customarily invited only the households of the Gao Family Hamlet to their ceremonies, and the same went for the Lus (H-I-17). Even within the Lu descent group, further fragmentation came with the hiving off of the South Hamlet. By the 1930s, most of the Lus no longer invited their kin from the other hamlet (H-II-11, 25).

There were of course gradations of closeness within the descent group. The sons (or the daughter where the husband had been adopted in) met for three years at their father's gravesite to honor him with a meal. This was the closest relationship, with the most stringent demands. After three years, the sons would simply make offerings annually, mainly of symbolic money in the form of tinfoil ingots (*xibo*). The obligation to make offerings extended up the patrilineal line to include four generations, up to one's great-great-grandfather. This was the second tier of closeness. Custom also called for offerings to paternal uncles, not at the gravesite, but just at their sons' houses, and usually not tinfoil ingots, but the less expensive paper ingots. This was the lowest tier of the annual *qingming* offerings. These three-tiered relations within the descent group made up the basic social referents of the Huayangqiao villagers (H-I-10, 12, 13).

VILLAGE POLITICAL ORGANIZATION

Shajing had a well-articulated internal political organization, centering around a group of nine village notables called *huishou*, or "association heads." Like other village leaders in North China (also called *shoushi* or *dongshi*), they tended to be the most prominent members of the community: all nine were substantial landowners of at least middle-peasant status (Huang 1985: 239). Such positions were often inherited and held for long periods of time. Sidney Gamble found that 37 of 48 leaders in five North China villages were

serving for the second generation, and 33 for the third; and in another sample, that the majority of the 141 leaders in twelve villages
had served for ten years or more (Gamble 1963: 323; see also Huang
1985: 238–42). In Shajing, as elsewhere in North China, the huishou
constituted a kind of informal council for village governance, their
purview extending from the oversight of internal affairs (e.g., heading up village groups like the temple association or funeral associations and settling disputes between groups) to systematic dealings
with the outside world (e.g., organizing crop-watching associations
and interacting with state agents; Huang 1985: 237–38).

In Huayangqiao, leadership was strictly ad hoc and informal, and
basically limited to the natural agnatic unit: when the need arose,
the most respected member(s) of a descent group might be called on
by others to settle disputes or extend a helping hand, but such authority was not formalized with a position or title. In Xue Family
Village, for example, Xue Bingrong enjoyed the greatest prestige, not
so much by force of seniority as by ability and character, and was
routinely called on to arbitrate disputes among his kinfolk. His prestige was such that it also extended to the Zhangs, the other descent
group in the village. The Zhang brothers, Huosheng and Shousheng,
apparently fought all the time. Since there was no senior male in
the family and the mother could not handle them, Xue Bingrong
was asked to mediate between them. After Bingrong died, his son
Xiansheng, also respected by fellow villagers as a just and responsible man, became the village leader. The fact that he was able to
keep accounts helped establish him in that position (H-I-13).

In the Middle Hamlet of Xilihangbang, the de facto leader in the
1930s and 1940s was a woman. Lu Danan (b. 1893) was by far the
eldest of the Lus of her generation, 26 years older than her brother
Guantong (b. 1919) and 19 years older than her cousin Gensheng
(b. 1912). (Danan had not married out; the family had adopted a husband for her, a quite common practice in Huayangqiao, but he had
died young, in 1929.) It was not seniority, however, but sheer force of
personality that had established Danan in her position. Even before
the deaths of her father and her aunt (Gensheng's mother), in 1939
and 1945, she was the one the younger Lus turned to. When Lu
Longshun's father died in 1938, he went immediately to his cousin
Danan for help. Why not to his uncle Yongzhou or to his elder
cousin Gensheng? Well, Longshun says, Yongzhou was not one to
help others, and Gensheng, only in his twenties, was too young.
Danan went to town to arrange for the purchase of the coffin and the
funeral clothes on credit. Longshun himself could not have obtained

the credit, but Danan was well known and respected in town. Later, it was she who got Longshun a job as a "little year-laborer" (*xiao changnian;* H-I-10).

Danan, the villagers say, was forthright, capable, and generous, a woman who always kept her word and "was a man's equal." Her brother Guantong, a calculating and rather unpopular man, clearly admires her deeply. When they divided up their father's land in 1939, he got all ten mu of the subsoil and six of the ten mu of topsoil. Danan's two sons, Hailai and Haitang, did not like the arrangement, but it was their mother's wish. This act earned Danan the lasting affection of Guantong, who says of his sister, "she was not one to count every catty" (H-I-10). The Lus of the Middle Hamlet all referred to her affectionately as Da Ajie (or Big Elder Sister), the person everyone turned to in an emergency. This included the one non-Lu member of the Middle Hamlet—Gao Yonglin. Danan's is a story that attests to the absence of formalized power structures in the Yangzi delta, and to the role that personality and character played in descent-group leadership.

Although we do not have this kind of oral-history information on the other delta communities studied in this book, it is clear that several of them fit the Huayangqiao pattern. Sunjiaxiang "village," in Wuxian, for example, only appears at casual glance to be a single community, surrounded on four sides by waterways. Up close, we find that the xiang (or administrative village) in fact comprised 29 separate and distinct hamlets. The original, agnatic grouping is reflected in hamlet names like Wu Spring Harbor (Wuquangang), On Zhou Lane (Zhouxiangshang), Gao Family (Threshing) Ground (Gaojiachang), Meng Family Place (Mengjiashang), and Sun Family Bridge (Sunjiaqiao).

In this case, the xiang had been almost wiped out by the Taiping wars. A few of the communities that Hayashi Megumi surveyed in the 1930s had been reconstituted by families that had returned after the Taipings (e.g., the Gaos), but most had been formed as individual settlers drifted in. Many had not proliferated into descent groupings; of the 154 farming households in the xiang in the 1930s, no fewer than 77 were the only representatives of their descent group. Yet descent-group clustering was still unmistakable: all of the 29 descent groups lived in clusters of two to seven households within their own small hamlet (Hayashi 1943: 34, 68–71).

Villages fortunate enough to escape the Taiping wars—three of the eight in this study—generally had larger descent groups, traceable for more generations. Yanjiashang appropriately retains the name Yan Family Place: fully 29 Yan households lived there at the time of the Mantetsu investigations, almost all of them clustered side by side at the east end of the community. Touzongmiao and Dingjiacun also had large descent groups of considerable longevity: 43 Zhangs and 17 Xus in Touzongmiao, and 18 Dings in Dingjiacun.

The paradoxical combination of strong agnatic grouping and weak community structures in much of the Yangzi delta has not been ac-curately grasped in the past, in part because of the vivid picture of community organization we have from Fei Xiaotong (1939; see Chap. 2 above). In fact, outside of religious groupings that were fast disappearing with the increasing secularization of village life in the twentieth century and with the economic distresses caused by the depression of the 1930s, the supra-agnatic community organization in Kaixiangong was limited to the single act of collective drainage. Even irrigation was done by individual households (Fei 1939: 160–62). And the natural hamlets of Kaixiangong, like those of Huayang-qiao, had no developed political organizations or leadership beyond agnatic groupings (pp. 8, 109–16).

LANDOWNERSHIP AND RELATIONS WITH THE STATE

We have, then, the paradoxical phenomena of strong descent groups but a weak supra-agnatic community in Huayangqiao, and weak descent groups but a strong supra-agnatic community in Shajing. The question is why. A big part of the explanation lies in the differ-ential landownership patterns of the North China plain and the Yangzi delta.

Taxed directly as owner-cultivators, the villagers of the North China plain had a distinct need for an organizational structure to cope with the Qing state. Before the twentieth century, it is true, the state rarely imposed special levies on village communities over and above the land tax on households. But the nineteenth-century Baodi county archives show that the state, lacking the necessary coercive apparatus to enforce its will down to the individual household level in the manner of modern states, often relied on descent-group and community leaders to enforce collection. The institutional system that evolved in Baodi centered around a quasi-official tax collector called the *xiangbao*, who oversaw an average of about 20 natural vil-lages each. These xiangbao, nominated by the community but for-mally appointed by the county government, were generally small fry—dependable middle peasants whom the local and village notables thrust forward as buffers against state authority to avoid having to answer directly to the state for tax arrears. Informal power and formalized state authority coexisted in delicate balance in the persons of these quasi-officials (Huang 1985: 224–33). Behind the xiang-bao were the village-level informal councils comprising the leading members of the community, usually at least one from each of its lineages. These councils usually took on the actual responsibility of collecting delinquent taxes and extraordinary levies, and by extension, for other community affairs, like the arbitration of disputes, the maintenance of roads and temples, and crop-watching.

This structure of village leadership was formalized, elaborated, and reshaped in the twentieth century. The first step in this direction came during the last decade of the Qing, under the so-called New Policy reforms. Hebei [Zhili], under Yuan Shikai, led the way with the establishment of modern schools and police forces, funded by new levies: the *xuekuan* (for schools) and the *jingkuan* (police). There, as eventually in the other provinces of North China, the new levies were imposed on the villages, rather than on individual households. To enforce collection, the state established subcounty administrative units called wards (*qu*) to oversee the selection and appointment of new village heads (*cunzheng* or *cunzhang*) and deputy heads (*cunfu* or *cunzuo*), who were in turn responsible for the new levies (Huang 1985: 275–76; Mackinnon 1980: 139–45).

What happened in most North China villages was that the existing village councils chose men from their own ranks to serve as the new village heads. Since their primary responsibility was to meet the new levies, they were generally from the wealthiest households, men who could afford the time for the service and, even more important, advance the taxes if need be. In Shajing, Yang Yuan, who owned 40 mu, served as village head from 1927 to 1936; his successor, Zhang Rui, owned 110 mu (KC, 1: 99–100, 146). In a few places, like Houjiaying (Changli county, Hebei) and Wudian village (Liangxiang county, Hebei), two of the six North China villages where Mantetsu investigators did detailed interviews, the designated village heads, buttressed by the state, came to dominate village communities and abuse their powers. In most instances, however, decisions continued to be made in a committee-like manner by the council, as in Shajing, with the village head acting only as its executive officer (Huang 1985: 270–74). Some places even tried for a time to institutionalize their village councils, converting them into a kind of legislative body—called the *jiancha weiyuanhui*—to check on the work of the village heads (Shunyi County Archives, 2: 374, July–Nov. 1926; 2: 507, Mar.–Aug. 1927).*

With these reforms, villages developed not only identifiable village heads and deputy heads but also semiformalized operating budgets. Customarily, the village heads, and sometimes also the informal leaders, advanced the special levies and then settled accounts after the fall harvest, allocating the appropriate tax shares to individual households, usually by the amount of land owned. An account sheet would be posted in a visible spot in the village for all to see (ibid.; see also 3: 42, Jan.–Dec. 1929, and 3: 170, Jan.–Sept. 1930).

Where state extraction and internal divisions in the community combined to make the preexisting village leaders' positions untenable, the old village political organizations collapsed. The special levies came to exceed the land taxes proper in many places by 1928 (Huang 1985: 278–79). Those increases occurred at a time when county governments were becoming more illegitimate in peasant eyes with the rise of local warlord or bandit power. Moreover, since it was left to village leaders to decide on the best way to apportion the levies, whether by landownership or by head, divisions of interests and opinion between landowners and others were unavoidable. The position of village head, never a lucrative post, became an ever-more-thankless one. In some communities, like Wudian and Houjiaying, the old leaders refused to serve, leaving power vacuums that were filled by "local bullies and evil tyrants." In those villages, community bonds dissolved and highly atomized societies resulted. More commonly, though, community organization grew even stronger in the face of a mounting external threat, as occurred in Houxiazhai, Lengshuigou, Sibeichai, and Shajing (Huang 1985: chaps. 14–15).

In the Yangzi delta, the process of state-stimulated village-level political organization did not advance nearly so far. The Qing state, as we have seen, was generally content to deal with the delta peasants through their urban landlords, so that communities like Huayangqiao never evolved even the most informal of village councils. Neither the New Policy reforms of the Qing nor the county-government reorganization efforts of the Nanjing government altered this state of affairs substantially. The new taxes continued, by and large, to be levied mainly on the absentee subsoil owners in the towns, rather

---

*These are archives of the county government kept at the Shunyi County Archive (Shunyi xian dang'an guan). The first number refers to the archive's classification category, the second to the volume (juan) number. Citations below follow this same format.

than the tenants. The villagers of Huayangqiao were not even aware of the New Policy school and police taxes.

Nor did the new requirement that each village identify a head, cunzhang, to deal with the state penetrate down to Huayangqiao. Instead, the four villages continued to rely on the old Qing *baozheng* system, by which the county had been divided into units called *tu,* each with a head called the baozheng. Huayangqiao was in Number Ten Tu, lumped in with nearby Shen Family Village (Shenjiada). Before the Japanese came in 1937, a man named Wu Yungang had been the baozheng. As was true of all baozheng, his main duty was rent collection, so that he represented the landlord more than the state. The baozheng also drew up the documents for the sales of subsoil rights and houses, for which they charged a fee—their prinicpal source of income. Since almost all such transactions involved urban landowners and not peasants, this activity brought them into little contact with the villagers. Beyond those duties, the baozheng were called on on occasion to mediate disputes that were too big for a descent group or lineage and too small for a town government. Where waterworks needed coordination at the tu level, the baozheng sometimes undertook that role, but not in Huayangqiao (H-I-5).

Not surprisingly, the baozheng figured very little in the memory of the Huayangqiao peasants. To their minds, there was simply no such thing as an organized community government like Shajing's. Hamlet and village leadership was strictly ad hoc and informal, based on consanguineous groupings. The baozheng was a remote figure, almost an abstraction, who was not tied in any way to a natural community, with a natural constituency. He was strictly an agent of the state, overseeing an artificial unit imposed from above, far removed from the hamlet and the village, and of little consequence in the day-to-day lives of peasants.

Only under Japanese occupation did this state of affairs change in Huayangqiao. New levies were imposed—a poll tax (*hukoujuan*) and army rice (*junmi*)—along with various requisitions of labor and material. The occupation government therefore needed and wanted stronger control. The method it chose was China's own baojia system, the artificial grouping of ten households into jia units, each under a jia head, and ten jias into a bao, under a bao chief (baozhang). Though similar in title to the Qing and Republican baozheng, the occupation's baozhang was a very different sort of state agent. In Huayangqiao, the man recruited for this role was twenty-five-year-old Xue Baoyi (an offense of collaborating with the enemy for which he was later imprisoned for 20 years, until 1979).

In the delta's higher-lying dry-farmed zones, where village social structures were more like those of the North China plain and the state had an incentive to strengthen its tax-collection apparatus, the village governments were probably comparatively bureaucratized. And the exigencies of counterrevolutionary mobilization under the Guomindang certainly powered high degrees of village political and military organization in certain places, notably in the vicinity of the Communists' Jiangxi Soviet base area (Huang et al. 1978). Even in Kaixiangong, the coming of a regional silk industry, coupled with the state's imposition of an administrative village structure, gave concrete substance to a xiang government that had till then existed in name only (Fei 1939: 106–9). But Huayangqiao exemplifies the prevalent situation in the delta, one in which the predominance of tenants and the absence of other incentives for state organization left intact an almost "natural" substratum of communities bound chiefly by kinship groupings, with little supra-agnatic political organization.

STABILITY OF LANDOWNERSHIP

How did commercialization affect these patterns and processes? It is on this question that the empirical reality turns out to be the most surprising of all. Land use in Huayangqiao, far from evincing a higher rate of turnover than in less-commercialized Shajing, as we would expect, shows remarkable continuity.

True, the subsoil rights turned over very rapidly, bought and sold almost like stocks and bonds. In 1940, no fewer than 80 absentee landlords shared the villages' subsoil rights; the largest were the Xu Gongji rice shop in town, which owned the rights to 26 mu, and the Gu lineage of Songjiang, with 34 mu (MT, Shanghai 1940: table 6). But such transactions had little effect on village life. A transfer was almost always made between one absentee owner and another; sometimes, it meant a change in the place where the peasant had to deliver the rent, but often, not even that, for the same rice merchant would continue to handle the rent collection. Beyond that, the matter was of so little concern to the peasants that they had difficulty recalling them. Indeed, the Huayangqiao villagers could recall for the Mantetsu investigators only one such transaction, and that no doubt because the purchasers were fellow villagers. In the early 1930s, Gu Mingzhi, of the wealthy Gu lineage of Songjiang and himself one of the major absentee subsoil owners in the county, with a total of 300 mu (73 mu in Huayangqiao), sold off his rights to finance a trip to the

United States to study. Perhaps because of the depressed economic conditions of the time, Gu did the unusual thing of selling mainly to villagers. That was how Lu Shoutang (20 mu), Lu Jintang (12), Gao Changsheng (8) and Gao Liangsheng (5) of Xilihangbang and Xue Bingrong (14) and Xue Peigen (14) of Xue Family Village came to be the only substantial owners of subsoil rights among the Huayangqiao villagers (with rights to 13 percent of the cultivated area between them). The other villagers owned only fractions of a mu, usually the land on which their houses stood.

From the cultivators' point of view, it was the topsoil rights that really mattered, for these determined who farmed which parcels. The outright sale of topsoil, constrained as it was by custom, was extremely rare. At the time of the Japanese survey, the Huayangqiao peasants could recall only two cases. In 1932, He Yougen of He Family Village, impoverished and under severe financial pressure, sold twelve mu of topsoil that his family had farmed for four generations to Gao Jintang and Gao Changsheng of Gaojiada to pay for his mother's funeral. In 1939, Gao Botang of Gaojiada, who had not been able to meet his rent payments for three consecutive years, sold eight mu to Gao Quansheng of the same hamlet (MT, Shanghai 1940: 58–9, 195, table 6).

Even conditional sales, with the right of redemption within a certain number of years, were rare. Again, the villagers could recall just two transactions. In 1935, Lu Shoutang of South Hamlet (Xilihangbang) pledged four mu to Gao Agen of Gao Family Hamlet, for six years, for a price of 26 yuan apiece (against a sale price of about 33 yuan). Yang Tusheng of Xubushanqiao pledged six mu to Yang Weisheng of the same village in 1935, also for a price of 26 yuan per mu (ibid.). Plainly, there was great stability in land use in these villages: most of the villagers farmed the same family plots generation after generation.

Our past data on villages like Huayangqiao have been skewed by the failure to understand this two-tiered system of landownership. Land relations have been mistakenly equated with subsoil relations, and owners of the topsoil taken simply for tenants because they rented the subsoil they farmed. Qing and Republican law, as we have seen, never recognized the sale of surface rights, despite its prevalence in social practice. Even Amano Motonosuke and his team, meticulous and expert in almost all other respects, did not fully grasp the nature of topsoil ownership and therefore overlooked a system called *hunzhong*, in which the topsoil was rented out. This occurred only infrequently, but the practice serves nevertheless to make the

point. Gao Shigen rented five mu of topsoil from his uncle, Liangsheng; for the use of the topsoil, he paid a rent of three dou per mu,
in addition to the 8.2 dou per mu for rental of the subsoil from the
landlord Gu Mingzhi. Lu Hailai, similarly, rented three mu of topsoil for 3.5 dou per mu from Tu Pinshan (H-I-5).

There was no equivalent to this two-tiered ownership in North
China. Land transactions and tenure relations involved just a single
layer of land. A seller might continue to cultivate the land he sold as
a tenant of the new owner, but this arrangement needed to be renewed every year (in northeastern Hebei) or two (in northwest Shandong, where a three-crops-in-two-years regime prevailed; Huang
1985: 209). More often a sale was accompanied by a change of cultivator, and the frequent land sales meant a high turnover in land
use as well. Consider the following against the scattered cases in
Huayangqiao. In 1937, the peasants of Michang recalled fully 73
land purchases by villagers between the 1890s and 1936, totaling
538.4 mu (of a total cultivated area of 2,237 mu); 424 alone had been
purchased in the last 20 years, during which the village had turned
to cotton cultivation (Huang 1985: 108−9). In fruit-growing Qianlianggezhuang, peasants recalled 74 transactions, involving 1,291.2
mu (out of a total cultivated area of 1,564 mu; MT, Kitō 1937c:
6−10). Even in little-commercialized Dabeiguan, peasants recalled
76 transactions, in which 402.2 of the 2,438 mu of cultivated land
had changed hands (MT, Kitō 1937a: 6−9). In the case of Qianlianggezhuang, the Mantetsu investigators were able to elicit fairly detailed data on land sales as well: 44 transactions totaling 691 mu.

We do not have comparable data for Shajing, but the map drawn by
the Mantetsu investigators showing the individual parcels and their
owners in 1940 leaves little doubt about the highly fragmented and
fluid state of landownership there. There was little contiguity of
ownership among members of the same descent group. Moreover,
426 of the village's 1,182 mu (36 percent) were owned by outsiders,
mostly small peasants in neighboring villages (307.4 by residents
of nearby Wangquan and Shimen; KC, 1: appended map; KC, 2:
464−72; see also Huang 1985: 82).

Incomplete as these data must be, compiled as they were from villagers' memories, they are certainly adequate for documenting the
high degree of fluidity in landownership and land use on the North
China plain. The fact that relatively uncommercialized Dabeiguan
and Shajing evince essentially the same pattern as highly commercialized Michang and Qianlianggezhuang, all in North China,
cautions us against a simple equation of fluidity with commer-

cialization. The stability of Huayangqiao in the delta, more highly commercialized still, underscores the point.

The explanation for the great turnover in landownership in North China, I have suggested, lies in the region's structural poverty and ecological instability. A harsh, dry-farmed agrarian regime combined with population density made for structural poverty. And structural poverty made for a low tolerance for disasters, whether natural or man-made. Like someone standing neck deep in water, the North China peasant could be drowned by the merest ripple. As one villager put it, one year of disaster meant three years of bitter existence on account of debts; but two consecutive years of disaster meant a bitter life with little hope of recovery (Huang 1985: 299). It was natural disasters above all else that forced peasants to sell their land. The villagers of Shajing experienced four floods and one drought in the short space of 23 years (1917–40): three of the floods were severe enough to destroy half to three-quarters of the year's crops (ibid., p. 213). At the worst, peasants stripped of all means of subsistence were forced to uproot and migrate—hence we find not only a high incidence of land selling but also a high rate of migration in and out of villages like this.

The social composition and residential patterns of Shajing shown in the map prepared by the Mantetsu investigators confirm this picture. The village comprised eighteen descent groups in all. Seven of the older ones (families that had lived in the village a century or more) were represented by only one household in 1940. Five households had come within the last two generations, from a variety of places and for a variety of reasons: Zhao Shaoting, around 1910, a resident in town (Shunyi) who owned land in the village; Fu Ju, in the 1910s, a peddler; Bai Chengzhi, in 1929, an ironsmith from Shandong who had affinal ties to the village; Ren Zhengang, around 1930, from neighboring Shimen village, because he had no place to live there and had affinal kin in Shajing; and finally Jing Defu, in 1939, again from neighboring Shimen, who had bought some land in Shajing (KC, 1: appendix).

In Huayangqiao, by contrast, the peasants could recall only one major natural disaster since the turn of the century: in 1939, when 20 percent of the crop was destroyed by insects. There had not been a major flood or drought in living memory. As we saw in Chapter 2, the delta, though not without ecological problems, was much less unstable than North China: a mere 20 major floods in the 500 years between 1401 and 1900 (Table 2.1), compared with the almost annual flooding of the Yellow River on the North China plain.

The delta also benefited from much richer soil. Indeed, this was what made the two-layered system of rents possible: the land was so productive that a man could still net something after paying rent on two layers of soil. Such a system was precluded in North China. At half of the yield per mu, a tenant barely eked out a living; there was no margin for yet another layer of rent.

Moreover, thanks to its relatively higher living standard, there was considerable resilience in the delta's family-farm economy. Lu Longshun (b. 1926) of the South Hamlet of Xilihangbang, for example, became a "little year-laborer" for a time after his father died. Unable to meet the payments on the four mu of subsoil land he rented, he had had to turn over the surface rights to the subsoil owner. Had Lu been in North China, he would have had little prospect of eking out enough surplus from his wages to climb back up the socioeconomic ladder (Huang 1985: 199–201). Happily for him, after hiring out for three years, he was able to redeem the four mu by paying off the back rent he owed (H-I-2). Wu Yucai (b. 1930) had a similar story to tell: after his father died, he went off to work as a "little year-laborer" at a nearby village, while his married elder brother attended to the family's farm. Yucai learned to raise ducks, and became so good at the job by age sixteen that another employer lured him away with a better offer: 240 catties of rice more a year than he was earning, plus a two-months' holiday. Yucai's skills made him a desirable son-in-law, and he was adopted into a Xubushanqiao family when he was twenty (H-I-4).

The more commercialized and diversified Yangzi delta economy offered yet other avenues of employment and upward mobility. Yang Weisheng (b. 1906) of Xubushanqiao was dirt poor, with only two mu of surface soil rights. But he was able to accumulate a good deal of money by digging for loaches (niqiu, eel-like fish up to eight inches long that are a popular delicacy in this area) in waterlogged low-lying rice fields during the fallow season. Yang and his four teenage children would get up before dawn, walk for three hours to the right spot (about eighteen kilometers away), and shovel up the loaches from under the water; each could dig up a little over ten catties in one day. The family would then go to Huayang town to peddle the catch at two and a half to four catties of rice per catty. Yang was able to acquire six mu of land by this means (H-I-8).

He Shutang (b. 1917) of He Family Village, for another example, farmed only six mu of land, just enough to feed his family until March. He supplemented his income by working in town at a restaurant during the winter months, earning the equivalent of 80 catties of rice a month. He further augmented the family income by peddling water chestnuts, which he bought at 100 catties a yuan and sold in Songjiang city for a 20 percent profit (H-I-4).

Subsidiary incomes like these did not take the place of family farming; instead, they augmented inadequate farm incomes and enabled small peasants who might otherwise have been unable to make ends meet to hang onto their family farms. They added to rather than undermined stability in the delta countryside.

CHANGE VERSUS INVOLUTION

The fact is, *pace* Smith and Marx, that the greater commercialization in the delta brought not greater intravillage differentiation between capitalistic farmers and proletarians but less, and not greater falling away from the community but less. In North China, the effects of ecological shocks and land scarcity were not counteracted by the same degree of commercialization and familization that lent the peasant farm in the delta its added resilience.

Under the circumstances, it comes as no surprise that Communist organizing should have met with little success in the delta. Despite the high incidence of tenancy, the Communists' call for a rural revolution against "feudal landlordism" met with little support there. By contrast, the instability and insecurity of rural life on the North China plain, despite a low incidence of tenancy, made the peasants much more receptive to revolutionary mobilization. Their support for the Communists was in fact to make the decisive difference in the civil war with the Guomindang. But that support might not have been so readily given had the party's original vision not been substantially revised to take account of social reality. Since less than 20 percent of the cultivated area was rented, no revolutionary program could have succeeded by emphasizing only the struggle of tenants against "feudal" land rents. Communist organizers on the scene had to adapt to the real world by adding tax resistance and community defense against external intrusion to their program (Perry 1980; Huang 1985).

2

AFTER 1949

CHAPTER 9

Restructuring the
Old Political Economy

For the late imperial and Republican states, the agrarian economy was chiefly an object of taxation, and the peasant chiefly a source of tax revenue. Beyond seeing to orderly tax collection, neither state interfered much with agriculture and peasant life. The new revolutionary state, however, was interested in far more than just the extraction of surplus from the countryside; it was also bent on reorganizing and developing the agrarian economy, in accordance with its program of "socialist transformation." The state was to become much more than just tax collector; it was to plan for and control rural commerce, and arrogate to itself almost complete power over household economic decision making. To do so, the state had not only to extend its vertical reach down to the village, but also to expand the horizontal scope of its powers, to encompass especially rural economic life. The three crucial steps in this revolutionary program were *land reform*, the *three-fixed policy* (of state-fixed grain production, grain purchase, and sale), and *collectivization*. Through this program, the old political-economic system based on a let-live peasant family-farm economy was transformed into a gigantic party-state based on a collectivized and planned economy.

LAND REFORM

Land reform came to Huayangqiao in the autumn of 1950. In contrast to the areas contested by the Communists and the Guomindang during the civil war, the process here was peaceful and orderly (*heping tugai*), carried out in accordance with the Land Reform Law formally promulgated in June 1950. As Shen Baoshun, head (cunzhang) of the administrative village (*cun*) of the time (Shenjia cun, which encompassed the four Huayangqiao villages, plus nearby Shenjiada), tells it, in June 1950 he was called to the county to study the land reform policies for half a month. At those sessions, the rationale and policies were explained in detail. On his return, his first job was to register all of the land and then calculate an average range of land per capita: 2.5–3.0 mu in this case. Peasants with more than the average high were allowed to retain the equivalent of 3.0 mu, called the "big average" (*da pingjun*); those under the range received enough land to make 2.5 mu, the "small average" (*xiao pingjun*). In addition to land, the reform called for redistributing draft animals, farm implements, houses, and furniture; together with land, these were the so-called "five major properties" (*wuda caichan*) subject to redistribution (H-II-13).

The organizational frame for implementing the reform was the administrative village, headed by Shen, a deputy (*fu cunzhang*), and the head of the militia. Under them came the natural villages, each headed by a "group head" (*zuzhang*). Shen, the deputy, and the militia head formed an "executive group" (*xingzhengzu*), responsible first for assigning all the peasants to one of the Land Reform Law's categories. In theory, each peasant household was to suggest an appropriate classification for itself, subject to revision and decision by the leaders (called *zibao gongping*), but since "poor peasant" constituted the most desirable category, practically everyone professed to fall in that class. Shen's executive group called in the villages' group heads for consultation and assistance in arriving at an appropriate classification for each household.

The general rule of thumb actually applied for the classification was as follows: "middle peasants" generally farmed an amount of land close to the upper average and generally possessed a draft animal and farm implements; "upper middle peasants" (*shang zhongnong*) were somewhat above this standard and hired in some labor; "rich peasants" hired in more labor and farmed substantially more land than the average, while "poor peasants" farmed less than the average amount of land and had to hire out to augment their income. It was not the most precise of schemes, or even the most Marxist. Here there was no attempt to adhere strictly to the letter of the law or to apply the calculus of the rates of "surplus extraction" to rent and wage labor relations, as was done in "Longbow Village" in Shanxi (Hinton 1966). The reality was that there was little intravillage stratification in Huayangqiao; almost all villagers rented the subsoil from town landlords, and almost all owned the surface soil they farmed. No one hired a year-laborer. An attempt to divide the villagers according to rent and labor relations would have placed almost everyone in the same category. However fuzzy and non-Marxist the

TABLE 9.1

Middle- and Poor-Peasant Households in Huayangqiao
at the Time of Land Reform, June 1950

Village/hamlet	Middle	Poor	Total
Xue Family Village			
(Xuejiada)	7	5	12
He Family Village			
(Hejiada)	0	9	9
Xubushanqiao			
East Hamlet	2	12	14
West Hamlet	0	4	4
Xilihangbang			
Gao Family Hamlet	3	4	7
Lu Family Hamlet	2	2	4
South Hamlet	2	5	7
TOTAL	16	41	57

NOTE: The classification was based on an average range of 2.5–3.0 mu per capita. There were no villagers in Huayangqiao who fit the Land Reform Law's "rich" category, i.e., hiring one or more long-term laborers.

categories applied might have been, they did reflect local realities (H-III-4).

The entire classification process took about a month, and the results were announced on posters, one for each natural village (Table 9.1). The poor peasants who received land (41 households) got a bamboo placard (*zhupai*) certifying their ownership, with which they staked out their new property. They also received some confiscated property. The middle peasants (16 households) were essentially untouched. There were no landlords or rich peasants.* The details of the classification and redistribution process are now hazy in the minds of both the cadres and the peasants, perhaps because the changes wrought by land reform were relatively short-lived and paled by comparison with the subsequent collectivization. But the numbers were all recorded carefully at the time, with land deeds showing the amount of land each household owned before land reform and what it received or gave up. Copies of the deeds are still kept at the County Archives (H-II-13, 18; H-III-3).

There was so little stratification in these villages that most of the additional land for the poor had to be carved out of landlord and rich-peasant holdings in other places. Take Wu Renyu of the generally

*In 1955, one villager, Lu Guantong (b. 1919), was reclassified a rich peasant, ostensibly because he had concealed land on which he collected rent at the time of land reform. The judgement was overturned in 1979 (H-I-3).

poor village of Xubushanqiao, for example. His household had only
ten mu of surface soil for five people, and he had been granted another three mu. But since there was not enough confiscated land in
Xubushanqiao to reapportion, he was given three mu of land located
in another village, really too far away to be useful to him, he says.
Others received fragments of rice land without access to a water
pump. They had no choice but to convert the land to cotton. It was
in part problems like these that motivated the collectivization
to come. In more well-to-do Xue Family Village, where there was
enough confiscated land to go around, Xue Gentao's family of eight
simply received the eight mu (of surface soil) that he had been rent-
ing. They were adjacent to the thirteen mu of surface soil he owned.
Land reform thus worked out well for him (H-III-3).

Since no "landlords" were identified in Huayangqiao or Shenjiada,
the villagers' only direct experience with the anti-landlord class
revolution was a mass struggle meeting organized for the whole of
Xinglong township (xiang), which encompassed Shenjia cun and
several other administrative villages. At that meeting, convened at
the Catholic church in the nearby town of Yangjing, three landlords
were "struggled": Lu Dirong, who owned about 500 mu of land; Lu
Zicai, who also had 500 mu; and Wu Shunyu, who had only 30 mu.
All three were Catholics, allowing the revolutionary leaders to join
the class issue with the issue of imperialism. The Huayangqiao villagers received instructions to attend; everyone over the age of sixteen was expected to go, men and women alike. But many said they
were busy and stayed home. In all, about 1,000 people from Xinglong
township attended the meeting, where the leaders announced the
landlords' crimes, tenants did their "speak bitterness," and "the
masses" were allowed to beat the three men. The meeting left no
great impression on the Huayangqiao villagers, as it happens, because none of the landlords was known to them (H-III-3).

Properties confiscated from the landlords were distributed at mass
meetings held afterward at the administrative-village level. The villagers recall that at the meeting in Shenjia cun, poor peasants received various items: some got a chair or bench, others bedding, another a chamber pot, and so on. But it is clear the meeting was no big
deal to them; only a few could recall it, and then with effort. This
and the meeting at the Catholic church in Yangjing were the only
two local mass meetings during land reform (H-III-3).

Subsequent revolutionary propaganda notwithstanding, there was
little in the way of intravillage class struggle in this area. For the Huayangqiao villagers, the overturn in class relations that came with the

Revolution was not a blood-and-guts affair involving mass struggles against specific, hated landlords with names and faces. Rather, it occurred almost unnoticed and at some remove from their daily lives. It was done chiefly by administrative fiat, the revolutionary authorities outlawing by a stroke of the pen the collection of rents on the subsoil.

In Shajing village in North China, by contrast, even though landlordism was much less pervasive, there was considerable stratification. Long-term labor was a fact of life there, with the result that three of Shajing's 71 households were classified as rich peasants (Ren Zhengang, Yang Yuan, Zhang Rui). One household was classified as a landlord (Zhao Limin), and 179.9 of the village's 1,182 mu of land were redistributed.

Land reform in Shajing began with the establishment of the Poor Peasant Association at the end of 1949, in which more than 30 households participated. A two-man work team of educated "intellectuals" (*zhishi fenzi*) was sent down from above. They stayed in the village fully half a year, and worked with the then-village head, Li Xianglin, to classify the villagers and redistribute the land. The results were announced by placards and at mass meetings. Since this village too fell within a newly liberated area, the process did not involve the kind of violent struggle that occurred in villages like Longbow, which witnessed seesaw contests between Guomindang and Communist armies (Hinton 1966; Shajing interviews, April 1980).

IMPLICATIONS OF LAND REFORM

Though pushed through with little fanfare, "peaceful" land reform wrought profound changes. In Shajing, it eradicated rent, equalized property differences, removed the basis for long-term wage labor, and set the stage for expanded state taxation. Because Huayangqiao was much less stratified than Shajing, the equalizing of landholdings within the village had comparatively little effect. But the impact of land reform was no less far-reaching, completely altering the villages' relations with the outside. Gone were the urban-residing absentee landlords' claims over the subsoil. The villagers became owner-cultivators pure and simple, like their counterparts in North China. Instead of rent payments to landlords, they now paid taxes to the state. For the Huayangqiao peasants, state extraction, and state power, penetrated directly into the natural villages for the first time in centuries.

In North China, the tax burden in imperial times had probably been no more than the national average of about 2–4 percent of the gross produce from the land (Yeh-chien Wang 1973). Even with the additional levies imposed by local governments to finance modern schools and a modern police force, and later paramilitary forces at the ward (qu) level, in three North China villages for which we have peasant tax receipts, taxes still took only about 3–5 percent of peasant gross income in 1937. As wartime inflation in food prices outran the tax rate, there was even a brief dip down to 2–3 percent by 1939 (Huang 1985: 280–82). But local governments soon caught up with rising prices, and tax rates climbed again. In the Japanese-occupied villages of North China, the tax burden reached 6–8 percent of peasant income in 1941 and then skyrocketed as the Japanese occupation authorities resorted to more drastic methods of taxation.

In the Yangzi delta, imperial taxes had been higher than in other areas of China, but had been borne by the subsoil landlords and not the tenant cultivators. Added taxes of the twentieth century were similarly borne by the absentee landlords and therefore left little impression on tenant cultivators. In Huayangqiao, dramatic increase came only under Japanese occupation, with the imposition of "military rice" (junmi) requisitions in both 1943 and 1944. In 1944, the demand was for one shi per mu, or about 50 percent of produce. Xue Baoyi, the Japanese-appointed baozhang, recalls that he and three other baozhang had great difficulty collecting the grain. When they reported the problems to Officer Kawada in charge, he flew into a rage, drew his sword, and slashed across the air at the four. He threw Baoyi in prison and released him only on the promise that he would do better. When Baoyi failed to deliver on his promise, Kawada had Baoyi's mother arrested. Baoyi gained her release only with the help of Xu Liang, the head of the collaborationist government in Huayang town (H-I-13).

Tax rates also rose in the Guomindang- and Communist-controlled areas in the later years of the war. The effective rate of taxation in the Guomindang-occupied areas might have reached 20 percent of produce after 1941 (Huang 1985: 281). In the Shaan-Gan-Ning border area, the average tax peaked in 1941 at just over 13 percent of total produce, imposed on a progressive scale ranging from 10 percent for the poorer peasants up to 30 percent for the rich (Selden 1971: 181–83).

Initially, the new revolutionary government taxed at rates far greater than anything seen under the imperial and prewar Republican governments. In Nanjing village, Guangzhou, the tax burden increased from 13 percent of output before land reform to an astronomical 30 percent under eager local cadres in the immediate aftermath of land reform (Yang 1969: 56–57, 155–56). Even in the fully recovered agricultural economy of 1953–57, the national rate amounted to 10.5 percent of grain output (Kenneth Walker 1984: 182). The agricultural taxes have since been largely frozen at the absolute amounts imposed in the early postrevolutionary years and have therefore increasingly shrunk as agricultural production expanded. Our earliest figures on Huayangqiao, for 1966, show a rate of 5.9 percent of income from crops (*nongye shouru*, exclusive of *fuye*, or sidelines, and *xumu*, or income from livestock). By 1983, the figure had declined to 4.7 percent.

If it is true that the new taxation at least began at exorbitant rates, it is also true that, in assessing what these rates meant for the livelihood of peasants, we need to keep in mind the trade-off between tax and rent. For the Huayangqiao tenant peasants, the new government's "gift" was the ending of rent payments to urban landlords, which in effect meant they gained 43.8 percent of total rice output. Under the circumstances, therefore, the new land taxes might not have seemed all that burdensome. Although the proportion of tenants was much lower in North China than in the Yangzi delta, in aggregate terms, what the new state took in expanded taxes probably did not exceed the combined total of taxes and rents of an earlier day.

In terms of state-village power relations, land reform and expanded taxation brought state power into the natural village to an unprecedented degree. The old triangular relationship between state, gentry or landlord, and peasant was replaced by a new bipolar relationship between state and peasant. The peasants of Huayangqiao were no longer buffered from state power by an urban landowning elite; those of Shajing were now taxed more heavily than before. For both, land reform and the new taxes represented the first steps in the massive penetration of state power into their lives.

THE "THREE-FIXED" POLICY

The next big step came with the extension of state control over commerce. On October 16, 1953, the Central Committee of the Chinese Communist Party adopted a resolution on the "Planned Purchase and Planned Sales of Grain," initiating the first of a series of major measures taken to bring rural commerce under control. According to this resolution, serious shortages in grain supply had developed despite great advances in grain production. On the one hand, the demand for grain had increased with the expansion of the urban and industrial population and the improvement in living standards. On the other hand, the state had not been able to purchase what was needed because merchant and peasant profiteers were hoarding grain in anticipation of scarcity and price rises. The party leaders therefore resolved that grain should be subject to unified purchase (*tonggou*) and unified sale (*tongxiao*). The resolution became official government policy with the State Council's "Commands on the Implementation of Planned Purchase and Planned Sale of Grain" of November 23, 1953 (Beijing nongye daxue 1981, 1: 129–30, 139–42).

What this meant in practice was, first of all, the compulsory sale at state prices of surplus grain produced by peasant households (later euphemistically called "commodity grain," *shangpin liang*, distinguished from the agricultural tax, *nongye shui*, or "public grain," *gongliang*). Kenneth Walker (1984: 182) shows that the state procured 17.1 percent of the gross output of grain in 1953–57 under this program. Between the 10.5 percent tax and this program, the state absorbed 27.6 percent of total grain output.

The procured grain was supplied or sold through state-managed outlets at state-set prices to about 200,000,000 consumers: 100,000,000 in the cities, and another 100,000,000 in rural towns and villages, including the 10 percent or so grain-short households in villages. Privately managed shops were not allowed to purchase or sell grain for themselves but could only act on behalf of the state's grain-control agencies. Peasants were not allowed to sell their surplus grain to private merchants but could only sell to state agencies or coops or in state-established markets (Beijing nongye daxue 1981, 1: 134–35).

The procurement quotas were set by taking into account needs and harvests, and then passed down from the top. The State Planning Commission first set the total needs for the nation as a whole, then the quotas were passed on down through the various administrative layers, each layer apportioning a quota to the next layer below it, all the way down to the administrative villages.* Given the crisis of supply that had impelled the new policy, officials felt pressed in the beginning to set the quotas as high as the peasants could bear. The resulting burden on peasant producers was to lessen only with increases in grain output in later years (H-III-20).

As Vivienne Shue (1976: 111–16) has shown, the policy was highly successful. State purchases of grain jumped about 80 percent between 1952/53 and 1953/54. In part, this was because of the effec-

* Oi n.d. is the most detailed study to date of the process and politics of procurement.

tiveness of the control measures. In part, it was because the state provided strong material incentives to secure peasant compliance. Prices were pegged at prevailing market rates, so that no one would lose from selling to the state. Peasants who had received advances from merchants before November 1953 for that year's crop did not have to repay the money if they sold to state stores, a policy that supplied a powerful incentive for peasants to break loose from the merchants. Peasants who deposited the proceeds from their sales of grain into accounts with the National People's Bank could earn a very favorable interest rate of 1.5 percent to 2.0 percent a month, for up to six months, which gave well-to-do peasants a lucrative way to put their surpluses to work without engaging in hoarding. Peasants who contracted with government coops to sell their crop in 1954, finally, received interest-free advances.

The control of the grain trade became complete on August 25, 1955, with the State Council's passage of a set of "Provisional Regulations on Unified Purchase and Unified Sale of Grain in the Countryside," formally calling for quotas on each household's grain production (Beijing nongye daxue 1981, 1: 142–51). Together, the fixing of compulsory purchase quotas (*dinggou*), unified sale quotas (*dingxiao*), and production quotas (*dingchan*) came to be known as the "three fixes in grain" (*liangshi sanding*).

Once implemented, the three fixes left little in the grain economy to chance or individual choice. Every household had to attend first to the state's procurement needs, and then to its own requirements for consumption, for feed, and for seeds (called the "three retains," *sanliu*). In setting the amount of compulsory sales, the state theoretically first deducted the household's "three retains" from the planned production quota. Procurement was not supposed to exceed 80–90 percent of the "surplus grain" left to the household. In practice, local cadres often set the production quotas at artificially inflated levels, so that little or nothing was left to the peasants' discretion. The policy in fact "tied" their hands tightly, as even the government acknowledged when, in the mid-1980s, the dropping of compulsory sales was justified as the "untieing" (*songbang*) of the country's farm households.

In Huayangqiao, the three fixes did more than bring the household economy under control; they played a powerful role in pushing unwilling households into the collectives. Production quotas for rice were set at 800 catties (unhusked) per mu on top-grade land, 700 on medium-grade land, and 600 on low-grade land, when the average yield in Songjiang county as a whole in 1953–56 was only 552 catties. Since procurement quotas were set by the target yields, not actual yields, peasants had to pay the fixed amount even if that left them with less than enough for household consumption. As the peasants put it, "the state came first." The result was immense pressure on peasant households. Some, apparently, were simply left with not enough to eat. One way out, as the peasants tell it, was to join a collective, because that transferred the immediate burden from the single household to the collective and, more important, because the state favored collectives over individual households in granting procurement reductions and waivers. In Xilihangbang, eighteen households joined the new Linked Stars (Lianxing) Collective in 1955 for that reason alone (H-III-3, 20).

State control was extended to the county's other major crop on September 14, 1954, when the State Council issued a set of "Commands on the Implementation of the Planned Purchase of Cotton." Except for what was needed for home consumption and taxes, cotton-growing peasants were to sell all of their produce to state agencies, under the unified management of the State Company for Cotton, Yarn, and Cloth. No private dealings in cotton were permitted, with the single exception of merchants dealing in cotton wadding, and even they were to be supplied only by the state. Even before the collectivization of agriculture, therefore, the state had brought the backbone of the rural economy under complete control (Beijing nongye daxue 1981, 1: 168–89).

COLLECTIVIZATION

In Huayangqiao, the first step toward collectivization came with the organization of mutual-aid teams, beginning in 1952. In Xubushanqiao, the young (former) poor peasant Yang Xiaofa led in organizing the first local team; its aim was merely the pooling of certain resources. But Yang was not recruited into the party; his position as mutual-aid team leader was informal, and his role chiefly that of community leader rather than state agent or party representative. This preliminary stage, in fact, appears relatively minor in comparison with the dramatic changes before and after it. It has paled in the peasants' memories; they can recall few concrete details about the mutual-aid teams.

That is hardly the case with the next steps of collectivization. Shen Family Village (Shenjiada) was the first "test point" for collectivization in Shenjia cun, because it was relatively poor and because it was the home of Shen Baoshun, at the time the only party member in the administrative village. Xubushanqiao lacked the necessary leadership, and relatively well-to-do Xue Family Village and the Middle Hamlet of Xilihangbang were reluctant, Shen recalls. The word "star" was favored in the naming of these first experiments in agrarian socialism. Shen Family Village's Star Group Collective (Qunxingshe), formed in 1954, was a so-called early-stage collective (*chuji hezuo she*), in which production was done in a group but the yield was distributed according to each household's contribution in land and labor. The following year, Xue Family Village, He Family Village, and Xubushanqiao were organized into the Three-Star Collective (Sanxing she), under the leadership of the former poor peasants Yang Xiaofa, He Huosheng, and Zhang Boren. Xilihangbang, with its three hamlets, was organized into the Linked-Stars Collective that same year, under the poor peasant Lu Longshun (H-II-13, 18).

In 1956 came the drive for higher-stage collectives (*gaoji hezuo-she*), and Shen Family Village and our four Huayangqiao villages were amalgamated into a single group, called simply the Number Two Collective of Xinglong township. Distribution was now to be on the basis of labor contribution only (ibid.).

With the Great Leap Forward in 1958, the Xinglong Number Two Collective was merged with another (present-day Xinyu Brigade) to form the "Ninth Battalion" of the enormous Chengdong (East of the City) Commune. Then, in 1959, as the dust of reorganization began to settle, the four Huayangqiao villages were brought into the Xinglong Brigade, along with ten other villages. Xue Family Village and He Family Village made up one production team, Xubushanqiao another, and Xilihangbang a third. That administrative arrangement was to last until 1978, when the four Huayangqiao villages were separated out to form a special Seed Farm Brigade (Zhongzichang dadui), which meant that it was responsible for growing and developing seeds for the entire brigade—something that took up about 4 percent of its cultivated area.

THE PARTY-STATE

In the Qing state, the lowest-level salaried officials were attached to the county yamen. Below them, the bureaucracy relied on such unsalaried, quasi-officials as the xiangbao (in Hebei) or the baozheng (in the Yangzi delta) for tax collection. The xiangbao of nineteenth-century Baodi county oversaw an average of 20 natural villages. It was here that state power met the endogenous interest groups of local society, in the nomination and appointment of the xiangbao and in the conduct of tax collection. With the coming of local government reform in the Republican period, the formal state apparatus was extended one level lower than the county government office. Shunyi county, for example, was divided into eight wards (qu) in 1928, each with a salaried ward head (quzhang), supported by an average of thirteen policemen and fifteen paramilitary guards. State power now stretched down to the administrative village cun (sometimes one large natural village, but usually encompassing several small ones); and the lowest state tax-collection agent, at least in North China, was now the administrative village head (cunzhang), answerable directly to the ward (Huang 1985: 276–77).

The successor to the Republican ward in the postrevolutionary government of the early 1950s was the township xiang; like the ward, it exerted state control through the oversight of the administrative village cun. The xiang remained the basic unit for both taxation and land reform until collectivization, when it gave way first to the higher-stage collective and, by 1958, to the commune (and the administrative village to the brigade). In time, the administrative staffs of the township or the commune came to dwarf the Republican ward, and sometimes even the old imperial county yamen.

State-paid administrative personnel, or state cadres (guojia ganbu) in the parlance of post-1949 China, are not found beneath this level. The new government had no wish to extend its formal power to the villages, and probably did not have the capacity to do so in any case. Indeed, the elaboration of the township (commune) administrative apparatus alone swelled salaried state personnel geometrically in the course of the years. In 1982, there were 54,352 communes in China. Ten state cadres for each commune alone would bring their numbers close to 550,000, more than sixteen times the number of centrally appointed officials in the first half of the nineteenth century (Chang 1955). Given an average of 13.2 brigades per commune at that time, to have extended the formal apparatus down one more layer, with just one state cadre assigned to each brigade, would have pushed the total well over the million mark (Zhongguo tongji nianjian 1983: 147). In 1984, with the move toward agricultural de-collectivization, the commune was done away with, and the xiang again became the lowest-level unit of state administration. (Since the structures of control of the collectivized period took shape under the communes, I will stick to that term in the pages that follow, rather than continuing with the awkward township/commune usage. But the reader should keep in mind that "township" is appropriate for all years except 1956/57–1983.)

TABLE 9.2
Late Imperial and Twentieth-Century Local Administrative Units

Imperial	Republican	To 1955	1956–57	1958–83
county	county	county	county	county
li/bao	ward	township	higher-stage collective	commune
—	administrative village	administrative village	early-stage collective	production brigade
				production team

What distinguished the revolutionary state from earlier ones was above all its resort to a second, informal apparatus of state control: the Chinese Communist Party. Party organization, which paralleled the formal apparatus of government at every level, stretched down to the production brigade, where the party branch committee (*dang zhibu*) took over for the state. The party branch committee secretary (*dang zhibu shuji*), or "branch sec" (*zhishu*) for short, became the postrevolutionary equivalent of the old administrative village head (cunzhang). The polite form of address for a village head of old was Village Head X (e.g., Li cunzhang); it was now Branch Sec X (Li zhishu).

The process of party building down to the village level had of course begun much earlier, in the days of the struggles against the Guomindang. Each side had propelled the other to deepen and expand its control over the basic levels of society. But it was only after the final victory in 1949 that the Communist Party was able to extend its apparatus fully in the newly liberated areas. Land reform soon brought it into every administrative village. In Huayangqiao, as we saw, the man charged with carrying out land reform was the administrative village head, Shen Baoshun. Shen was a party member but not a state-paid employee; his link to the new state was through the party organization and not the formal state apparatus.

It was collectivization that finally brought the party to extend its apparatus to the production team, or the smaller natural villages and hamlets of Huayangqiao. Yang Xiaofa of Xubushanqiao, He Huosheng of He Family Village, and Lu Longshun of Xilihangbang were the first villagers to be recruited into the party. All three joined in 1956. Party membership in these villages was eventually to grow to thirteen by 1985 (H-III-28).

One advantage of relying on the party organization for local control was that it avoided bloating the bureaucratic apparatus still further and shifted the burden of paying for the administrative personnel to the local community. Under the communes and the brigades, a clear distinction was always made between the cadres who ate "state rice" (*chi guojia fan*) and those who ate "collective rice" (*chi jiti fan*).

Huayangqiao reveals one pattern of state-village relations. The Huayangqiao brigade, with its four natural villages, was largely an artificial grouping with little natural basis. Consequently, the crucial point of intersection between state power and the village community occurred at the level of the production team. In other areas, where the brigade was the natural village (e.g., Shajing in North China), state and community met at the higher level. In still other areas, where groupings of small natural villages and hamlets were linked by extended lineage ties (e.g., "Chen Village" in Guangdong studied by Anita Chan et al. 1984), state power met with community interests at both levels.

In Huayangqiao, the tug between the party-state and the community at the brigade level was very much tilted in favor of the former. For one thing, the other key brigade leaders besides the party branch secretary—the brigade head and the chief accountant—were generally party members, as shown in Table 9.3, subject to the pull and

TABLE 9.3
Party Membership and Brigade Leadership in Huayangqiao, 1956–85

Start of tenure	Party secretary	Brigade head	Accountant
1956	Shen Baoshun[a]	Shen Baoshun, P[a]	—
1960	Lu Defa, O	He Huosheng, P[b]	Xu Mujin, P, O
1964			Huang Xiyu, P, O
1967	Tong Jiahong, O	Xu Mujin, P, O	
1968		Huang Xiyu, P, O	Zhang Bingyu, P[c]
1971		Ye Shilin, P, O	
1972	Xu Mujin, O		
1975	Huang Xiyu, O		
1977	Ye Shilin, O		
1978	Wang Shunzhong, O	Chen Donglin, P, O	He Yonglong, P[d]
1981		He Yonglong, P[d]	
1982			Zhang Bingyu, P[c]
1983	He Yonglong	Xue Delong, P[e]	
1984	Chen Donglin, O		
1985	Xue Delong	He Deyu, P[f]	

SOURCE: H-III-28.
    NOTE: "P" in columns 2 and 3 indicates party membership. "O" indicates someone from outside Huayangqiao. The year of admission to the party is given where known.
    [a]Pre-1949.   [c]1975.   [e]Party member later, in 1984.
    [b]1956.   [d]1971.   [f]1984.

TABLE 9.4
Party Membership and Team Leadership in Huayangqiao, 1956–85

Start of tenure	Xuejiada (#1) team head	Xubushanqiao (#2) team head	Xilihangbang (#3) team head
1956			Lu Haitang, P[a]
1957	Zhang Boren		
1958	Xue Peigen	Yang Xiaofa, P[b]	
1959	He Huosheng, P[b]		
1961	Xue Shunquan		
1968	He Dexing		
1969			Gao Yonglin
1972	Xue Shunquan		
1973			Lu Longshun, P[b]
1974			Lu Jinquan
1975			Li Peihua, P[c]
1977			Wei Guoqian, P?, O
1978	He Deyu[d]	Wu Mingchang	
1979	Zhang Shunyong		Lu Jinquan
1980		Yang Yinlong	
1981			Gao Jinyun
1982	Xue Renxing	Wu Mingchang	
1983		He Guohua	Gao Huojin
1984	He Deyu, P[d]	Wu Renyu, P[e]	
1985	He Xiudi		

NOTE: See Table 9.3.
[a] 1974.   [d] 1984.
[b] 1956.   [e] 1964.
[c] 1975.

pressures of "the organization." For another, brigade administration was largely desk work, pulling the leaders away from production work for about 80 percent of the time; they generally put in only 100 workday equivalents a year (of an average total of 500) in productive labor. They were thus not nearly so close to their fellow workers as the team leaders, whose ratio of cadre work to productive labor was just the opposite: generally no more than 20 percent time spent away from production. Moreover, since brigade leaders had to be educated, they tended to be younger men. As such, they had much more opportunity to move up the bureaucratic ladder than the older and generally illiterate team leaders under them. Table 9.3 shows the very high turnover rate in brigade leadership in Huayangqiao over the 30-year period. Without the countervailing pull of the ties born of the natural community, the Huayangqiao brigade leaders tended to be more agents of the state than representatives of their villages.

As we see in Table 9.4, most of Huayangqiao's production team heads (*shengchandui duizhang*) were not party members; and unlike the brigade cadres, they tended to stay in their positions for many years. On occasion, recruitment into the party might coincide with appointment as team head, as in the case of Li Peihua of Xilihang-bang. It might also follow service in the position, after a person had demonstrated an exceptional capacity for leadership, as in the case of He Deyu. Such overlaps attest to the party's intent and effort to incorporate team leadership into the organization. At the same time, the fact that the majority of team heads were not party members at-tests to the delicate balance at this junction point between party au-thority and local community. For reasons to be detailed later, these team heads were almost always people from their own commu-nities, respected and trusted for their knowledge of production. In Huayangqiao, these were the people who were truly Janus-faced, subject at once to pressures from above and the pull of community interests from below.

In places where the brigade was itself a natural community, the brigade leaders sometimes stood at the intersection between state and rural community. That was true, for example, in Shajing. This first tier of intersection, of course, tended to buffer the small produc-tion teams of the tier below from direct party-state power, with the result that they were more nearly purely community-oriented units than in Huayangqiao. That appears to have been the case in Chen Village (Chan et al. 1984).

Whether the crucial intersection between party-state power and the community occurred at the level of the brigade or the team, or both, postrevolutionary political power had a far greater vertical reach than the imperial state. Whether in the person of the party branch secretary or the production team leader, the power of the state was felt directly by every peasant—a very different situation from the imperial days when the emperor and his agents were far removed from village life.

MANAGERIAL AND DISTRIBUTIVE POWERS

Even as the party-state extended its vertical reach down to the pro-duction team, it extended its horizontal reach into realms far be-yond mere taxation. The brigade leaders' chief responsibility was the management of production. It was up to them to transmit and imple-ment the quotas, targets, and development plans from above. Accord-ing to the Huayangqiao brigade cadres, each year, after the July–August rush to harvest the early rice and plant the late rice, they would draw up the next year's production plan. They would begin by computing the "three retains" of consumption grain, seed, and feed, and the agricultural tax, then tack on the amount of grain the brigade was obliged to sell to the state under the compulsory-purchase program. That would set the total grain output target, which determined how much land the brigade would put under grain, as well as the target yields per mu. The target yields, in turn, determined not just the cropping choice, but to a great extent also the way in which the grain would be grown: whether single-cropped rice followed by wheat or double-cropped rice followed by barley, what kind of seeds to use, how to plow and sow, how much fertilizer to use, and so on. All these things too generally came down from above, consistent with the party-state's aggressive presence in economic decision making. The successful patterns, once test-pointed (*shidian*) and shown to work, would be pushed vigorously across the board (*quanmian tuiguang*), with the decision and initiative coming from upper levels. Then came the "planning" of the other crops to grow, which, again, followed closely tested patterns sanctioned by higher authorities. In Songjiang, for example, double-cropped rice, followed by barley, was pushed across the board between 1965 and 1976 under the slogan "Wipe out single-cropped rice!" (*xiaomie danjidao!*). This was modified in 1976–77, when the leadership adopted the three-thirds cropping system (one-third double-cropped rice, one-third single-cropped rice, and one-third cotton). This kind of approach left no room for cropping choices by the villages and producers themselves (H-II-1, 7, 20).

Within the brigade, power was concentrated in the party branch committee, which normally comprised the branch secretary, the brigade head, the chief accountant, and, for a kind of "affirmative action," the "woman chair" (*funü zhuren*). This group, which the brigade cadres conceptualize as the "overall leadership" (*zonglingdao*), as opposed to "line" work (*tiaoxian gongzuo*) and leaders, met as often as twice a month and made most of the important decisions, including the selection and appointment of the production team heads. Day-to-day decisions on implementation rather than policy were made by the party branch secretary and the brigade head (H-II-21).

There were three main categories of line work and leadership, according to the cadres. Agricultural production made up the "first line," under the leadership of the party branch secretary and the brigade head. Industry and sidelines made up the "second line." The "third line" was led by the secretary of the party youth league, the "woman chair" (who oversaw, among other things, birth control), and the head of the militia (*minbing lianzhang*). Together the leaders of the three lines made up the larger brigade management committee (*dadui guanli weiyuanhui*).

This larger group did not meet nearly so often as the party branch committee. Its role was confined largely to implementing decisions already taken by the smaller "overall leadership." It customarily convened, along with the heads of the teams and their accountants and "woman team leaders" (*funü duizhang*), at the three busiest periods of production: the "double rush" (*shuangqiang*), between July 25 and August 10, that is, the rush to harvest the early rice (*qiangshou*) and the rush to plant the late rice (*qiangzhong*); the "three autumns" (*sanqiu*), from early November to mid-December, the autumn harvest of cotton and late rice (*qiushou*), the autumn planting of rape and wheat (*qiuzhong*), and the autumn payment of taxes (*qiuzheng*); and the "three summers" (*sanxia*), from May 15 to the end of June, the summer harvest of the wheat and rape (*xiashou*), the summer planting of the early rice and cotton (*xiazhong*), and the summer payment of taxes (*xiazheng*). During each of these periods, the larger group typically met three times, chiefly for the purpose of announcing goals and plans and mobilizing the second-tier brigade leaders and the production team leaders to work (H-II-21, H-III-2).

The organizing principle in brigade leadership, as with everything else in party affairs, was that of democratic centralism. That is, to allow as much "democratic" discussion as possible before a decision, but once higher authorities took the decision, to act in centralized unison. Each successive level in the hierarchy, then, mainly played the role of fleshing out, layer by layer, decisions handed down to them.

The party-state's control extended also to the distribution of the product. With collectivization, the team replaced the household as the basic unit of ownership and distribution. Where households had once reaped the rewards to their labor chiefly in the form of an undivided product from the land they farmed, the total product now went first to the collectivized team and was only later divided among the workers by workpoints.

Huayangqiao had a five-grade system of workpoints, pegged to the worker's age and sex, as shown in Table 9.5. These grades were intended to be only rules of thumb; someone who was unusually weak for his or her age could be assigned a lower grade. Among the elderly, particularly, there was so much individual variation in physical condition that my informants refused at first to suggest any correspondences between age and grade. They would point to the example of

TABLE 9.5
Labor Grades and Workpoints for Members
of Huayangqiao's Production Teams by Age and Sex, 1983

			Points	
Age		Labor grade	Males	Females
Males and females				
16		5	6.0	6.0
17		4	7.0	7.0
18		3	8.5	8.5
19		2	9.5	8.5
20		1	10.0	8.5
Males	Females			
61–62	57	2	9.5	8.5
63–64	58	3	8.5	8.5
65	59	4	7.0	7.0
66	60	5	6.0	6.0

SOURCE: H-III-2.
NOTE: All ages are in Chinese sui, which counts from two on the first New Year's after birth. An unusually weak young worker would be assigned a lower grade, and an unusually strong elderly one a higher grade.

seventy-five-year-old Yang Shougen (b. 1910), who was still able to carry a 150-catty load like any young male worker and therefore still earned ten points for each workday. It was only after my repeated pleas for help in dealing with the rigidities of the computer that they provided the rough correspondences between age and work grade shown here.

The workpoint system did not apply to all farmwork. For the rush periods, Huayangqiao turned to a piecework system that provided higher incentives for longer hours and more intense work. Transplanting, for example, was assigned the value of 3.0 workdays (gong) per mu (each equivalent being translated into the person's usual workpoint rate). In harvesting work, single-cropped rice was worth 2.5 workdays per mu, early or late rice (which is lighter than single-cropped rice), 2.0, and wheat 2.5. Other tasks to which a fixed value of workdays was assigned were carrying the rice shoots to the fields for transplanting (*tiaoyang*), transporting the harvested rice (*tiaodao*), and carrying the compost fertilizer (*tiaoxie*). The normal workday ran around six hours, but at these busy times, workers generally put in twelve to eighteen hours a day and thus could earn as much as three times the points they normally got in a single day. During these rush periods, the work recordkeeper (*jigongyuan*) went to the fields, notebook and charts in hand, and kept track of each person's work (H-III-2).

At the end of the year, the team would first deduct the present amounts for the agricultural tax and the "three retains" from the total product before handing out the workers' shares. The computation for the first "retain," seed, was fairly straightforward, based on production plans. The usual allowances were 30 catties for each mu of single-cropped rice, and 40 catties for early rice, wheat, and barley (H-III-20). Feed was figured on the estimated number of pigs per mu of land under grain. At the start of collectivization, the planners put the figure at 0.32 of a pig per mu. In Songjiang county, the figure was raised to 1.57 pigs in 1975–80, then set back to 1.31 in 1981. In Huayangqiao, these state plans translated into a quota of some 250 catties of feed per mu under grain; in terms of population, this anticipated more than one pig a person, but the figure was adjusted down to only one per person in 1983. The feed quotas were paid mainly with the winter barley crop (H-II-21, H-III-1, 8, 9).

The consumption grain was computed according to two state-set scales. One was based on a per capita average pegged to the amount of consumption grain to be retained per cultivated mu under grain. The amount varied from area to area, and over time. In Huayangqiao, the range in the 1950s was 480–520 catties (unhusked) per person. In the early 1980s, the range was increased to 520–86 catties, reflecting the country's improved grain supplies at the time (H-III-20). The second scale, shown in Table 9.6, differentiated among age groups, and ranged from eight catties a month for a one-year-old infant to 67 catties for an adult male worker (twenty years old and up).

Cash distributions were made from the sale of the team's "surplus." Generally, all the surplus was sold to the state at a set price in fulfillment of the team's compulsory-purchase quota. Each house-

TABLE 9.6

Monthly Consumption Grain Allowances in Huayangqiao, 1985

Age	Catties	Age	Catties	Age	Catties
1	8	8	22	15	36
2	10	9	24	16	38[a]
3	12	10	26	17	48
4	14	11	28	18	52[b]
5	16	12	30	19	63[b]
6	18	13	32	20	67[b]
7	20	14	34		

SOURCE: H-III-2.
NOTE: See Table 9.5.
[a]If still in school; a 16-year-old worker got 44 catties.
[b]From age 18 on, the allowance was pegged to the labor grade. 18 = grade 3, 19 = 2, 20 = 1.

hold received a share of the cash income based on its total work-points, less the value of the consumption grain that it received in kind.

Between its managerial and distributive functions, the state left little to chance or to the discretion of the peasants. State procurement quotas continued to be set high. As late as 1984, the goals for Huayangqiao were put at 500 catties per mu of grain under cultivation for consumption grain, 250 catties for feed, and 560 catties for compulsory purchase. The anticipated total yield, which did not include seed, then, was 1,310 catties of grain per mu (H-II-21, H-III-20). Actual yields for the three teams the year before, 1983, amounted to only 1,314 catties per mu. The planners and their agents clearly saw to every last catty.

THE LIMITS OF PARTY-STATE POWER

The party-state's power over the village was never total, to be sure, and a good deal has been written about community resistance (Oi n.d.; Shue 1988). But we should have no illusions about how much latitude over economic decisions a production brigade or team enjoyed under normal circumstances. Cropping decisions were passed down from above. Even if, as occasionally happened, those decisions contradicted village realities, the brigade/team leaders usually had to comply with them. One rather extreme example, from the experience of Shajing in North China, was the attempted switch to late maize in 1976–79. Shajing brigade had been interplanting wheat and maize for decades. But the provincial leaders had apparently gotten the idea that yields would be better if the maize was sown only after the wheat was harvested, and the decision was made to push late maize across the board. The trouble was that the late maize, planted after the wheat harvest in June, did not have time to grow tall enough to withstand the North China plain's torrential rains of July and August. In the first summer of the experiment, 1976, the decision seemed well taken: there was relatively little rain, and yields were high. But even after the customary heavy rains returned the next year, severely damaging the young maize shoots, the policy was continued for another two years. The Shajing peasants, when asked for examples of "bureaucratism" (*guanliao zhuyi*), pointed to this as a case of "giving orders blindly" (*xia zhihui*), which to them was the central meaning of the term "bureaucratism" (Shajing interviews, Nov. 1980).

In Huayangqiao, the 1969 decision for the across-the-board double-cropping of rice (followed by wheat) was no less impractical. The planners simply assumed that the higher the intensity of land use, the better. From their point of view, the larger the total output, the larger the state procurement; neither production costs nor net returns were of any concern. The overintensified agrarian regime was only achieved at the cost of severely diminished marginal returns to factor inputs, especially labor. Once alternative employment for farm labor became possible under the reforms of 1977/78, the three-crops-a-year system no longer made rational sense, and a less-intensive cropping regime of one-half double-cropped rice and one-half single-cropped rice was adopted. In 1985, double-cropped rice was given up completely. In the words of one team leader, with the advantage of hindsight and the encouragement of the climate of reform, "the policy benefited the state but not the peasant."

The planners set the production quotas according to the cropping decisions taken. The decision to double-crop rice across the board, for example, meant higher target yields per mu, which could not be met by single-cropped rice. And cropping choices and production quotas in turn determined just what kind of seeds were to be used, how intensively planting and fertilizing were to be done, and so on. A team head's job was chiefly to see that the planners' decisions were carried out. He had no say in those decisions.

Yet it will not do to imagine push-button, "totalitarian" control, as if peasants were mere automatons. That would be to fall prey to the propagandistic effects intended by the military language of "brigade" and "team." There may not have been much room for individual teams to choose crops or to farm as they liked, but the degree to which they complied with state plans was still very much up to them. Resistance could take the form of laziness or poor performance.*

From the state's point of view, quality compliance could only be secured with the willing cooperation of the peasants, and the key here was the team head. As the Huayangqiao team cadres point out, the team head's chief responsibility was assigning the day's work to each team member. During the regular farming season, this took up about one hour of his time every morning, usually from 6:00 A.M. until 7:00. In the busy seasons, he would have to start earlier, usually by 4:00 A.M., and would need two hours to allocate the work, since there was so much more to be done. At those times, the afternoon's work would also have to be allocated systematically, and the

---

*Shue 1988 spells out well the inadequacies of the old totalitarian model and the reasons for favoring a model that posits a two-way interactive relationship between state and society.

team head would have to do that before lunch at noon. Someone who did not command the respect of the people in his hamlet would have trouble getting them to work, so the state had to take peasant sentiment into careful account in selecting a team head (H-III-4).

For this reason, the brigade cadres routinely consulted with team members on who should be selected or reappointed. As He Yonglong, a key brigade leader since 1978, tells it: whenever there was an opening, the branch party secretary would normally "go down" to the team for a day or two and meet with the influential members of the team (primarily men but always including a woman or two) before the branch committee arrived at a decision, which would then be announced at a meeting of the team members (H-III-4).*

From the point of view of the peasants, the team head was the person who affected their interests most immediately and directly, much more so than a brigade cadre. Incompetent or lazy leadership at this level affected everyone's pocketbook. Peasants thus took seriously their role in the selection of a team head. According to the Huayangqiao villagers, the first and foremost consideration was the person's farming skills and willingness to jump in and lead everyone in work, regardless of his (or rarely her) political qualifications (H-II-13, H-III-4).

Xue Shunquan of Xue Family Village served as the head of the Number One Team for almost the entire period 1961–77 (he was replaced only in 1968–71, when he was sent north to give instruction on rice cultivation), even though he was never a party member. In Xubushanqiao, Yang Xiaofa led his team for 20 years, from 1958 to 1977, not so much because he was a party member, but because he was respected by his constituency for the good worker that he was. Lu Haitang led Xilihangbang for fourteen years, from 1956 through 1968, even though he was not admitted into the party until 1974. His knowledge and skills in farming were so exceptional that he was recruited into the Municipal Agricultural College as an instructor in 1979 (Table 9.4; H-II-13, H-III-4).

Team heads were normally reviewed every two or three years. In the case of both the Xuejiada team (Number One Team, made up of Xue Family Village and He Family Village) and the Xubushanqiao team (Number Two Team), the relative cohesiveness of the commu-

---

*There was always the possibility, to be sure, that an authoritarian brigade branch secretary would impose his will on the branch committee and pick only yes-men. But one should not underestimate the structural constraints against any such attempt, for poor performance by team leaders would reflect immediately on the brigade cadres who chose them.

nities, plus the presence of a respected leader whom everyone could agree on, made for great continuity in leadership. Xue Shunquan's and Yang Xiaofa's long years of service attest to the relatively smooth functioning of the system. Xilihangbang (Number Three Team) enjoyed the same kind of continuity until 1969. But once Lu Haitang departed, no one was able to command the same degree of respect from the villagers, with the result that the leadership turned over regularly.

The Xilihangbang record is instructive. The frequent changes in team leadership after Lu Haitang were due not to arbitrary actions from above, but to internal dissension in the community. As we have seen, this village actually comprised two hamlets that, in the minds of the peasants, were really very nearly separate villages. By the twentieth century, the Gao Family Hamlet (Gaojiada) and the Lu Family Hamlet (Lujiada) no longer crossed over for weddings or funerals. The Lu Family "village," moreover, was itself divided by rather deep animosities between the Middle Hamlet (Zhongda) and the South Hamlet (Nanda). The selection of a team head, therefore, was a difficult and intricate balancing act. As the list of the three key team leaders in Table 9.7 shows, every effort was made to attain some balance in representation between the Lus and the Gaos. If the team head was a Lu, then the deputy head or the accountant, at least, would be a Gao, and vice versa.

TABLE 9.7
Key Leaders of Xilihangbang Team, 1956–84

Start of tenure	Team head	Accountant	Deputy head
1956	Lu Haitang, M[a]	Lu Hailai, M	Gao Laigen, G
1965		Zhang Houxin, G	Gao Yonglin, M
1969	Gao Yonglin, M	Lu Maoyuan, S	
1970			Wei Guoqian[b]
1973	Lu Longshun, S[a]		
1974	Lu Jinquan, S		
1975	Li Peihua, S[a]		
1977	Wei Guoqian[b]		Gao Jinyun, G
1979	Lu Jinquan, S		
1981	Gao Jinyun, G	Lu Jinquan, S	Gao Huojin, G
1982			Gao Jindi, M
1983	Gao Huojin, G		

SOURCE: H-II-19.
    NOTE: G signifies Gao Family Hamlet, M Lu Middle Hamlet, and S Lu South Hamlet.
    [a]Party member (from 1974, for Lu Haitang).
    [b]Outsider; possibly a party member.

So deep were the fissures within Xilihangbang that they led to the unusual appointment of a woman as team head in 1975—the only woman in such a position in Huayangqiao in all those years—as a compromise candidate. Li Peihua was one of the most respected and powerful people in these villages; recruited into the party in 1975, she became the brigade's "woman chair" in 1978 and was thus on its powerful four-member party branch committee. But even so, she had a terrible time as team head. Some of the men on the team, the women say, refused on purpose to cooperate. Li could only get the women to work, and she ended up doing a great deal of the work that others should have done. She lasted only two years as team head and lost much weight in the process. After her, an outsider, Wei Guoqian, who had lived in the village as a "sent-down educated youth" (*xiafang zhishi qingnian*), was appointed team head. Wei had no better success. He had pretty good connections in the Gao Family Hamlet, where he lived, but had trouble getting the Lus out to work. He too lasted only two years (1977–78). Appointments like these, and their rapid failure, tell about the difficulties the state faced in its attempt to merge divided communities into a single collectivity (H-III-4, 33).

Villagers like Xue Shunquan, Yang Xiaofa, and Lu Haitang, who were informal leaders of their communities to begin with, made the best team heads. But for that very reason, they tended to identify at least as much with their home hamlets as with the state. They were subject to the bonds of kinship and community, and could not easily act only as agents of the party-state. At this level, more than at any of the higher ones, the leaders were Janus-faced, at once answerable to external power and internal community ties.

From the Huayangqiao experience, service in one of the key team roles appears to have been a truly thankless position. Where there was an identity of interest between the state and the community, these jobs could be relatively painless. But the moment friction developed between the two, the team leaders would be the first to feel the stress. The tribulations of Yang Xiaofa and He Jinlin (who served as the accountant of Yang's Xubushanqiao team for most of his tenure, 1962–77) speak volumes about the vicissitudes of team leadership. According to them, the worst time they had in their careers as cadres was during the "small four cleans" (*xiao siqing*) movement, which came to Huayangqiao in 1964. County leaders had decided to send out work teams to uncover what was called the "three one-thousands" of cadre corruption in each production team: 1,000 catties of embezzled grain, 1,000 yuan of embezzled funds, and 1,000 unearned workpoints. An officious young woman named Mu, from the Shanghai Normal College, was responsible for Huayangqiao. Determined to fill her assigned quota, she began by gathering information from various team members, and then proceeded to interrogate Yang and He at length. In the end, she "uncovered" a number of "corrupt" acts. The cadres had gone to get their hair cut during work hours: their workpoints should be docked for those hours they took off from work. The cadres had received full credit for time spent at meetings: they should get only half the credit because meetings required less exertion than farmwork; and if the meetings had taken place during off-hours, then none at all. In the end, Mu managed to dig up 30–40 undeserved workdays each for Yang and He (H-II-18).

After this experience, neither Yang nor He wanted to serve any more. As accountant, He was expected to go to the brigade office at the end of the year and pick up a new account book for the coming year. Now he just refused to do so. But the brigade leaders came down and brought him the book, and worked on him to continue. This went on year after year, with the request that he serve just one more year. Meanwhile, Yang had tried to get someone else to take his place, but that man (Yang Xiutang) did not do the job well, and the brigade leaders came down to work on him too (in his words, *shangmian xialai zuo gongzuo*). In this case, they appealed to him in terms of a party member's obligations to serve. Thus he, like He, continued in the job for many more years (H-II-18).

Here we see most plainly the critical differences between team leaders and the higher-level cadres appointed by the state. Yang and He were chosen for their technical know-how and their influence among their constituencies. As team leaders, they still worked alongside the rest of the team most of the time. They remained very much full-fledged members of their communities. Moreover, an illiterate peasant like Yang Xiaofa had little chance of advancement. He remained at his post for fully 20 years.

The relationship between individual team heads and their teams varied from one village to the next. Some heads, no doubt, lorded it over their communities, although we have no examples of that in Huayangqiao. As the cadres point out, organizationally the team was an administrative and not a party unit, so that a team head was not constrained by the party's routinized style of doing things by committees (i.e., "collectively"). Within the scope of his powers, a team head could go his own way without consulting his colleagues.

There was substantial scope for abuse, for the power of a team head like Yang encompassed considerably more than the management of production. He was expected to mediate conflicts that could not be settled within a descent group (such as a dispute between a mother-in-law and a daughter-in-law) but were too small to take up with higher authorities (who had to be brought into any disputes involving personal injury or substantial damage to property). He was also expected to name the deputy head and the accountant, subject only to what was usually pro forma approval from the brigade party branch committee. He pretty much handpicked the other members of his "administration": the "woman team leader," the work recordkeeper (*jigongyuan*), the treasurer (*jingji baoguanyuan*), the grainkeeper (*liangshi baoguanyuan*), and the militia platoon leader (*minbing paizhang*). Not least, as the crucial link between his community and higher authorities, he was generally the one who nominated people for off-farm positions, assignments, or educational opportunities when they came up (H-II-18, H-III-4).

But as Branch Secretary He Yonglong pointed out, even with this power the position of the team head was on the whole more work and worry than it was worth. There was a crucial difference between serving as the leader of an artificial unit like the brigade and being the head of a natural community like the team; the first was often a coveted position, the second a chore that few people wanted. Perhaps for this reason, there appear to have been few complaints from below in Huayangqiao about a team head. When criticisms were made, they usually came from above, as in the "small four cleans" movement. But even then, there were constraints on how far the state would or could go, since team leaders were so hard to replace. In the end, the party had to work to persuade Yang Xiaofa to continue to serve (H-III-4).

THE NEW POLITICAL ECONOMY

There are striking continuities, to be sure, between the imperial and the postrevolutionary politico-economic structures. The centralized imperial state was formed in the first instance by its linkage with a high-density small-peasant economy, the source of both revenues and military recruits. The fully articulated bureaucratic state apparatus, in turn, developed the imperial civil service examination system, which gave rise to a distinctive Chinese gentry elite. Despite periodic shifts of power from state to elite, the centralized state would reassert itself, on the founding of a new dynasty, by strengthening the small-peasant economy against the elite estates. In such a perspective, the postrevolutionary state might be seen as a gigantic reassertion of state power against century-long centrifugal tendencies, and its land reform as a gigantic expansion of the smallholder economy against larger landlord holdings. The postrevolutionary state's claims to total power unchecked by organized interests, moreover, can be seen as bearing a strong resemblance to the imperial institution's intentions to monopolize political power. The analogy could even be pushed to predict centrifugal tendencies involving a shift of power from the centralized state to a new bureaucratic elite.*

But the discontinuities seem to me to be even more striking. The imperial state never achieved the party-state's vertical reach down into the natural village and to the individual household, its declared intentions notwithstanding. We must not confuse the postrevolutionary state, whose cadres extend down to the level of the commune/township, with an imperial state whose bureaucracy reached only the county seat. Even more important, we must not equate the Communist Party, which had 17,000,000 members by 1961 and party branches in every administrative village, with an imperial gentry of a mere 1,100,000 members in the middle of the nineteenth century (Schurmann 1968: 129; Chang 1955).

Perhaps most important of all, the horizontal scope of the new party-state is qualitatively different from that of the imperial state in both theory and practice. The imperial state was concerned chiefly with taxation and order, expressed institutionally by the lijia and baojia systems. To be sure, the state intervened in the economy to an exceptional degree for premodern states. The emperor performed symbolic rites and, on occasion, even gave instructions on farming. To that extent, the imperial state expressed its concern over the rural economy. It also maintained a monopoly over salt and iron and sought to keep a lid on grain prices. But the imperial state never arrogated to itself the power, even in theory, to control directly the exchange of such staples of peasant life as cloth and grain, to plan for and manage directly all sectors of the economy, or to make decisions for every peasant household on what to grow and how to grow it. To the extent that the new state had to take into account the realities within peasant communities, its power was less than total. But in the long perspective the big story that jumps out at us is the replacement of a let-live small-peasant economy by a planned economy and, with that change, the transformation of a relatively nonintrusive

---

*Shue 1988: chap. 3 argues at length the analogy between the imperial gentry and the cadres of the present day.

imperial state into a party-state that not only reached down to the individual household but took over its powers of economic decision making.

Orthodox Marxist theory urges us to focus on social relations in thinking about the nature of the state. The official Chinese view, therefore, portrays the imperial state as the organized agency of the "landlord ruling class." Land reform supposedly brought an end to landlordism and the "feudal" relations of production that underlay the imperial state; and the collectivization that followed put an end to "petty bourgeois" private property and the exploitation of one class by another, thereby ushering in "socialism" and a state that represents the interests of the laboring classes.

In historical hindsight, we can see that those changes in social and property relations, sweeping as they were, do not tell the full story of the crucial changes that have taken place in state-society power relations. Land reform in itself does not tell about the extension of state power down to the level of the administrative village, just as collectivization does not tell about its further extension inside the natural village to the household. Those vertical extensions of state power can only be understood through the distinctive characteristics of the Communist party-state.*

More important, the state's intervention into the realm of property relations does not necessarily imply the dramatic horizontal expansion of state power that has taken place. After all, peasant owner-cultivators—and hamlet collectives—could be left to make economic decisions on their own. The crucial vehicle for this horizontal expansion was not the state's intrusion into social relations so much as its aggressive intervention in the economic realm, first to control commerce, and then to take economic decision making out of the hands of individual peasant households. Those interventions are not adequately conveyed by the word "socialism"; they need to be understood in terms of a planned and controlled economy.

The interventions have some premodern roots, to be sure. To the extent that the postrevolutionary Chinese state still perceives the peasant and the agrarian economy as above all a source of tax reve-

*Here I agree in emphasis with Andrew Walder's (1986) analysis of the relationship between the Leninist state and the factory worker. But there is a major difference between the shop floor and the village: the "clientelism" model for analyzing party relations with atomized factory workers seems to me to require major qualification when applied to the natural village/hamlet, where the team head is so often an uncle, cousin, or nephew of his constituents. The role that kinship ties played in shaping state-peasant relations in Huayangqiao is shown by the vicissitudes of team leadership in Xilihangbang.

nue and military recruits, it most certainly resembles the old agrarian state. The countryside remains the source of surplus for feeding the nonfarm population. But the scale of the extraction has dwarfed any by the imperial and Republican states: though the proportion of agricultural output extracted by direct agricultural tax is probably comparable, the proportion extracted by compulsory purchase vastly exceeds any amount contemplated earlier. Total state procurement took a whopping 27.6 percent of grain output in 1953–57, as has been seen. More important, the party-state's intervention into the rural economy has gone far beyond the mere appropriation of the surplus, characteristic of the premodern agrarian state, to include management and distribution.

In the multiple relationships among the triangular configuration of state, elite, and peasant, the most important set for imperial China was that between elite and peasant. The state's role in society paled in comparison with the all-pervasive influence of the elites. With the great expansion in the scope of the state's powers in postrevolutionary China, however, the crucial relationship has shifted to that between the state and the peasant. Today's elite is far more dependent on the state apparatus than the gentry of old. We will need to take greater account of the role of the state in our analysis of postrevolutionary China than we did for imperial China.

CHANGES AFTER 1978

Reforms have brought a substantial contraction in the role of the team heads in Huayangqiao, and hence in the vertical and horizontal reaches of the party-state. The process began with the party's call in December 1978, after the third plenary session of the Eleventh Central Committee, for lowering the age and raising the educational level of team leaders. The result, in Huayangqiao, was an across-the-board replacement of the longtime team heads. In Xubushanqiao, Yang Xiaofa (b. 1931) stepped down in favor of the next generation: first Wu Mingchang (b. 1950) in 1978, next Yang Xiaofa's son Yinlong (b. 1960) in 1980, then Wu Mingchang again in 1982, followed by He Guohua (b. 1960) in 1983. The same pattern obtained in Xuejiada, where Xue Shunquan stepped down after seventeen years. In Xilihangbang, younger men also came to the fore, though the contrast with the earlier years was less sharp because the heterogeneity of this team had already led to the appointment of a young woman and a sent-down youth.

The frequent turnover in leadership in Xuejiada and Xubushanqiao, four times in the six years between 1978 and 1985 (Table 9.4), stands in sharp contrast to the earlier continuity. As it turned out, the younger men seldom made good leaders. According to Yang Xiaofa, he chose Wu Mingchang because "Mingchang knew about farming, and also seemed serious and responsible." Yang had already made him his deputy leader back in 1974. But, as team leader, Yang says, Wu Mingchang turned out to be selfish and unable to command the respect of the other members of the team. So he was replaced by Yang Yinlong in 1980. But how could a mere twenty-year-old do the job? Well, says He Yonglong, the brigade branch secretary responsible for the appointment, "He's an enthusiastic worker. Besides, his father could help him out." The same logic applied in the choice of Yang Guiming as the accountant in 1982: Guiming's father, Xingcai, was the only villager outside of He Jinlin who was educated and could do the bookwork. So Secretary He chose Guiming to comply with orders from above for younger leadership, with the thought that his father would help him out in the job.

These proxies for the old team leaders clearly did not work out too well. Yang Yinlong and Yang Guiming were both replaced in 1982. Wu Mingchang, who had admitted his errors, was asked to serve again as team leader, while Yang Yinlong, now twenty-two, who was still not really knowledgeable about farming but educated enough to learn to keep the books, was asked to serve as accountant. Once again, the arrangement was not to last. This time it was because Wu Mingchang, who was especially skilled at rabbit raising, a household sideline that was sweeping the Yangzi delta at the time, was recruited as a brigade cadre in charge of sideline production.

The entire system of collectivized farming was undergoing fundamental change by this time. In the fall of 1982, in a system called "linking output [targets] to the household" (*lianchan daohu;* also called "linking production contracts to output" or *lianchan chengbao*), responsibility for maintaining all fields planted in dry crops was turned over to individual households. The following year, rice was included as well.* The individual plots were assigned by lot. Each came with a specific output target and had a certain value in ten-point workday equivalents, depending on the crop: 30 per mu for

---

*The transition to the individualized farming of rice was particularly difficult because of the tremendous time pressures surrounding the late July/early August rush in harvesting early rice and planting late rice. The rice also had to be husked under extreme pressure, for rain would quickly rot the unhusked grain. Before, rice husking had been done around-the-clock and coordinated by the collective. Under the household-responsibility system, the harvesting, husking, and planting schedules all became much harder to coordinate.

early rice, wheat, and barley, 35 for late rice, 80 for cotton, and so on. At the end of the year, the responsible household was paid the cash value of its total workpoints. Those who exceeded the production quota for their plots received a 50 percent bonus on the surplus; those that were below quota paid a 50 percent penalty on the deficit (H-III-20).

In 1985 a new system called "contracting production to the household" (baogan daohu) or the "big contracting of production" (dabaogan) was put into effect. Output targets and bonuses and penalties were done away with, and a household now contracted for plots based on the number of mouths to feed and its available labor supply. In theory, households retained most of the produce from their "responsibility field" (zeren tian), to do with as they pleased. In practice, there were still specified obligations. The agricultural tax, of course, remained. Compulsory purchase was abandoned in 1985 and 1986, but this owed not so much to a desire to leave more to individual household choice as to a glut in state grain and cotton supplies from several successive years of bumper harvests. That glut soon disappeared, and compulsory sales returned with shortages in 1987–88, though they were now euphemistically termed "contracts." Huayangqiao's obligations for compulsory sales to the state, which had fallen from 500 catties per mu to 100 catties in 1985–87, climbed back up to 300 catties (H-III-22, H-IV-4).

Plainly, neither system should be mistaken for free-market family farming. In Huayangqiao, cropping choices, though ostensibly left to the households, were in fact still very much passed down from above. For one thing, tractor plowing, electrified irrigation, and spray application of insecticide still had to be done at coordinated times for the different plots and were therefore placed under brigade-organized teams. For another thing, in Huayangqiao the first step toward de-involution in rice cultivation had already come under collective leadership in 1977–78, with the retreat from two crops of rice to one. Further adjustments came in subsequent years, still under collective planning, to the point where high-labor and low-return double-cropped rice and cotton had been almost completely done away with by 1987. But in 1988, with national shortages developing in both crops, the party-state ordered the peasants to begin growing cotton again (H-IV-1).

In Shajing, the scope for household choice was even more limited. Household responsibility was not introduced until 1985 and remained in effect for only two years. In 1987–88, Shunyi county became a testing ground for recombining household plots into larger units. Shajing was formed into a 435-mu collective farm, under the direction of a farm manager (*changzhang*), who took orders on what to grow directly from the township above and was rewarded or penalized depending on whether "his" eighteen farmworkers met the designated output targets. The new system is reminiscent of the old production team organization. Even the 10:8 ratio of rewards to male and female farmworkers returned, in substance if not in name (Shajing interviews, June 28, 1988).

It is clear that the Huayangqiao and Shajing "semi-collective" patterns are not unique to villages near major metropolises. Putterman (1989), for example, reports that in relatively remote Dahe commune in Huailu county in Hebei province, plowing and planting also continued to be performed by service teams (for a fixed fee, in this case), and the cadres continued to instruct farm households on the specifics of crop production.

Still, in some areas of the country, the reforms brought considerable scope for individual household choice, certainly greater scope than in Shajing. In Zengbu brigade in Guangdong, the state went on in 1985 to allow peasants to work their allotted land for a period of fifteen years, instead of the annual rotation system adopted in Huayangqiao. The state also allowed the peasants to meet the compulsory rice purchase quotas in cash, or even by purchases on the market. And collective tractors and threshing machines were sold outright to individual peasants (Potter and Potter, n.d.).

At the time of this writing, official Chinese sources do not permit fine distinctions among different forms and degrees of household responsibility. The 1984 *Statistical Yearbook* shows simply that 94.2 percent of all households were under the "big responsibility for production" system by the end of 1983 (*Tongji nianjian*, 1984: 131). We must await more field research before attempting even to guess how the program works in different parts of the country. For now, we can do no more than note the different degrees of household responsibility and maintain a healthy skepticism toward equating the development with free-market family farming.

Nevertheless, so far as state-peasant relations are concerned, the reforms plainly reduced the duties and powers of the team head, even in Huayangqiao. Unlike their predecessors, the new team heads there were not called on to coordinate and hand out work assignments: each household now maintained its own field, and plowing, irrigation, and insecticide application were the responsibility of the brigade. One interesting result is that a person did not have to be all that good in farmwork to become a team head. Wu Mingching's replacement, He Guohua, for example, attained the position because he had been identified by the brigade party organization as a "target of cultivation" (*peiyang duixiang*). He had shown leadership qualities as the secretary of the brigade's Youth League and was being groomed for higher position. As Secretary He explained, under the reforms, all the team head had to do in the domain of farmwork was to transmit the orders from above.

The younger leaders also bore a different relationship to their communities and to the party-state. Unlike their fathers and uncles before them, they were educated and could look forward to a career higher up in the hierarchy. The massive opening up of off-farm employment opportunities in the late 1970s to "the best and brightest" of the countryfolk stirred the young to dream of breaking out of the confines and drudgery of village life. Consequently, team leadership came to be seen as an opportunity for advancement rather than an unwanted chore for the committed. Yang Xiaofa had grown up under the old system and rose up to team leadership through revolutionary mobilization. As a former poor peasant, he was deeply committed to the party, but as an illiterate, he had no chance of moving up in the party-state hierarchy. The young men of the 1980s were of a different breed altogether. They did not have the same faith in either the revolution or the party as their elders. And they had sufficient schooling to aspire to something more than the life of a peasant. The apprenticeship of the party's "target of cultivation," He Guohua, lasted only a year. And Yang Guiming just wanted to get out of the village. Since he had not been able to do so through the examination route, he hoped to move up and out as a cadre (H-III-4).

To the peasants of Huayangqiao, the party-state could only seem to shrink in stature when its on-site agent changed from a middle-aged longtime leader like Yang Xiaofa to short-term young leaders like Wu Mingchang and Yang Yinlong. And organized authority could only seem to recede when the team head's powers dwindled from telling everyone what to do on a daily basis to mere record-keeping and transmitting messages from above. Nevertheless, the planned and collective economy persists to a considerable degree in agriculture in Huayangqiao. And if the Shunyi experiment foreshadows changes to come, the Chinese peasant might yet witness the return of something more like the old politico-economic system.

CHAPTER 10

Collective, Family, and
Sideline Production

Though of much-diminished importance, the family production unit persisted through the collectivized years in various kinds of sidelines. A comparison of the coexisting family and collective forms of labor organization not only allows us to take a close look at some of their shared and contrasting characteristics, but furthers our understanding of the dramatic return of the family production unit to farming.

PROPENSITY TO INVOLUTE

The collective farm was in some respects a mere enlargement of the old family farm. The production team grouped together a number of family farms (30 households on average in 1982; *Zhongguo tongji nianjian* 1983: 147) to form a single ownership unit.* Like the family farm, it was at once a unit of consumption and a unit of production. A large part of its grain went to meet the consumption needs of its members. Decision making for the collective was thus similarly shaped by considerations of consumption as well as of production.

Like the family farm, the collective could tolerate much lower marginal returns to labor than a capitalist enterprise. Indeed, under subsistence pressures and given abundant labor, the collective could be made to put in labor until, logically, its marginal product approached zero. The marginal costs of labor would not be a consideration since, for the collective as for the family farm, the quantity of labor was a given and not something hired on a free market as profit

---

*The collective was quite clearly different from state farms and state industrial enterprises in this respect. The latter are in theory owned "by the whole people"; their workers are paid a nationally standardized wage. The collective (production team) formed an individual accounting unit whose net income was apportioned to the workers regardless of the income of other collectives or state enterprises.

maximizing decreed. A collective, like a family farm, could not fire its surplus labor.

I suggested in *The Peasant Economy and Social Change in North China* that perhaps one-third of the labor in the prerevolutionary family-farm economy of the North China plain (Hebei and northwest Shandong) was surplus, relative to the more nearly optimal organization of labor along capitalist lines on the managerial farms that occupied about 10 percent of the cultivated area. This means that, all things being equal, the imposition of a capitalist form of labor organization there would have left a third of the peasant labor unemployed. From this perspective, the collective form of labor organization was consistent with the revolutionary program of guaranteeing subsistence to everyone. It would provide employment for all, even at the cost of relative inefficiency and underemployment. It would not tolerate the unemployment of some, even if that meant the more efficient use of the labor of others. Given such a form of labor organization, a collective's surplus labor in fact had a near-zero opportunity cost. It therefore made perfectly good economic sense to continue to put in labor so long as its marginal product remained more than zero.

This involutionary propensity was reinforced by yet another characteristic of the collective. From the planners' point of view, what mattered was the absolute level of output, to which state quotas for tax and compulsory purchase were pegged. The higher the output, the larger the state's take. Overzealous planners, therefore, pushed the collective to maximize output regardless of its members' welfare. In a later chapter, we will look at some specific instances of state-imposed involution.

Members of collectives, for their part, tended to be tolerant of state-imposed involution. They were paid according to the cash value of their accumulated workpoints, which were arrived at by dividing the collective's total net product by the combined workpoints of all the members. Their incomes, therefore, were pegged to the average product of their labor input and not to its marginal product.

LABOR CALCULATIONS

On family farms, labor could not easily be broken down into units—the men worked with the ebb and flow of the seasons, and women and children helped when needed. The labor of the entire family for the year formed something of an organic whole, rewarded by the year's total harvests. That kind of productive organization did not lend itself to a capitalist accounting of unit labor costs and unit labor returns. The collective was similar to the family farm in the sense that the reward for the labor of all the members was the total harvest minus taxes and expenses. But the resemblance ends there, for that labor was calculated and remunerated in workpoints. Member households were paid a share of the collective product according to their total labor contribution, not simply in the form of the harvested product of the family farm.

This system dramatically changed things for peasant women. As we have seen, in both North China and the Yangzi delta, women had served mainly as auxiliary farm labor, to be drawn on to differing degrees depending on need. Even in the Yangzi delta, where farm production was comparatively more familized, women were far from being involved full time in agriculture month in and month out. The coming of the collective workpoint system brought women fully into production and remunerated them according to their labor (although payment was made in practice to the head of the household). Most of the older women of Huayangqiao trace this change back to the mutual-aid teams and early-stage collectives of the early to mid-1950s: from that time on, "if you did not go out to work, you did not get paid" (H-III-10).* In North China, where women had done relatively little farmwork, this meant a virtual doubling of the farm labor force. Even in the Yangzi delta, it amounted to a dramatic increase in the labor pool. This led, as will be seen in the next chapter, to great spurts of labor intensification in agriculture during the late 1950s and the 1960s.

Women were not remunerated at the same rate as men, to be sure. In Huayangqiao, they earned at most 8.5 points per workday, compared with the men's 10.0, as has been seen. This gender distinction extended to the work assignments: in Huayangqiao, for example, cotton cultivation became strictly women's work. Only plowing, the heaviest part of the work, was done by men—and that by machine under contract with the brigade. The chief responsibility of the "woman team leader" (*funü duizhang*), in fact, became cotton cultivation. As women's work, it was lower paid than grain cultivation.

Feminists have pointed out the inequities in the treatment of men and women under the collectives. At rice transplanting time, peasant women say, the men often just sat around after they did the

*But the Xubushanqiao women remember that even before that they had shouldered more farmwork, because land reform gave most of the households in the village additional land (H-III-14).

"heavy work" of carrying out one load of shoots, on which the women then spent half a day transplanting. At husking and milling time, similarly, the men only hauled out the machine, leaving it to the women to do the work for the rest of the day. Such divisions of labor were ostensibly based on physical strength requirements. But the argument falls flat when we note how the electric pump station operator, who had only to switch the power on and off, sat around puffing on cigarettes, while the women charged with directing the flow of the water sloshed around to move wet earth (see also Wolf 1985: chap. 4); or how, when insecticide was being applied, the lone male operator of the electric pump sat in leisure while a dozen or so women dragged around a heavy rubber hose and braved the harmful effects of the spray. In those situations, gender differentiation based ostensibly on strength was joined by the still less defensible argument of technical know-how.

Nevertheless, in historical perspective, we need to keep in sight two facts: women were much more involved in production under the collectives than in the family-farm economy; and they were rewarded for their work. There was stratification by gender, to be sure, and reality remained far from the revolutionary ideal of complete equality between the sexes, but that needs to be seen in conjunction with the social effects of women's complete involvement in production.

Although payment was still made to the head of the household, a family could not overlook, for example, the additional workpoints of a sixteen-year-old daughter newly entered into production. This principle of separate remuneration for male and female workers alike should not be underestimated. In 1985, young women who worked in the rural industries of Huayangqiao began to be paid a regular cash wage directly, where before, as in farming, they had accumulated workpoints. That gave them financial independence comparable to that of their urban counterparts. But the change was barely noticed, because of the already long-standing practice of crediting each woman for her labor.

Moreover, female labor was generally valued more highly under the collective than it had been under the family farm. In Huayangqiao, the women had traditionally helped with farmwork and done the household handicrafts almost imperceptibly, without the family's consciousness of the costs of their labor. The collective, however, had to pay for such labor in regular workpoints. That is why, during the collectivized years, a number of low-return, spare-time or auxiliary jobs continued to be done by individual households rather than the collective. From the collective's point of view, family labor was cheaper.

SIDELINES UNDER THE COLLECTIVES

Family production persisted chiefly in what was called *jiating fuye* (household sideline production).* It was an apt term, for it conveyed immediately the central logic of such production: it was subsidiary to the main work, farming, and was generally based on spare-time labor and spare materials from farming.

The Private Plot

A major and obvious form of sideline production was the private plot, used chiefly by families to grow their own vegetables and, sometimes, also for "nickel-and-dime" sales on the free market. Vegetable growing is relatively labor intensive in much the same way that gardening is: it requires countless small tasks and continual care. A small vegetable plot near the home, on which one could grow several crops of different vegetables in succession, was therefore especially well suited to spare-time cultivation. The man might fertilize the plot some mornings before joining the production team for the day's work, and irrigate or weed during the midday break or after work in the early evening, while his wife was preparing the meal. On occasion, the children and the old and retired can be mobilized to weed and to pluck. For planting, the only time when labor demands are considerable, the family might work as a unit, calling on all available hands, the incentive being the product to be harvested, just as in the prerevolutionary family farm.

The one time in all the collectivized years when the private plots were done away with in Huayangqiao was during the Great Leap. In the attempt to turn the countryside into factory-like production units, all private plots were transferred to the commune, and a special brigade was created to grow vegetables for all the households.

---

*The term "sidelines" (*fuye*) has two different usages in Chinese. Local statisticians at the county, commune, and brigade levels include under sidelines all production outside of crop production (*nongye*, or "agriculture" in the narrow sense) and industry (*gongye*). Household cultivation of private plots and pig keeping, in addition to household handicrafts, are included, as are collective operations like dairies, forest products, and fish ponds. This is the sense in which I am using the term here. The State Statistical Bureau, on the other hand, defines sidelines more narrowly, excluding from it animal husbandry, forestry, and fishery.

But the new enterprise quickly ran into difficulties in organizing labor, and in storing, transporting, and supplying the vegetables. The
brigade was terminated, and the private plots restored within three
years, by 1962. Thereafter, most vegetables for rural consumption
were home-produced. There was one exception in Huayangqiao. In
1966, the team leaders of Xubushanqiao formed a special vegetable
team of six elderly and exceptionally skilled peasants to grow vegetables for a profit. It turned out to be a viable way to use elderly
labor, and the team was able to turn a profit regularly, for nearly
20 years. In 1984, the team members decided to disband as the gap
between state-purchase prices and free-market prices widened, and
began producing vegetables for the market on their own. In Huayangqiao, the average size of a household plot was 0.15 mu after the
readjustments of 1962 (compared with 0.05–0.08 mu in the years
before the Leap), and then 0.12 mu after 1979. These plots were not
challenged even during the Cultural Revolution years (H-III-23, 26).

Surplus from the private plots was sold on the "free," periodic
markets (jishi). In Huayang town, vegetables led all commodities in
1982–84, accounting for 20 percent of the total volume of trade.
(Other major items were fish at ca. 17 percent and poultry and eggs,
10 percent). A typical private seller might gross ten yuan at one such
periodic gathering, which usually began by 4:30 A.M. and broke up at
seven or eight. These free markets accounted for a total of perhaps
5 percent of all commodity sales,* and helped fill in the cracks in the
state supply system. As prices for vegetables in the free markets
rose, the activity became increasingly profitable. Huayangqiao peasants interviewed in 1985 and 1988 said they were able to net 200 yuan
a year from this spare-time activity; this compares with 400 yuan a
year for those who had worked full time on Xubushanqiao's collective vegetable team until 1984 (H-III-26, H-IV-1).

Where collectivized production triumphed over the family production unit in Huayangqiao was in more highly specialized and
capitalized sidelines. In most areas of the Yangzi delta, the capital
accumulation under collectives continued to be favored over capitalistic accumulation under "specialized households" (zhuanyehu)
in the reformist 1980s. The policy makers justified the choice in
terms of socialist ideals of equity: the "southern Jiangsu model"
stood for the path of "getting rich together" (gongtong zhifu; Tao
Youzhi 1988).

* This figure, from Zhang Yulin and Shen Guanbao 1984, is for the Zhenze area, in
nearby Wujiang county.

The commune-operated pear orchard is one example of a collective sideline. Begun in 1958, it survived a disastrous flood in 1962 and was able to turn a profit by 1964. By the 1980s, this collective sideline employed eighteen workers on its 70 mu of land. It grossed 80,000–90,000 yuan a year, with a net profit of 3,000–6,000 yuan. It managed to weather the movement toward agricultural "de-collectivization" (H-III-23).

Another collective sideline activity in Huayang commune was mushroom growing—specifically, straw mushrooms, for which there was considerable export demand. The optimal scale is apparently a hothouse of three rooms totaling about 2,000 square feet. In the most labor-intensive stage, 30,000 catties of compost fertilizer and 10,000 of (wheat) straw must be applied in one day. It takes about twelve workers to do the job, and is not something that can be done by a single household. Mushroom growing began here in 1971 and went through several volatile swings: the total area devoted to the enterprise reached 160,000 square feet in 1973, dwindled to a mere 20,000 feet in 1978, and then jumped up massively in the next few years, to stand at 230,000 feet in 1983 (H-III-23).

Other examples of collective sideline enterprises are the Xilihang-bang team's fifteen-mu nursery for decorative saplings, begun in 1980, and the brigade's more recent (1984) twelve-mu flower nursery and 50-mu fish pond. Instituted in the middle of the "de-collectivization" of agriculture, these enterprises attest to the persistence and efficacy of collective organization in the Yangzi delta for larger-scale and more-capital-intensive sideline production. But it is also clear that family production was more economical than collective production when it came to vegetable growing for home consumption and for peddling on the free market.

Hogs

Substantially the same logic applied to the raising of hogs. The Huayangqiao households fattened their animals in part on feed processed by collective stores from the brigade's barley crop and in part on their own side products, especially the chaff from their stock of consumption grain (which was distributed unhusked), augmented by a "coarse feed" (*cu siliao*) of ground-up rice straw and grass. Most of the work was done in the spare time before or after meals.

During the Great Leap, all hog raising was concentrated under a single, commune-operated "factory." More than 300 makeshift mud pens were built for the "factory," each housing seven or eight animals. One problem immediately cropped up: the commune did not have access to the chaff from household consumption grain for feed. It tried burning cow dung for feed, but that did not work. Similarly, the commune could no longer rely on spare-time household labor for its compost, made by repeatedly adding grass to pig manure. The hog "factory" on its own was not able to generate more than minimal amounts of the organic fertilizer so vital to agriculture in this area. The makeshift pens finally collapsed under rain (and some pigs even ran off, or so the story goes). The entire misguided enterprise was given up within two years (H-III-23).

Thereafter, the collectives undertook only specialized hog raising: studs were raised by the commune, sows by the brigades. Locally, the commune's large stud farm had more than 90 animals by 1985. Each sired some 20 male offspring a year, and about 40 percent of these were of sufficiently high quality to be sold or raised as studs. The rest were used for meat. Huayangqiao brigade also had some success in its sow-raising enterprise. In 1985, it maintained 40 sows, which farrowed at least 600 piglets a year—enough to meet the assigned quota of one pig per person. As for the common pig, the chief source of meat for the Chinese people and the chief source of organic fertilizer for Chinese agriculture, once the Leap was over, they were once again entrusted entirely to the household (H-II-6, H-III-23).

Throughout the collectivized years, the state's approach was to set prices for pork so low that, even with the use of cheap spare-time household labor for maintenance and of household leftovers for feed, pig raising did not pay, as the Huayangqiao peasants were quick to point out. A piglet cost 30 yuan in 1984. It required three catties of processed feed a day, for four to five months, or a total of 360 to 450 catties of feed; this item had to be purchased at a cost of 0.14 yuan per catty, for a total of 50 to 63 yuan. On top of this, the young animal consumed about 200 to 300 catties of chaff, worth 16 to 20 yuan, and 200 to 300 catties of coarse feed, costing 7 to 9 yuan for processing. So if the piglet was fed for four months, it cost the household a total of 103 yuan, and the figure could rise as high as 122 yuan if the animal was fed for a full five months. Since the average four-month-old pig weighs about 150 catties, and the state's purchase price was 68 yuan per 100 catties, the animal typically brought only 102 yuan. Most peasants, therefore, did not even break even, let alone make a profit. From their point of view, pig raising only made sense for the compost it produced. But that was a rather indirect incentive during the collectivized years, since the collective took responsibility for the supply and application of fertilizer. That is why, with one exception, the peasants I interviewed spoke of hog raising as an unwanted burden imposed by the state (H-II-6).*

Nevertheless, in the three and a half decades after 1949, the state managed to increase the number of hogs raised in Huayangqiao from an average of one per household to one per person (MT, Shanhai 1940: table 8; H-III-1). Nationwide, in roughly the same period, the number of hogs more than quintupled, from 58,000,000 to 301,000,000 (Liu and Zhang 1981: 105). The state achieved these results by administrative fiat and in the cheapest way possible from its point of view—by drawing on household sideline products and spare-time household labor, rather than relying on commercial feed and remunerated full-time labor.

Where the collective prevailed over the family production unit was in raising dairy cows, which requires greater capitalization, and, for the Chinese peasants, rarer skills. The peasants of Huayang commune had made numerous attempts to raise milk cows, both collectively and individually. During the Great Leap, the commune invested in a herd of 24 dairy cows and even paid 3,000 yuan for a special Dutch breed. But the project never got off the ground. In late 1963, the herd contracted a disease, apparently from rotten potatoes, and almost all the animals died. The eleven calves that survived were sold to the "factory" workers. It was only in 1976 that the effort took off, after the leadership gave proper recognition to Shen Xuetang, who was particularly knowledgeable about cows. By 1985, thanks to Shen's technical know-how, the commune dairy had expanded to more than 200 cows, each producing upwards of 50 catties of milk a day, and was supplying nearby Songjiang. It employed 40 workers, grossed 1,000,000 yuan a year, and brought in a net of 120,000 yuan. Almost a showcase success story, this collective enterprise provides a sharp contrast to low-return individualized hog raising (H-III-23).

Household Handicrafts

Some household handicrafts managed to survive collectivization. Cotton spinning and weaving, the traditional household sidelines, virtually disappeared in the 1950s because of the state's imposition

---

*The lone dissenter among the nine Huayangqiao peasants who discussed this subject (H-I-7, H-II-6, H-III-1, 8) was Wu Renyu, who is apparently especially skilled in raising pigs. He boasts of being able to get his pigs up to 200 catties in four months. The key to lucrative pig raising, Wu observed proudly and somewhat mysteriously, lies in the proper intermixing of fine and coarse feed, and in a precise grasp of mating times for the sows. But this was clearly a fund of specialized knowledge that few other peasants shared.

of compulsory-purchase quotas on cotton and the rapid development of state-operated, modern textile factories. In Huayangqiao,
rope making and straw-basket weaving took their place.

There had been only a limited straw-products industry here before
the Revolution. Straw-shoe making, still quite prevalent at the time
of the Japanese investigations, had already seen its day by 1949, as
peasants turned increasingly to rubber shoes. All that remained was
a small industry in straw-rope making: a household, for a long day's
work, could turn out perhaps ten catties of straw rope by hand,
worth a meager 0.75 yuan.

Collectivization, paradoxically, injected new life into this household industry. The collective could purchase machines that had
been beyond the reach of the individual household. With the hand-
turned straw-rope-making machine (yaoshengji) and the foot-pedaled
straw-basket-weaving machine, a family could take 100 catties of
straw and, in two long days of work in which the man and the
woman operated as a team on the machines and the children put the
buckles on the baskets, turn out 70 catties of rope and 30 baskets. At
0.08 yuan per catty of rope and 0.35 yuan per straw basket (of average
quality), the total product was worth about 16 yuan. This was almost all net income, if we do not count the cost of the machines,
for as a by-product of rice, the straw was very cheap—1.20 yuan per
100 catties (H-III-16).

The Xubushanqiao team acquired five sets of these machines in
the early days of collectivization. Though it had the option of setting
up a workshop-type production unit, with all the machines and the
workers concentrated in a single location, the team decided in the
end to adopt a household piecework system, which was cheaper in
terms of labor costs from the point of view of the collective and the
state. The state-assigned quota of 300 baskets a year was shared out
to the team's member households along with the straw, and the payment rate was set at six ten-point workday equivalents (gong) for
every 30 baskets. As the peasant women point out, 30 baskets actually required substantially more labor than this allowed. The norm
for the farm workday was six hours, and collective workpoints were
computed accordingly, but basket making typically took two twelve-
hour days of very intense work, about the same as agricultural work
during the busiest times of transplanting and harvesting (for which
the peasants generally received credit for at least two workday equivalents). The labor of the man and the woman alone, therefore, should
have been worth at least seven workday equivalents; the auxiliary
labor of the children, who helped with the light chores, did not fig-

ure in at all. By the piecework system, therefore, the state and the collective made a considerable savings in labor costs.

Still, the state-set prices on these straw goods were relatively generous. The average cash value of a ten-point workday equivalent was just about one yuan in Xubushanqiao during most of the collectivized years (see Table 11.4); straw handicrafts brought in about 1.50 yuan per worker for a day's work. In addition, since the state-assigned quota was set well below the village's productive capacity, and the demand of the state stores was higher than the assigned quotas, the peasants were able to augment their collective incomes by private handicraft production. According to them, each household netted about 200 yuan a year from this source—for about a month's intensive work (H-III-16).

Two changes in the mid-1960s sent the straw industry into decline. First, as national economic development proceeded, other kinds of materials for rope and baskets became available, and consumer demand for the straw products dwindled. The state stores curtailed their purchases accordingly. And second, a supply problem developed when single-cropped rice was practically terminated under the state's aggressive push for double-cropping. Double-cropped rice, the peasants say, does not produce straw of comparable texture and usefulness. The result was that straw-basket production in Songjiang county dropped from a high of 12,000,000 baskets in 1957 and 17,000,000 in 1964 to fewer than 1,000,000 in 1971. (The industry recovered somewhat, but never came close to achieving the 1950s and 1960s levels; the 1979 output was still only around 5,000,000; H-III-16, 23.)

Thereafter, all that was left of the old tradition of household handicrafts was women's spare-time crocheting and knitting under contract to collective or state enterprises in search of cheap labor. This kind of work came to Huayang in the late 1960s and at first was mainly confined to the women residing in town. It consisted chiefly of crocheting lace for the Shanghai Industrial Arts Import-Export Company, which farmed out the work to the commune, which in turn let out the work to individual pieceworkers. A woman who spent all available spare moments on it could average one yuan a day. This was incentive enough at the time to induce 2,000 women in the commune to take up the work (Table 10.1). But as new small industries began to spring up in the town in the late 1970s, bringing increased employment opportunities, the town women were no longer willing to do the work. The village women came to do most of it (along with some knitting of hats and mats, for a time). A good

TABLE 10.1
Crocheting in Huayang Commune and the Huayangqiao Brigade, 1968–85

| | Huayang commune | | Huayangqiao brigade | |
Year	Number of workers	Value of output (yuan)	Number of workers	Value of output (yuan)
1968	1,000	53,900		
1969	1,300	85,773		
1970	1,450	72,834		
1971	1,030	49,587		
1972	1,200	73,316		
1973	1,400	87,789		
1974	2,300	108,231		
1975	2,000	81,328		
1976	2,700	213,124		
1977	2,900	257,175		
1978	2,100	92,606	80	5,500
1979	3,000	215,495	90	7,100
1980	3,400	321,923	90	7,600
1981	4,600	693,229	93	9,300
1982	6,100	811,722	93	11,200
1983	6,000	339,418	60	5,100
1984	2,900	164,000	20	1,050
1985	1,260	17,700	2	250

SOURCE: Data supplied by commune and brigade accountants.

worker, the peasant women say, could earn about 100 yuan a year to augment the household's income from farming. This was the third major item in household sidelines for the Huayangqiao villages.

THE CONTRACTION OF THE FARM LABOR FORCE

The household sidelines persisted alongside collective agriculture until they were challenged by the coming of rural industrialization and the concomitant rise in the opportunity costs of auxiliary and spare-time rural labor. The rural labor force had exploded with the full mobilization of women for production in the 1950s, then stabilized until the mid-1960s, when it began to balloon again as the postrevolutionary baby boomers reached working age. As Table 10.2 shows, the proportion of farm laborers to population mounted steadily in the Huayangqiao villages, from about 40 percent in the mid-1960s to more than 60 percent by the end of the 1970s, placing enormous pressures on the brigade's fixed amount of farm land. Only minimal relief was provided by the movement of labor out of agricul-

TABLE 10.2
Farm Laborer-to-Population Ratios in Huayangqiao, 1965–84

Year	Xuejiada team	Xubushanqiao team	Xilihangbang team	Combined total
1965		0.43		
1966		0.41		
1967		0.42		
1968		—		
1969		0.44		
1970		—		
1971		0.59		
1972		—		
1973		—		
1974		0.52		
1975		0.52		
1976		0.54		
1977	0.54	0.66	0.55	0.58
1978	0.53	0.66	0.60	0.59
1979	0.63	0.57	0.60	0.61
1980	—	0.61	0.68	—
1981	0.49	0.58	0.61	0.56
1982	0.47	0.59	0.62	0.56
1983	0.57	0.38	—	—
1984	0.39	0.33	0.38	0.37

SOURCE: Laborer and population data supplied by brigade accountants.

ture into industry. Just a handful of villagers obtained off-farm employment in the 1950s and 1960s. Things improved modestly in the 1970s, chiefly for well-connected Xue Family Village, but far from enough to reverse the long-term trend of growing underemployment.

It was only in the 1980s that industrialization came full force to Huayangqiao, to such stunning effect that, by 1985, more than one-half of the 308 laborers in the three teams were employed off-farm. Most of these jobs were divided evenly between commune enterprises and brigade industries. On the commune level, the most dramatic impact came with a boom in house construction, which accounted for 23 jobs. On the brigade level, the big change came with the opening of a "lock factory"; no fewer than 58 workers from the Huayangqiao villages found employment there. (See Tables 10.3 and D.4.)

Off-farm employment on this scale finally relieved the pressures on the land, providing some breathing space until the vigorous birth-control program launched in the 1970s could make its mark on the labor force.

TABLE 10.3

Population and Full-Time Laborers in Huayangqiao, 1965–87

Year	Xuejiada Population	Xuejiada Laborers	Xubushanqiao Population	Xubushanqiao Laborers	Xilihangbang Population	Xilihangbang Laborers	Total Population	Total Laborers
1965	144		120	[51]	137		401	
1966	145		120	[49]	139		404	
1967	153		118	[50]	141		412	
1968	160		122	—	149		431	
1969	160		124	[54]	159		443	
1970	167		128	—	158		453	
1971	167		127	75	158		452	
1972	166		134	—	156		456	
1973	176		134	—	159		469	
1974	175		135	70	164		474	
1975	185		141	73	164		490	
1976	189		141	76	169		499	
1977	197		143	—	171		511	
1978	202	122	145	80	171	100	518	302
1979	199	126	148	100	177	115	524	341
1980	196	122	143	101	184	116	523	339
1981	190	120	144	99	184	120	518	339
1982	196	120	150	84	186	117	532	321
1983	191	106	154	97	184	120	529	323
1984	[179]	98	[155]	90	[186]	122	[520]	310
1985	—	105	—	96	—	107	—	308
1986	—	108	—	91	—	111	—	310
1987	—	103	—	89	—	106	—	298

SOURCE: Data supplied by brigade accountants.
    NOTE: Bracketed numbers are estimates from household income data supplied by the brigade.

The Peasant-Worker Household

Off-farm employment in collective industrial enterprises typically did not remove the laborer completely from the farm. In most instances, some members of a household took off-farm jobs and the others continued to farm. Moreover, even the workers employed in collective industry continued to help out in farming during the busy seasons. These part-peasant part-worker households (*bangong bannong*) continued to live in the villages, holding their official registration there, and still depended in varying degrees on farming for their subsistence. The advantage of such an arrangement, from the point of view of the state and the collective, was that rural families were much less expensive to maintain than those completely severed from the farm.

In many villages, off-farm employment removed much of the surplus and spare-time labor, causing a rise in the costs of that labor. In the more fully industrialized versions of the part-peasant part-worker household, only the auxiliary labor continued to be employed on the farm, and in the most advanced version, agriculture itself became just a sideline activity, dependent almost entirely on spare-time labor; all working-age members were employed in industry, and the household contracted for just a fraction of the land that it was capable of farming, strictly for the purpose of growing its own consumption grain.

The Huayangqiao villages are good illustrations of the first pattern, by far the most common one in the delta. More than half of all the full-time laborers in these villages had come to be employed off-farm by 1985 (172 of 308). The vast majority were men: their representation ranging from 82 percent in the most coveted state enterprises to 64 percent in the commune enterprises and 58 percent in the brigade enterprises (see Table D.6). In all, men outnumbered women two to one in off-farm employment.

By the mid-1980s, in fact, rural cadres were inclined to joke about how farming was being done mainly by the "Three Eight Team" (*sanba duiwu*)—a reference to March 8, Women's Day. But this perception exaggerates the degree of change and overlooks the very real efforts of the leadership to achieve some semblance of equity between the sexes. The brigade's lock factory, for example, the largest employer of off-farm labor from the Huayangqiao villages, has studiously tried to give equal opportunity to women. Indeed, women have even been favored to some extent: they accounted for 52 percent of the 58 villagers employed there in 1985. For all that, gender stratification is still plainly very much a fact of life in these villages, as the proportion of men in the off-farm labor pool attests.

The example of Fengqiao commune, on the outskirts of Suzhou city, however, suggests that the "feminization of agriculture" does not completely capture the direction of change. The commune's economic structure was completely reversed in the course of the years: where agriculture and hand-produced sidelines had accounted for 83.1 percent of total output in 1958, their share was a mere 16.9 percent in 1984. Industry now accounted for 83 percent. For official statisticians, the villagers of Shenxianglang are part of the "population working in industry who farm only consumption grain land" (*zhizhong kouliangdi de wugong renkou*). Each person here received 0.5 mu of land to cover his or her grain consumption needs, plus 0.2 mu to meet state tax requirements; hence the appropriately named "consumption grain land" (*kouliang tian/di*). From what the peasants say, they took off from industrial work only six days a year, during the busiest agricultural periods, and were able to do the rest of the farmwork in their spare time.

There was considerable incentive for continuing to farm for consumption in the late 1980s. The supply of rice on the open market was limited, and the price, at 0.25 yuan a catty, was prohibitively high. An adult male would have had to spend 150 yuan a year to maintain his accustomed consumption. The spare-time growing of consumption grain was quite a high-return activity in the circumstances. No villager was likely to find employment that would pay anything close to that amount for just six days of full-time work plus spare-time labor.

The Shenxianglang pattern typifies the sidelining of agriculture, not its feminization. At the time of my visit (1985), nearly all the village women, as well as the men, had off-farm jobs. And farming had become not women's work but simply spare-time work. In fact, according to the peasants, the men tended to do more of the farming than the women, who still bore the main responsibility for housework (H-III-38, 39).

Researchers (led by Fei Xiaotong) in Wujiang county have noted a pattern of increasing separation from farming as off-farm employment moves up the hierarchy from brigade to commune to state enterprises. In brigade enterprises close to home, workers typically work only five to seven hours a day; in the busy farming periods, they spend four hours a day on agriculture. In commune enterprises farther away, workers typically work eight-hour days and spend only two or three hours in agriculture during the busy periods. In state enterprises, still more distant from home, workers are typically completely severed from farming (Zhang Yulin 1984: 284).

The New Sidelines

As agriculture itself became more and more of a sideline, the older household sidelines fell away, unable to compete with farming for labor. Hog raising, for example, had been maintained at artificially high levels because of state-imposed quotas. In 1985, however, the state decided to experiment with lifting the quotas. Once given the choice, many peasants promptly opted out of that unprofitable activity. In Xubushanqiao village, for example, the number of hogs fell from 150 head in 1984 to a mere 70 in 1985. (This was a matter of

great concern to the commune cadres I interviewed in the summer
of 1985; H-III-8).*

The upward pressures on labor costs were such that even the
lower-paying collective sidelines fell to the wayside. Mushroom
growing in Huayang declined from its high of 230,000 square feet in
1983 to just 10,000 or so in 1985. Mushroom prices dropped, and
more stringent standards were set with the increased supply. The
500–600 yuan income per worker per year became less attractive as
alternative employment opportunities became available (H-III-26).

Feminists are of course correct to deplore the persistence of gender
stratification in productive activity, despite the decline of the old
household sidelines. Nevertheless, the combination of industry as
mainline and agriculture as sideline represents a step forward from
the old combination of agriculture as mainline and household handicrafts as sideline. The full sidelining of agriculture, moreover, as we
saw in the Fengqiao case, did not bring stratification between males
working off-farm and females working in agriculture so much as the
relegation of agriculture to spare-time work, by both men and
women.

The household vegetable garden was one of the few old sidelines
that managed to survive in the face of rural industrialization. More
than that, thanks to the rising prices of vegetables on the private
market during the late 1980s, vegetable growing was able to thrive
as never before. In fact, the widening gulf between state and private
market prices has almost completely undermined collectivized vegetable growing. In Xubushanqiao village, as we saw, the old vegetable team was disbanded in 1986 because of the higher returns to be
had on the private market (H-IV-1, 5).

A related boom took place in petty commercial activity. Someone
who peddled vegetables (or poultry and fish, whose prices also rose
sharply with increased prosperity and demand) could profit hand-
somely: buying cheap in the country and taking the produce to sell
in the town or city. One peasant in Xubushanqiao (Yang Hongqiang)
actually gave up his job in the village lock factory to make his living
as a peddler. In 1988, he was able to net an average of ten yuan a day
(H-IV-5).

---

*The household-responsibility system instituted in 1983 contributed to this devel-
opment. With plots reallocated every year, peasants ceased to be so concerned about
the long-term health of the soil and began to rely more heavily on chemical fertilizer,
which is much easier to use than compost. The soil damage worked by chemicals
does not show up for several years, the peasants claim.

For the most part, however, the household sidelines pursued shifted to producing high-return specialty items, usually for the urban and/or export market. Crocheting fell into this catetory. At the height of the industry in 1982, fully 93 women in Huayangqiao engaged in this activity. The sideline came to a skidding halt thereafter (for reasons to be discussed later), so that, by 1985, only two women still did any crocheting. In Huayang commune as a whole, meanwhile, the number of workers dropped from a high of 6,100 to 1,260 workers (Table 10.1). But crocheting then rebounded, so that, by 1988, about one-third of the Huayangqiao households were once more engaged in the activity (H-III-16, 24, H-IV-5).

Another item of this sort was rabbit fur, which was in much demand outside China. Table 10.4 shows the quantity of rabbit fur purchased by state stores in Songjiang county between 1966 and 1984. The decline in the numbers after 1982 reflects not an absolute decline in the production and sale of the product, but only the loosening of state controls and the increased participation of private traders. Rabbit raising in fact spread dramatically until 1985.

Cute animals with pink noses and lily-white coats, the rabbits raised for fur are delicate animals that must be kept caged indoors. They require considerable attention, to feed and to keep clean. Their urine discharge must be drained off every day, for they can easily become diseased if allowed to soak in their own urine, the peasants say. But all this is light, incremental work—expecially well suited to household auxiliary and spare-time labor. Each rabbit can be sheared four times a year, to yield about three ounces of fur at a time.

Rabbit raising began in Huayang in 1978 under fairly tight state control. The price for the highest-grade fur was set at 27 yuan a catty at the collective- or state-managed purchase stations. In 1984, however, the authorities relaxed their controls and permitted private

TABLE 10.4

Rabbit Fur Purchased by State Stores in Songjiang, 1966–84

Year	Catties	Year	Catties	Year	Catties
1966	361	1973	1,151	1980	16,778
1967	494	1974	1,575	1981	39,357
1968	396	1975	1,753	1982	124,303
1969	296	1976	2,127	1983	70,246
1970	224	1977	2,610	1984	36,777
1971	251	1978	2,958		
1972	415	1979	4,654		

SOURCE: Data supplied by Songjiang County Statistical Bureau.

traders to operate. In Huayang, the peasants say, traders from Zhejiang (who export to Taiwan) came every three or four days. One household would be visited by as many as five or six groups in a single day. Demand so exceeded supply that prices rose sharply. At their height in February–March 1985, a catty of top-grade fur fetched 110 yuan.

At 100 yuan a catty, a villager could net as much as 120 yuan from one rabbit. Two little old ladies in Xilihangbang, Gao Yindi and Gao Meiying, managed to net 2,000 yuan in 1984. Thereafter, every household in Xilihangbang took up this sideline, raising anywhere from four to five rabbits to as many as 60. Nearby Xubushanqiao was slow to follow Xilihangbang's lead; in 1985, only five or six households kept hutches, Wu Mingchang heading the list with 25 rabbits. And the members of Xuejiada team, with their greater access to employment opportunities in town and generally higher incomes, were mostly uninvolved. Unfortunately for the Huayang rabbit keepers, supply soon caught up with demand, and prices slid badly—to 72 yuan per catty in August 1985 and to a mere 40 yuan in 1988. By the summer of 1988, virtually everyone in Huayangqiao had gotten out of the business (H-III-1, 6, 26, H-IV-2).

Another specialty item that attracted much attention for a time was the dried earthworm (*qiuyin*, used as medicine for apoplexy). There was tremendous demand for the worms in 1984 (again from Taiwan). A catty sold for 1.75 yuan, and traders were not too concerned about the quality. Two Xubushanqiao villagers (Wu Achang and He Xiaomao) managed to net 150 to 200 yuan that year. But again, supply quickly caught up with demand, and the prices dropped to 1.60 yuan in 1985. The traders then began setting more stringent standards, demanding that the worms be cut only in a certain way and rejecting any that were severed or dirty. That summer, virtually no one in Huayangqiao went out to gather worms. But then market conditions turned around and, by the summer of 1988, earthworm gathering was once more a boom activity. Fully 21 of the 37 households in Xubushanqiao were engaged in it that year (H-III-1, 6, H-IV-5).

We might speculate here on the logic of these pursuits. All seem to follow the same pattern. When there is a demand for some unfamiliar product, only a few pioneers turn to it, demand exceeds supply, and prices are high, enough to make the activity more worthwhile than farming. The relatively high returns, however, quickly attract more producers, and sooner or later prices are pressed downward. When prices drop below what peasants will tolerate for spare-time work, they simply stop producing the item until the market recovers. To judge by the examples of crocheting, rabbit raising, and earthworm gathering, despite the rather violent swings that seem to characterize the specialty market, the farm household production unit is able to adapt readily to the changes. The shocks are cushioned by the fact that the production is only a sideline, so that the household can move out of the activity without devastating consequences to its fundamental livelihood. At the same time, its low-cost and spare-time nature enables the household to move back into production rapidly once the market shifts.

It is interesting to note how the term "sidelines" is taking on new connotations. Rural cadres today boast about the climbing share of sidelines and industry in total rural output. For them, a "sideline" is no longer a low-return activity that is secondary to agriculture, but a pursuit that, like industry, ranks above crop planting. What they have in mind when they speak of sidelines are of course the more highly capitalized collective sidelines and the new individual sidelines, not hog raising and rope making.

The transformation in the nature and function of sidelines is easy to overlook because of the way statistics are kept. The category "sidelines" lumps old household sidelines in with the new glamorous ones and the highly capitalized collective activities. So though we know that sidelines averaged about 17 percent of the gross value of rural output in Huayang commune and hovered around 20 percent nationally in the 1970s and early 1980s (Appendix Table E.1), we have no way of knowing the precise degree to which the old low-cost household sidelines have been replaced.

FAMILY PRODUCTION IN THE
NEW ECONOMIC STRUCTURE

The family unit, as has been seen, has two distinct organizational advantages over the collective: it is particularly amenable to a two-tiered remuneration structure, usually stratified by gender between the man and the woman; it is also particularly amenable to the use of unremunerated spare-time labor. It is therefore a lower-cost form of labor organization for small-scale sideline production than the collective. For the same reasons, it is a more economical organization for spare-time farming than the collective. The cultivation of consumption grain land is most cheaply done in spare moments by the family unit working under the incentive of meeting its own con-

sumption needs. The logic here is similar to that of the private vegetable plot.

Thus we witness the seemingly paradoxical coincidence of the return of the family production unit with the rise in the opportunity
costs of rural labor. The latter stems from the development of rural
industry and, to a lesser extent, of new high-paying sidelines. The
former comes from the continued interlinking of two kinds of production, one higher paying than the other.

Once in place, the family form of labor organization brings with it
its own imperatives with respect to farm labor use. Even without
the incentive of alternative employment opportunities, the family
production unit can have a different attitude toward work efficiency
from the collective's. Under the collective, leisure was a negative incentive. For team and brigade cadres, idleness looked bad to their su-
periors. For individual team members, no work meant no labor
points. But in the absence of alternative employment, there was no
incentive to finish a task quickly. So long as someone put in his
hours and the work got done, that was good enough. Given surplus
labor, the collective system led to the phenomenon of what the
peasants in Huayangqiao call "loitering work" (*langdang gong*). It
was better to do the job slowly, stand around, loiter about, and so on,
than to take time off. The result was inefficiency and underemployment that tended to increase with time and pressures on the land.

For the family farm, by contrast, leisure acts as a positive incentive. Rewarded in the form of product rather than by workpoints,
there is no reason for family laborers to loiter around on the job. The
laborer who gets the farmwork done early can get on to other tasks
or simply relax at home or in the shade of a tree, go shopping, or visit
the teashop. Leisure is more appealing than loitering around in the
fields. Even without alternative employment possibilities, therefore, the leisure incentive propels efficient work on the family farm.

This difference between the family farm and the collective is not
readily quantifiable. The laborer under the family-farm system who
finishes his work in a morning instead of an entire day, or in two
hours instead of three, does not report or record that fact. There is no
reason to, since the payment for work is not in workpoints but in
product. As for the collectivized team, it was well-nigh impossible
for the recordkeeper to differentiate between efficient farm labor and
loitering labor, especially if almost everyone was loitering. (Piecework arrangements during busy periods, of course, did differentiate
by work efficiency.) My efforts to get team accountants to help

record how much time each household and laborer spent in the field each day resulted only in rough records of full days and half days. Such data will not, cannot, document the point being made here.

My best evidence is qualitative: the fact that all peasants interviewed on the subject agree that there had been much loitering work under the collectives, that people tend to finish their work much more quickly under the family-responsibility system, and that once finished, people will go off to do other things, including resting and "playing." Pressed for a quantitative scale of the difference in work efficiency between the two kinds of work organization, most say that for normal farmwork outside of the busy periods, the same jobs now take only about two-thirds as much time as in the old days (H-II-3).

THE FAMILY PRODUCTION UNIT VS. THE COLLECTIVE

The popular media would have us believe that China gave up family production completely after the Revolution, and that in the 1980s the country just as radically reversed its ways, giving up collective farms and socialism for family farms and capitalism. But the record shows that changes after the Revolution were never so abrupt and complete as we imagined. Even at the height of collectivization, as has been seen, the family production unit persisted in private vegetable plots, hog and poultry raising, and handicrafts.

The same applies to the "de-collectivization" after 1978. Collective organization actually thrived as never before in new sidelines and industries, even if the administrative nomenclature changed from brigade to administrative village (cun) and from commune to township (xiang). In Huayangqiao and indeed in the Yangzi delta area as a whole, almost all industrial enterprises and highly capitalized sidelines were still under collective auspices as the 1980s came to a close. Private enterprises may have played a larger role in places like Fujian-Guangdong and Wenzhou in Zhejiang, but collective enterprises still accounted for two-thirds of the gross income of all rural enterprises in China in 1986. (See Appendix Table F.1.) Even in crop production, collective organization persisted in the Yangzi delta for such tasks as plowing, irrigation, and insecticide application. Household responsibility remained limited to the maintenance (weeding, fertilizing, and harvesting) of the fields and did not include the choice of crops.

What the 1980s brought to the Yangzi delta, then, was a mixed collective-family system. In industry, collective organization continued to predominate. In sidelines, collective organization predominated in highly capitalized production, leaving the family unit to conduct lower-return, more labor-intensive production. In crop production, the collective dominated in those domains requiring relatively high capitalization, leaving the family unit to carry out the more-labor-intensive tasks of keeping up the fields and harvesting. It is an intricate mixture that defies simple dichotomizing between collective and family production.

The popular media would also have us believe that the key difference between collectives and family farms in China is the latter's profit-orientation in marketed crop production. But the Yangzi delta record shows us that the crucial difference consists instead in the family production unit's superior ability to diversify into low-return and/or high-risk sideline production by mobilizing auxiliary and spare-time household labor. That is the key to its persistence through all the changes in sideline production and agricultural collectivization and de-collectivization.

CHAPTER II

Growth Versus Development in Agriculture

As in the chapters on agricultural change during the Ming-Qing period, "growth" refers to any kind of expansion in total output; "development" to growth accompanied by increased productivity per unit labor, and "involution" to growth accompanied by decreasing productivity per unit labor. This chapter first reviews the record of changes in agriculture (i.e. crop production)* in Songjiang, then examines the dynamics for those changes, and finally, relates the Songjiang story to national trends.

THE COLLECTIVIZED YEARS

The record of agricultural change in Songjiang county is principally the story of four crops: rice and wheat or barley, the two main grain crops, and cotton and rape, the two main cash crops. Tracing the story of each permits us to cut through the ideological baggage surrounding policy debates to the actual record of change.

Rice

According to elderly peasants and team cadres, the first step forward in rice production after the Revolution was a modest one that came with the upgrading of poor-peasant production. Just before the Revolution, the yields on poor-peasant farms had been lower than those on average farms. In part this was because of underfertilization. In Huayangqiao, poor peasants usually applied one cake of soybean fertilizer (ca. 50 catties) per mu, purchased on credit at the price of two cakes per shi of husked rice, while the more well-to-do applied one and one half to two cakes, purchased at half the price, or

---

*The Chinese State Statistical Bureau includes under "agriculture" not only crop production but forestry, animal husbandry, sidelines, and fishery, plus brigade and team industry. Such usage has caused much confusion. I am using "agriculture" here in the stricter sense of crop production only.

four cakes per shi of rice. The poorest peasants often could not afford any soybean cake at all. Additionally, most poor peasants hired out during the busy seasons, from 50 to 100 days a year, as did eight of eighteen households in Xubushanqiao and five of nine in He Family Village. Even in more well-to-do Xilihangbang and Xue Family Village, three households each (of nineteen and thirteen, respectively) hired out. These short-term laborers had to work their own plots with auxiliary family labor or after they had completed their contracts. Some of them would not transplant until mid-May, two or three weeks later than most of the other peasants in these villages. This delayed planting also affected yields. Whereas the more well-to-do peasants using lots of beancake fertilizer could get up to three shi of rice per mu, poor peasants often fell below the average of two shi (H-I-1−4, 7, H-II-6).

Land reform equalized farm holdings and almost completely eliminated hiring. Then in the early-stage collectives, the state loaned money to the poorer households in the collective for fertilizer. The result was modest increases in average yields—reaching the vicinity of 550 catties of unhusked rice by the mid-1950s (H-II-6, 7, 13; Table 11.1).*

Thanks to several technological factors, yields climbed in the following two decades. Huayangqiao's arterial irrigation canal (Daminggou) and two major east–west drainage ditches were dug in 1959 during the mass mobilization for waterworks under the Great Leap Forward. Electrified pumping also began at that time. Chemical fertilizers, insecticides, improved planting methods, and scientific seed selection followed, all contributing to steady, though modest, increases in yields. By 1963, each crop yielded more than 650 catties (H-II-7).

Water control was improved even more with the systematic "checkerization" (*gezihua*) of the fields after 1969: ditches were dug every 60 to 70 meters to form squares of about 4,000 square meters (or ca. one acre), which were further subdivided into rectangular north–south plots about 20 meters wide (about two mu, or a third of an acre each). The 20 × 70 meter size was dictated by technical considerations: when the fields are flooded for transplanting, that size permits a rapid and even flow of water; a wider field is harder to fill, and a longer one harder to grade evenly. Furthermore, in transplanting, the shoots are first tossed to their approximate location from the ridge between the plots; 20 meters is optimal for controlled toss-

*The ratio of unhusked to husked rice is usually about 10:7. All rice yield figures in the rest of this book refer to unhusked rice.

TABLE II.I

Yields of Major Crops in Songjiang and China, 1952–87

(catties per sown mu)

	Rice[a]		Wheat		Cotton		Rapeseed	
	Song-jiang	China	Song-jiang[b]	China	Song-jiang	China	Song-jiang	China
1952	504	321	98	98	23	31	67	67
1953	551	336	128	95	26	30	75	70
1954	525	337	117	115	21	26	70	69
1955	548	357	112	115	47	35	80	55
1956	[526][c]	330	181	121	26	31	43	57
1957	[450][c]	359	112	114	39	38	85	51
1958	[555]	338	126	117	50	47	75	58
1959	[591]	319	214	125	62	41	113	62
1960	[598]	269	209	108	—	27	—	41
1961	[543]	272	129	74	—	28	—	35
1962	[548]	312	161	92	—	29	—	48
1963	[656]	355	164	104	—	36	—	48
1964	[679]	374	207	109	—	45	—	70
1965	[614]	392	253	136	—	56	—	80
1966	660	417	157	141	96	63	195	69
1967	699	410	201	150	112	62	167	81
1968	642	422	262	149	161	63	218	86
1969	722	417	221	145	143	57	217	82
1970	616	453	269	153	112	61	212	89
1971	551	440	348	169	85	57	245	102
1972	613	430	366	182	130	53	251	95
1973	723	463	181	178	136	69	146	86
1974	651	465	472	201	139	66	237	89
1975	622	469	233	218	136	64	162	89
1976	700	463	429	236	128	56	169	77
1977	614	483	228	195	114	56	128	70
1978	752	530	511	246	190	59	279	96
1979	797	566	638	285	142	65	289	116
1980	576	551	587	252	116	73	204	112
1981	659	576	575	281	100	76	268	143
1982	811	652	591	327	136	82	312	183
1983	696	679	544	374	141	102	236	156
1984	818	716	582	396	197	122	289	164
1985	876	700	574	392	110	108	306	166
1986	778	712	594	406	140	110	232	160
1987	730	722	546	406	132	116	280	168

SOURCES: China, Zhongguo tongji nianjian 1983: 155–56, 158–59, 1984: 153, 1987: 175, 1988: 253. All Songjiang figures here and in the following tables were supplied by county authorities.
[a] No yield data are available for late-rice in Songjiang for the decade 1956–65. The bracketed figures are estimates: they assume the same acreage and yields for late-rice as for early-rice.
[b] Songjiang figures are for wheat and barley.
[c] The drop in yields was due to the vigorous push to raise cropping frequencies by planting more double-cropped rice.

ing. The same principle applies to the spraying of insecticides and to fertilizer application, again tossed in from the ridge. These refinements raised rice yields to a high of nearly 800 catties per mu in 1979 (H-II-7). Between 1952–55 and 1976–79, yields per sown mu increased by a third (from an average of 532 catties to 716 catties). Improved cultivation techniques, then, were one major component of the total growth in rice output per cultivated mu.

The other major component was the switch to double-cropping. Before 1955, there had been no double-cropping of rice to speak of in Songjiang. As Table 11.2 shows, more than 80 percent of the county's total cultivated acreage was under rice, and almost all of that was single-cropped. (In Huayangqiao, 94.8 percent of all cultivated acreage was under single-cropped rice in 1940.) By 1975–77, acreage under single-cropped rice in the county had declined to 3.9 percent of the total cultivated area, versus 57.1 percent for early rice and 72.8 percent for the late crop.

Double-cropped rice was first tried on a large scale in Songjiang in 1956 on about 15 percent of the cultivated area. But this intensification created immense pressures between the first and second rice crops and between the second rice crop and the winter crop. The winter wheat/barley from the preceding year had to be harvested and the early-rice planted by about May 25, the early-rice harvested and the late rice planted by August 10, and the late-rice harvested and the wheat/barley planted by November 10. Any delay in one affected all the rest of the schedule. Retreat followed almost immediately after the experiment of 1956: acreage under double-cropped rice dropped by more than half the next year. The double-cropping of rice was not tried on a large scale again until tractor plowing was introduced in the mid-1960s (H-II-7). Just as in North China, it was a labor-saving device, ironically, that permitted further labor intensification in the form of increased frequency of cropping (Huang 1985: 143, 181, 183).

Large tractors had come to Songjiang county earlier, in 1958, during the Great Leap Forward, but it was only after the brigade procured hand-held, small tractors (mostly, twelve horsepower) in 1965–66 that mechanized plowing delivered its full impact. From 1969 on, double-cropped rice was pushed across the board in the county, dramatized in the slogan "Wipe out single-cropped rice!" (*xiaomie danjidao!*; H-II-7). The acreage under single-cropped rice declined dramatically, from 513,989 mu in 1963 to a low of 19,146 in 1977.

TABLE 11.2

Acreage Sown Under Single-Cropped, Early-, and Late-Rice in Songjiang County, 1949–84

(mu)

Year	Total cultivated area	Single-cropped rice	Percent of total	Early-rice	Percent of total	Late-rice	Percent of total
1949	872,658	702,826	80.5%	30,078	3.4%	—	—
1950	872,041	709,408	81.4	31,496	3.6	—	—
1951	871,349	704,554	80.9	27,798	3.2	—	—
1952	870,560	703,219	80.8	26,870	3.1	—	—
1953	867,559	713,122	82.2	26,790	3.1	—	—
1954	878,461	739,189	84.1	24,100	2.7	—	—
1955	866,392	646,605	74.6	10,274	1.2	—	—
1956	863,459	527,241	61.6	123,560	14.3	131,839	15.3%
1957	860,641	617,093	71.7	45,243	5.3	54,299	6.3
1958	848,533	492,596	58.1	60,239	7.1	50,291	5.9
1959	848,533	473,993	55.9	54,905	6.5	52,057	6.1
1960	861,103	457,687	53.2	60,878	7.1	76,729	8.9
1961	850,636	460,528	54.1	48,310	5.7	52,973	6.2
1962	850,814	476,392	56.0	32,009	3.8	23,830	2.8
1963	832,711	513,989	61.7	18,082	2.2	19,561	2.3
1964	832,652	469,904	56.4	62,730	7.5	72,624	8.7
1965	830,393	392,364	47.3	108,175	13.0	140,445	16.9
1966[a]	585,285	384,611	65.7	114,632	19.6	152,184	26.0
1967	583,813	438,191	75.1	79,045	13.5	104,027	17.8
1968	584,395	385,074	65.9	116,845	20.0	152,893	26.2
1969	581,497	270,128	46.5	174,026	29.9	246,543	42.4

Year						
1970	583,827	131,053	22.4	274,009	46.9	377,913	64.7
1971	599,652	108,040	18.0	299,621	50.0	381,126	63.6
1972	598,955	97,786	16.3	303,964	50.7	388,960	64.9
1973	597,889	58,809	9.8	323,493	54.1	427,041	71.4
1974	—	41,861	—	330,236	—	439,885	—
1975	592,944	28,255	4.8	331,662	55.9	442,753	74.7
1976	591,416	21,286	3.6	332,977	56.3	434,913	73.5
1977	589,738	19,146	3.2	349,062	59.2	414,425	70.3
1978	587,305	42,813	7.3	299,646	51.0	373,947	63.7
1979	584,171	83,568	14.3	244,656	41.9	322,211	55.2
1980	582,680	112,540	19.3	187,399	32.2	245,638	42.2
1981	581,360	129,569	22.3	154,641	26.6	202,198	34.8
1982	580,143	102,186	17.6	174,757	30.1	230,051	39.7
1983	578,790	94,058	16.3	193,325	33.4	260,215	45.0
1984	576,933	97,385	16.9	191,903	33.3	254,622	44.1

NOTE: Percentages are of sown area to total cultivated area; data on total sown are not available.
[a]The decrease in total area reflects an administrative redivision in 1966: Songjiang lost five communes (Shanyin, Caojing, Zhuxing, Fengwei, and Tingxin) and two zhen (Fengjing and Tinglin) to Jinshan county, and that county's Maogang Commune was transferred to Songjiang (H-II-24).

The two sets of data in Tables 11.1 and 11.2 give us a rough sense of the relative roles played by expanded yields and increased cropping frequency in the total growth of rice output. Average yields per cultivated mu placed under rice were 1,222 catties in 1976–79, compared with 532 catties in 1952–55, or an increase of 130 percent. Improved yields accounted for about a quarter of this increase (184 catties of 690), and increased cropping frequency the rest.

Wheat/Barley

The planting of winter wheat/barley after rice pushed foodgrain output per cultivated mu up higher still, to a total of 1,477 catties by 1976–79, or 173 percent above the 1952–55 figure (541 catties) (Tables 11.1–11.3). These dry crops had not been grown much in prerevolutionary Songjiang because they do not do well in the soggy soil of rice fields. The water table of wet-rice fields is normally about 20 centimeters, and wheat roots, which drive down a meter or more, cannot take that much moisture (H-II-7). Before the Revolution, therefore, wheat was planted chiefly on high, "dry land" (*handi*). In Huayangqiao, single-cropped rice was typically followed by a crop of green fertilizer (alfalfa), not by wheat. In Songjiang county in 1952–55, only an average of 6.5 percent of the cultivated area was planted under wheat/barley (and 9.3 percent under rape).

Winter wheat was first tried in wet-rice fields in Huayangqiao in 1953, but yields were only a discouragingly low 70 catties per mu. According to the peasants, the first advance came with collectivization, when the pooled oxen were formed into teams that could pulverize the soggy soil, allowing it to dry up some. With that method, yields increased to about 200 catties per mu. But they could not go much beyond that, for the high water table remained a problem. It was only with the adoption of new drainage methods that yields advanced again. Deep ditches were dug to lower the water table for the winter cropping, and drier soil, in turn, made plowing easier. The coming of tractors accelerated the entire process, permitting a second plowing that further improved the soil for sowing. Together these changes pushed yields up to 327 catties by 1970–74 (H-II-7).

Even greater gains were made after 1978, when a new system of underground drainage ditches was instituted. First, about eight inches of the topsoil was removed by tractor, and then ditches in the shape of inverted triangles were hand-cut about eight inches deep, then mounded over. This underground system had the advantage of requiring little capital input, only intensive labor: three workday equivalents (gong) for each mu every few years (if not redone, the

TABLE 11.3
Acreage Sown Under Wheat/Barley, Cotton, and Rape
in Songjiang County, 1949–84
(mu)

Year	Wheat/barley	Percent of total	Cotton	Percent of total	Rape	Percent of total
1949	31,859	3.7%	77,205	8.8%	56,755	6.5%
1950	36,566	4.2	67,689	7.8	65,933	7.6
1951	34,479	4.0	77,577	8.9	75,978	8.7
1952	54,811	6.3	80,791	9.3	100,348	11.5
1953	53,703	6.2	46,064	5.3	75,374	8.7
1954	59,574	6.8	44,228	5.0	55,913	6.4
1955	56,904	6.6	17,732	2.0	92,237	10.6
1956	77,264	8.9	19,319	2.2	96,976	11.2
1957	193,921	22.5	14,843	1.7	59,553	6.9
1958	146,285	17.2	13,857	1.6	53,536	6.3
1959	81,170	9.6	11,297	1.3	47,983	5.7
1960	84,388	9.8	9,709	1.1	75,563	8.8
1961	142,473	16.7	15,385	1.8	95,465	11.2
1962	125,771	14.8	14,842	1.7	73,757	8.7
1963	109,240	13.1	15,064	1.8	77,964	9.4
1964	154,890	18.6	20,000	2.4	79,296	9.5
1965	263,925	31.8	58,253	7.0	65,561	7.9
1966	284,820	48.7	27,486	4.7	70,014	12.0
1967	216,044	37.0	21,804	3.7	69,444	11.9
1968	243,331	41.6	23,904	4.1	70,986	12.1
1969	296,942	51.1	42,183	7.3	77,001	13.2
1970	280,241	48.0	46,723	8.0	84,735	14.5
1971	267,386	44.6	59,729	10.0	83,772	14.0
1972	277,913	46.4	58,200	9.7	91,357	15.3
1973	292,887	49.0	58,200	9.7	91,235	15.3
1974	274,532	—	58,200	—	90,874	—
1975	266,784	45.0	58,200	9.8	89,257	15.1
1976	253,579	42.9	68,086	11.5	84,129	14.2
1977	224,943	38.1	86,300	14.6	78,072	13.2
1978	228,520	38.9	86,366	14.7	82,809	14.1
1979	242,882	41.6	86,300	14.8	84,790	14.5
1980	260,203	44.7	124,300	21.3	75,119	12.9
1981	230,802	39.7	149,300	25.7	107,503	18.5
1982	231,678	39.9	145,303	25.0	106,234	18.3
1983	230,893	39.9	119,946	20.7	90,264	15.6
1984	244,803	42.4	119,700	20.7	82,251	14.3

NOTE: See Table 11.2.

earth on top of the ditches collapses). It also permitted fuller use of the topsoil than the earlier system, since the underground ditches did not take up any cultivated surface. These underground drainage ditches, coupled with improvements in cropping patterns with the introduction of the "nutrient bowl" transplanting system for cotton

and the three-thirds cropping system (discussed below), raised wheat
and barley yields to an all-time high of 638 catties per sown mu in
1979 (H-II-7).

Acreage sown under wheat and barley in Songjiang expanded from
6.5 percent of the total cultivated area in 1952–55 to 40.4 in 1976–
79. On fields where wheat/barley was combined with single-cropped
rice, the foodgrain yield per cultivated mu rose to nearly 1,200 catties, and where it was combined with double-cropped rice, to as high
as 1,800 catties. Planted on more than half of all acreage under
foodgrain, wheat/barley accounted for perhaps one-third of the total
increase in foodgrain output per cultivated mu between 1952–55
and 1976–79.

Cotton

The systematic efforts to make wet-rice fields hospitable to dry
crops also improved the yields of cotton and led to increased cultivation. In prerevolutionary Songjiang, cotton had been grown chiefly
on dry land without access to irrigation. Yields were a mere 29 catties (ginned) per mu in 1952–55 and brought lower net returns than
rice under the existing price structure. With the expansion of irrigation facilities, many cotton fields therefore gave way to other spring-
sown crops, including rice, and acreage under cotton declined steadily through the early 1960s. A mere 1.8 percent of the cultivated area
was under cotton in 1960–64 (Tables 11.1, 11.3).

Thanks to the great improvements in drainage during the Great
Leap Forward and Cultural Revolution years, cotton could be rotated
with rice for high yields. Improved seed (the "big flower," or *dahua*
variety) also helped to increase yields. The coming of chemical
fertilizers, finally, allowed the development of an intensive and
complex fertilization schedule: 30 dan (there are about 100 catties
in a dan) of pig manure compost; then two chemical fertilizers,
50 catties of ammonia water (*anshui*) followed by 20 catties of urea
(*niaosu*); and finally, ten dan of human manure. These methods
raised cotton yields to something of a plateau of 144 catties per mu
in 1976–79 (H-II-7; Table 11.1), and acreage under cotton increased
to 15 percent of the cultivated area in the late 1970s (Table 11.3).

The year 1979 saw the introduction of a new transplanting system
that got cotton off to an early start in hothouse conditions. By the
old method, winter wheat had been put in in October–November,
interplanted with the cotton while it was still being harvested. By
the new method, cotton was started in March 15–25, a month earlier than before, grown in glasslike "nurturing bowls" (*yingyang bo*)

covered by plastic until the plant was about a foot high, and then transplanted in the ground. This not only allowed the cotton to be harvested about ten days earlier, thereby gaining a safety margin against cold-weather damage, but also allowed wheat to be sown over the entire field, rather than in alternating rows between the cotton, thus adding significantly to the wheat output. Although the transplanting system did not push cotton yields up past the plateau achieved earlier, it is said to have stabilized them and to have improved the quality of the harvest (H-II-20).

Rape

The yield story of rape, the other major commercial crop of this area, is much like cotton's. A dry crop, its yields are crucially dependent on drainage. The systematic digging of deep drainage ditches in the rice fields alone increased the per-mu yields of rapeseed from 73 catties in 1952–55 to over 200 catties by the end of the 1960s.

Acreage sown under rape did not fluctuate nearly so violently over time as the cotton acreage did. In part, this was because it is a winter crop, so that it was competitive with wheat/barley rather than with rice. The first contraction in rape acreage, to under 7 percent of the total in 1957–58, coincided with a substantial expansion in wheat/barley. But then improved drainage methods, especially after the fields were checkerized, led to growth in both. The rape acreage increased to about 15.0 percent by the mid-1970s. Together rape and wheat/barley attest to a dramatic rise in cropping frequency through winter-cropping: from a mere 15.8 percent of the cultivated area under these crops in 1952–55 to 54.4 percent in 1976–79.

The Dynamics of Agricultural Change

In hindsight, four structural factors jump out at us as having been fundamental to Songjiang's agricultural change down through the late 1970s. The first was the increased supply of farm labor, a factor that most of the cadres I interviewed, political and technical alike, were slow to mention. Much of the expansion in yields was achieved through labor intensification, in terms of both labor input per crop (especially for cotton and wheat) and increased frequency of cropping. According to the Huayangqiao team leaders, labor input jumped from about 30 workday equivalents (gong) per cultivated mu in the early 1950s to 100 by the late 1960s. That labor supply came in part from the mobilization of women for full-time farmwork. But it could not have been sustained without the absolute increase in labor power that came with population growth. The labor force, as we have seen, expanded even faster than the population from the mid-1960s on. With the entrance of the baby boomers of the 1950s into the labor force, the laborer-to-population ratio rose (Table 10.2). The great increase in the labor supply underlay the dramatic labor intensification of the postrevolutionary years.

The second factor was state-coordinated water control. Under the imperial and Republican states, water control had been largely left to the haphazard initiative and coordination of the local and village elites. The key to postrevolutionary water control was a coordinated effort that extended from multi-province regional projects down to intravillage ditches. Given the Yangzi delta's geology, effective drainage of the central basin required coordinated flood prevention and drainage in the entire basin.

In the 1950s, state-coordinated water-control efforts in Songjiang county concentrated primarily on large projects: the building of seashore, lakefront, and river dikes (summarized in the slogan *zhutang xiuyu*), and the digging and dredging of large canals and rivers (*wahe shuhe*). In all, sixteen kilometers of seawall and 80 kilometers of river embankments were constructed, seventeen rivers dredged, and "10 million cubic meters" of artificial canals dug during that decade. Much of the work was done during the Great Leap Forward, under the coordination of the communes.

In the 1960s, the main attention shifted to lower-level water control. Electrification had begun during the Great Leap. Now electric pumping stations were established in every commune. The mazes of embankments around individual fields were rationalized and linked, and the ditches that served them were systematized and coordinated with larger rivers and canals by the extensive use of sluice gates. By the end of the 1960s, large-scale water control and plot-level water use had been linked up into a single system, summed up by the expression "checkerization" of the farm fields.

Subsequent programs of the 1970s and 1980s were chiefly elaborations and refinements of this new infrastructure. A host of pumping stations was built throughout the county, 230 for drainage and 331 for irrigation. Huayang commune alone had 32 stations. And some 2,300 bridges were built in the villages to improve local transport. The entire system was in place by the end of the 1970s. Water-control efforts of the 1980s were limited to improving the management and maintenance of the system. These advances were necessary preconditions for the expansions in output of the different crops (H-II-17, H-III-24).

The third major factor was modern agricultural inputs. Triple-cropping would have been quite unthinkable without the use of tractors. At the same time, increased yields per cropping depended to a considerable extent on the use of chemical fertilizers. This applied to virtually all the crops. Electrified pumping, finally, was a crucial part of the new irrigation and drainage networks.

The fourth structural factor was collectivization, something that political cadres were slow to discuss with me, given the current preference for de-collectivization. Collectivization furnished, for one thing, the organizational framework for the all-out mobilization of female labor. Collectivization also likely contributed to the population explosion of the postrevolution years. It was through this organizational framework that the state deployed "barefoot doctors" in every village by the 1960s. Improvement in health services sharply reduced mortality rates, thereby contributing powerfully to the population growth rate of the period. At the same time, in shifting the basis for rural income from land to labor (paid by workpoints), collective organization probably made large families more desirable, since the household's income now became dependent solely on its labor supply (whereas earlier there had been the constraint of having to share out the limited land to all sons). To that extent, collectivization might help explain the rise in fertility rates through the early 1960s (except for the years 1958–61). The combined effects of declining mortality and increased fertility led to very high population growth rates, which were only partially checked by delayed marriage. The sharp increase in fertility rates topped out only after 1963, first because of later marriage, and then because of the state's vigorous birth-control program (Coale 1984).

Collectives also furnished the organizational framework for virtually cost-free labor for the new water-control projects. The state supplied the modern capital inputs, such as electric pumps, sluice gates, and the cement required for the new seawalls,* but the projects were built by the "obligatory labor" (*yiwu gong*) of the peasants. On the average, the peasants of Songjiang contributed more than 10 percent of their total labor, or 50–60 workday equivalents per year, to state-coordinated water control. Theoretically, the figure was supposed to be 7.5 percent, but actually they contributed more, according to the local water-control cadres. The work went largely uncompensated, simply deducted off the top before the collective computed

---

*At least off and on. From 1958 to 1964, the communes bore all the cost for such items. However, the state repaid them in 1964 and began routinely picking up the costs. Then, in 1975, it shifted ground, and about one-third of the burden reverted to the collectives (H-III-7).

and distributed income to its members at the end of the year. The
state contributed only minimally, in the form of a subsidy for non-
staple food (*fushi butie*): 0.35 yuan (of which 0.05 was allocated to
the collective for its administrative costs) per cubic meter of earth
construction in the case of county projects (affecting two or more
communes). This amounted to about one-fifth of the actual workpoint value of the work, according to the peasants. The rest was
simply borne by them. In the case of commune projects, the state
contributed only 0.10 yuan per cubic meter of construction, while
the commune provided 0.15–0.20, and the production teams were
responsible for the rest. Brigade projects, like the irrigation and
drainage ditches for the Huayangqiao villages, were entirely the responsibility of the peasants (H-III-7).

No doubt the larger projects could have been built without collective organization, through a state-imposed corvée tax, as was inter-
mittently done in imperial times. But local irrigation and drainage
ditches were quite another matter. It is hard to imagine how these
improvements could have been made for so little cost and so systematically in a laissez-faire family-farm economy. Collectivization,
and with it the reach of state and party control down to the level of
the natural village, provided the organizational framework for virtually cost-free plot-level water control.

Maintenance of water control also relied heavily on the collectives. In the Huayangqiao brigade, for example, 200 workday equivalents were required each winter to dredge the irrigation ditches, and
another 300–400 for dredging and weeding the drainage ditches.
These jobs were done by mobilizing the members of the production
teams. Even with the agricultural de-collectivization of the mid-
1980s, collective "service teams" (*fuwu dui*) continued to keep up
Huayangqiao's irrigation network. Maintenance of the drainage
ditches began to be contracted out to households in 1985, with problematic consequences (H-III-7).

Collective organization, of course, was crucially important also in
funding some of the modern inputs. Chemical fertilizers and improved seed varieties may have well been within the reach of individual households, but tractors and electric pumping stations
clearly were not. The collectives represented one practical way of
saving for the costly items. Though alternative organizations for
such investments are possible (e.g. state-sponsored projects or localized coops or the highly capitalized family farm), it is difficult to
imagine them in the context of an atomized family-farm economy
near the margins of subsistence.

In looking back at the entire record of agricultural change in Songjiang, it is tempting to try to single out one factor as more important than the others. Water control, for example, was clearly crucial. Yet the projects undertaken in Songjiang were unthinkable without the other factors outlined above: low-cost mass labor, collective organization, and modern inputs. Water control, like agriculture itself, depends not on any single factor, as one might expect with the mechanical world, but on multiple interdependent factors, as in the organic world.

Seed Selection and Climate

We need to consider also two second-order factors, both of which were strongly emphasized by the technical cadres. One is scientific seed selection, innovations that, in their description, produced something of a "punctuated equilibria" growth pattern: a good new seed raises yields substantially when it is introduced, but its effect then levels off. The "Green at Old Age" (Lao lai qing) seed developed by the agro-hero Chen Yongkang contributed to the advances in single-cropped rice in the 1950s. After yields leveled off, it was replaced by the "Agricultural Reclamation No. 58" (Nongken 58 hao) seed in 1963, which brought further advances. In early-rice, one outstanding variety used in the 1960s was the "Short-Legged Southern Special Number" (Aijiao nan tehao) from Guangdong. It was replaced in the 1970s by "Short Southern Early Number One" (Ai nan zao yi hao), which was in turn replaced by yet another variety in the 1980s. The same pattern obtained in late-rice, where the search was for tolerance of low temperatures, in addition to high yields and pest resistance (H-II-14, 15).

The other factor the technical cadres liked to emphasize was climate. Early-rice is susceptible to damage from too much rain in June, and single-cropped rice to too much near the end of September. Late-rice is at risk in early October from both unseasonable rain and unseasonable cold. Winter wheat and rape are both vulnerable to uninterrupted rain in the spring. And the chief fear for cotton is an early cold snap. It is also vulnerable to too much rain in the spring and autumn and to typhoons (H-II-20).

In the view of the technical cadres, it is weather conditions above all that cause sharp fluctuations in yields from year to year. Deng Zhengfan, for 30 years a technical cadre in the county Bureau of Agriculture, pointed to the recent record: near perfect weather in 1978 led to the highest yields ever for single-cropped and late-rice. But both fell off badly in 1980 and 1981, when the cold season started in early September, the earliest in a hundred years. Even hog raising in 1981 was affected, because of the drop in the quantity of feed available (H-II-14; Table 11.1).

The late 1950s and early 1960s saw similar ups and downs in rice yields. There were record rains in 1957, including one day of torrential downpours that reached a record-setting 157 millimeters (6.1 inches). The resulting floods caused extensive damage to rice. Advances in rice yields then resumed until 1961, when drought—90 days without rain, which is exceedingly unusual for this area—combined with an early cold spell again cut sharply into the yields (H-II-14).

Growth Without Development

Despite the very impressive record of agricultural advances outlined above, our peasant informants were well aware that there had been little overall change in income per workday. Gao Youfa, a middle-aged peasant of Gao Family Hamlet, put things the most clearly of all: from the earliest days of collectivization, apart from the abnormal years from the Great Leap through 1962, the value of each ten-point workday equivalent had hovered between 0.9 yuan and 1.0 yuan. Why? Because "although output went up, so did the number of people."

There were of course minor fluctuations with climatic conditions, technological changes, capital inputs, price adjustments, and the like, all of which affected crop yields. But the amplitude of those swings seldom exceeded 20 percent of total output, and changes in one factor were often offset by changes in another. By contrast, when a son or daughter reached age sixteen (sui) and entered the labor force, the impact on household income was immediate and dramatic, dwarfing by far the fluctuations resulting from those external factors.

That is why peasant informants, when asked to remember the years they did best financially, invariably pointed to the years during which their children earned an income and had not yet split off to form separate households. Gao Shitang (b. 1925), for example, said things were best for him in the ten years from the mid-1960s on, because his household had four labor units: himself, his wife, his adopted daughter, and the adopted son-in-law who married into his household in 1965. The arrival of two grandsons, in 1967 and 1968, did not affect his fortunes that much, since he still had four income earners in the household; the real blow came in 1974, when his daughter and son-in-law set up their own household. Lu Guantong

(b. 1919) told basically the same story: things were good for him after the mid-1960s (despite his political misfortunes) as his many children (except the eldest son, who married out in 1963) entered the labor force one after another: the second son in 1966, the third in 1968, a second daughter in 1970, the fourth son in 1977, and the fifth in 1981. Even with the household partitions of his second and third sons, in 1975 and 1977, he was still in good shape financially because of the multiple income-earners in the household.

The household fortunes of the much younger Gao Youfa (b. 1937) had taken a turn for the better only in the last few years, with the entrance into the labor force of two sons and a daughter, all unmarried and living at home. The same went for Wu Hugen (b. 1917). Though his first two children had died young, a third had married in 1983, and the couple still lived in his household. Things had been best for him, he told me, because he had "four people working and four people eating." Wu Genyu (b. 1917), similarly, said things had taken a turn for the better recently, when his daughter started working in the brigade lock factory. A son, born in 1968, was also about to begin earning an income at the time of the interview.

Examples like these could be continued at great length. Of the twelve peasants queried on this point, only two had a different story to tell. He Jinlin (b. 1933), the kind of person for whom the glass is always half empty, said things had never been all that good for him, because his father (d. 1965) and first wife (d. 1980) were sick for a long time; he was the only healthy one in his household. (What is more, in 1984, his eldest son had just split off to establish his own household.) He Kuifa (b. 1925), whose memory was fading, said things had been best for him since the institution of the responsibility system. But his testimony was contradicted by the income data on his household furnished by the brigade; I can only conclude that He was trying to gain favor with the brigade party secretary by mouthing what he thought to be the current policy line. All the others singled out the time when the employment structure of their households changed with the entrance of their children into the labor force. None pointed to a technological breakthrough or a change of policy as marking a dramatic turn in the financial fortunes of their households (H-II-3, 6, 8, 9).

What these peasants took for granted and did not bother to mention, of course, was the fact that it was only under the collectivized economy that household income came to depend not on property ownership but on labor. It was collectivization, and the introduction of the workpoint system, that brought Chinese reality in line with

the model of "demographic differentiation" that Chayanov had outlined in the 1920s for prerevolutionary Russia: the economic well-
being of a peasant household varies with the household's life cycle
and changing laborer-to-consumer ratio (Chayanov 1986 [1925]:
chap. 1; see also Huang 1985: 13–14). A household reaches the top
of its economic fortunes when its children come of age and work,
until they marry and set up on their own. Then the cycle begins all
over; the new household experiences the nadir of its fortunes as its
children grow bigger and consume more, until they enter the labor
force and begin to earn an income.

The peasants' testimony can be checked against data on the "cash
value of each workday equivalent" (the *gongfenzhi*). The workday
equivalent, or gong, is intended to be a measure of a typical agricultural workday, of about six hours, for a ten-point laborer. Long and
intense days of work during the planting and harvesting periods are
rewarded with two or even three gong, based on observations in the
field by the team's work recorder and accountant, who work alongside other peasants and are thoroughly familiar with actual work
conditions. The cash value of the gong is arrived at after deducting
production expenditures, and is a measure of net income, not gross
income. In the absence of more precise data, it is the best gauge for
peasant income per workday during the collectivized years.* Where
prices were stable and a team had little other income outside of
crops, the gong can also be taken as a fair indicator of labor productivity in agriculture.

Table 11.4 shows the cash value of the gong in Xubushanqiao from
1965 to 1983. As is readily apparent, the quantitative data confirm
the peasants' testimony: the gongfenzhi indeed hovered around one
yuan in most of the collectivized years. One notable exception was
1970, when Xubushanqiao cut back drastically on single-cropped
rice (from 112.9 mu to 36.8 mu) and greatly expanded the acreage
under double-cropped rice (from 81.5 mu to 138.1 mu). This shift
to a more intensive cropping regime required increased labor input: total workpoints accumulated by team members jumped from
18,629 to 21,067, an increase of 13 percent. But total output did not
increase commensurately—a result of diminished marginal returns
to labor that came with such extreme intensification. The team
managed to do better only after it had gained more experience with
triple-cropping. In the years 1975–77, the value of the gong declined

---

*The annual income of a laborer, of course, depends also on the number of days
worked a year; and, of a household, the number of days worked by other members of
the household, especially the women. But there was little change in these respects
during the collectivized years.

TABLE 11.4

Cash Value of Workday Equivalent (Gong) in
Xubushanqiao Team, 1965–83

(yuan)

Year	Yuan	Year	Yuan
1965	0.94	1975	0.79
1966	0.94	1976	0.85
1967	1.11	1977	0.80
1968	1.06	1978	0.92
1969	1.04	1979	1.14
1970	0.83	1980	1.03
1971	1.01	1981	0.71
1972	1.01	1982	1.08
1973	1.00	1983	1.27
1974	0.97		

SOURCE: Data furnished by brigade authorities.

well below one yuan again, but this time for reasons external to agriculture: until 1974, team members had earned substantial cash income off-farm helping to load and unload earth used in house construction, but this source of employment dried up as the housing industry shifted to the use of manufactured materials.

It would be a mistake, however, to conclude from the above that what happened in Songjiang was a simple matter of straight-line intensification, of a one-to-one relationship between increased labor input and expanded output. There is in fact incontrovertible evidence of capitalization and development. Improved water control, tractor plowing, chemical fertilizers, and new seeds all contributed to increasing the productivity of land and of labor. Under different conditions, genuine development with rising returns to labor might well have resulted.

But the introduction of those modern inputs was accompanied by extreme labor intensification, which inevitably resulted in diminished marginal returns. Two crops of rice generally require twice as much labor (and capital) as one crop, but do not bring twice the yields. Moreover, pound for pound, early-rice is worth much less than single-cropped rice, in part because local consumers consider long-grain rice much less desirable than short-grain. As for late-rice, its straw is not as usable for sideline products as the thicker straw of single-cropped rice. The vigorous push for across-the-board triple-cropping in the late 1960s, therefore, brought unavoidable declines in average returns per workday.

The same applied to some of the refinements in wheat and cotton cropping. The use of hand-dug underground drainage tunnels for wheat, for example, assuredly made for more efficient land use, but only at the cost of highly intensive labor input. Such intensification, like triple-cropping, might appropriately be labeled involution, for its diminished marginal returns to labor.

The fact of involution is confirmed by the behavior of the Huayang-qiao brigade in the 1980s. Once allowed by higher authorities to give top priority to "economic benefits" (jingji xiaoyi) rather than just total output, the brigade chose to give up double-cropped rice alto-gether. This made good economic sense. Yields from double-cropped early-rice generally ran about 20 percent lower than those from single-cropped rice, because 20 percent of the cultivated area was taken up by seedbeds for the late-rice; and late-rice yields were lower still, because of diminished returns in a second cropping. One would expect a total per-mu yield from double-cropped rice plus winter barley of about 1,600–1,700 catties, compared with 1,300 for single-cropped rice plus wheat (800 rice, 500 wheat). The difference in the yields was worth only only about 24–28 yuan. For that extra incre-ment in yields, the production teams would have to put in 10+ yuan in fertilizer and seeds and 20+ workday equivalents. Obviously, the proposition made sense only if the opportunity costs of the added labor input were very low. Once those costs rose with increased off-farm employment and rural industrialization, double-cropping rice was no longer rational. Thus, once the state eased its procure-ment requirements for the Huayangqiao brigade in 1984, the brigade "opted" enthusiastically for discontinuing triple-cropping (H-II-21).

Output growth without an increase in returns per workday, then, was the result not of simple intensification, but of the coincidence of development with involution. Gains in labor productivity from capitalization were almost entirely whittled away by losses from extreme labor intensification. Development was canceled out by involution.

It is important, however, to sort out these overlapping and yet sepa-rate phenomena. It is tempting to speculate on what might have happened to rural China if collectivization had not been accom-panied by demographic growth. The water-control projects of the late 1950s and 1960s could probably still have been built; after all, the expansion in the labor supply of those years stemmed far more from the mobilization of women for work and of men and women for off-season capital construction than from population growth. It was the postrevolution baby boom that propelled the involuted triple-cropping of the late 1960s and the 1970s. If the accomplishments of the 1950s and 1960s had had the opportunity to exert their full effect without the countervailing influence of overpopulation and extreme labor intensification, the countryside of the Yangzi delta might well have broken out of its underdeveloped poverty. In this respect, the record of the three collectivized decades telescoped and repeated the pattern of agricultural growth without development that character-ized the six centuries between 1350 and 1950.

THE DE-COLLECTIVIZED YEARS

The Songjiang Record

The unexpected result of the rural reforms in Songjiang was that crop yields either dropped or stagnated (see also Putterman 1989 on Dahe township, Huailu county, Hebei). As shown in Table 11.5, yields in all the major crops in Songjiang reached something of a peak in 1979: rice yields were at nearly 800 catties per cropping, wheat surged above 600, cotton climbed above 140, and rapeseed ap-proached 300 (Table 11.1).* But yields turned downward in 1980 and 1981, falling well below 1979 levels in all the crops, and then stag-nated into the late 1980s.

We have not far to look for the reasons. There were no major tech-nological changes in the four major crops during the 1980s. The big steps had been taken in 1978–79, when the underground drainage tunnel system had been adopted for wheat, the "nutrient bowl" transplanting system for cotton, and earlier planting for rape. Those advances were largely responsible for the spurt in yields in those years.

Another factor was the adjustment in cropping patterns imple-mented in 1978. The new combination was summed up in the ex-pression "the three-thirds [cropping] system" (*san san zhi*), with three-year rotations of three different combinations of croppings: Year 1, cotton, rape; Year 2, single-cropped rice, wheat; and year 3, early-rice, late-rice, barley. The formula called for putting one-third of the cultivated acreage each under cotton, single-cropped rice, and double-cropped rice in the spring, and rape, wheat, and barley in the same proportions for the winter. Thus, only one-third of the culti-vated area would be triple-cropped at any one time.

The system represented a substantial reorientation on the part of the planners. On the eve of the adjustments (1975–77), 57.1 per-cent of the cultivated acreage was under double-cropped rice and

---

*In 1978 and again in 1984, cotton yields were exceptionally good because of un-usually dry weather.

TABLE II.5

Index of Yields of Major Crops in Songjiang and China, 1952–87

(1979 = 100)

Year	Rice Song-jiang	Rice China	Wheat Song-jiang[a]	Wheat China	Cotton Song-jiang	Cotton China	Rapeseed Song-jiang	Rapeseed China
1952	63	57	15	34	16	48	23	58
1953	69	59	20	33	18	46	26	60
1954	66	60	18	40	15	40	24	60
1955	69	63	18	40	33	54	28	47
1956	[66]	58	28	43	18	48	15	49
1957	[57]	63	18	40	28	59	29	44
1958	[70]	60	20	41	35	72	26	50
1959	[74]	56	34	44	44	63	39	53
1960	[75]	48	33	38	—	42	—	35
1961	[68]	48	20	26	—	43	—	30
1962	[69]	55	25	32	—	45	—	41
1963	[82]	63	26	37	—	55	—	41
1964	[85]	66	32	38	—	69	—	60
1965	[77]	69	40	48	—	86	—	69
1966	83	74	25	50	68	97	68	60
1967	88	72	32	53	79	95	58	70
1968	81	75	41	52	113	97	75	74
1969	91	74	35	51	101	88	75	71
1970	77	80	42	54	79	94	73	77
1971	69	78	55	59	60	88	85	88
1972	77	76	57	64	92	82	87	82
1973	91	82	28	63	96	106	51	74
1974	82	82	74	71	98	102	82	77
1975	78	83	37	77	96	99	56	77
1976	88	82	67	83	90	86	59	66
1977	77	85	36	68	80	86	44	60
1978	94	94	80	86	134	91	97	83
1979	100	100	100	100	100	100	100	100
1980	72	97	92	88	82	112	71	97
1981	83	102	90	99	70	117	93	123
1982	102	115	93	115	96	126	108	158
1983	87	120	85	131	99	157	82	135
1984	103	127	91	139	139	188	100	141
1985	110	124	90	138	77	166	106	143
1986	98	126	93	143	99	169	80	138
1987	92	128	86	143	93	178	97	150

SOURCE: Table II.I.

[a]Wheat and barley.

42 percent under winter wheat/barley, with only 12 percent under cotton. A literal and complete implementation of the three-thirds system would have reduced double-cropped rice and winter wheat/barley considerably and raised cotton almost threefold. It would have meant adjustments both in the direction of de-involution (to a less-intensive cropping regime) and diversification (with less of the cultivated acreage under grain and more under cash crops) in the cropping portfolio.

This strategic rethinking led to the following actual adjustments in 1978–79: acreage under single-cropped rice was raised from 3.2 percent in 1977 to 7.3 percent in 1978, and then to 14.3 percent in 1979; and acreage under double-cropped rice was reduced from 59.2 percent in 1977 to 51.0 percent in 1978 and 41.9 percent in 1979. The result was a considerable easing of the time pressures from planting two crops of rice. Meanwhile, cotton acreage was adjusted upward to nearly 15 percent in 1977–79. This amounted to a shift away from the great emphasis placed on grain production earlier.

These adjustments in Songjiang's cropping portfolio no doubt played some role in the impressive advances of 1978–79. But care should be taken not to give too much weight to this factor, since further adjustments in the direction of the three-thirds system in 1980–81 (single-cropped rice and cotton rose to more than 20 percent of the cultivated acreage, and double-cropped rice fell to less than 33 percent) did not produce increases in the yields of those crops.

The stimulative effects of adjustments in state procurement prices should also be considered. In 1979, the government raised the price of early-rice and wheat 21 percent, and the price of single-cropped and late-rice 19 percent. These were the first adjustments in grain procurement prices in more than ten years (Lardy 1983: appendix 3). In cotton, quota procurement prices were increased 9 percent in 1978 and raised another 15 percent in 1979. The procurement price for rapeseed was raised a similar 27 percent in 1979. Moreover, the state increased the premium for above-quota sales in grain from the 30 percent set in 1972 to 50 percent in 1979; it also instituted a 30-percent premium for above-quota sales of cotton and rapeseed that year (H-III-27; Lardy 1983: 91–92; Sicular 1986). These measures substantially improved peasant incomes and the terms of rural-urban trade.*

---

*Lardy (1983:89) estimates that average purchase prices paid to peasants nationwide rose by 42 percent between 1977 and 1981. See also his Table 3.4, p. 108.

Once again, however, the effects of price adjustments should not be overestimated. In Songjiang, cropping decisions continued to be made by higher authorities and not by the peasants, as has been seen. We must not confuse the officially planned cropping adjustments of 1978 and after with peasant responses to price and market incentives. Moreover, when asked about the reasons for the changes in crop yields, none of my peasant informants ever pointed to price incentives. For one thing, the intricacies of computing standard quota and premium prices were difficult for them to grasp. For another, as they pointed out, a big part of the grain produced in Songjiang was self-consumed; for that portion of their produce, changes in procurement prices mattered little, affecting only the computations of the total value of output on the books, and not actual peasant income. In any event, if we are to judge by the Songjiang record, the price adjustments appear to have generated at best a one-shot stimulative effect that was not sustained into the 1980s.

Finally, the form of organization of labor for crop production, whether collective or family, does not seem to have mattered much.* The household-responsibility system, when it came to Songjiang in 1983, at first merely linked output quotas to households rather than production teams. Then, in 1985, the quotas were done away with, and farm plots were simply contracted out to individual households to maintain and harvest. State procurement quotas were also basically done away with in 1985–86, because of the glut in state supplies of grain and cotton (but they returned in 1987–88, as has been seen).

In Songjiang, these changes clearly did not bring anything like the spurt in production claimed by the official press for China as a whole. At best, crop yields stagnated. If we can trust the testimony of the peasants and the technical cadres, as opposed to the political cadres, crop yields in Songjiang were shaped principally by technological and climatic factors, and only secondarily by policy choices involving cropping patterns and procurement, and least of all by the reorganization of farm labor.

Development Without Growth

This is by no means to deny that profound changes came with the reforms, only to point out that the reasons for those changes are not the ones claimed by official propaganda. Consider what happened to

---

*Lardy 1983 reaches this same conclusion from his examination of the national record in the early years of the reforms (see especially pp. 220–21).

the cash value of the workday equivalent in Xubushanqiao in 1983: although crop yields in the village dropped that year, the gongfenzhi jumped dramatically, breaking clearly away from the one yuan value of the preceding two decades. Why? Because, as Gao Youfa explained, "the year before each family got to send one worker to the brigade factory. Thus the number of people who shared in the total agricultural output decreased" (H-II-9). Chapter 14 will review the record of industrialization in Huayangqiao and show how dramatically and quickly the lock factory changed the employment patterns in the villages. In the first year alone, fully 34 villagers obtained jobs in the new factory. The outflow of overcrowded labor from the land had been but a trickle in the 1950s and 1960s because industrialization had been largely limited to state-owned enterprises in the cities, which drew their labor force almost entirely from urban residents. The outflow increased somewhat in the 1970s with the establishment of commune industries, which drew part of their labor force from the villages. But it was only with the coming of village industries in the 1980s and the vigorous development of small-town industry (at the level of the commune seat and commune towns) that large numbers of villagers were finally diverted out of overcrowded agriculture. By 1985, more than half of the laborers in the Huayangqiao villages had come to be employed in rural (commune town and village) enterprises. And by 1988, only those villagers above age fifty still remained entirely in farmwork; all the younger men and women were working in higher-paying and less-strenuous off-farm jobs.

What off-farm employment in large numbers meant for Huayangqiao was a reversal of the centuries-long pattern of agricultural (output) growth without (labor productivity) development. As surplus labor got diverted off-farm, labor productivity and income per workday in farming went up markedly, both because of the end to the "loitering labor" under the collectives (when everyone went out to work the entire day in order to earn workpoints, even when there was not that much to do) and because of the great flexibility in using spare-time and auxiliary labor. Thus, even with the diversion of more than half of the full-time labor force from farming, crop yields were maintained at levels close to the collectivized years. The result was a sharp rise in the cash value of the workday equivalent in farming.

The data on these values end with the breakdown of the old accounting systems after 1983 in Huayangqiao. Under the "big contracting" (*dabaogan*) system implemented in 1985, peasant households sold their surplus grain directly to the state rather than through the collective, and team accountants no longer kept a precise record of crop output. In fact, as has been seen, the production teams became but shadows of their earlier selves.

But there can be no mistaking the steady expansion in rural incomes: though crop output from the villages remained close to the earlier levels, thanks to off-farm employment in industries and new sidelines the peasants' new combined incomes dwarfed the old. This new prosperity in Huayangqiao is documented by the 97 percent surge in the gross value of output between 1979 and 1984, and by the radically new composition of that value (from 84.7 percent in crops in 1979 to just 55.6 percent in 1984; Table E.3). Even more, it is evidenced in a new penchant for conspicuous consumption by the villagers and in the dramatically changed appearance of the villages as huts and shacks of straw and earth came to be replaced by two-story houses of stucco and cement in the late 1980s.

For the peasants of Huayangqiao, there can be no mistaking the difference between the earlier pattern of growth without development in crop production and the new pattern of development without growth. In the one, absolute output increased, as did the state's take in taxes and procurement, but farm labor productivity and peasant incomes stagnated. In the other, crop yields have stagnated, as has the state's take in taxes and procurement, but farm labor productivity and peasant incomes from farming have risen dramatically. Nor can there be any mistaking the cause of the change: it comes not from any dramatic breakthrough in crop yields as a result of the supposedly superior incentive power of marketized family farming, but rather from the diversification of the rural economy and the diversion of surplus labor from farming into off-farm employment.

SONGJIANG IN THE NATIONAL CONTEXT

Can the Songjiang story teach us anything about national trends? If we look at only the national record in crop production, it is hard to see any correlation at all: national crop yields continued to grow (after a setback in 1980) after Songjiang's topped out, advancing through 1984, before leveling off in 1985–87.

The advocates of reform imputed these advances mostly to the increased incentives under family farming. In the heady days of 1984, they claimed that family farming had been the "detonator" of the rural development of the 1980s. Moreover, carried away with the 5–6 percent annual growth in crop production between 1979 and 1984, they proclaimed that China had finally solved its problem of feeding and clothing the people. Growth in grain output, they predicted confidently, had only to be sustained at half that rate for the rest of the century to more than adequately supply the nation and support dynamic economic development (Fazhan yanjiusuo 1985: 1–3; Fazhan yanjiusuo zonghe keti zu 1987).

The leveling off of crop yields in 1985–87, however, led to some serious reassessments of these assumptions. For one thing, major flaws of family farming were exposed. In the compensation-obsessed new rural economy of the 1980s, the peasants had allowed irrigation and drainage canals and ditches, which had been dug, dredged, and maintained virtually cost free under the old collectivized organizations, to go almost completely neglected. Additionally, by 1988 the wanton use of chemical fertilizer had finally caught up with the peasants of Songjiang and brought things to a crisis state: the "burnt" soil was caking badly, promising to sharply reduce crop yields. (Local cadres talked about the problem openly, but at the time of my last visit, they had not received any clear directive from above on how to go about rectifying the situation.) Finally, atomized and minuscule family farms that were still close to the margins of subsistence had not been able to generate the accumulative capacity for the capitalization of farm production, all the hulabaloo surrounding "specialized households" (*zhuanye hu*) notwithstanding.

It is in this context that the Chinese leaders turned to experiments with larger farms of "appropriate scale (economies)" (*shidu guimo*). As we have seen, Shunyi county in the outskirts of Beijing became a testpoint for the new approach. In the summer of 1988, there was still much experimentation with different organizational forms for these new larger-scale farms, with unclear outcomes. But if Shajing village (brigade) is at all representative, the new organization will bear much in common with the collectivized production teams and brigades of old. All of the village's farm land was reconsolidated into a single large farm (*nongchang*), its "manager" (*changzhang*) operating in ways little different from the team or brigade head of old. As under the old collective, he took his orders from above and was responsible for seeing that the farm met its assigned quotas. What was new was the relative scarcity of farm labor because of the growth of off-farm employment. The village's 435-mu farm was worked by just eighteen full-time workers, as against more than 40 in the years before rural industrialization. Moreover, the farm no longer had to bear the main burden of the village's expenses, including not only the sustenance of the population, but also cadre compensation, services, welfare, and accumulation for investment.

Village industries now carried the bulk of the burden. Most of the crop output after taxes went to pay the farmworkers. The result was a threefold to fourfold increase in their annual income, which stood at about 2,000 yuan in 1988 (Shajing interviews, May 11, June 28, 1988).

What allowed the sharp reduction in labor was the use of mechanical harvesters, which effected a saving in labor of 2.5 workday equivalents for every mu of wheat. In 1987, the village hired harvesters from the commune at a cost of eight yuan per mu, or about 3.2 yuan for every workday equivalent saved. In the old days, when the cash value of each workday equivalent was well below this level, using the machines would have only added to the costs. Now, however, with ten yuan per day the normal expectation of a laborer, the hiring of the harvesters made good economic sense. In 1988, Shajing village actually purchased a harvester of its own.

In rice-growing Huayangqiao, the search for larger, "appropriate scale" farm production was still under way at that point. As in pre-reorganization Shajing, plowing, irrigation, and insecticide application had all been mechanized earlier. But no mechanized solution had been found for the transplanting and harvesting of rice. Unlike the tractor, which can be put to many jobs other than plowing, the transplanter can have no other use. It was therefore prohibitively expensive, even under the current costs of labor. As for mechanical harvesting, though the same harvesters used for wheat can be used for rice, they chew up the rice stalks, which were still the peasants' main source of fuel for cooking and heating. The fact is that as late as 1988 the countryside of even our very "advanced" Yangzi delta was still very far away from being in a position to convert to coal for fuel. Family organization for transplanting, weeding, and harvesting seemed likely to remain for some time (with plowing and irrigation continuing to be done collectively; H-IV-4).

In the end, the reform leaders have been forced to acknowledge the limitations on what can be done through crop production alone. In this light, Theodore Schultz's meeting with then-party General Secretary Zhao Ziyang (*Renmin ribao*, May 17, 1988) takes on special meaning. Schultz, understandably, has seen in China's agricultural de-collectivization vindication for his long-held thesis that marketized family farming, not collective agriculture, is the way to achieve the modern transformation of peasant economies. As might be expected, at one point in the interview, Schultz praised "the great success" of China's rural reforms. But Zhao pointed out in reply that marketized family farming alone could not be the long-term solu-

tion to rural China's underdevelopment: further progress would require that China overcome the weaknesses of "atomized family
farming" by diverting a substantial proportion of farm labor into off-
farm rural enterprises.

It is in this context of reassessing the record of the reforms of the
1980s that the Songjiang (or Shanghai) approach (currently dubbed,
along with southern Jiangsu, the "Southern Jiangsu model" [*Sunan
moshi*]) takes on special significance. The relevance of the model for
sidelines and for industry are discussed in other chapters; here I re-
strict my attention to the realm of crop production.

In Songjiang, as has been seen, collective organization made possible the dramatic mobilization of women for farmwork, very low-
cost construction of irrigation and drainage networks, and accumulation for "lumpy" modern inputs like tractors and electric pumping
stations (as opposed to "divisible" inputs like chemical fertilizer). It
also allowed for an incentive system much like a small cooperative's, since rewards to team members were tied immediately to the
team's output, rather than to independently standardized wages as
in a state farm or factory. Twofold to threefold increases in crop
yields per sown mu and more than threefold increases per cultivated
mu were attained under collective organization—not at all bad by
any standard (Tables 11.1–11.3).

The problem came not from the collective structure as such, but
from overcrowding. The overabundance of farm labor, conjoined
with the collective structure of remuneration by workpoints, caused
the phenomenon of "loitering labor," such that by the late 1970s,
the same farm tasks (outside of busy-season tasks) were taking one
and a half times as long to accomplish as they required under family
management. Overcrowding plus loitering work, in the context of
artificially low prices for agricultural commodities, in turn, caused
the stagnant returns to farm labor of the 1960s and 1970s, despite
the very high yields attained per unit area.

The Songjiang record suggests that it would be a mistake to expect
a mere change in the form of labor organization from collective to
family farming to power dramatic advances in crop yields. With all
the propagandistic hype on marketized family farming, it is easy to
overlook in the national record the fact that crop yields advanced not
just in the reform period of 1979 to 1984, but throughout the collectivized years, attaining a twofold to threefold increase by late 1970s in
a pattern similar to Songjiang's. Even the years immediately prior to
the wave of implementation of the household-responsibility system
saw advances in yields that approximated those of 1979–84; more

250 AFTER 1949

TABLE II.6

Index of Chemical Fertilizer Input in Shanghai Municipality
and China, 1952–86

(1979 = 100)

	Shanghai		China	
Year	Catties by nutrient value per mu	Index	Catties by nutrient value per mu	Index
1952	0.5	1	0.1	1
1957	1.8	4	0.3	3
1962	4.7	12	0.6	6
1965	15.3	38	1.8	18
1970	20.7	51	—	—
1975	28.6	71	—	—
1978	34.3	85	7.9	81
1979	40.3	100	9.8	100
1980	43.4	108	11.6	118
1981	43.9	109	12.3	126
1982	42.9	106	13.9	142
1983	41.1	102	15.4	157
1984	39.5	98	16.1	164
1985	33.8	84	16.5	168
1986	40.9	101	17.9	183

SOURCES: *Shanghai tongji nianjian* 1987: 183, 201; *Zhongguo tongji nianjian* 1987: 139, 164.
    NOTE: In 1985–86, the ratio of nutrient value to weight was 1 : 4.1 (*Zhongguo nongye nianjian* 1987: 343–44).

than 20 percent in rice and wheat yields between 1976 and 1979, as shown in Tables 11.1 and 11.5.

The difference between the national record and Songjiang's is not one of substance but of a time lag. It is the difference between an advanced area quick to take advantage of new inputs and technological breakthroughs and less-advanced areas slower to follow. The steady improvement in crop yields after the 1960s topped out in Songjiang by the late 1970s but continued in many areas of the nation down to the mid-1980s.

The pattern can be illustrated with the differential records of chemical fertilizer input. As Table 11.6 shows, it would take the nation 20 years to match the rate of chemical fertilizer use in Shanghai municipality in the late 1960s. In Shanghai, something of a plateau appears to have been reached by 1979–80, when nutrient input reached 40+ catties per mu. To judge by the Huayang experience, the leveling off thereafter was more a matter of cost effectiveness than of availability. The local peasants say that by the early 1980s, one could basically purchase all the fertilizer one wanted. But for China as a whole, there was clearly room left for more fertilizer use.

As Table 11.6 shows, the application of chemical fertilizer increased fully 64 percent between 1979 and 1984, from 9.8 catties per mu to 16.1 catties. Given the generally good climatic conditions that prevailed in those years, and assuming that crop yields responded in "normal" ways to the added input (Perkins 1969: 73),* this change alone would be sufficient to explain an average increase of some 75 catties of grain per mu—or one-half of the advance in rice yields and three-fourths of that in wheat yields between 1979 and 1984. But the rate of increase and the response of crops yields at the margins were to diminish in the mid-1980s, as they had in Songjiang some years earlier.

If the Songjiang story does indeed represent a preview of national trends, we would do well to look less to the form of labor organization and more to technological and climatic factors for the explanation of the national advances of 1979–84. There is nothing necessarily magical about either marketized family farming or collective agriculture. The Songjiang story suggests also that advances in national crop yields would level off, as indeed they seemed to do in 1985–87. Most important, it tells us that, given the very highly involuted condition of Chinese agriculture, the impetus for long-term rural (labor productivity) development, as distinguished from mere (output) growth, would have to come from outside crop production. In Songjiang, it was rural industrialization, not marketized family farming, that finally brought real productivity development, after six centuries of growth without development.

*At a rate of three times the multiple of fertilizer to nutrient value (in this case, 4.1), or 12.3, or more.

CHAPTER 12

Rural Industrialization

"Rural industry" is used here to refer to small town and village industry owned by communes/townships (xiang) and brigades/administrative villages (cun), or private groups and individuals. It should be distinguished from state-owned enterprises and county or provincial "collective" industries, usually sited in larger towns and cities. It should also be distinguished from private industries in those urban areas. "Urban industry" generally draws its labor force from urban residents and has little direct impact on rural employment. Rural industrial enterprises, by contrast, employ mainly villagers.

Huayangqiao illustrates the very different effects of urban and rural industrialization on village employment patterns. State-owned urban enterprises accounted for only 33 of the 185 villagers who moved into off-farm jobs between 1950 and 1985; two of 46 from Xubushanqiao; thirteen of 55 from more "advanced" Xilihangbang, which had closer contact with Huayang town; and 18 of 84 from Xuejiada, which is directly adjacent to the town (Appendix Table D.4).* From the peasants' point of view, state enterprises were understandably still perceived as something "outside," rather far removed from the concrete realities of their existence.

It was commune and brigade industrial enterprises that really made the important difference in the villagers' lives. (As earlier, I shall stick to the terms communes and brigades for convenience, even though the units were officially changed to townships and administrative villages after 1983). The commune factories came first, employing increasing numbers of peasants from the 1970s on. By 1985, commune enterprises accounted for 80 jobs in Huayangqiao,[†]

*The figures throughout are totals. They include temporary positions and people who at some point moved elsewhere; these cases are identified in the Appendix D tables.

[†]Includes nonindustrial commune units like the Town Sanitation Group and the Culture Factory, as well as very small units like the Furniture Factory and the Town

or 43 percent of all the off-farm jobs there. Brigade enterprises came to employ a significant number of the villagers in the 1980s (chiefly in 1982 with the opening of the lock factory) and by 1985 accounted for 72 of all the jobs off-farm.* If our concern is with transformative change for China's peasants, we need to focus on rural industrial enterprises rather than urban ones.

GROWTH OF INDUSTRY IN HUAYANG COMMUNE

Rural industry in the Yangzi delta generally began as one of four types of "factories": (1) those linked directly to agriculture or local resources and handicrafts (e.g., the production and repair of agricultural tools, processing of industrial crops and food, brick making, textiles); (2) those using either old equipment phased out by higher-level industries or waste materials (e.g., bits and pieces of plastic left over from the larger factories, worn rubber tires, low-grade cotton rejected by the large factories, scrap iron) to produce small commodities not provided by state industries (e.g., plastic basins, elastics, coarse cotton sacks, locks); (3) those operated in conjunction with larger state-owned industrial enterprises, especially for the use of cheap village labor in the processing of factory-produced goods; and (4) those linked to foreign capital and the export market. In Nantong municipality in 1985, for example, farm machinery and implements repair accounted for about 20 percent of total rural industrial output, recycling production another 40 percent, and processing contracts with larger factories or foreign capital for the remaining 40 percent (H-III-44).

Huayang commune illustrates the path that rural industrialization has generally taken. The first industrial enterprise, the Agricultural Implements Factory (Nongji chang), was established during the Great Leap. The main activity at first was the repair of agricultural hand tools, with some small-scale production of tools in "backyard furnaces." Other locally rooted items were gradually added—straw rope, furniture (separated out in 1979, when the Furniture Factory, or Jiaju chang, was established), bricks and tiles (with separate accounting dating back to 1958), metal products (later to be merged into the Printing Factory]—all involving mainly hand production. This conglomerate "factory" employed 130 workers by 1968.*

Household handicraft sock making, which had emerged in the greater Shanghai area in the twentieth century with the coming of machine-spun yarn, was the basis for another commune workshop. The enterprise began as a collective undertaking in 1950, was taken over by the state in 1957, only to be disbanded in 1960–62 during "the three difficult years" (when people could no longer afford socks), and was then reestablished by the commune in 1964. It employed almost all of the 400–500 people in Huayang commune who had been involved in the activity before 1949.

These locally originated handicraft industries were mechanized only after they were linked with, and aided by, higher-level industrial enterprises. In 1971, for example, the Agricultural Implements Factory contracted with a Shanghai factory to make a nozzle for fire hoses, a clamp for irrigation pumps, and bushings for spinning machines. The Shanghai factory supplied the equipment and materials and saw to the marketing; Huayang furnished the labor and the processing site. It was really a kind of putting-out arrangement, termed *weituo jiagong* ("commissioned processing"). The addition of this new component increased the workshop's labor force to 400. Similarly, the commune Sock Factory (Wa chang) made arrangements in 1972 to begin processing work for the Shanghai Number Six Sock Factory, using 45 old machines that the factory was phasing out. In 1981, the commune unit bought those machines for 300 yuan each and added 56 new, more sophisticated ones that cost 3,000 yuan apiece. By 1983, the factory employed 683 workers.

The Sock and Agricultural Implements factories gave the commune enough of a start in industrialization to allow it to establish the Printing [Machine] Factory (Yinshua [jijie] chang) on its own in 1979. Its activities in this field had begun two years earlier with the purchase of a small electric press for something over 3,000 yuan. The Printing Factory, in turn, expanded two years after it opened its doors by contracting with the Shanghai Camera Factory, located nearby at the east gate of Songjiang city, to make backs for box cameras. Later, the link was expanded to cover the first rough grinding of camera lenses. The success of those two activities formed the basis for the new Optical Parts Factory (Guangxue lingjian chang), built

*The information in this section, unless otherwise identified, is based on interviews conducted by Joseph Esherick, one of the four members of our research team. I am grateful to Joe for allowing me to use his data.

jointly with commune and Shanghai Camera capital, which opened in 1983. It employed 235 workers in 1984.

A fifth important commune factory, the Wool Yarn Factory (Maotiao chang), had a similar history. It grew out of a processing arrangement with the Shanghai Number Two Wool Yarn Factory in 1981. As in the other arrangements, the commune provided the land, the building, and the labor, and the Shanghai factory furnished the capital equipment and the materials, and saw to the marketing. The profits were shared according to complex formulas. The factory employed 223 workers by 1984.

Subcontracting was similarly crucial for the brigade's main enterprise. In this case, the capital equipment (four lathes) was purchased from a commune enterprise, and the processing contract was made with another brigade-level enterprise. The raw material was scrap metal, and the product was parts for locks, hence the informal name lock factory (suo chang) for this enterprise, formally called the Mechanical Electrical Factory (Jidian chang). In 1985, the lock factory employed 58 workers and was the principal source of off-farm jobs in our four villages.

In 1986 Huayang advanced to yet a higher stage of industrial development. Together with the Shanghai Meat Products Foreign Trade Company and Songjiang county's Dajiang Company, it entered into a joint enterprise with a Thai finance group (Zhengda) to start a chicken-processing plant at an initial investment of U.S. $6,000,000. Huayang supplied 30 percent of the Chinese side of the investment (the Shanghai Meat Products Foreign Trade Company 20 percent and Songjiang's Dajiang Company 50 percent), and furnished the land and most of the labor. The new plant, the Meat Products Company (Roushipin chang), supplied baby chicks and feed to the peasant households in the area, then bought them back full-grown, to be slaughtered and frozen for export. In 1988, the plant was processing 20,000 chickens a day (H-IV-1, 3).

This enterprise gave a powerful boost to the industrialization of the township. By providing an output worth in excess of 50,000,000 yuan a year, it doubled the gross value of Huayang's industrial output practically overnight. In 1987, it employed more than 700 residents of the township, including ten Huayangqiao villagers, pushing the villages yet further along the path of industrialization. In the summer of 1988, plans were afoot for yet another joint enterprise with foreign capital, this time with a Japanese company to manufacture jackets and pants, at an initial investment of U.S. $1,300,000 (H-IV-3).

CONSTRUCTION AND TRANSPORT

Employment in these workshops and factories produced substantial increases in peasant incomes, both because of the somewhat higher industrial salaries and because of improved distributions per unit labor in agriculture as a result of the removal of surplus labor. Increased peasant incomes, in turn, sparked more spending, especially in the area of housing. The tendency was reinforced by state policy, which in the 1980s raised housing construction to top priority. It was also reinforced by the changing age structure of the population: the baby boomers of the 1950s and 1960s were getting married and demanding housing for their newly established households. The combined effect was a boom in the rural construction industry, shown by the fact that the commune's Construction Station employed fully 23 Huayangqiao villagers by 1985.

Another source of new employment, linked closely to rural industrialization, was transport. There had always been some hiring out by the villagers for transport work during the collective era. Xubushanqiao team, for example, had three transport workers. But the spread of trading among rural production units in equipment, raw materials, and products brought a greatly increased demand for transport. By 1988, six people in Xubushanqiao were employed in this work. Though usually heavy work, transport jobs paid well, ranging from 2,000 to 4,000 yuan a year in 1988 (H-IV-5).

Capitalized sidelines, housing construction, transport, and most of all, rural industry between them absorbed a large proportion of the rural labor pool. According to my peasant informants, by 1988 every male and female laborer under fifty in Huayangqiao was employed outside of agriculture; only older people still remained in farming.

CAPITALIZATION AND WAGE COSTS

One key to the earlier stages of rural industrialization in the commune is that it used relatively little capital investment per laborer. We can get an approximate indication of the difference in capitalization between the Huayang factories and the state-owned urban industrial enterprises by comparing their investment-per-employee figures. As Table 12.1 shows, the national average for state enterprises in 1983 stood at 13,422 yuan, compared with some 7,000 to 4,000 yuan in the three relatively highly capitalized Huayang factories, and 2,000 or less in the rest. If the cost of buildings could be

TABLE 12.1

Capitalization, Income Produced, and Wages Per Employee
in Huayang Enterprises Compared with the Average
in State Industrial Enterprises, 1983

(yuan)

Enterprise	Fixed capital[a]	Number of employees	Capital per employee	Income per employee[b]	Average wage[c]
State-owned industry	—	—	13,422	12,401	878
Commune-owned industry					
Printing Factory	2,168,455	318	6,819	5,773	528
Wool Yarn Factory	998,620	195	5,121	4,451	679
Optical Parts Factory	998,840	235	4,250	—[d]	—[d]
Furniture Factory	193,000	83	2,325	5,360	498
Sock Factory	1,233,256	683	1,806	4,789	800[e]
Bricks and Tiles Factory	622,135	365	1,704	2,303	651
Brigade-owned industry (lock factory)	89,502	60	1,492	1,989	628

SOURCES: State-owned industrial enterprises, Zhongguo tongji nianjian, 1984: 108, 264, 265, 459. Commune and brigade data were furnished by the local units in 1985.

NOTE: No data available on the Agricultural Implements Factory as a unit. Both the Furniture Factory and the Bricks and Tiles Factory are offshoots of the original factory.

[a]The Chinese accounting category is guding zichan yuanzhi, or "original value of fixed capital," which is based on actual expenses at the time of installation. It includes building costs in addition to capital equipment.

[b]The State Statistical Bureau uses a different category: "labor productivity" (laodong shengchan lü), computed by dividing the value of total output of state-owned industries by the number of employees. I have used here the slightly different figure of "gross income" (zong shouru), as opposed to "total output" (zong chanzhi), to make the figure comparable with the local data, which are given in terms of gross income and not total output.

[c]Including bonuses.

[d]The factory was only founded this year. The income per employee (1,064 yuan) and the average wage (161) are therefore low because they apply to only a period of months.

[e]This represents a substantial jump over previous years. The figure for 1980 is 573, for 1981, 577, and for 1982, 585. The factory began producing synthetic socks in 1981–82, with additional capitalization. The high wages of 1983 reflect that change.

deducted from these data to compare only the relative value of the capital equipment, the contrast would be greater still. The low level of capitalization makes understandable the price tag attached to jobs in collective factories: in Huayang in 1985, peasants could secure a position in the planned Meat Products Factory for 1,500 yuan (in addition to passing an examination)—a procedure

called "using capital to lead the way for labor" (*yizi dailao;* H-III-27).
It was a way to raise start-up funds for industries with few financial
sources to draw on.

These capital-cheap industries often carry a junkyard dimension.
The Huayang Sock Factory, as we saw, got going by taking over 45
"K-type" sock-knitting machines from the Shanghai Number Six
Sock Factory, and the brigade's lock factory was established with
lathes phased down from a commune enterprise. For capital-scarce
China, milking every machine to capacity instead of junking it fig-
ures importantly in the program of rural industrialization.

Table 12.1 also compares the "gross income" per employee in the
different kinds of industrial enterprises. The amount of income
produced was of course very much influenced by state pricing policies and the nature of the industry, but the correlation between the
rate of capitalization and earnings is clear enough: the more highly
capitalized factories generated more income per employee.*

The differential, though narrowed considerably, also held in wages.
The average wage per worker was substantially higher in the state-
owned enterprises than in the Huayang factories: 878 yuan a year in
1983, compared with an average of 630 for the factories (Table 12.1).
Peasant informants estimated that other off-farm employment in
brigade units paid 500 to 700 yuan a year (H-III-1).

As the cadres and peasant informants pointed out, there were substantial differences in benefits as well. In state enterprises (and
county collective enterprises) workers continued to get 70 percent of
their salary during retirement, compared with only 40 percent for
the Huayang enterprises, and generally nothing at all for brigade enterprises. The state enterprises covered all medical expenses and permitted disability leave with full pay for up to six months. The commune employee usually had to pay for medical services (in Huayang
in 1985 a bed in the commune clinic cost 0.9 yuan a day and each
injection 0.4 yuan), and there was a one-week limit on disability
leave at full pay (thereafter, the worker got 70 percent of his salary,
for a maximum of six months). The brigade enterprises provided no
benefits of this sort at all. Death benefits, finally, were similarly differentiated: the state enterprises paid 300 yuan for funeral expenses,
plus two to three months' salary; the commune enterprises gave

---

*Many village enterprises, to be sure, have outperformed state enterprises in this
regard, especially some of the joint-stock enterprises in Guangdong and Fujian enjoying overseas investment. I am referring here to the general pattern in collective
industry.

only 180 yuan for funeral expenses; and the brigade enterprises, once again, provided no benefits at all (H-III-5).

From the point of view of the state factories, the main reason for dispersing parts of the production process to the rural areas was to get rid of money-losing or low-return operations. Lower wage costs made those operations viable for the rural units, even if they were not for the state enterprises. Indeed, from the point of view of a commune and brigade with abundant surplus labor, low returns might still prove attractive: even if the enterprise brought no greater return than agriculture, it still had the value of relieving the pressures on the distribution of agricultural income. Both sides to a processing contract, therefore, stood to benefit.

HUAYANG IN THE NATIONAL CONTEXT

Huayang commune, to be sure, cannot be considered "representative" of China as a whole. Inland peripheral areas do not have the access to links with metropolitan industry or foreign capital and markets that the Shanghai area has enjoyed in recent years. Those links, as has been seen, were crucially important to the rapid industrial development of Huayang township in the late 1970s and 1980s.

Nonetheless, the Huayang record tells a much larger story. We must not underestimate the scope of China's rural industrialization in the 1980s. By 1986, industry accounted for more than 40 percent of the gross value of output in rural China (Appendix Table E.1), excluding the value of new housing, transport fees, commercial profits, and the gross revenues of the many new eateries. If the latter categories are added to the gross value of output in rural China, industry still accounted for more than 30 percent (Table E.2).

Huayang commune was well ahead of the rest of the nation, for its industrial development reached those proportions of total output by the mid-1970s. The subsequent spurs to development from joint enterprises with metropolitan factories and, in the mid-1980s, from joint enterprises with foreign capital, raised industry's share of total commune output to over two-thirds. To the extent that such development represented opportunities not open to areas at some remove from the eastern and southeastern coast or from major cities, Huayang cannot be considered representative even of the trends to come. Yet, by the mid-1980s, efforts were being made to bring inland units into the industrial network by linking them to townships on the eastern coast. Huayang's leaders, for example, were ordered to get together with the leaders of Xingguo county in Jiangxi province to establish a joint enterprise (H-IV-3). The nation's economic planners, it is clear, hope to extend the successful development experience of the coastal areas to inland peripheral areas by having coastal townships play the same role for the interior that the coastal cities had performed for them at an earlier stage.*

COLLECTIVE VS. PRIVATE ENTERPRISES

Most industries in Huayang, as the foregoing discussion suggests, continued to be collective enterprises, whether owned and managed by the communes and brigades of old, or by the current township and administrative-village governments. In 1986, collective enterprises still accounted for fully 93.5 percent of the gross income of all rural enterprises in Shanghai municipality and 88 percent in Jiangsu province, compared with a mere 1.4 percent and 7.8 percent, respectively, for private individual enterprises (Appendix Table F.1; cooperative enterprises of various sorts accounted for the balance). There can be no mistaking the continuing primacy of the collective organization unit in the rural industrialization of the Yangzi delta area.

What little individual "enterprise" there was lay largely outside of industry. Two Xubushanqiao villagers, He Huoyun and Yang Xiutang, purchased their own boats and relied entirely on transport work for a living. A fellow villager, Yang Hongqiang, gave up his job in the lock factory to engage full time in peddling watermelons, vegetables, and fish. (Yang netted 2,000 yuan in 1987 from this petty trade.) And Zhang Yinlong of Xue Family Village was quick to join in the national proliferation of private eating establishments during the 1980s by setting up a restaurant (H-IV-5).

Elsewhere in China, collective organization has lost some ground, certainly much more so than in Huayangqiao. Individual and private cooperative enterprises in Guangdong province, with its access to overseas Chinese capital, for example, accounted for more than 30 percent of the gross income of all rural enterprises in 1986. In Sichuan province, which spearheaded the 1980s reforms, the private sector's share was more than 43 percent. In Hebei and Henan, such

*Note, in this connection, that in 1986 the research group led by Fei Xiaotong, which studied small towns and urban-rural relations in the Yangzi delta in 1981–85, embarked on a new five-year study of the relations between the coastal and inland areas, in an enlarged conception of urban-rural relations (interview with Zhang Yulin, May 20, 1988).

ventures accounted for more than 50 percent. Nationwide, individual enterprise (*geti qiye*) has clearly been the most dynamic of all the organization forms in rural industry. From a mere 7.7 percent share in 1984 (when these businesses were officially included under "rural enterprises" and systematic records of them were first kept), they surged to 17.5 percent in 1985 and 23.5 percent in 1986 (C. Wong 1988: 12; Table F.1).

Individual enterprises seem generally most prevalent in poorer localities (*Zhongguo nongye nianjian* 1987: 3). As William Byrd and Alan Gelb (1988) have shown convincingly, this is largely due to the financial straits of their township governments. Townships with well-developed industries enjoy large revenues from the retained profits of the enterprises. In these townships, government expenditures for public services consume only a small part of the total revenues, leaving a large share for investment in other industries, producing still more revenues and more investments. Poorer townships without strong industries have sparse revenues, sometimes not even enough to cover the relatively inelastic requirements for public services. Some of these townships engage in a kind of "fiscal predation" on their enterprises, even if unprofitable, forcing them to borrow to meet payments to the governments. The result is a vicious cycle of poverty. It is in backward areas like these that low-investment private enterprises have flourished the most relative to collective enterprises.

A few of these areas have in fact seen their private enterprises go on to vigorous development and capitalization. The Wenzhou District (embracing Wenzhou city and nine counties in southeastern Zhejiang province, with a total population at the end of 1986 of 6,400,000) is the example par excellence. The key to success there is the district's 133,000 small household enterprises. Those enterprises, with an average of three labor units each, employed some 15 percent of Wenzhou's work force in 1985 (400,000 in a total of 2,670,000) and accounted for fully 60 percent of the gross value of output of all rural enterprises (Guo 1987: 86; He et al. 1987: 1–4).

The Wenzhou household enterprises are chiefly of the capital-cheap, labor-intensive variety, which take advantage of the distinctive qualities of the family production unit. One major product line, for example, is cheap acrylic sweaters and bags. In 1985, some 380 buyers scouted the nation for raw material and managed to purchase in bulk a total of 17,000 tons of leftover odds and ends of the synthetic material, at 0.5 yuan per catty. Shipped to Yishan, the center of the acrylic recycling industry, these bulk purchases were sorted by 600 households, fluffed by another 1,200 households, spun, woven, and knit by 6,400, and finally sent to 2,900 others for tailoring. All together, these small producers manufactured some 150,000,000 items of clothing (including sweaters that sold at the incredible price of just 1.60 yuan apiece), 68,000,000 acrylic knit bags, and 3,000,000 bolts of acrylic fabric. Their combined products were marketed by some 8,000 traveling salesmen all over the nation, each of whom typically sold several hundred to several thousand items at a time; these agents each grossed from 30,000 to 300,000 yuan in sales that year and made a net profit of a few thousand yuan (He et al. 1987: 26, 33–34).

Other major product lines in Wenzhou are plastic shoes, elastic waistbands, shoelaces, aluminum school badges (more than half of all those used in the nation), and buttons, all "petty commodities" that can be efficiently produced for low cost by the household unit (He et al. 1987: 19–31).

What is interesting about the Wenzhou story is the specialization and capitalization that has developed within this household-based industry. In the production of badges, for example, households specialize variously in design, drawing, carving, cutting the model, cutting the material, painting, drilling the hole, and so on (He et al. 1987: 10), much as in the production of acrylic sweaters. Typically, the spinning and weaving/knitting of the sweaters are done by machine rather than by hand, each household owning its simple spindles and looms.

Scholars committed to arguing the intrinsic superiority of marketized family enterprise, in industry as well as in farming, will of course find much support for their predilections in the Wenzhou experience. Given suitable market conditions and a sufficient surplus, the small-scale family production unit, to be sure, can be a unit for accumulation and capitalization, no less than the successful mom-and-pop business in the United States. "Petty commodity production," *pace* Marx, can become capitalist production even as it continues to rely on the household unit. But the potential of the Wenzhou type of development, under present conditions in China, should not be exaggerated. The area has a special history: opened as a treaty port in 1876, and pressed by its very low land-man ratio (0.44 mu of cultivated area per capita in 1985, compared with 1.5 mu nationwide), Wenzhou had a strong tradition of petty commerce and production. The family enterprises of the mid-1980s are sustained by an army of no fewer than 140,00 petty traders roaming all over the nation in search of opportunities and cracks in the bureaucratized economy. Few other areas enjoy this kind of tradition and commercial network. The market for low-cost petty commodities such as those produced by Wenzhou, moreover, is not an indefinitely inflatable one: the district has a virtual monopoly on its school badges and cheap acrylic sweaters and bags. There may not be room for many more Wenzhous.

More important, it will not do to exaggerate the scope and importance of the Wenzhou type of family enterprise in China as a whole. Even within Zhejiang province itself, Wenzhou is unique; provincewide in 1986, private individual enterprises accounted for a mere 8.4 percent of gross income of all rural enterprises (against 83.5 percent for collective enterprises; Table F.1). And despite the dynamic spread of such enterprises, collective enterprises still accounted for the lion's share of the gross income generated by rural enterprises nationally: 66.1 percent, compared with 23.5 percent for private enterprises. Most of all, we need to keep in mind the singular preponderance of collective organization in the successful rural industrialization experience of areas like the Yangzi delta.

The Classical English Experience

Rural industrialization and small-town development of the Huayang type provide a sharp contrast with the classical experience in England. In England and, to a lesser extent, continental Europe, industrialization proceeded from the bottom up, from village handicraft home industry to small-town handicraft manufacturing to big city machine manufacturing. Jan de Vries (1981, 1984) urges that a distinction be made between a premodern pattern of urbanization, which saw the growth of large, old administrative-commercial cities (with populations of 40,000 or more, like Paris and London), and a "new urbanization" that took place chiefly in smaller new towns and cities (of sizes between 5,000 and 39,000). For de Vries, this was a Europe-wide pattern that began around 1750. Between 1750 and 1800, the proportion of Europeans living in larger cities remained stationary (growing by only 0.2 percent over the period), while the proportion living in the small cities and towns exploded fourfold. E. Anthony Wrigley (1985) has refined de Vries's data and argument to show that this "new urbanization" was first and foremost an English phenomenon, traceable to the dynamic rise and expansion of towns after about 1670.

In China, industrialization and modern urbanization proceeded instead from the top down: first through the transplanted urban factories in the era of imperialism, and then through aggressive state-sponsorship of large-scale factories in the postrevolutionary decades. (One result, as we shall see, was a widening urban-rural gap that extended across the economic realm to the social and cultural.) China did not see the sort of vigorous small-town development that occurred in England in the period 1670–1800 until the 1980s. G. William Skinner (1977: 229) estimates the proportion of Chinese living in towns of 2,000 or more in 1843 at just 5.1 percent, rising to 7.6 percent in the most advanced "Lower Yangzi" region, compared with the 27.5 percent (in towns of 5,000 or more) in England in 1801 estimated by Wrigley (1985: 688, table 2). Even as late as 1980, only 19.4 percent of the population lived in towns of 2,500 or more.*

Thus, China's rural industrialization is "late," totally unlike the "early industrialization" of England. And so is its modern small-town development. Large cities (like Shanghai and Tianjin) led the way in modern urbanization, not small towns as in the English and European experience. And industrialization occurred not first in small rural industries, giving way later to large urban factories, but rather the reverse, occurring first in urban factories, whose worn equipment and lowest-paying operations then trickled down into the towns and villages.

The Contemporary Developing Countries

If we turn our comparative searchlight from the classical English experience to the contemporary developing world, a different contrast comes to the fore. The top-down pattern of industrialization and urbanization is common to Third World countries that began the processes after imperialist intrusion. What is distinctive about rural development in China is not the top-down pattern but the active role played by village and township collectives. Typically in most Third World countries, rural populations have passively waited for urban industry to expand to the point where it can absorb them into the labor force. Industry is typically sited almost entirely in urban and town centers, and industrial development is typically accompanied by massive out-migration from the rural areas. This is

---

*More precisely, towns of 2,500 or more, with 85 percent of the population off-farm, or towns of more than 3,000, with 70 percent of the population off-farm. This definition of town (zhen) was adopted by the State Statistical Bureau in 1964. Before that, the standard was a population of 2,000 or more, with 50 percent off-farm (*Zhongguo tongji nianjian*, 1983: 104, 576).

quite unlike the modern Yangzi delta story, where rural collectives took the lead in accumulation for rural industrialization, first at the commune level and then at the brigade level. Beginning early on, industries were sited in the countryside, not only in the small-town seats of government, but also inside the natural villages themselves, and the rural population was kept in place by a rigid registration policy.

The Huayang example shows how the basis for township industrialization was first laid through commune accumulation, with a small farm tools workshop linked to local agriculture during the Great Leap, and a sock workshop built on the prerevolutionary handicraft industry of the area in 1964. Given a powerful boost by subcontracting arrangements with larger state factories in the 1970s, commune industrialization began to stimulate brigade industrialization in the 1980s, following the same pattern of collective accumulation and trickle-down mechanization. Thus the Huayangqiao brigade acquired the "obsolete" capital equipment of a commune enterprise to establish its lock factory.

Huayang gives concrete illustration to the kind of industrialization described in a saying associated with Fei Xiaotong (1984): in contrast to industrial development under capitalism, where "the big fish eat the little fish, and the little fish eat the shrimps" (*dayu chi xiaoyu, xiaoyu chi xiami*), in "socialist" China, "the big fish help the little fish, and the little fish help the shrimps" (*dayu bang xiaoyu, xiaoyu bang xiami*). This construction is excessively moralistic, to be sure, but it does capture a central reality of the top-down pattern of industrialization in China.

With all the press being given to agricultural de-collectivization, to capitalistic industrial development in the home communities of the overseas Chinese in Guangdong and Fujian, and to free-market and family enterprise in a place like Wenzhou, it is easy to distort or forget the reality of collective industry. But that is in fact the dominant mode of rural industrial organization in the Yangzi delta, and indeed in most of China. It is the form of productive organization that powered most of the rural industrialization that took place in the 1970s and 1980s, and it is what distinguishes the China experience from that of most other Third World countries.

CHAPTER 13

Capitalism Versus Socialism
in Rural Development

Debates over China's rural development are often framed in terms of a struggle between capitalism and socialism, particularly in crop production, which is what most people immediately associate with the word "agriculture." The recent reforms supposedly turned China decisively toward the capitalistic approach by agricultural decollectivization and the return to family farming. The reformers called on the enterprise and initiative of rational family farmers, and dramatic advances in crop production were the prompt result. Their socialist predecessors, by contrast, are portrayed as having relied on overplanned, collectivized agriculture, to the neglect of individual incentives, the sure path to stagnation.

THE ROLE OF IDEOLOGY

We do not have far to look for the roots of such a highly ideological way of posing the issues. Decades of revolution-making solidified a particular kind of attitude toward the role of political agency among the party leaders. To begin with, a revolutionary is almost by definition someone who believes in the primacy of individual choice, of the capacity of human agency to reshape the structure of society. That attitude was strengthened through the actual experience of triumphing against overwhelming odds. Once in power, the restructuring of society through land reform and collectivization further confirmed the faith, while the vast expansion in the scope and apparatus of the state lent institutionalized expression to the power of human agency, at least of the leaders. Indeed, the revolutionary tradition forged the assumption that political agency is determinative. It is an assumption running so deep in Chinese political discourse as to be taken for granted, too obvious to require justification.

Within that faith is a particularly strong emphasis on the role of ideology. It is once again an emphasis that is reinforced not just by Marxism-Leninism, but by concrete historical experience. For twentieth-century China's elite intellectuals, the difference between choosing to become an underground revolutionary and becoming a successful official, businessman, or professor was often just a matter of a sliver of political consciousness. Then, after the seizure of power, it was ideological choice that powered the restructuring of society, in land reform and collectivization. The cumulative effect was to elevate ideology to center stage in all political discussion in China.

Maoists and reformers alike have operated within this structure of discourse. The Maoists set the terms of the debate with their insistence on "the struggle of the two roads" between socialism and capitalism. They harped on the theme of "politics [i.e. ideology and morality] in command." Their reformist critics felt impelled, even as they criticized the Maoists' excessive emphasis on ideology, to stress the importance of ideological choice. They harped on the negative consequences of Maoist ideological choice and the positive results of their own, all the while condemning "politics in command" as "ultra-leftist."

The propaganda emanating from official China in the 1980s struck ready chords in the American mass media. The American public showed, once again, that what it wants to see in China is not so much the complex reality that is China, as the confirmation of its own cherished values. What could be more alluring than the thought that, after a decade of ideological ranting against capitalism, the Chinese Communists had finally realized the folly of their ways, criticized the "radicals" as Americans might, and adopted the American way to agricultural development?

WORK INCENTIVES AND CROP PRODUCTION

Within this ideological discourse on both sides of the ocean, the issue of incentives, especially, has been elevated to a position of great symbolic significance. The Maoists had insisted on the paramountcy of work incentives: whether other-serving moral incentives or self-serving material incentives operated was nothing less than part of the struggle between "the two roads of socialism and capitalism." Their critics emphasized the opposite: for them, the pursuit of material gain was the very stuff of economic "rationality," and the resort to revolutionary exhortations of working for the public good represented the heart of "ultra-leftism."

Once again, it is a line of argument that strikes deep chords in the

American consciousness. After all, the idea that the "rational" pursuit of self-interest powers modern development constitutes the very core of the capitalist faith. In addition, we Americans, given the scarcity and high cost of labor in our economy, are greatly concerned with the question of how well incentives motivate work. From our point of view, it is perfectly understandable to place great emphasis on this question. Indeed, most of us would assume that the issue of incentives is too obviously crucial to require justification or explanation.

We assume, furthermore, that profit maximizing in a market economy has got to be the main motivation for work. American farmers choose what they grow, how to grow it, and how much of it is to be sold. And in this land of plenty, the farmers have long enjoyed (at least by Chinese standards) a great potential for profit and gain. We therefore assume that the profit motive must figure centrally in farming in China no less than here.

It is easy to forget that for the Chinese farm family, given the great surplus of human labor in the rural economy, the work incentive was—and is—of less concern. In the days before agricultural collectivization, the surplus peasants produced above subsistence was minimal, and sheer survival, not profit maximizing, had to be the primary concern of most peasants. With collectivization, little room was left for individual choice, and the surplus above subsistence in any event still remained minimal. Under those conditions, collective survival, not market profit, was the primary motivation for work. Even under the 1980s reforms, as has been seen, agriculture was far from being as marketized, and its surplus far from being as great, as in American farming.

In the supposed struggle between capitalist and socialist incentives, the tendency on both sides of the ocean has been to focus especially on crop production. The Maoists, once again, set the terms of the debate in the Great Leap Forward, with their millenarian hopes for the magic of other-serving incentives in crop production. The reformers responded in kind: the socialist planning of crop production led to agricultural stagnation, whereas capitalist incentives powered dramatic breakthroughs. For Maoists as for their critics, labor organization in crop production occupied center stage in the debates over rural development.

We Americans have been quick to accept official China's emphasis on crop production. Given the relatively non-intensive nature of our agriculture, we accept readily the notion that crop production can expand greatly and make a decisive difference for development. It is easy to forget that in other places, including most parts of China, crop intensity has already been raised as high as the land can bear.

The rest of this chapter examines what actually happened during the Great Leap Forward, the Cultural Revolution, and the early rural reforms, to see where and how the capitalist-versus-socialist debate on crop production has distorted the real issues in China's rural development.

THE GREAT LEAP FORWARD (1958–60)

In Huayang, according to the peasants, the "big mess halls" (*da shitang*), in which everyone simply ate as much as he or she wanted without paying, operated for some four months, from October 1958 to January 1959. This was the height of Leap radicalism, when the ideological line moved from the socialist "to each according to his labor" to the communist "to each according to his need," and when the incentive for work moved from the material to the moral/ political plane. But the commune quickly ran short of food, and a system of "small mess halls" (*xiao shitang*) was introduced. People were now issued coupons and took the rice home, to apportion out as they saw fit. That system lasted until the middle of 1960. Then private plots returned, as did private hog raising. In 1961, the team replaced the commune as the basic unit of ownership, accounting, and production, essentially returning the administrative structure to what it was before the Leap. Thus, the organizational features commonly associated with the Leap were basically in effect only in the years 1959 and 1960 (H-II-7, 12).

Crop yields remained high through those two years. To be sure, in these villages the Leap brought the romantic notion that the land could be made to yield almost infinite amounts in response to labor and capital inputs. But the commune was not willing to test this romantic notion on more than a few mu of land. In Xuejiada, twice the usual amount of seeds and fertilizer was used on two mu. In Xubushanqiao, the team leader Yang Xiaofa recalls, they called the experimental fields "satellite" plots (*weixingdi*) and farmed them with "rocket squads" (*huojiandui*). On those plots, they plowed the land to the depth of a person and "tossed in whole cakes" of bean-cake fertilizer. (The results? Well, the rice did grow very big and tall, Yang says, so big and tall that the plants simply toppled over. Did he really think the experiments would work, seasoned farmer that he was? Well, he knew they would not work, but the atmosphere of the time was such that he dared not say so.) These experimental plots were limited to only six mu of the team's land; the rest was farmed as it had been before the Leap (H-II-7).

The Huayangqiao peasants' and team leaders' testimony is confirmed by the commune's statistics: average yields for all the major crops continued to advance through 1958 and 1959, and most of them remained high through 1960. Single-cropped rice, the most important crop at the time, broke 600 catties per mu in both 1959 and 1960 (Table 13.1).

TABLE 13.1

Yields of Major Crops in Huayang, 1956–83

(catties per sown mu)

Year	Single-cropped rice	Early-rice	Late-rice	Wheat/barley	Cotton	Rapeseed
1956	570	455	225	182	—	42
1957	509	403	128	122	—	92
1958	532	505	230	127	—	95
1959	614	484	333	208	—	150
1960	613	494	214	201	—	117
1961	572	498	235	130	—	79
1962	558	419	217	158	—	102
1963	665	484	398	160	—	65
1964	698	473	409	206	—	139
1965	593	577	347	235	116	208
1966	785	481	550	139	121	175
1967	774	537	649	158	135	144
1968	715	484	596	196	170	184
1969	786	608	659	192	150	225
1970	691	620	573	236	122	207
1971	626	550	490	311	97	207
1972	687	669	499	327	127	224
1973	739	733	647	146	147	116
1974	712	621	592	405	142	231
1975	—	681	535	165	139	127
1976	—	720	616	388	127	171
1977	831	610	545	159	119	123
1978	967	682	693	430	192	266
1979	757	869	696	621	152	269
1980	758	676	434	499	119	184
1981	670	784	502	561	113	225
1982	782	687	652	488	122	256
1983	769	552	589	539	153	215

SOURCE: Data supplied by commune authorities.

But how representative was this experience, after all? By the account of the leaders I interviewed, Huayang commune's party secretary of the time, Wang Deming, was partial to Peng Dehuai and stoutly against the Maoist Leap. He and five other commune party secretaries had joined together to criticize the county party secretary, Zhao Ren, in the spring of 1959, when the upper levels had invited people to speak out against the "boastful tendencies" (*fukua zhi feng*) triggered by the Leap mentality. But with Mao's triumph over Peng at the central level, Zhao counterattacked and succeeded in having Wang dismissed from his post as Huayang's party secretary at the end of 1959. Until then, Wang seemingly managed to cushion the commune from the full destructive impact of the Leap policies (H-III-25).

Even so, Huayang's advances in crop yields were not unique for Songjiang county, as a quick comparison of Tables 13.1 and 11.1 will show. In the county, just as in the commune, rice and wheat yields reached a peak in 1959–60. Despite the evidently quite fierce political struggle between the "Maoist" Zhao and the "Pengist" Wang and his group, their policies do not seem to have had much effect on yields. In fact, in China as a whole, the most radical reorganizations associated with the Leap do not seem to have made themselves felt immediately in this respect. In part this was surely due to local resistance to the Leap's most extreme notions; Huayang would not have been alone in that. But the initial enthusiasm for the Leap itself, even with its destructive aspects, probably also helped sustain crop production.

For the most part, crop yields declined only after 1960 in Huayang and Songjiang, ironically at a time when the organizational excesses of the Leap had been given up. They hit rock bottom in 1961–62 (Table 11.1), just as the earlier organizational forms were reinstated. How do we explain this rather curious coincidence of sustained or peak yields with radical reorganization and drastic declines with a return to earlier organizational forms?

I believe that we need to look outside of labor organization in crop production for the answer. First of all, it was in the realm of sidelines, not in crop production, that the Leap had its most immediately destructive effects. Cadre mentality at the time of the Leap, as Shen Baoshun (brigade party secretary at the time) points out, was "the bigger the better" (*yue da yue hao*) and "first, big; second, public" (*yi da er gong*). Just as the mammoth communes were the result of the emphasis on bigness, so private plots and sidelines fell to the emphasis on "public" ownership. The slogan, which came from Mao himself (Lau et al. 1973), was intended to convey the notion that the communes would represent the sprouting of communism and the transition from small-scale collective ownership to large-scale "ownership by the whole people." It was on that rationale that the Leap put an end to private plots and household hog raising.

But vegetables and pigs, it turned out, were more economically produced by individual households than by large collectives. As we have seen, both utilized low-cost, spare-time household labor. Moreover, private vegetable growing avoided the problems of storage and distribution, just as household pig raising shifted the problem of feed to the individual. Collectivized vegetable growing and hog raising could not match those features of household management. They were given up in two years, but not before they caused significant damage.

Yet if the Leap failed in its attempt to collectivize household sidelines, it nonetheless succeeded in launching some larger-scale, more highly capitalized collective "sidelines."* Two of the Huayang enterprises, as we saw in Chapter 10, proved to be particularly successful (after rather tortuous beginnings): by 1985, the dairy-cow farm and the pear orchard between them employed 58 workers and grossed over 1,080,000 yuan. Both survived the policies of de-collectivization. The Leap's destructive impact on household sidelines must be weighed against these collective successes.

That destructiveness must also be weighed against what in the long view must be considered the Leap's most important achievement. It was at this time that Huayang's industrial development began, with the establishment of the Agricultural Implements Factory; as we have seen, it was to spawn several other commune industries. Here, as in many other communes in China, the origins of rural industrialization can be traced to the Great Leap.

None of this is to deny that the Leap caused serious disruptions. The principal charge that Wang Deming's group leveled against the "Maoist" Zhao Ren was that, in making exaggerated claims for Songjiang's crop production, he had led the authorities to impose excessive burdens on the peasantry. Although we lack the statistical data on the agricultural tax and quotas in Songjiang county during those years, the national figures suggest that procurement was

---

*Straw-basket weaving is in a class of its own, sharing a little of both kinds of sidelines: the collective purchased and owned the equipment, but turned to a household piecework system in order to retain the distinct organizational advantages of the family production unit.

increased substantially (Lardy 1983: 104). The combination of increased state procurement with uncontrolled consumption in the "big mess halls" drastically reduced the cash incomes distributed to the peasants at the end of 1958. The Huayangqiao peasants recall this as the height of the "equalize everything" (*quanmian laping*) mentality; only 0.03 yuan was distributed for each workday equivalent, compared with about a yuan the year before. In 1959, the figure returned to the 1957 level, but that year peasant households could no longer supply their own vegetable needs from their plots or augment their incomes by selling pigs and the surplus of their private plots.

In addition to losses in cash income, the peasants recall steep increases in obligatory labor. A work team, headed by a certain Shen Huaming, was sent down to oversee the commune during the year 1959. The man assigned to Huayangqiao was Wang Yongquan, described by He Jinlin (the most outspoken of the Xubushanqiao informants) as a pompous activist who pushed everyone else but himself to work super hard. At the busiest times, Wang insisted that everyone work into the night, leaving the teams to struggle on by the light of lanterns while he himself went back to the commune headquarters to get a full night's sleep. The peasants were so overworked that their hands and feet swelled up. In the end, they resorted to a kind of sabotage: they would go home on time, but leave the lanterns lit and hanging, swaying with the wind. Wang caught them a few times and would blow up in anger; that did not prevent it from happening again. He graded the three teams for their work performance by the use of three flags: a red flag for good work, a white one for mediocre work, and a flag with the picture of a turtle to shame the team doing the worst work.*

The capital construction projects of these years were also directed by overzealous outsiders. The Huayangqiao women recall the especially heavy water-control work in the winter of 1958–59, when they were called on first to dredge and improve the Dongjinggang River, and then the Yangjinggang. The man in charge was Chen Shoulin, who, the women say, stood around in his padded jacket and did nothing while insisting that everyone else work hard. At one point,

---

*He also inspected the communal mess halls periodically, still insisting on the villagers eating in the halls rather than at home. Yang Xiaofa recalls that by then, all the members of his Xubushanqiao team had taken their tables and chairs home and were eating in their own houses. When they saw Wang coming, Yang and He Jinlin, the team's accountant, would run to everyone's house, getting each family to bring back its tables and chairs and make a show of collectivized eating (H-II-18).

lunch breaks were reduced to 20 minutes, and sometimes the provisions were too skimpy to fill people's stomachs. In all, the work lasted two months. The next year, work concentrated on the digging of the brigade's irrigation and drainage ditches (H-III-10).

When we consider the 1958–60 crop yields against the background of such Herculean efforts, it seems clear that even modest advances would have been seen as disappointing failures. The Leap called on selfless sacrifice for a soon-to-come millennium to motivate peasants to work. In light of the promise and the exertions, the achievements in crop yields were far too minuscule.* Disillusionment was unavoidable.

It was greatly aggravated by natural disasters: excessive rains in October 1960, which cut down Huayang's late-rice yields; excessive rain again in April–May 1961, which reduced the yields of rapeseed and wheat; an early cold wave later that year, which damaged both the single-cropped rice and the late-rice; excessive rain once more in the spring of 1962, adversely affecting the two winter crops for the second year in a row; and, finally, excessive rain yet again in the spring of 1963, reducing the yields of the same two crops for a third time. The Maoist vision had emphasized the indomitable power of the human will and the infinite responsiveness of the land to human effort. Nothing reminded people so much of the fallacy of that vision as climatic disasters entirely beyond human control. The torrential rains and early cold winds demonstrated to everyone human limitations.

It is clear that declining peasant and cadre morale, climatic factors, and organizational failures all contributed in some measure to disasters in Huayang and Songjiang after 1960, just as they did in the rest of the nation. Recovery was to begin only in 1963, starting with the rice crops, followed by wheat and rape a year later.

Climatic stability in Songjiang was helped by technological advances. In single-cropped rice, for example, the seed variety "Green at Old Age" gave good yields for a time, then became susceptible to disease. The renewed advance in 1963 came from good weather and the adoption of a new variety—"Agricultural Reclamation No. 58." Impressive advances continued into 1965, but then the effects of the new seed leveled off. The next year saw unusually good weather, and the start of another climatic cycle. In 1973, another new seed variety was adopted. Through all these punctuated advances, the twists and turns in ideological and policy lines mattered little.

*It was precisely in this context that local cadres reported fantastic yields, though pressures from above no doubt also played a role.

To portray the Leap as an unmitigated disaster caused by ultra-leftist political choices alone—the standard line among the political cadres of the 1980s—is to leave out so much as to distort the historical record. It disregards the great advances in water control, rural industries, and capitalized sidelines that would turn out to be crucial to the later rural development. Even within the narrow realm of crop production, it leaves out the role played by climatic disasters. It was the coincidence of natural disasters with mismanagement that caused the huge setbacks in crop yields.

To equate all of collective agriculture with the Leap—another standard line of the political cadres of the 1980s—is a more serious distortion still. The basic collective structure of ownership and distribution by the production team, disrupted only in 1958–60, should be clearly distinguished from the Leap's disregard for material incentives. The team tied rewards directly to work—in a system best likened to a small cooperative that holds property in common and rewards members according to their work contribution. It bears no resemblance to the Leap's exclusive emphasis on moral incentives.

THE CULTURAL REVOLUTION DECADE (1966–76)

The political campaigns that accompanied the Cultural Revolution were turned mainly upward and outward from the villages. Their main impact in Huayang commune was on the cadres, not the peasants, and in the town, not the villages. Team cadres felt the shock waves first, in the "small four cleans" (*xiao siqing*) movement. In the summer of 1964, about 50 college students, most of them from the Shanghai Normal College, came down to Huayang commune to root out corruption. They were led by a certain Professor Liu. Once they arrived, they divided up into work teams, one for each brigade. All the brigade cadres were called in for questioning, a process that went on for about a month and a half. At our brigade (then still part of the larger Xinglong brigade), only one instance of "corruption" could be found at first: the leader of Team Number Five, Xue Shoulin, was said to have gotten five workpoints more than his due. Brigade Party Secretary Lu Defa tried to brush the matter off and protect the cadres under him.

But the county party secretary, Zhao Ren, had by now translated the movement into the formula of "the three one thousands" (*sange yiqian*): the work teams sent to the villages ought to be able to uncover 1,000 catties of grain, 1,000 yuan of cash, and 1,000 workpoints of "corruption" in each production team. Zhao himself had "squat-

ted" at the Red Star brigade, and this formula "summed up" his findings there. The Huayang work team now divided up into smaller
work groups of two to three people each, assigned to look into the
operations of two or three teams. As we have seen, the Xubushanqiao leaders claim that the young woman who was responsible for
their team was bound and determined to uncover "three one thousands." According to Yang Xiaofa and He Jinlin, she pushed them
until they had no place to go (*zoutou wulu*). Outraged that they had
not deducted workpoints when they took two hours off for a haircut,
and that they had given themselves full workpoints for meetings,
though these required much less exertion than farmwork, and were
sometimes not even held during work hours, she managed to "dig
out" 300–400 workpoints each from Yang and He (H-II-18).

The investigators also uncovered a couple of instances of "male-
female problems" (*nannü wenti*) among the brigade and team cadres. These were considered especially grave if the woman involved
was married to someone in military service or was single. Either offense called for dismissal from cadre service and expulsion from the
party; illicit relations with just a normal married woman were not
considered all that serious (H-III-25).

Despite the stormy experiences of the team cadres, however, there
was little change of leadership at this level. In Huayangqiao, as has
been seen, the same team leaders stayed on, however reluctantly.
Leaders like Yang Xiaofa and He Jinlin felt disgruntled about the un-
justness of the complaints against them and wanted to resign, but
bent to pressures "from above." Yang especially, being a party member, was urged to put personal sentiment aside for the public good.
He and others like him helped to buffer the teams, the real locus of
peasant day-to-day life, from the political storms above.

The "big four cleans" (*da siqing*) followed the next summer (1965).
About 30 outsiders came to the commune this time, again mainly
from Shanghai Normal College. The target now was not the cadres,
but "class enemies." To attack them, a "mass organization," the
"Poor, Lower-Middle Peasant Association," was established, with
two representatives from each team. In the course of this campaign,
two Huayangqiao villagers were "struggled": the former "rich" peasant, Lu Guantong, and Gao Yongnian, an unruly man with a fiery
temper (who would throw things, yell at people, and insult women
during his tantrums). The "masses" tried to get both men to admit
their "crimes." Though Lu "confessed" readily enough, Gao refused
to do so, saying: "If I laugh, you struggle me; if I cry, you also struggle
me. What is there left for you to do but put two holes in me? Then

I'll stop laughing." For that posture, Gao earned the lasting grudging concession from the others that he was a "hard bone" (*ying gutou*). In the end, both men were made to pay for their "crimes" by "supervised labor" (*jiandu laodong*), which meant that they had to be the first to work and the last to quit, that they had to work every day, even when others were not working, that they had to put in twice as many obligatory service days as the others, and that they got only nine workpoints for a normal day's work, not the ten they should have earned. Neither could leave the village without permission. For the others, life went on much as before (H-II-1-3, 26).

The Cultural Revolution itself came to the area in August 1966 in the familiar pattern. Big-character posters were plastered around, attacking the commune leadership in both principled and ad hominem terms. The party secretary, Qian Pu, was the focal point of the criticisms. Factional divisions followed, between the group out to "seize power" and the one trying to retain it. The rebels soon gained the upper hand, and the top cadres in the commune's party committee were "struggled." Qian Pu was "sent down" to work in the Huayangqiao brigade for a year and to write his self-examination. The same thing happened to Zhang Xiulong, the first deputy secretary (H-III-25).

The "rebels" set up a governing "small group," originally called the "Seize Revolution and Promote Production Small Leadership Group" (Zhua geming cu shengchan lingdao xiaozu), later renamed the Fire-Line Command Post (Huoxian zhihui bu). But they interfered little with village production, for their attention was concentrated mainly on continuing factional struggles in the towns and at higher levels. At the start of 1967, armed groups of "ins" and "outs" fought it out in the town of Huayang, each side trying to capture the opposing leaders. The strife eventually culminated in a massive armed confrontation on December 28, 1968, in Songjiang city that involved tens of thousands of people. Dozens were wounded in the fighting on that cold winter day (H-III-25).

The change in commune leadership brought a change in brigade leadership. The Poor, Lower-Middle Peasant Association, now renamed the Poor, Lower-Middle Peasant Rebel Team (Pin xiazhong nong zaofan dui), convened a big "mass meeting," attended by six or seven people from each team, and "struggled" the brigade cadres. The party branch secretary, Lu Defa, and the head of the brigade, He Huosheng, were interrogated, paraded around with dunce caps, and deposed. But the upheaval did not reach down to the natural village (team) level, where the same leaders remained (H-III-26).

Though only peripherally involved, the villages did see the coming of the inevitable Red Guard organization. All together, fifteen people from our four villages participated, all aged fifteen to twenty. For a period of seven or eight months, during 1967, they attended meetings in town, generally in the evenings, and occasionally went to Songjiang to bulk up some movement or march (H-III-26).

But these peasant Red Guards also turned their attention mainly toward the town and the upper levels, not to the villages. The one concrete action they took on the village level was to rake over the "class enemies" still one more time. To ensure fervor and "impartiality," the young Red Guards were organized to act not in their home villages but outside. The unfortunate Lu Guantong saw his house ransacked and the door removed. All his good furniture was taken, and his pigs were sold. After being paraded around for three hours, stripped to the waist, in the cold, he was subjected to sleepless interrogation, to compel him to reveal where he had hidden the gold and silver he was thought to have. He was finally imprisoned for four years. On his release, he was kept under supervised labor for several more years, until 1979 (H-III-26). This was the petty and mean-spirited side of the Cultural Revolution, rationalized by the slogan of "class struggle."

Yet it is clear that for most peasants life went on much as before. Struggling "class enemies" like Lu Guantong, after all, had become almost a ritual of postrevolutionary life. Beyond that, most of the action of the "four cleans" and the Cultural Revolution concerned higher-level cadres and the towns and cities, above the basic stuff of rural life. The continuity in team leadership in Huayangqiao attests to the basic calm in the villages through those years. To hear the peasants tell it, in fact, the "four cleans" movement and the Cultural Revolution merely swept across the ocean of peasant life like so many waves on the surface. Political meetings took place mainly in the evenings after work, and they were discontinued after a couple of years. Cropping choices changed chiefly in the direction of greater labor intensification, and the checkerization of the fields laid the basis for significant advances in crop yields. Income distribution and household sidelines were untouched. The attempt of the Leap to reorganize rural life was not repeated.

The statistical record bears out the overall impression of stability and growth in agriculture. Crop yields advanced steadily, and in some cases dramatically, in both Songjiang and the nation as a whole between 1962–66 and 1972–76 (Table 11.1). That is why peasants and technical cadres alike emphasize that the Cultural Revolution was a *political* movement that had little disruptive impact on crop production.

In the realm of sidelines, the Cultural Revolution did not repeat the excesses of the Leap and left private plots, at least in Songjiang, untouched. Downward adjustments in the size of the plots (from an average of 0.15 mu per household to 0.12 mu) came only in 1979, in response to population pressure, and in spite of the economic reforms. Though household basket weaving declined, this was primarily because of the switch away from single-cropped rice, with its superior straw. Household hog raising in fact increased steadily, and collective mushroom growing was begun. There was nothing like the systematic attack on private sidelines that had occurred during the Great Leap.

In industry, the Cultural Revolution years saw new advances similar to those during the Great Leap. It was during these years that Huayang's Agricultural Implements Factory expanded to include an electroplating shop, thereby tripling its work force to more than 400,* and the Sock Factory began using the 45 machines that had been discarded by its "partner" in Shanghai. As noted earlier, the local growth of rural industry in Huayang during these years was repeated nationwide.

Overall, then, the Cultural Revolution managed to avoid the worst economic excesses of the Leap, while achieving major advances in crop yields, sidelines, and industry. This is not to deny the great human toll that the Cultural Revolution took in its indiscriminate attacks on innocent victims, especially in the cities. It is only to point out that the political radicalism of the Cultural Revolution was not accompanied by extremist economic policies in the countryside. The "Maoists" seem actually to have learned some lessons from the failures of the Great Leap.

THE MAOIST CHOICES OF CROPS

Policy cadres today are wont to criticize their predecessors, especially those in charge of the Cultural Revolution, for their supposed "irrational" emphasis on grain, to the exclusion of commercial crops (like cotton, rape, peanuts, sesame, sugarcane, tobacco, and sugar beets). The problem, they say, was summed up in the slogan "take grain as the key link" (*yiliang weigang*), which, they would like us to think, meant something like "don't bother with cash crops."

---

*Huayang lost this shop to Chedun commune in 1978.

But this picture is contradicted both by the statistical data and by peasant testimony. In Songjiang, as Tables 11.2 and 11.3 showed, the three major Maoist pushes were not so much for exclusive emphasis on grain as for intensification, especially by raising cropping frequency. The first of these, in 1956, saw the acreage for early-rice pushed up from 1.2 percent to 14.3 percent. But this was not done at the expense of cotton, the main spring-sown cash crop, which hovered at less than 2 percent from the mid-1950s to the mid-1960s, chiefly because cotton simply could not do well in soggy rice fields. That year also saw the expansion of acreage under winter wheat/ barley from 6.6 percent of the cultivated area to 8.9 percent. But again this was not done at the expense of rape, the chief winter cash crop, whose acreage was also pushed up: from 6.4 percent in 1954 to 10.6 percent in 1955 and 11.2 percent in 1956. The figures fell off substantially in 1957, except for wheat/barley, which, as has been seen, achieved productive breakthroughs with the introduction of collective plowing.

The second push, in the Great Leap years of 1958–59, brought only very modest increases in early-rice, which climbed back up to around 7 percent from 5 percent, while wheat/barley was substantially reduced, falling to under 10 percent. Otherwise, the outlines of the county's cropping portfolio remained unchanged.

The third big push came with the "four cleans" (and the socialist education movement), followed by the Cultural Revolution. Acreage under early-rice went back up to 13 percent in 1965 and then increased steadily to a top of 59.2 percent in 1977. Once again, this was not done at the expense of cotton, whose acreage also mounted, from around 5 percent in 1966 to 14.6 percent in 1977. The increased cotton acreage was due to the productivity breakthroughs achieved by effective drainage of the rice fields with checkerization in the late 1960s. As for the winter crops, wheat/barley acreage rose dramatically from 1965 on, to peak at 49 percent by 1973. But once again, this was not done at the expense of rape, which simultaneously expanded from 7.9 percent in 1965 to 15 percent in the early 1970s.

The record therefore bears out the pointed statements of one dissenting political cadre in Songjiang: the slogan *yiliang weigang* did not mean an exclusive emphasis on grain, but was associated from the start with an attempt to "develop all facets" (*quanmian fazhan*) with "multiple undertakings" (*duozhong jingying*). From this perspective, the usual translation—"take grain as the key link"—comes quite close to capturing the real policy; and the reformers' attempt to equate the slogan with a singular emphasis on grain is clearly a propagandistic distortion.

In point of fact, the agricultural policy in Songjiang during the Cultural Revolution years had two dimensions: the intensification noted above, and the push for capitalization associated with checkerization. It was the mid-1960s that saw the spread of hand-held tractors down to the brigade level and the establishment of electric pumping stations in every commune. The checkerization of the fields in the late 1960s, finally, capped off the entire effort to co-ordinate higher-level irrigation and drainage with plot-level water use. Only then were wet-rice fields able to accommodate cotton, wheat/barley, and rape, the three dry crops that together accounted for the bulk of Songjiang's agricultural growth in the postrevolutionary years.

Though the great push for triple-cropping in the late 1960s is certainly traceable to some extent to the Leap mentality about the infinite inflatability of agricultural yields, it reflected to a still greater extent the very real structural pressures on agriculture. As has been seen, the Cultural Revolution decade saw mounting pressures on the land as more and more baby-boomers entered the labor force. The kinds of intensification (and involution) that characterized policies like "Wipe out single-cropped rice!" were propelled in good measure by the logic of using otherwise underemployed and unemployed labor. To characterize the Cultural Revolution's intensification and checkerization drives as simply an irrational and excessive emphasis on grain to the exclusion of other crops, just as the criticism that it emphasized crop production to the exclusion of sidelines and industry, is to distort the historical record.

How representative, we must once again ask, was Songjiang of China as a whole? Table 13.2 gives the relative proportions of sown acreage under grains and cash crops for all of China from 1952 to 1986. As can be readily seen, there is little substance to the charge that the Cultural Revolution decade unduly emphasized grain. Before the beginning of the decade, 83.5 percent of the sown acreage was under grains, and 8.5 percent under commercial crops; at the end the respective figures were 80.9 percent and 9.0 percent. The last year (1976), in fact, compares "favorably" with 1957, which saw 85.0 percent under grains and 9.2 percent under cash crops. Though the ideological predilections of the planners no doubt did affect cropping choices to some extent, they do not seem to have made nearly the difference claimed in the official propaganda. Truly dramatic changes

TABLE 13.2

Acreage Sown Under Grains and Cash Crops in China, 1952–86

(percent)

Year	Rice	Wheat	All grains[a]	Cotton	Rape	All cash crops[b]
1952	20.1%	17.5%	87.8%	3.9%	1.3%	8.8%
1953	19.7	17.8	—	3.6	1.2	—
1954	19.0	18.2	—	3.7	1.2	—
1955	19.3	17.7	—	3.8	1.5	—
1956	20.9	17.1	—	3.9	1.4	—
1957	20.5	17.5	85.0	4.1	1.5	9.2
1958	21.0	17.0	—	3.7	1.5	—
1959	20.4	16.6	—	3.9	1.4	—
1960	19.7	18.1	—	3.5	1.6	—
1961	18.3	17.9	—	2.7	1.0	—
1962	19.2	17.2	86.7	2.5	1.0	6.3
1963	19.8	17.0	—	3.1	1.0	—
1964	20.6	17.7	—	3.4	1.2	—
1965	20.8	17.2	83.5	3.5	1.3	8.5
1966	20.8	16.3	—	3.4	1.2	—
1967	21.0	17.5	—	3.5	1.1	—
1968	21.4	17.6	—	3.6	1.0	—
1969	21.6	17.9	—	3.4	1.0	—
1970	22.6	17.7	83.1	3.5	1.0	8.2
1971	24.0	17.6	—	3.3	1.1	—
1972	23.8	17.8	—	3.3	1.3	—
1973	23.6	17.8	—	3.3	1.4	—
1974	23.9	18.2	—	3.4	1.4	—
1975	23.9	18.5	80.9	3.3	1.5	9.0
1976	24.2	19.0	80.6	3.3	1.6	9.2
1977	23.8	18.8	80.6	3.2	1.5	9.1
1978	22.9	19.4	80.3	3.2	1.7	9.6
1979	22.8	19.8	80.3	3.0	1.9	10.0
1980	23.1	20.0	80.1	3.4	1.9	10.9
1981	22.9	19.5	79.2	3.6	2.6	12.1
1982	22.8	19.3	78.4	4.0	2.8	13.0
1983	23.0	20.2	79.2	4.2	2.5	12.3
1984	23.0	20.5	79.3	4.8	2.4	13.4
1985	22.3	20.3	75.8	3.6	3.1	15.6
1986	22.4	20.5	76.9	3.0	3.4	14.1

SOURCES: *Zhongguo tongji nianjian*, 1983: 154–56, 1987: 164.

[a]Includes also such food crops as soybeans and potatoes.

[b]Includes peanuts, sesame, hemp, sugarcane, tobacco, sugar beets, etc., as well as cotton and rapeseed.

in cropping patterns were to come only in the 1980s, with structural changes in the rural economy.

As we saw in Chapter 11, the switchover to household responsibility in farming did not bring any significant increase in Songjiang's yields. Yields had topped out in the late 1970s under collective production. The big change that came in the 1980s consisted rather of expanded labor productivity in crop production with the removal of its surplus labor, without increases in the absolute levels of crop yields—or, in other words, of *development without growth* in agriculture.

Songjiang's record in the late 1970s actually foretold what was to come in the 1980s in the less-advanced areas of the nation. Yields in those areas had also advanced impressively under collective farming, but instead of topping out in the late 1970s as in Songjiang, they continued to advance, in good measure because of the increased availability of chemical fertilizer with the full development of a Chinese petrochemical industry. Greater inputs of fertilizer, combined with extended good weather in 1979–84, almost guaranteed sustained growth in those areas, so whether and to what extent the introduction of the household-responsibility system in farming made a real difference is hard to fathom. Since crop yields had advanced nationwide earlier under collective farming and declined in the advanced areas under household responsibility, the burden of proof, it seems to me, lies with those who insist that the new incentive structure contributed decisively to increased yields.

We also need to be on the lookout for the possibility that in at least some of the backward areas the advances of 1979–84 resulted from involution rather than from development—in a manner similar to what had happened in Songjiang. There the use of chemical fertilizers involved labor intensification as well as capital intensification, since they were applied as "chase fertilizer," used in addition to, not in place of, the customary applications of organic fertilizer. And technological advances like underground drainage tunnels and the transplanting of "forced" cotton seedlings were also based on greatly intensified labor. Is it not possible that, in the lessadvanced areas of the nation during the period 1979–84, we are merely looking at the results of a technology that was introduced earlier in places like Songjiang? Much detailed local research would be needed to verify this hypothesis. For now, the Songjiang record of output growth without labor-productivity development throughout the 1960s and 1970s argues for caution against making excessive claims for the national trends of 1979–84.

In any case, as the preceding chapters have shown, the really significant changes of the 1980s were in off-farm employment. The loosening of bureaucratic control permitted the emergence of new kinds of higher-paying household sidelines, like the crocheting, dried earthworms, and rabbit raising taken up in Songjiang. At the same time, collective accumulation generated the development of more highly capitalized commune sidelines, like the dairy farm, the pear orchard, and the fish ponds in Huayang. The result was that sideline production was able to grow at roughly the same rate as the overall rural economy. It maintained its earlier proportion of gross rural income, at about 20 percent, while crop production's share shrank from more than 70 percent in the early 1970s to less than 40 percent by the mid-1980s. This is one source of increased off-farm as opposed to farm employment.

But of course rural industry was by far the most dynamic and important source of off-farm employment. By 1983, industry accounted for two-thirds of the gross value of output in Huayang, compared with just one-third a decade earlier, while the share occupied by crop production shrank from one-half to just one-fifth. Nationwide, the share of rural industry rose from under 10 percent to more than 40 percent in the years 1973–86 (Appendix E.1). It was rural industry, more than anything else, that accounted for the increased rural prosperity of the 1980s.

Rural prosperity and rural industrialization, finally, go a long way to explain the changes in the national cropping portfolio of the 1980s. As Table 13.2 shows, it was only in the 1980s that the proportion of acreage devoted to cash crops moved decisively above 10 percent, to stand at 15.6 percent midway through the decade, while the proportion occupied by food crops shrank about 5 percent. We do not have far to look for the reasons: increased rural prosperity raised peasant consumption of auxiliary foodstuffs (fushi), like vegetables, eggs, poultry, pork, and fish, and rural industrialization as well as expanded rural consumption have increased the demand for commercial crops. The prime examples are rape, sugarcane, and tobacco, whose sown acreage rose dramatically between 1980 and 1986: 73 percent, 98 percent, and 126 percent, respectively (Zhongguo tongji nianjian 1987: 164). Planners' strategies and ideological predilections made some difference in the shape of the cropping portfolio, to be sure. But the scale of those factors is surely dwarfed by the massive change wrought by the altered economic and employment structures of the 1980s.

THE COLLECTIVE PAST VS. THE
REFORMIST PRESENT

In the current climate of opinion, it is fashionable to dismiss China's collective past as a complete failure and to claim for the reformist present spectacular advances. Every change in Chinese leadership since the Revoluton has produced similar charges against predecessors and similar claims for new policies, and the latest has been no different. The preceding four chapters have shown that, except for the years of the Great Leap, collectivized agriculture was by no means so "radical" or "irrational" as it is often made out to be. Ownership under the collective system was in the hands of the relatively small production team. Distribution was not by standardized wage as in a factory system, but always based on output. What team members received was directly linked to what they produced. That was a very "materialistically" oriented incentive structure, even though a collective one, and not a particularly "political" or "moral" one.

The performance of collective agriculture was also not nearly so disastrous as the reformers would have us believe. We should not confuse the stagnation in per capita peasant incomes, which resulted above all from population pressure on the land, with stagnation in crop yields, which apart from the setbacks during the post-Leap years, advanced steadily throughout the collectivized years.

The Leap failed miserably in sideline production, by its irrational insistence on large-scale production where spare-time work using spare materials worked best. Its radical distribution policies and millenarian strivings led in the end to disillusionment, made all the worse by a series of climatic disasters, and to severe setbacks in crop production. But those failures must be weighed against the Leap's vigorous initiatives in water control, capitalized collective sidelines, and rural industry.

The Cultural Revolution did not repeat the Leap's errors in household sideline production and income distribution. Continued advances were sustained in crop production, and significant initiatives were undertaken in rural industry. The massive human hardship the Cultural Revolution worked on the cities needs to be seen in conjunction with the relative stability of the countryside.

Casting the debates over the 1980s in terms of a struggle between capitalism and socialism in crop production misrepresents the reformist present no less than the collectivist past. The greatest success of the 1980s lay in rural industrial development, not in crop production. Mere advances in crop yields tell little about development in labor productivity and cannot account in themselves for the rural prosperity of that decade.

Given the above record, it is particularly misleading to insist on the crucial importance of altered incentives in crop production and changed ideological predilections in cropping-portfolio planning. That kind of emphasis obscures the central historical reality about Chinese farming—of involuted cultivation and stagnated incomes per laborer. And it diverts attention from the truly significant changes that have come with rural industrialization and the diversion of surplus labor from farming.

Once we place crop production and rural industry into their proper perspectives, we cannot help being struck with some of the fundamental continuities between the collectivist past and the reformist present. There is a straight line in rural industrial development from the Great Leap to the Cultural Revolution to the 1980s. Collective accumulation had powered the first commune and brigade industries, and they continued to power the advances of the 1980s, now helped by the trickle-down effects of large-scale urban industries.

All this is not to deny real differences between the two eras. The 1980s reforms, it is true, advocated in unprecedented ways dispersed as opposed to centrally planned initiatives. Leaders of collectives were encouraged as never before to seek out contacts and opportunities to establish rural industrial "enterprises." There was an official recognition that, in the countryside at least, dispersed initiative could be better than planned, and small-scale production more rational than large. The result was a flurry of opportunity-hunting by enterprising rural cadres, for processing contracts and joint operations with other units, small and large, near and far, foreign as well as domestic.

Out of all this emerged the southern Jiangsu model that dominated rural development as the 1980s drew to a close. It is a model that stands apart from the "Maoist conservatives," since it advocates de-control of the economy. But it also stands apart from the "radical" reformers who would have a simple turn to a private-property and free-market economy. It is, in short, a model and vision for entrepreneurial initiatives within a socialist system of ownership, a mixture of elements of capitalist and socialist principles to fit the realities of rural China. To cast the issue in terms of a simple dichotomy between capitalism and socialism, focused on crop production, is to completely miss the reality and significance of the changes we have traced in the Yangzi delta.

CHAPTER 14

Peasant-Worker Villages

Social science models based on the historical experience of the developed world teach us to expect urbanization with industrial development, and social stratification with commercialization. Industrialization, we assume, will trigger rural–urban migration. At the same time, commercial opportunity will bring forth rural entrepreneurs, causing increased social differentiation. To some of us, these expectations seem confirmed by media reports on the reforms in China, and we have given much attention to small-town growth and the rise of the new "ten thousand–yuan households" in our research.

This chapter argues that such research runs the risk of obscuring what is truly distinctive about the recent changes: that there has been *rural industrialization without residential urbanization* and *stratification by bureaucratic hierarchy* rather than by market opportunity.

The Chinese government has forbidden uncontrolled rural–urban migration since 1958. The policy was born of the need to keep the vast rural population from inundating the cities, whose employment opportunities could not begin to match the population pressure in the countryside. Unchecked, rural–urban migration would have produced urban slums and massive unemployment, as has happened in most of the densely populated Third World countries. Promulgated in January 1958, the Household Registration Regulations required every urban household to register with Public Security offices, and every rural household with the collectives. Unauthorized changes of residence were strictly forbidden. Children of villagers had to follow the mother's registration, rather than the father's (lest rural households with urban-employed fathers swell the urban population; *Zhonghua renmin gongheguo gong'an fagui xuanbian* 1982: 83–87; see also S. Potter 1983). Adherence to the regulations was ensured by the state's tight rationing of basic necessities like grain, oil, and cloth, which were available in towns and cities only at state stores and only by rationing coupons distributed to registered households. Legitimate housing and employment could be obtained only with proper registration.

With the liberalization of the economy in the 1980s, unregistered urbanites found it easier to purchase basic necessities on the market and to obtain jobs in private enterprises and housing through private channels. Official agencies, moreover, tended to close an eye to illegal residents. As a result, there are larger numbers of unregistered people living in the towns and cities than ever before. Nevertheless, official state law remains a powerful constraint on uncontrolled movements of population. In areas like the Yangzi delta, where the private sector remains relatively undeveloped, opportunities for peasants to find long-term housing and employment outside of the officially regulated channels remain very limited.

This means that despite rural industrialization, peasants by and large continue to be tied to their home villages. Villagers employed in industry do not as a rule move into the towns. Some new industries, moreover, are simply sited in or near the villages themselves, not just in "central places" like the township seats. The result is the emergence of massive numbers of peasant-worker villages.

The Huayangqiao villages fit this description. Though well over half the laborers (172 of 308) were employed off-farm by 1985, the composition of the villages remained substantially as it was before the coming of rural industrialization. Almost all those employed in town (172 of 185) continued to live in their home communities and to farm, either part-time themselves or with their household members. Rural industrialization thus occurred without the predicted removal of villagers to the urban areas.

These villages, to be sure, are relatively highly industrialized. Xubushanqiao and Xilihangbang, farther from town and less "advanced" in this respect, had 46 percent and 49 percent, respectively, of their labor force employed off-farm in 1985, compared with 72 percent for closer-in Xuejida (Tables 10.3, D.4).* How closely this

---

*The Dongbang brigade of Fengqiao commune on the western outskirts of Suzhou city is an example of a still-more-industrialized peasant village. Here in the summer of 1985 fully 698 of the 748 laborers in the village were employed in either commune (158) or brigade (540) enterprises, and 45 others were self-employed in household enterprises. As we have seen, all agriculture had by then become spare-time work on "consumption grain land" (kouliangdi; H-III-39).

might conform to the national picture we do not know, for as yet there are no reliable national statistics.* For now, we must rely on local studies for any national extrapolations.

The most systematic of these is the survey carried out by the group of researchers associated with Fei Xiaotong (Jiangsu sheng xiaochengzhen 1984, 1987). Between 1983 and 1985, this group selected for detailed study representative counties in Jiangsu province's seven subregions. Among other things, the researchers censused the population of every small town in the seven counties on June 30, 1985. In an attempt to record the social changes, they divided the townspeople into three categories: registered town residents, unregistered town residents (consisting mainly of unemployed dependents of the registered town residents), and nonresidents who came to town to work during the day.† As Table 14.1 shows, the last category of people ranged in 1985 from a low of 13.3 percent in least-advanced Suqian county in northern Jiangsu to 43.0 percent in the delta's more-advanced Jiangyin county, with a seven-county average of 27.6 percent. There are about half as many dayworkers as legal residents, and they outnumber the unregistered residents two to one.

These figures show that the much-touted small-town growth in the 1980s was due mainly to the daily influx of workers from the villages. Dubbed the group that "leaves the soil without leaving the village" (litu bulixiang), these workers have been the fastest-growing occupational/social group in China. In 1986, they numbered an estimated 70,000,000 nationwide, or about 20 percent of the total "rural" labor force (Jiangsu sheng xiaochengzhen 1987: 7; Zhongguo tongji nianjian 1988: 153).

THE HIERARCHY OF VILLAGE EMPLOYMENT

The amazing growth of off-farm employment, within the context of a state-enforced encapsulation of village populations, has given rise to a distinctive pattern of social stratification in the countryside. Within every peasant-worker village there is an elaborate hierarchy

*The State Statistical Bureau long assumed that almost all "rural" people would be engaged in "agriculture" (including farming, forestry, animal husbandry, handicrafts, and fishery), and that industry would be of minor importance in the countryside. It therefore simply lumped brigade and team industry under "agriculture" for its national statistics. Rural industrialization has altered the social reality, but the bureau has yet to adapt fully and to record systematically the numbers of villagers employed in industry (or of town workers who are village residents).

†They also attempted to include transients based on the average occupancy rate in 1984 in the town's hotels and guest houses and the average number of tourists in town each day that year (Jiangsu sheng xiaochengzhen 1987: 303, 475).

TABLE 14.1

Census of 190 Small Towns in Seven Counties of Jiangsu Province, June 30, 1985

County	County population[a]	Town residents: Regis-tered	Town residents: Unregis-tered	Nonresident dayworkers	Total censused population
Wujiang	730,519				
Number		121,006	35,437	56,098	212,541
Percent		56.9%	16.7%	26.4%	100.0%
Jiangyin	1,022,612				
Number		178,170	22,148	150,926	351,244
Percent		50.7%	6.3%	43.0%	100.0%
Lishui	370,282				
Number		39,817	12,083	27,216	79,116
Percent		50.3%	15.3%	34.4%	100.0%
Hai'an	941,490				
Number		94,955	35,716	70,553	201,224
Percent		47.2%	17.7%	35.1%	100.0%
Yancheng suburb	1,074,415				
Number		96,506	34,573	27,062	158,141
Percent		61.0%	21.9%	17.1%	100.0%
Suqian	944,374				
Number		170,604	32,126	31,099	233,829
Percent		73.0%	13.7%	13.3%	100.0%
Peixian	885,908				
Number		136,538	15,710	27,892	180,140
Percent		75.8%	8.7%	15.5%	100.0%
Total	5,969,600				
Number		837,596	187,793	390,846	1,416,235
Percent		59.1%	13.3%	27.6%	100.0%

SOURCE: Jiangsu sheng xiaochengzhen 1987: 302–3, 454–55.

NOTE: The census covered all towns (zhen, generally ranging in population from 3,000 to 50,000) in seven typical counties; they represent 10 percent of the towns in the province (1,901).

[a] As of Dec. 30, 1985.

of jobs, differentiated by their levels of capitalization and remuneration, their accessibility, and their prestige. At the top of the ladder are the jobs in state enterprises, which require higher education or special qualifications. Next come those in commune/township units, with somewhat lower wages and benefits, but still substantially higher than farming, and normally requiring a lower-middle-school (*chuzhong*) education. Below these are the jobs in brigade/administrative-village enterprises, where the wages and benefits are sometimes no better than those in farming, but where the work is less strenuous and the pay is more stable. These jobs usually require a primary-school education. At the bottom is farmwork, strenuous, poorly remunerated, and subject to the vagaries of the weather. For this, young peasant men and women need little in the way of formal schooling.

In the postrevolutionary years, only one Huayangqiao villager had achieved the distinction of gaining admission to a university by national college-entrance examination: Xue Bulin, who in 1966 was admitted to the Nanjing Academy of Mechanics. On graduation, he became an engineer in a Songjiang factory, and his registration transferred out with that position.

The second most-respected route for gaining urban registration is admission by examination into a special middle school (zhong-zhuan), more often than not a school of education. Xue Chunhua, for example, was admitted to the Shanghai Number Four Normal School and was assigned after graduation to the Songjiang (County) Fangta Grammar School. Zhang Jinlong, a teacher in the commune grammar school, similarly got his job after graduating from a normal school. All together, five villagers had obtained urban assignments and registration through this route by 1985; three others were attending such institutions. This group, we might say, represents "the best and the brightest" of these villages (H-III-5, 21; Table D.5).*

Villagers could also qualify for jobs in state enterprises by examination in special skills. Ma Dalong, a skilled bricklayer, managed to get a permanent position this way in the Songjiang Construction Engineering Corps. He was able to move his registration out of the village—the only person in Huayangqiao to do so by this avenue. Three others obtained employment as temporary contract workers (hetong gong) in state units because of their special skills: the carpenter He Xiugen, for example, got a job in the Shanghai Number 703 Engineering Corps. But like all contract workers, He Xiugen remains registered in his home village (H-III-5, 21).

Until 1986, the state allowed a parent in a state enterprise to pass his job on to a child.† Zhou Jianhua and Xi Xiufang (both of Xuejiada) "replaced" (dingti) their fathers in the County Industrial Art Products Factory under this provision. Six villagers obtained state jobs this way. Urban registration was inherited along with the jobs (H-III-5, 21).

The state also gives preference to former cadres in assigning state jobs. He Shunyu had served as a brigade party secretary; when his

---

*Table D.5, which shows the different avenues to off-farm employment, lists 185 jobs, but in five cases, I was unable to find out how the workers procured the jobs. In the following discussion, the figures include people who had moved away and temporary workers.

†The practice was abolished by the Standing Committee of the Sixth National People's Congress on September 2, 1986 (Zhonghua renmin gongheguo quanguo renmin daibiao dahui changwu weiyuanhui gongbao 1986: 66).

cadre appointment was not renewed (making him a so-called *luo-xuan ganbu*), a position was arranged for him in the County Water Control Engineering Corps. He Yonglong, party secretary of Hua-yangqiao brigade, succeeded in getting a permanent assignment in the Songjiang Highway Company, thereby moving his registration out of the village. Another villager obtained a position through pref-erential assignment for veterans (although, as will be seen below, most veterans get placed in lower-level jobs; H-III-5, 17, 21).

In all, by 1985 26 Huayangqiao villagers had obtained state jobs through one of these avenues. Of those, 21 were permanent posi-tions that came with urban registration. Nine of the 21 had moved out; the others continued to live in the villages.

Access to commune-level jobs is similar to that for state-level jobs in that peasants can qualify variously by examination (14 of 80), spe-cial skills (8), priority for veterans or former cadres (5, 1), and inheri-tance (1). But these jobs are often also assigned under quotas set by the commune party organization, making them much more acces-sible to villagers than state jobs. This process is called "[objective] assignment by the organization" (*zuzhi anpai*). Various considera-tions guide the handing out of this kind of "principled assignment." Preference may be given to households that already have two or three people engaged in agriculture. This was the formula the Xue-jiada team used when it received a quota for five slots in the Printing Factory in 1982. Or a team may give special consideration to house-holds in difficulty. Zhang Bamei, a widow with three children, was given a job in the Sock Factory in 1980 on this account. For this rea-son, also, Lu Shuifang, a deaf-mute, got his job in the Clothing Fac-tory in 1985. In all, "objective assignment" accounted for 21 of the 80 commune jobs held by the villagers.

Brigade jobs, the lowest of the off-farm jobs, generally do not re-quire an examination, or more than a grammar-school education. Most are apportioned out as principled assignments. The lock fac-tory, for example, hired one worker from every willing Huayangqiao household in 1982. Fully 58 of the 72 villagers employed in the bri-gade industries obtained their jobs this way.

THE "BACK DOOR"

The peasants consider all of the above avenues legitimate means of obtaining off-farm jobs. They refer to it as "getting out the hard way" (*ying chuqu*).* But the stratification of employment has prompted

*Though in its narrowest meaning, the term refers to someone who has moved his registration out, it is applied broadly to anyone who has a job outside the village.

elaborate maneuverings to obtain off-farm jobs by irregular means. The Huayangqiao peasants refer to the process of using connections to get jobs as "boring one's way out" (*zuan chuqu*) of the village.

Two of the 23 Huayangqiao villagers with permanent jobs in state units, and three of the eight with temporary jobs, had obtained their positions through personal connections rather than legitimate avenues. He Shutang, for example, obtained his permanent job in the County Good Seed Factory through a friend. Friends also helped Lu Guiquan and Lu Mingqiang get their temporary jobs in the Songjiang Mail and Telegraph Office and the County Cotton Ginning Factory, and Zhang Zhengyun got a temporary job in the Songjiang School of Public Health through his brother-in-law (H-III-5, 17, 21).

The intercession of relatives or friends was a common route to jobs in commune enterprises as well. The biggest influence-wielder in all these villages in the 1980s was Xue Huilin, who got himself the job of foreman of the Construction Team, after having first served for six years as a temporary worker (*linshi gong*). Xue could hire unskilled short-term workers at his discretion. In 1984, he hired six of his fellow team members as temporary workers on the team's construction projects. In all, 24 of 72 Huayangqiao villagers permanently employed in the commune's industries (and five of the eight temporary workers) "bored" their way out through connections.

Back-doorism is less rampant among jobs at the brigade level, no doubt because the stakes are not so high, but also in part because at this level the community is more closely knit and less open to influence-mongering. Only two of the 72 brigade workers can be explicitly identified as having "bored" their way through personal contacts: Lu Minghua secured a relatively soft job in the factory of nearby Xinglong brigade through the influence of his father, Lu Haitang, who had served for some years as the head of Xilihangbang team. Haitang had also secured a soft job in the brigade's mill for his brother Hailai (H-III-5, 17).

Getting jobs by pulling strings (*la guanxi*), then, occurs chiefly on the commune level. Few peasants have contacts in state units through which to "bore" themselves all the way out of the village. The commune enterprises, on the other hand, are close enough for some to have special contacts in them, yet far enough removed from the strictures of the immediate community to provide the necessary elbowroom for back-door maneuvering. As has been seen, in all, 36 of the 180 off-farm jobs for which access can be identified had been obtained through the back door. Of those, 29 were commune positions.

RURAL—URBAN DIFFERENCES

This stratified employment structure has implanted in the villagers a new value system. No one misses the point: only the best and the brightest are allowed out of the village; and only the least-talented and skilled, or least−well connected, continue to work in agriculture.

Farmwork, by its very nature, is open to a host of negative associations. Busy-season work is backbreaking. One has to handle manure fertilizer and cope with the stench. One has to go barefoot, slosh around in wet soil, get dirt under one's fingernails and toenails, and wear the unmistakable permanent sunburn of the peasant. By Chinese standards of beauty, the contrast between the fifteen-year-old girl, still in school, and her elder sister who has worked in the fields for a number of years is striking: the one fair-skinned and to all appearances indistinguishable from a town resident, the other darkened, barefoot, and unmistakably "peasant." By middle age, after the physical stress of farmwork and prolonged exposure to the sun have taken their full toll, the contrast is sometimes greater still.

Maoist ideology had tried to turn the tables on the urban intellectuals. Peasants might be physically smelly and dirty, but in spirit they were much cleaner than corrupted urbanites. It was the toilers who had genuine class sentiment (*jieji ganqing*), a feeling that those who did not work with their hands could only internalize with effort. The revolutionary intellectuals must live and work with the peasants to cleanse themselves (Mao Zedong 1964 [1942]: 853).

But though the Revolution made much of the "three great differences" between city and countryside, industry and agriculture, and mental and physical labor in its propaganda, the government favored the city and the urbanites in its concrete actions. Urban advantages were reinforced by a strategy of forced-draft industrialization that favored urban industry over rural production in state investments. The industrial workers were favored far above the peasants in wages and benefits, consistent with the orthodox Marxist emphasis on the proletariat, Maoist sentiments notwithstanding. One result, in socialist China no less than elsewhere, was a mass exodus from the countryside, a trend that led to the rigid household registration law of 1958. Despite all the Maoists' pro-peasant talk in the Great Leap and the Cultural Revolution, the state in fact enforced throughout the strictest restrictions on access to cities and towns.

Encapsulated within a stratified structure, villagers themselves have almost without exception come to believe that rural life is vastly inferior to urban. Parents pressure their children to study hard, just as the urbanites do, so that they will have a chance to leave the drudgery of agricultural life. The villagers who make it are seen, among other things, as more desirable mates. The most prized mates are those with "good" off-farm jobs, preferably in the commune factories. The attitude toward an employee of a state unit is ambivalent, for that person is perceived as someone who would surely be too good and haughty to consider marrying a mere peasant. There is, moreover, the very real problem that marriage does not entitle a person to change to the spouse's registration. The rural partner would thus not be entitled, for example, to grain, oil, and other rationing coupons, or housing assignment in the urban locale of his/her spouse. Consequently, the couple would have to live in the rural partner's village, representing a downward step for the urban partner (H-III-6, 16).

Almost all my village informants said they did not know of any young or middle-aged person who did not want to leave agriculture and get out of the village. Asked why, they consistently pointed to the superior salaries and benefits, lighter working conditions, and greater security of off-farm jobs. But one gets the impression, in the end, that those material calculations are only part of the reason. The fact is that peasants in semi-industrialized villages like Huayangqiao have internalized the urban bureaucracy's attitude toward village life. One former peasant woman in her mid-thirties who had successfully left the village, for example, was simply horrified by the thought of going barefoot or uncovered under the sun. She would go down to the village only if she was well-shod and completely protected from the sun under an umbrella. From her point of view, she must never, never allow her skin to darken like a peasant's.

Pressed for an example of someone who did not want to leave the village, my informants came up with Tan Meijuan (b. 1949), the wife of Lu Maoyuan. Apparently illiterate, she seems to be one of those who slipped through the new education system. She is painfully shy and afraid of the outside world (H-III-9).

We have in the "peasant-worker village," then, a community that is maintained chiefly by restrictions imposed by the state. Except for the elderly, most members of the village live in the community not by choice but by state-imposed encapsulation. Almost all look upward and outward from the village, aspiring to the "better" off-farm and urban life. They speak of "getting out" of the village, either by their own ability or by "boring" their way out through special contacts—the illegitimate, back-door way, but no less envied for that.

The more purely peasant village of the past had also seen the "townpeople" (jieshang ren) as in some ways superior to themselves. But at the same time, the old village had a strong sense of "we" as opposed to "them," insider as opposed to outsider. Village identity was reinforced by multi-stranded kinship and community ties. It was also reinforced by the shared assumption that most of those who left did so out of desperation, not hope and upward mobility. They left, as long-term laborers or itinerant peddlers, not because they had "made it," but because they had failed to make ends meet and had lost their land. Those who remained felt more fortunate than their neighbors or relatives who had had to leave. And the long-term village resident felt a distinct sense of superiority over the transient in the village, someone who had been uprooted for whatever reasons from his original home village. It took generations for newcomers like the Jins of Xilihangbang or the Zhangs of Xue Family Village to be accepted by the community. But all that is gone. These days, those who leave do so from the top, for jobs and lives that are presumed to be better. Gone is the dual sense of inferiority-superiority of old. The peasants of the peasant-worker village today, for all the improvements in living conditions, are perceived not only by others but also by themselves as being at the very bottom of society.

This second-class condition of the peasant-workers, like the second-class status of village and town industries, is both the blessing and the curse of bureaucratized industrialization. It is a blessing in providing, for the first time ever, the opportunity for these villages to de-involute and attain genuine development in productivity per capita. But it is a curse in relegating the villagers to the bottom of a bureaucratically imposed social and economic hierarchy.

INTRAVILLAGE AND INTRAFAMILY STRATIFICATION

Stratification in employment has also brought status differentiation within the villages themselves. The top of village society is occupied by those working in state units and enjoying urban registrations. (Overseas Chinese are often puzzled when their village relatives go to great lengths to show off an urban-registered family member.) There were fourteen urbanly registered people in the Huayangqiao villages in 1985; they either lived in the villages or returned regularly to visit their families (Table D.4). Below them were those employed in town, at the commune industries, followed by those working in the brigade factory. The villagers engaged only in farming, two-thirds of them women, usually the middle-aged and older women, were at the bottom.

With 172 of 308 laborers employed off-farm in 1985, these differences affected almost every household in the Huayangqiao villages. For some, the differences were manifested in male-female relations, especially where the man was employed off-farm in a "superior" job, thereby reinforcing his superior position in the relationship. For others, the differences were generational: the young were educated and employed off-farm; their elders were illiterate and knew only agriculture. Tensions were sharpest between mothers-in-law and daughters-in-law, a difficult relationship even under the best of circumstances.

Before the Revolution, the lowest-status person in the village had in many ways been the daughter-in-law. Detached from her natal family and a stranger to her marital family, she was often at the mercy of her mother-in-law. As several informants noted, the daughter-in-law was usually the first one up in a household, charged with lighting the breakfast fire. She was also usually the one assigned to dump the family's chamber pots (H-III-16).

Collectivized agriculture considerably altered this state of affairs. Women gained a sense of independent economic worth, even though the income from their workpoints was usually paid to the male heads of households. But the change was a "mixed blessing" from the standpoint of the mother-in-law. It placed the younger woman in a stronger position once the older woman retired from work. Under the collective workpoint system, the retiree ceased to draw any income. The result, for the older woman, was a divergence between expectations and economic realities: she herself had put up with subservience to her mother-in-law in her youth and naturally expected the same from her own daughter-in-law; but economic realities now placed her in an inferior position. As for the younger woman, schooled under the new system and growing up with a sense of economic independence and worth, she was much less easily cowed than the daughter-in-law of old. This applied all the more when it fell to her to help support the retired old woman.

The problem is aggravated when the two work in occupations of different status. The young woman who finishes middle school and obtains a commune job feels herself definitely among the better and brighter of the village. Those who move into such jobs shortly after school have virtually no experience in farmwork. In appearance, dress, and outlook, they identify much more with the townsfolk than the villagers. Moreover, now that they are able to pocket their pay themselves, rather than receiving it through their fathers or husbands from the collective at the end of the year, they have an even greater sense of economic independence and worth. In their eyes, the

mother-in-law appears not only as a "dependent," but also as someone of inferior status.

The result is added stress on the already tension-fraught relationship between mother-in-law and daughter-in-law. The peasants speak
of this as the number one source of social friction in the villages, and
the cadres speak of it as the main task of the old team leaders and
woman team leaders in their attempt to maintain social harmony
within the community (H-III-33). Interviewed about 31 mother-in-
law and daughter-in-law relationships in the three teams, my village
informants ranked nine as "no good" (*buhao*) and twelve as "so so"
(*keyi*); only ten were pronounced "good." The most common explanation given for a good relationship was that "the daughter-in-law
has a good heart." For our purposes, it is significant that, of the ten
good relationships, six were in Xubushanqiao, the most "backward"
village of the Huayangqiao cluster, with the smallest proportion of
people in "desirable" off-farm jobs. In Xuejiada team, the most "industrialized" of the three teams, only one of ten relationships was
said to be "good" (H-III-14, 15, 17).

The stresses have begun to have an impact on family structures as
well. As Yang Shougen (b. 1910), the strongest and most clearheaded
of the older men in Huayangqiao, put it, in the old days, parents invariably ate with their sons in their old age; if they had several sons,
they usually ate with the youngest, generally the last to marry. But
now, because of the stresses between mothers-in-law and daughters-
in-law, the old folks often eat alone. Couples with only one son were
more likely to eat with him, because the old ethic of taking care
of the old holds with greater force in those cases. Couples with
more than one son, however, were very likely to eat by themselves
(H-III-14). Thus in Xuejiada team, three of the four single-son households ate together, but the parents ate separately in five of nine
multiple-son families. In Xubushanqiao, both single-son families ate
together, against only three of six multiple-son families. In Xilihangbang, though all of the six multiple-son families still ate together, two of the seven only-son families ate separately because of
impossible relations between the mother and the daughter-in-law
(H-III-14, 15, 17).

The story of the elderly couple Lu Genshan (b. 1912) and his wife
Ping Yajuan (b. 1919) illustrates several of the themes considered
above, albeit with a twist. Genshan had gotten a job as a cook in the
dining hall of the commune's Printing Factory in 1970. When he
stopped working a decade or so later, he was faced with the choice of
simply taking his retirement, with 40 percent pay, or giving up his

retirement for the prerogative of passing on a slot in the enterprise to one of his children. Everyone, Genshan recalls, advised him to hang on to his benefits, but Genshan wanted to give the youngest of his four sons, Maosheng (b. 1957), whose health was not too good, the privilege of a soft off-farm job. In the end, he sacrificed his retirement benefits for Maosheng. Genshan and his wife lived with Maosheng and the daughter-in-law in one household, fully expecting to be taken care of for their remaining days.

But as things turned out, Genshan and his wife could not get along with their daughter-in-law, Xie Xuefang (b. 1957). Things got so bad that the old folks wanted to split off and form their own separate household, to avoid the friction. But Xuefeng would not agree to the arrangement, perhaps because she was used to having the old folks take care of the granddaughter, Yulian (b. 1982), or perhaps because she was reluctant to let go of the extra consumption grain left over from the share allocated to the household for the old folks (because the old lady often ate with her daughter living nearby), or perhaps just out of spite. Since the young couple were the breadwinners and officially the heads of the household, the local police office would not approve of the household division without their agreement.

Relations between the two couples had gotten so bad by 1985 that they simply could no longer eat together. The arrangement they came to was for the mother to cook the rice for everyone, but for each couple to make the rest of the food separately and eat separately. Was that not rather awkward? Well, Genshan said, it was a desperate arrangement in an impossible situation. The way things used to be, the daughter-in-law would be the first one up to make breakfast for the entire household; now the mother-in-law did it. Before, the daughter-in-law was the one who generally dumped the chamber pots; now each woman dumped her own. As for the men, well, many of them, especially retired men like Genshan, did wash clothes and cook, though none would think of dumping the chamber pot (H-III-16, 17).

What we are witnessing in Huayangqiao is the intermixing of patterns of social relations characteristic of both the old world of agricultural peasants and the new world of industrial workers. The old remains in the continued importance of the family as the basic economic unit, despite off-farm employment. The new consists in the independence of the young wage workers, shown most graphically by the young women receiving their wages directly from the factories. The old remains in the persistence of the young's obligation to take care of the old and of the men's superiority over the women; the new is evidenced in the stresses on the old arrangements, especially in the relations between mothers-in-law and daughters-in-law. Particularly problematic for elderly people like Lu Genshan is that they cannot turn for security either to the old value system or the new retirement benefits. Some would no doubt argue that in many ways the communities and families remain basically "traditional" or "Chinese," while others would emphasize the emergence of characteristics common to all modern "urban" societies. My emphasis in this chapter has instead been on the intermediate character of these rural communities and families, for it is precisely their twin peasant-worker nature that shows the distinctive phenomena in contemporary rural China of industrialization without residential urbanization and intravillage occupational stratification by bureaucratic hierarchy.

3

CONCLUSION

CHAPTER 15

A Summing Up

The historical record of the Yangzi delta in the period 1350–1850 runs counter to the classical model of Smith and Marx, as well as the "early modern" and "incipient capitalism" views derived from that model. There was widespread commercialization, to be sure, but the expansion of the market economy, far from undermining the peasant household production unit, actually strengthened it. Commercial growth in the Yangzi delta during the Ming and Qing, in fact, was undergirded by peasant household production and peasant petty trade, especially of cotton products and grain. Instead of the rise and spread of large-scale wage labor–based production units in agriculture, we witness their demise after the seventeenth century and the complete predominance of the small family farm. Instead of a breakdown of the so-called "natural division of labor" within the peasant household, embodied in the expression "the men farm and the women weave," we witness its further elaboration through commercialization and the full familization of rural production. Instead of a social division of labor between agriculture and handicraft industry and between countryside and town, we witness the strengthening of the bond between agriculture and handicraft industry within the peasant household. Instead of the entrance of merchants into production, the transition of "merchant capital" into "industrial capital," we witness the continued separation of merchants from production and their dependence on the circulation of goods and capital for profit. Five centuries of commercialization brought not incipient capitalism or early modern development, but an elaboration of the peasant economy and its household production unit.

It is a record that speaks against simplistically equating the Chinese experience with a model abstracted from the classical English experience. In fact, the record should call our attention to those parts of the Western experience that are obscured by a hindsight shaped by later capitalist development. It directs our attention to a resistance to capitalist organizational forms rather than their inexorable development. Europeanists have begun noting the differences between England and most of the countries of continental Europe (e.g., Wrigley 1985; Brenner 1982). The Chinese example shows with enlarged clarity some of the tendencies in the late-developing parts of Western Europe.

There was expansion in the commercializing peasant economy, to be sure, but that expansion was largely the result of involutionary growth rather than development in rural production. The spread of cotton and the expanded cultivation of mulberries for silk were both accompanied by increased labor input, disproportionate to the increase in capital input, so that capital input per unit labor shrank, as did average returns per workday. There was an expansion in the absolute values of output and, to some extent, even in annual incomes per household, but this was due to more days worked by household members, especially the women, children, and elderly, not greater net returns per workday. This involutionary growth was undergirded by the familization of agricultural production, its diminished marginal returns to labor absorbed by the hitherto unused reserve labor in the peasant household.

The roots for involutionary commercialization are to be sought in part in the earlier history of the delta's peasant economy. Long before the coming of the Ming–Qing cotton revolution, the small-peasant economy of the Yangzi delta had reached an advanced state of growth with the perfecting of the yutian system of embanked wet-rice fields and the gridlike system of rivers and canals under the "medieval" Tang and Song. The cultivated land-to-population ratio had probably dwindled to no more than three to five mu per person by the height of the Song—a density quite unthinkable to a Europeanist or Americanist. In the Ming and Qing, the population continued to increase, by perhaps 135 percent in Songjiang and Suzhou prefectures. Yet agricultural productivity had long since reached something of a plateau, especially in rice. Further labor intensification in agriculture, therefore, took mainly the form of the spread of still-more-labor-intensive commercial crops, especially cotton and mulberries, rather than added labor input to rice cultivation.

The special ecology of the delta, of course, was what enabled such a form of involution. It was the distinctive transport network of the delta and its low-cost water links to the middle and upper Yangzi regions and the southeastern seacoast that permitted a higher degree of involutionary commercialization of the peasant economy than in a region such as North China.

Home industries based on the new cash crops were part of the overall process of involutionary commercialization. In addition to cotton picking and silkworm feeding, the auxiliary labor of the peasant households took on cotton spinning and weaving (and silk-reeling in the case of Suzhou). The lighter work of spinning was done by the children and the elderly, while the more demanding work of weaving was done by the women in their prime and by the men in their spare time.

The resulting combination of home industry with farming was no mere "natural economy," in which the men farmed and the women wove for home consumption, but highly commercialized production. Home consumption for a peasant household of five required only about ten catties of ginned cotton a year, enough to produce about eight bolts of cloth in about 56 workdays. But the weaving household of the mid-nineteenth century, averaged nationwide, did twice that amount of cotton handicraft work. In Songjiang prefecture, the average weaving household did perhaps eight times as much. The surplus beyond home consumption was traded on the market, usually for the surplus grain produced by the nonweaving peasant households.

Most of these weaving households labored under the pressure of farm incomes that were inadequate for household subsistence and undertook home industry with the auxiliary household labor not otherwise employed. For them, there was a positive incentive to engage in home industry so long as the net returns were better than zero. They took no account of either market wages, since there was no labor market for such labor, or subsistence costs, since such costs were part of the household's daily necessities.

Sustained by such labor, net returns for cotton spinning leveled off, and by the eighteenth century, a worker earned nothing more than a day's subsistence grain for a day's work. Weaving, since it was largely done by adult men and women, approximated the net returns from agricultural wage labor, which generally amounted to about two times the worker's daily grain needs. But weaving accounted for only about one-seventh of the total peasant labor input into cotton handicrafts. At those returns, and given the minuscule farms, neither home industry nor farming alone was sufficient to ensure peasant survival. Each depended on the other. For the delta peasants, commercialized home industry became the chief way to augment the household's farm income to a level sufficient for subsistence and reproduction. It was the interlocking of the two that was the key to peasant survival and reproduction in the Yangzi delta.

Such an organization of farming and handicraft industry, of course, was predicated also on certain technological conditions of production. Hand-spinning and weaving used simple and cheap tools that even poor peasant households could afford. And only the coming of the mechanical spinning wheel and loom permitted the economies of scale sufficient to overcome the cost efficiency of the peasant household labor unit.

Under those conditions, small peasant production was able to snuff out virtually all other forms of work organization in the Yangzi delta. In agriculture, wage labor–based farms could not compete with familized peasant cultivation. In industry, urban workshops could not compete with low-cost home producers. The result was the complete predominance of the small-peasant household production unit in agriculture and handicraft industry in the Yangzi delta.

Against all expectations, it was in less-commercialized and less-urbanized North China that larger-scale, wage labor–based managerial agriculture developed. By the classical Smith-Marx model, anyway, we would expect to find larger-scale production and free wage labor associated with commercialization, not the opposite. But in fact it was precisely because the growth of the North China small-peasant economy was comparatively less involuted and the household production unit comparatively unelaborated that managerial farms were able to rise. And by the same token, it was precisely the relatively advanced involutionary growth of the smallholding family-farm economy that precluded the rise of managerial units in agriculture or the handicraft cotton industry in the Yangzi delta.

MARKET STRUCTURES UNDER INVOLUTIONARY COMMERCIALIZATION

The commodity trade built on this involuted small-peasant economy resembled the "petty commodity production" scheme of Marx in that the goods traded were mainly produced by small-peasant producers and exchanged in nickel-and-dime transactions in the local market. But the resemblance stops there, for unlike the petty commodity trade envisaged by Marx, this petty trade did not lead to a capitalist economy. It was also unlike the two-way trade of rural "rude products" for urban manufactures in the vision of Adam Smith. In this petty-trade market, the flow of goods was either among peasant producers (primarily cotton goods for grain and vice versa) or unidirectional from countryside to town, with very little in the way of urban-produced goods reaching the countryside.

Factor markets of the involuted peasant economy should similarly be distinguished from the perfectly competitive factor markets envisaged by neo-Smithians like Theodore Schultz. Farm labor, first of all, was not a scarce resource whose use would be optimized by the market forces of supply and demand. Instead, a substantial amount of the farm labor remained outside the market system, without the "opportunity cost" of alternative employment through the market. In effect, peasant farms drew on a labor pool distinct from that of the managerial farms using hired labor. That was how peasant farms could outcompete and then snuff out the wage labor-based farms.

The markets for labor, land, and credit in the delta economy actually operated by a very different logic from that postulated by our neoclassical economists. The nearest thing to the freely competitive market were the markets for short-term day labor, for subsoil rights, and for extravillage merchant loans, although even those tended to be highly localized. The markets for long-term labor, for topsoil rights, and for informal intravillage credit were all subject to severe constraints. Employment as a long-term laborer almost always required personal connections; the sale of topsoil was usually constrained by the customary prior rights of purchase of kin and fellow villagers; and intravillage credit operated generally by "good feeling" and reciprocity, rather than by considerations of costs and returns. Market development during the Ming and Qing, in other words, was accompanied by the persistence of the logic and practices of an involuted, subsistence peasant economy.

Commercialization in this peasant economy was in fact driven more by extraction and survival than enterprise. The bulk of the marketed grain in the delta originated as rent payments, and not as peasant exchange for gain. And most peasant households undertook commercialized cotton and mulberry cultivation and yarn and cloth production, not because those were the most rational ways to maximize profit and accumulation, but because they were the most rational ways to survive, given inadequate farm incomes and surplus household labor. This kind of commercialized agriculture and home industry, far from engendering upwardly mobile rich peasants and entrepreneurs bent on the pursuit of profit, worked to perpetuate the small-peasant economy. Our quantitative data suggest that entrepreneurial trading by peasant producers amounted at best to a small proportion of the total commodity trade that delta villagers engaged in.

Such commercialization differs from that schematized in the classical model because it pointed not toward transformative development but rather toward an involutionary elaboration of the existing system. There was little surplus above subsistence after rents or taxes and production expenses, and little accumulation. The "cotton revolution" of the Ming and Qing thus led not to a "transition to capitalism" or "early modern development," but only to an intensification of family production and reproduction at bare subsistence levels.

INTERNATIONAL CAPITALISM AND THE
INVOLUTED PEASANT ECONOMY

The highly advanced and yet involuted peasant economy of the Ming and Qing shaped powerfully the nature and patterns of change to come from China's forced encounter with international capitalism. A big part of that story is told simply by the interlinking of a labor-abundant peasant economy with a capital-abundant industrial economy. In the new international sericulture industry that emerged out of this linkage, for example, the peasants of the delta took on the most-labor-intensive and lowest-return parts of the production process: mulberry cultivation and silkworm raising up to the cocoon stage. In the cotton industry, similarly, once machine-spun products reached the scene, peasants undertook mainly the labor-intensive work of cotton cultivation.

Chinese industries that developed out of this interlinkage were generally built one way or another on low-cost peasant production. Thus, filatures for reeling peasant-produced cocoons and mills for spinning peasant-grown cotton constituted two of the major industries of modern China. And within the internationalized system, Chinese industries tended to congregate around the low-capital, labor-intensive ends of the production process. Thus, Chinese filatures undertook relatively non-capital-intensive machine-reeling, while American and French factories dominated more-capital-intensive machine-weaving. And Chinese mills similarly took on spinning, while British and Japanese factories dominated more-capital-intensive weaving. The key to Nantong's Dasheng company was precisely its combination of labor-cheap peasant production (of cotton and cloth) with capital-cheap machine production (of yarn).

The peasant economy was profoundly affected by the new system. No one should make the mistake of presupposing, as "economic dualism" does, the complete separation of the "traditional" and "modern" sectors. Almost all peasants were intimately involved in the cotton and grain markets. The breakup of the old unity within a single household of cotton cultivation, yarn spinning, and cloth weaving greatly accelerated the commercialization of the cotton economy and, by extension, also the grain economy. Now cotton cultivators sold their cotton to be spun by machine in the cities, and then repurchased the machine-spun yarn to weave at home. It was a change that left no peasant household untouched.

But international capitalism did not bring transformative development to the countryside. Low-cost peasant household production simply became further elaborated, while net returns to rural labor remained at the margins of subsistence. The peasant economy continued to involute in a pattern similar to that under the earlier commercialization, even while the cities saw the beginnings of modern development.

THE ROLE OF MERCHANTS

In this interlinking of international capitalism with the peasant economy, of urban development with rural involution, merchants played chiefly the role of connectors between the two systems. In cotton cultivation and mulberry growing and silkworm raising, low-cost peasant household labor acted as a disincentive to labor-saving capitalization and to the formation of larger-scale enterprises capable of economies of scale. There was no incentive for the merchants to invest directly in production. Their function consisted chiefly of supplying raw materials produced by cheap Chinese peasant labor to foreign industry. They acted as "compradors," to the extent that they served the needs of foreign capital, and as "parasites" and "exploiters," to the extent that they profited from exchange and not from investment in production. Those aspects of their role formed the empirical basis for the Revolution's deep distrust of commerce—an attitude that it shared with Confucianism.

On the other hand, the new "industrial crops" required and stimulated new productive investments; it was up to the merchants to supply the soybean cake fertilizer, and establish the new hongs for drying the cocoons for the new filatures in Wuxi and Shanghai. In these respects, theirs was a development-generating role. (But their "exploitative" face remained with their new productive roles, as, for example, in the usurious rates they charged for supplying fertilizer on credit.) In the scattered pockets producing the "improved native cloth," merchants also came to play new and innovative roles. It was up to them to supply the machine-spun yarn and improved looms to the countryside, and up to them to see to the development of new products and new markets. They still drew on the advantages of dispersed peasant household production, but they entered the productive process in unprecedented ways: putting out yarn for designated types of woven cloth intended for particular markets. As we saw in Nantong, merchant capital even occasionally made the transition into industrial capital.

COMMERCIALIZATION AFTER 1850

The accelerated commercialization under imperialism was strikingly different from the earlier process in that it took place within a world commodity market. Cotton, silk, and grain were internationalized commodities whose prices now responded as much to worldwide supply and demand as to domestic factors. The rice, cotton, and mulberry grower, the cloth-weaving peasant, and the silk producer were subjected to the violent swings of the world market, shown most dramatically in the whiplash effects of 1920s prosperity followed by 1930s depression.

Yet the patterns of commercialization retained fundamental continuities with the past. The old handicraft industry held on with great tenacity. The coming of machine yarn, it is true, profoundly altered the structure of the cotton economy by breaking apart in many places the old trinity of cotton cultivation, spinning, and weaving within the peasant household. Yet that breakup did not completely wipe out the old handicraft industry. In 1920, handweaving still accounted for fully two-thirds of all the cloth consumed in China. Even hand-spinning, in which the productivity gap between hand and machine was enormous, held on to account for fully one-half of all yarn consumed in 1920. The peasant household continued to combine farming with home industry.

It was only in the 1920s and 1930s that machine yarn and cloth overtook hand-spinning and weaving. Yet even as late as 1936, 30 percent of all peasant households continued to weave. The combination of farming and home industry within the peasant household proved to be powerfully resistant to machine industry.

The coming of machine-spun yarn clearly pushed the commercialization of peasant household industry further, since nongrowing peasants could now purchase yarn to weave, and weavers were no longer constrained by the limited supply of hand-spun yarn. The further commercialization of the cotton economy meant also that more peasants came to depend more heavily on the market for grain. The result was a great expansion in the volume of small-peasant exchange. But the main content of that exchange continued to center around cloth and grain.

New metropolises and towns in the Yangzi delta, it is true, took on more of a production dimension than ever before, for they became the centers of the new industries: cotton mills, silk filatures, wheat flour mills, and the like. But the structure of rural-urban relations remained much as before. The cities and towns still produced chiefly for urban, not rural, consumption. Machine-reeled and -woven silk, and machine-polished wheat flour found little market in the countryside. Even machine-woven cloth pushed into the rural market only with difficulty, for the majority of peasants continued to wear peasant-produced native cloth down into the 1920s.

Outside of cloth, other urban products, to be sure, came to be consumed by peasants, notably yarn, matches, and kerosene. But the peasants' consumption power for new products remained very limited, since net income per workday in agriculture had improved little, and peasant production for the market had continued to be chiefly for survival and not for capitalist accumulation. In the peasants' eyes, towns and cities remained chiefly centers of administration and of trade, not of production. It was a commodity structure very different from the "integrated" modern capitalist market envisaged by Adam Smith.

The difference was reflected concretely to some extent by the low level of small-town development. China had long had large cities, to be sure, but never quite the kind of small towns that came with the bottom-up industrialization of the early-modern English example. Industrialization came to China in the century after 1850 chiefly from the top down, through foreign transplants and state sponsorship, and even then there was never the kind of interlinkage through small towns between large cities (mainly of the treaty ports) and the countryside as in modern England. That is why, as late as 1893, less than 11 percent of the Chinese lived in towns of more than 2,000 population even in the highly developed Yangzi delta. This contrasts sharply with a much more urbanized England in 1801, when nearly a third of the population lived in towns of more than 5,000.

Herein lies one of the frequently neglected differences between the classical development pattern of England and that of the more backward Third World, where rural (or agricultural) development generally comes well after urban (or industrial) development— where peasant poverty persists in the face of modern urbanization, and subsistence farming in the presence of modern power (even nuclear power) plants. This is the empirical basis for the rural-urban gap that formed one of the central rallying cries of the Revolution. It is a gap that underscores the need for us to separate out urban from rural development in our thinking about change in the modern Third World.

Commercialization worked much the same kind of effects on the village communities in the delta as it did on the peasant-household economy. It brought not transformative change, but greater continuity and stability. Sideline and off-farm employment opportunities did not transform the rural economy, but instead helped to sustain it. The household that could not otherwise make ends meet could augment its farm income with sideline and off-farm employment, and thereby hang on to its family farm. The result was much greater continuity in land use than on the North China plain. The typical cultivator, especially in the rice and rice-silk zones of the delta, farmed the land that his father and grandfather before him had farmed. This was in sharp contrast to the North China plain, where frequent natural disasters unmitigated by a commercialized and diversified economy produced a very high turnover of land and much migration in and out of villages.

Stability and continuity, however, did not make for strong community organization, nor fluidity its opposite. In the Yangzi delta, relatively high surpluses from the land sustained a multi-tiered landownership system, in which village cultivators owned the topsoil, while absentee urban landlords owned the subsoil. The subsoil came to be bought and sold freely, but trading in the topsoil remained severely constrained by custom. Thus did the delta peasant economy adapt itself both to the commercialization of the period and to the tenacity of landholding rights. After the tax reforms of the second quarter of the eighteenth century, the mostly tenant delta peasants were not taxed by the state. The absence of interaction with the state's bureaucratic apparatus, in turn, removed both the stimulus and the imperative for evolving village-level political organizations to cope with external demands. In North China, by contrast, where the overwhelming majority of the peasants were owner-cultivators, state taxation supplied both the stimulus and the imperative for the evolution of well-articulated supra–descent group community organizations.

The fluidity of the North China plain also furnished fertile soil for social unrest and disorder, hence another imperative for community organization against outside intruders. There the main focus of peasant collective action was external intrusion, whether in the form of banditry, excessive taxation, or Japanese invasion. In the ecologically and economically more stable delta, the threshold for collective violence was substantially higher, but when it did occur, it conformed more closely to the predictions of "class action," taking the form of tenant rent resistance against absentee landlords and, in the century after the Taipings, the state that backed rent collection.

In short, we find a paradoxical coincidence in the delta of high commercialization and little state presence, with weak community organization but highly stable common-descent groupings, and just the opposite in North China: low commercialization and an intrusive state presence, with a high turnover in village membership but strong supra-agnatic community organization.

The supreme paradox, of course, is that the Communist movement turned out to be far less successful in the Yangzi delta than on the North China plain. Revolutionary doctrine predicted greater class differentiation in village populations with commercialization, so by rights there ought to have been greater receptivity to Communist organizing in the delta than in the North. But the fact is that, though the Yangzi delta had a far higher tenancy rate and, in that sense, greater rural social stratification, the differentiation was chiefly between village cultivators and their urban landlords, not among the village populations themselves. Despite their greater commercialization, the delta communities were more homogeneous, not less, than the North China villages, and more resistant, not less, to Communist organizing.

COLLECTIVIST INVOLUTION

The new revolutionary state was distrustful of the free-market economy and peasant family production for both ideological and empirical reasons. Marxist orthodoxy taught that commercialization was inevitably accompanied by the social ills of capitalism, and that socialism was the only alternative way to ensure both development and social justice. But ideology aside, considering the stubborn persistence of peasant poverty in the face of six centuries of vigorous commercialization, it would have been surprising if the new state had not opted for a radically different approach from the marketized family farming of old.

The new state acted quickly to institute a planned economy and collective production. It took over the marketing of grain and cloth under the policy of "unified purchase and unified sale." And it steadily extended its control over rural production, first by fixing quotas for production and for compulsory sale to the state, and then by organizing all peasant households systematically into collectives. The production teams took over the economic decision-making powers of the households, and the state in turn directed the production teams through every last detail of production and procurement.

The vastly expanded powers of the state enabled an unprecedented buildup of the rural economy's infrastructure. In Songjiang, the state launched gigantic efforts at water control in 1958, embracing everything from the most important arterial rivers down to the smallest village irrigation and drainage ditches. The entire effort was to climax in the checkerization of the delta's rice paddy into plots of an optimal size for irrigation, transplanting, and insecticide application.

The state also made modern and industrial inputs available to the collectives. Chemical fertilizers first came to Songjiang in the 1960s. By the late 1970s, the state managed to supply all the fertilizer that peasants could use. Small hand-held tractors reached the production brigades in 1965–66, permitting more efficient plowing and further labor intensification in the form of triple-cropping. The 1970s saw expanded wheat cultivation with improvements in underground drainage. Modern agronomy produced punctuated advances throughout these decades, periodically introducing new higher-yielding and/or more drought-, cold-, or insect-resistant seed varieties.

These inputs, combined with an intensification of such traditional inputs as hand labor and organic fertilizer, powered impressive increases in per-mu yields between 1952–56 and 1975–79 in all four major crops in Songjiang: of 103 percent in rice, 172 percent in wheat/barley, 291 percent in rapeseed, and 355 percent in cotton. These achievements in yields per sown mu were augmented by a greatly increased frequency in cropping. Once mainly a one-rice-crop-a-year region, Songjiang had more than half of its cultivated acreage under three crops a year by the late 1960s.

Under different conditions, modern inputs like chemical fertilizer, tractors, electrified pumping, and the like probably could have helped raise workday incomes significantly. But the relentless expansion in the agricultural labor force prevented even small gains. Farmland had to bear first the explosive expansion of the farm-labor supply as women were pulled into agriculture in the mid-1950s, and then the steady increases beginning in the late 1960s as more and more baby-boomers attained working age.

The vast farm-labor supply removed incentives for labor-saving capitalization and dictated that change take the direction of labor-intensifying involution. Capital inputs increased, to be sure, but not at a fast enough rate to outstrip the increased labor input per cropping and the increased frequency of cropping. Net returns to labor at the margin stagnated, even declined, and the cash value of the work-day equivalent hovered at the same level throughout the 1960s and 1970s.

The collectivist institutional framework, far from discouraging involutionary tendencies, served only to reinforce them. Like the family farm, the collective could not fire its surplus labor. Given surplus labor and subsistence pressures, it would intensify labor input until, logically, its marginal product approached zero. Or, put differently, the collective as an economic decision-making unit, like the family farm, was concerned chiefly with the average product of labor, not the marginal product. The postrevolutionary Chinese state, moreover, had a vested interest in involution. State tax and compulsory purchase were pegged to total crop output, not to income or productivity per unit labor. From the point of view of the state, procurement was maximized by the highest possible level of involutionary expansion, regardless of the net returns to labor input at the margins. The state, finally, was for ideological reasons deeply distrustful of rural petty trade and, by extension, also the peasant household's "petty commodities production" of old. It therefore imposed severe constraints on those outlets for rural surplus labor, which put still more involutionary pressure on the land. Thus in the first three decades after the Revolution, Songjiang repeated once more the pattern of involutionary growth (without labor productivity development) of the preceding six centuries.

In the end, collectivization did no better than the free-market approach before it. Despite the state's vigorous efforts, agriculture failed to break out of its involutionary pattern. In the late 1970s, returns to rural labor remained barely above the margins of subsistence, just as in the centuries before the Revolution.

RURAL INDUSTRIALIZATION AND ECONOMIC DIVERSIFICATION

What finally powered genuine development in Songjiang's rural economy was diversification, especially by industrialization. The collectives had started several "industrial" enterprises in the late 1950s, during the Great Leap, but they had remained modest, hand-production activities tied directly to agriculture: the production and repair of farm implements, straw-rope making, brick-and-tile making, and the like. Significant advances were made in the late 1960s and early 1970s, during the Cultural Revolution years, as urban industry began to forge processing links with communes or to send phased-out equipment to the communes. Brigade-level industry followed in the 1980s, trickled down from the commune in the same way as the state industries had trickled down to it.

From the villagers' point of view, the industrial enterprises high up in China's administrative hierarchy mattered little. State and collective enterprises of the county level and above take their labor force almost exclusively from the urban areas. Only commune and particularly brigade enterprises employ significant numbers of peasants. In Huayangqiao, state enterprises provided only a meager 33 off-farm jobs for the villagers during all the years between 1949 and 1985.

It was the opening up of commune and brigade jobs that finally reversed the six-centuries-long pattern of involution in Huayangqiao's crop production. By the mid-1980s, with more than half the villages' resident labor force employed off-farm, farm labor finally became a relatively scarce resource. Adjustments were accordingly made in cropping patterns to de-involute to more nearly optimal levels of labor use that would take account of the returns to labor. In Songjiang county as a whole, the double-cropping of rice was scaled down from a high of nearly 60 percent of the cultivated area to just one-third by 1985.

At the same time, the household-responsibility system of labor organization in crop production permitted more use of spare-time and auxiliary household labor for farming (whereas the collectives, given their workpoint system of remuneration for regular work, offered little incentive for such labor). It also furnished strong incentives for getting farmwork done more efficiently, whether to use the remaining time for off-farm employment or just for leisure, which had not been possible under the collective system. The state, finally, raised substantially the purchase price for major crops. The combined result was dramatic rises in incomes per workday and per laborer in crop production, even without any increases in crop yields per unit area. Added to the incomes from new and old sidelines stimulated by the enlivened rural petty-commodities economy and the incomes from the new rural industrial employment, these increases powered the new prosperity of peasant households in the Songjiang countryside.

For the first time in centuries, peasant incomes began to rise substantially above the margins of subsistence. And peasant consumption, for the first time ever, created a major market for urban manufactures and processed goods. The new prosperity produced a wave of conspicuous consumption in the countryside in the late 1970s and 1980s, shown most dramatically by the spiraling norms for wedding banquets, betrothal gifts, and dowries. The peasants became major consumers of "luxury" items like watches, electric fans, artificial fabrics, and even television sets, in addition to the thermos bottles, radios, and bicycles popular before the reforms.

Peasant prosperity, petty trade, and local industrialization underlie the small-town development of the late 1970s and the 1980s. Songjiang, like the Yangzi delta as a whole, finally began to witness the mutually generative pattern of rural-urban development that powered the growth of English small towns in the eighteenth century. Songjiang also finally began to experience the two-way rural-urban exchange of goods and services that we associate with modern development. But this "modern" form of development occurred under neither the capitalism of the classical view nor its socialist alternative. The economy remained predominantly collectivized in its industrial sector and dispersed to the household in its agricultural sector; and the new market system was similarly mixed, combining rural petty trade with planned distribution and allocation. In a rapidly spreading system of exchange, neither capitalist nor socialist, collective units sought out contractural arrangements with other collective units or state/private enterprises. The precise nature and logic of all these phenomena have yet to be studied systematically.

THE RETURN OF FAMILY FARMING

Much has been made of the return of household organization to farming, but its true significance in the delta consists in its capacity to make more flexible and efficient use of labor for the diversifying rural economy, not in supposedly superior incentives powering increases in crop yields. In Songjiang, crop yields per unit area in fact topped out by 1978–79 under collective organization. The household-responsibility system has actually seen stagnated unit-area yields down into the late 1980s. The real advance has come not in crop yields, but in savings of labor in crop production.

The huge surplus of farm labor of the 1960s and 1970s was tolerated by the collectives, which paid workpoints to "loitering labor" just the same as they did to more productive labor. So long as there was an overabundance of farm labor, and so long as the required job got done, there was little reason to search for more efficient ways to organize farm labor. Once industrialization drained off the excess labor from farming, however, a tightening up became imperative. Family labor motivated by opportunities for alternative employment, or even just by the incentive of leisure, works more efficiently than collectivized labor paid in workpoints: the same amount of farmwork, peasants say, gets done these days in about two-thirds of the time it took under the collectives. Moreover, much of the work is being done with spare-time or auxiliary household labor, or both. The more efficient and flexible use of family labor (along with the upward adjustment of state prices for major crops) is the real secret to the farm family's new prosperity, which has occurred without an expansion in crop yields.

At the end of the 1980s, returns to crop production (and household sidelines) still lagged behind the returns to industry (and the more highly capitalized collective sidelines), to be sure, but there can be no mistaking the upward shift in peasant incomes. Or the fact that farming had ceased to be the peasant household's mainline where rural industrialization had taken hold. The lowest-paid household sidelines of old are fast disappearing, replaced by farming as the new sideline.

The family form of labor organization has proved its resilience in the midst of these changes. Its major difference from the collective team is its ability to use spare-time and auxiliary labor without the constraints imposed by standardized remuneration in workpoints. That ability had ensured its survival during the collectivized years (except at the height of the Great Leap) in low-return household sideline production. The same ability now ensures its survival in low-return farming.

For all this, it remains to be seen whether the family unit is the best organizational form for large-scale, highly capitalized enterprises. The late 1980s saw experiments in the North China county of Shunyi that regrouped households into larger production units for capital accumulation and further mechanization, especially in the use of harvesters for maize and wheat. In rice-farming Songjiang, mechanical transplanters and harvesters have so far remained uneconomical, not worth the cost at present wage scales, and there has been no move to regroup the peasants into larger production units at this writing. The precise organizational form that crop production will take in the future is still an open question.

Although the thinking during the early reform years appeared to

lean toward "the smaller the better" in crop production, to counter-
act the Great Leap's dogma of "the bigger the better," that policy
began to lose ground in the late 1980s to something close to
Chayanov's old idea of "differential optimums." Different kinds of
production are optimal at different scales under different technological conditions. There need be no dogmatic attachment to either small-scale or large-scale production, the inclinations of the
classical views of Smith and Marx notwithstanding. At this point,
official thinking seems to be tending more and more toward flexibly
conceived "appropriate scale economies" that vary with different
conditions of production.

THE VILLAGE AND THE STATE

In terms of the state's claims to power vis-à-vis other organized
groups in society, imperial and postrevolutionary China share much
in common: like the imperial state, the contemporary state claims
"despotic power," to borrow Michael Mann's (1984) term, and permits no organized opposition, although it is no less subject in practice to the checks of an elite interest group (the cadres having replaced the gentry in that role) and of centrifugal tendencies in the
bureaucratic apparatus. The resemblance stops, however, when it
comes to the contemporary state's "infrastructural power" (to borrow Mann's other term) to impose its policies at the grass roots. The
postrevolutionary party-state has succeeded in penetrating every
natural village to the individual household.

It has also succeeded in broadening its reach across all sectors of
social and economic life. Where the imperial state claimed by and
large only the power to tax and to maintain order, the party-state has
asserted its right to restructure society by social revolution, to direct
trade and production by organized planning, and to maintain ideological conformity by party propaganda and control.

The power of the collectivist party-state, to be sure, was never
total. Many team leaders, brigade and commune cadres, and even
county officials had double loyalties, to their localities as well as to
the state. Some analysts have emphasized the limitations of the
state's control over its local cadres, especially at the team level, and
the tug-of-war between state intent and local interest. But we must
not exaggerate the scope of a village production team's independence. Paternalism more accurately describes the relationship. The
Huayangqiao example demonstrates the very complete control that
the state held over production decisions down to every team.

It also shows the high degree of identification among cadres above the level of the natural village/hamlet (i.e., the team in most of the Yangzi delta, but the brigade in North China) with the state and the party. Brigade cadres in Huayangqiao, with good prospects of advancing up the bureaucratic ladder of the party-state, tended to identify more with the state apparatus than their home communities. This was all the more true of commune and county cadres; most of them, in any case, came from other localities, a modern version of the good old-fashioned rule of avoidance for county magistrates. Only the team leaders in Huayangqiao were truly Janus-faced, as committed to their home communities as to the state. Usually of poor or middle-peasant background and at best semiliterate, they tended to serve for long periods, with little chance for advancement.

The implications of the post-1978 reforms for the relationship between the Chinese state and the peasant need to be understood in these terms. To the extent that the power of production team leaders today is but a shadow of what it was during the decades of collectivized agriculture, the administrative reach of the state has been retracted upward and away from the individual peasant household. And to the extent that more elbowroom is being allowed for a free-market economy and for peasant household decision making, the functional spread of state power has also contracted.

On the other hand, to the extent that postrevolutionary collectivization helped forge a new organizational frame for the natural hamlet/village, de-collectivization has weakened that community organization. To some degree, the peasant household now stands alone and isolated before state power, its prerevolutionary descent group as well as its postrevolutionary collective community very much diminished in importance. The precise shape that state-peasant relations will take with the new social-economic changes remains to be seen.

One impact of those changes is already clear. As more villagers come to be employed off-farm, village populations are coming to be stratified increasingly by occupation, with workers in the state enterprises at the top and farmworkers at the bottom. Some stratification has also come with the enrichment of a few through market opportunity, to be sure, but the main differentiating mechanism has been the state-imposed hierarchy among enterprises. It seems to me truly ironic that peasant cultivators should be feeling like the low person on the totem pole just when their incomes per workday are genuinely increasing.

A Summing Up   323

THE YANGZI DELTA MODEL IN THE NATIONAL CONTEXT

As one of the most advanced areas of China both industrially and agriculturally, the Yangzi delta is hardly typical. Nevertheless, its early record in reform clearly foretold some of the national trends discernible in the late 1980s. In hindsight, we can see that the dramatic national advances in crop yields between 1979 and 1984 probably resulted in good part from the extension to the less-developed areas of inputs (especially chemical fertilizer with the maturation of China's petroleum industry) that had reached the delta by the mid-1970s. The gains from the reorganization of farm labor that came with the household-responsibility system resulted at best in one-shot advances that could not be sustained so long as the technological levels of cultivation remain largely unchanged. By the mid-1980s, national crop yields leveled off, just as they had earlier in the delta.

Moreover, the dramatic consequences for peasant livelihood of rural industrialization and small-town development, already evident in the delta by the early 1980s, became much clearer nationwide in the following years. By 1986, rural industries had come to account for 40 percent of the gross value of commune/township output. At that point, they were well on the way to playing the role for rural development in the whole of China that they had played in the delta.

In terms of approaches to reform, the delta provides a sharp contrast to Wenzhou. Its rural industries remained predominantly collective, with private enterprises accounting for a negligible part of the gross income of all rural enterprises. Because of the industrial base built up during the collective years, the delta's township governments enjoyed substantial budgetary surpluses after the required expenditures for social services and were therefore able to take the lead under the reforms in developing additional collective enterprises. In Wenzhou, by contrast, community governments had been relatively poor and therefore lacked the capacity to develop collective industries. Lower-cost private initiative was the alternative. As it happens, enterprising peasants were able to take good advantage of the area's distinctive legacy from prerevolutionary days of household handicrafts and commercial contacts throughout China. The result was vigorous petty capitalist development, of production by small household units, concentrated in specific locales, with considerable specialization and some measure of mechanization.

Wenzhou's type of private household industry, to be sure, constituted the most rapidly growing sector in China in the mid-1980s, leaping to account for almost one-quarter of all income from rural enterprises by 1986. But the collective economy clearly still held the predominant position and accounted for two-thirds of the gross income. To that extent, Songjiang's is more the mainstream approach of broad relevance for China as a whole than Wenzhou.

We must not, in any event, lapse back into the simplistic classical alternatives between capitalism and socialism in considering the issues posed by the Songjiang and Wenzhou examples. The two "models" are actually intermixed in most localities and represent approaches that are by no means mutually exclusive. Most community governments have been busily engaged in operating or trying to start up industrial enterprises in the manner of the delta model, while their constituent households just as busily seek ways to augment their incomes with household production for the market in the manner of the Wenzhou model. The relative mix and successes of the two approaches have varied from place to place. Even in Songjiang itself, despite the predominance of the collective in industry, household production is the order of the day in agriculture, and household petty-commodities production an important contributor to the county's rural development. The mixing of household with collective production, and planned with market allocation and distribution, is forging new problems and possibilities that cannot be understood in the old terms. To cast the issues simply in terms of the classical alternatives between capitalism and socialism is to miss the true significance of the reforms and the historical background leading up to them. The delta's past and present cry out for new categories of understanding and new approaches to rural development.

CHAPTER 16

Some Speculations

At the end of this rather long book, I would like to engage in a few pages of speculative hypothesizing about three major issues that were raised but not discussed in detail in the text: the roots of China's high population density, the structure of its distinctive political economy and social system, and the paradoxical coincidence throughout so much of Chinese history of advanced urban "development" with backward rural involution. What follows builds on and elaborates observations in my earlier North China book (1985: esp. 246–48).

CHINA'S POPULATION DENSITY

Given the available evidence, we will probably never be able to know for certain why and how China came to have the density of population that it has. Nevertheless, this phenomenon has had such a profound impact on Chinese history and plays such a central role in the analyses of this book that I feel we must attempt some intelligent guesses about its origins, no matter how speculative.

I believe that the lowland core areas were already densely populated by the early empire. The rise of the centralized Qin-Han imperial state in the Warring States period (475–221 B.C.) was in fact predicated on a high-density smallholding peasant economy. Most states of the time were quite aware that their power rested on maintaining a large army, and that this rested on a large population. The Qi state under the Duke of Huan (685–43 B.C.) had decreed that males should be married by the age of twenty, and females by fifteen. The Yue under King Goujian (496–65 B.C.), similarly, had decreed that parents would be held guilty if any son should be unmarried by the age of thirty, and any daughter by seventeen. Those who bore lots of children were to be rewarded (Wu Shenyuan 1986: 24). Confucius himself (551–479 B.C.) had occasion to praise the state of Wei for its dense population, and Mencius (372–289 B.C.) later explicitly pointed to the useful role Confucian "humane government" (ren-zheng) played in helping the state to "expand territory and increase population" (guangtu zhongmin). The Guanzi (by miscellaneous authors from the later Warring States period down to the Western Han) put the whole matter the most straightforwardly of all: "the way to hegemony is a large territory and a wealthy state, and lots of people and a strong army" (quoted in ibid., p. 43).

The Qin state, especially, pursued a coherent and well-elaborated set of interconnected policies to these ends, thanks to its famous counselor, Shang Yang. Lord Shang sought actively to develop a smallholder economy by offering land and giving tax exemptions to encourage in-migration to the Wei River Valley. He also articulated explicitly a policy favoring the division of households and family property among brothers: "those households with two or more males that remain undivided will have their taxes doubled" (Takikawa 1960, 68: 8).

The logic implicit in these policies was, first, that a smallholding peasantry would make the best source of recruits for mass armies. We might observe further that smallholders also posed much less of a threat to centralized state power than large estates. Second, Shang appears to have made the conceptual connection between a small-holding peasant economy, partible inheritance, and high population density. Though he did not spell out the logic in so many words, it is clear that his goal was very high population density in the areas under Qin control. In his vision of an optimal balance of land and labor in (the Guanzhong plain of) the Wei River Valley, he projected 50,000 farm laborers working an area of 100 square li, 40 percent of which would be good cultivated land, 20 percent poor quality land, 10 percent hills, 10 percent lakes, 10 percent rivers, canals, and streams, and 10 percent towns and roads (Wu Shenyuan 1986: 31). This works out to 20.7 mu (present-day shi mu) of good cultivated land and 10.4 mu of poorer quality land per farm laborer,[*] or a density already quite close to the estimated 15 mu per farm laborer in the Han (Wu Hui 1985: 128; Hsu 1980; Ning Ke 1980a), and to the average of 25 mu per household (usually of not more than one or two farm laborers) for the fully settled Hebei–northwest Shandong plain in the eighteenth century (Huang 1985: 60–61, 185–87).

---

[*] 100 square li equaled 9,000,000 small (xiao) Han mu, or 2,592,000 contemporary (shi) mu (one Han small mu = 0.288 shi mu; Wu Hui 1985: 18; on the large [da] Han mu, see Liang Fangzhong 1980: 547).

Let me pause here to bring out the underlying connections. Under a system of primogeniture (or unigeniture), the heir cannot become economically independent until he inherits the farm on the death of the father. That may cause later marriage, as it did in Europe before protoindustrialization provided alternative sources for economic independence (Levine 1977; Tilly 1978: "Introduction"). All the siblings, moreover, have to seek alternative sources for economic independence. That may lower the rate of the proportion ever marrying, as it did in Europe before the coming of protoindustrial employment (Weir 1984; Goldstone 1986). Partible inheritance, on the other hand, ensures the economic survival of all siblings, even if at lowered standards of living, and hence enables higher nuptiality. Where it is accompanied by household partitions during the lifetime of the father, it also encourages earlier marriage. Early and universal marriage, of course, produces higher fertility rates in the population.

The ability of the peasant economy of the Warring States period to support an entire household with as small a farm as Shang Yang envisioned was due at least in part to technological advances that came with the "iron age." Contemporary sources document an already well-advanced and highly intensive agricultural regime, with planting in furrows; iron plows pulled by animals; hoes and spades for weeding, turning, and pulverizing the loess soil to preserve moisture; irrigation; crop rotation; and so on (Hsu 1980: esp. "Introduction"). The perfecting of the curved-iron moldboard for the plow during the Han was not to be matched in European agriculture until the eighteenth century (Bray 1984: 576–87; see also 186–93). It was this combination of technological advance and the active promotion of early and universal marriage that produced the high-density small-peasant economy.

The triumph of the Qin entrenched the formula of combining centralized state power with high-density peasant farming in China. Subsequent dynasties were to follow largely the same policy. Each new dynasty typically set out to check the growth of large estates and reinvigorate the small-peasant economy. The Tang instituted the "equal field" system of small cultivators. The Ming decreed that those who resettled the vast areas devastated by the wars of dynastic transition were not to claim more land than they could farm themselves. The Qing, along the same lines, undertook vigorous measures to check the *touxian* practice of the late Ming, by which smallholders sought shelter from taxation by placing themselves under the big gentry estates (Huang 1985: 86, 246–48). Likewise, Shang Yang's policy of partible inheritance became the standard social practice among most of the population by Tang times. The Tang code, which served as the model for the later dynasties, contained detailed provisions on how to divide up family property among brothers under all sorts of circumstances (Niida Noboru 1964: 234, 245–46).

Let me suggest, then, that the entrenchment in China of a centralized imperial state based on a high-density peasant economy under partible inheritance perpetuated early and universal marriage among the population, and that this in turn ensured relatively high rates of fertility. Combined with "normal" peacetime rates of mortality, fertility was high enough to sustain a population growth of as much as 1 percent or even more a year. China did not require, as early modern England did, the protoindustrialization that would break down late marriage and low nuptiality to usher in population growth of such an order.

We must remember that a 1 percent per year increase is sufficient to double a population in 72 years, and quadruple it in 144, and that given the sustained periods of peace during China's long imperial era, population expansions of several-fold were not at all uncommon. In this perspective, the nearly threefold increase in population between 1700 and 1850 in China, so often referred to as "the population explosion," was actually but the most recent of a series of peacetime population expansions in Chinese history. Each expansion was interrupted, and sometimes reversed, by the wars and famines of dynastic transition. Thus, the Qin-Han saw Chinese population reach possibly 60,000,000. It then dropped severely during the long centuries of division that followed, then expanded again during the Tang-Song, to reach perhaps 110,000,000 (Hartwell 1982; see also Ning Ke 1980b), only to be drastically reduced once more and then expand again during the Ming. What was different about the final wave of expansion of the imperial era, in the 150 years between 1700 and 1850, was not the rate of growth but the starting base of 150,000,000. The nearly threefold expansion to 430,000,000 (Ho 1959; see also Perkins 1969) in fact required only a growth rate of 0.7 percent,* modest even by premodern standards, and puny in comparison to the more than 2 percent rate of postrevolutionary China (Coale 1984) and most of the contemporary Third World, societies in which modern medicine has sharply reduced the mortality rate be-

* A rate that would see the population double in 103 years and quadruple in 206 (72 divided by the growth rate gives the number of years required to double the population).

fore social-economic change has had a chance to usher in the lower fertility rates associated with the modern "demographic transition."

If the above speculations are valid, they suggest that China's demographic change was driven by alterations in the mortality rate, not in the fertility rate as in early modern Europe. Early and universal marriage saw to the doubling of populations in a century or less during peacetime, until drastic rises in mortality curtailed the rate of increase or reduced the total population. In early modern Europe, by contrast, late and less-than-universal marriage saw to low fertility rates and little population growth, until protoindustrialization raised fertility rates by lowering the age of marriage and increasing the proportion ever-marrying. With the "modern demographic transition," during which families began to opt for fewer children, the fertility rate declined and population leveled off. Early modern and modern Europe's demographic change, in short, was principally fertility-driven, whereas China's was mortality-driven.

CHINA'S SOCIAL SYSTEM AND POLITICAL ECONOMY

The political and economic structure outlined above was integrally linked to a social system (or "social formation," *shehui xingtai*) that Chinese historians have dubbed "feudal landlordism." One of its key distinguishing features, according to Hu Rulei (1979), was private landownership and the relatively free buying and selling of land, this in contrast to medieval European "feudal manorialism." I believe Hu is correct in spotlighting this difference, and I would argue that it was born of the freeholding small-peasant economy promoted by the Qin and perpetuated by the dynasties that followed it.

A second distinguishing feature of "landlordism," according to Hu, is the separation of proprietary right over land from military, administrative, and judicial powers over the cultivators of the land, this again in contrast to the European manorial system, in which the lords also wielded noneconomic powers over their domain. Under Chinese "landlordism," the state monopolized the other powers, thereby overcoming the "parcelized sovereignty" that characterized European manorialism. This feature of Chinese landlordism is also traceable, I believe, to the Qin's active promotion of a freeholding small-peasant economy.

The institution of partible inheritance, I would further argue, was closely linked to Chinese "landlordism." A manorial system must be maintained by a single-heir system if the estate is not to break apart within a few generations. Partible inheritance, on the other hand, leads almost unavoidably to fragmented smallholdings. But once a certain density is reached, a peasant economy under partible inheritance requires a land market to reproduce itself: a peasant inheriting less land than his household can survive on has to be able to purchase or rent land.

The imperial system born of the interlinking of this social system with a centralized state and a high-density peasant economy gave rise to an elaborate bureaucracy recruited through civil service examinations. That system, in turn, formed the basis for a ruling elite that Western scholars commonly term "the gentry." As a status group, the gentry/degree holders were separated by law from commoners by virtue of their achievement in the state-administered examinations. As a class, the gentry were most often drawn from landowners who held sufficient landed property in the small-peasant economy to lease out their land (hence "landlords") and be liberated from the burdens of farmwork.

The concept "gentry society," used in Western scholarship (e.g., Eberhard 1965), seems to me to be perfectly compatible with the Chinese notion of "landlordism." The difference between the two categories is only a matter of emphasis. The Chinese historian stresses the landowning and rent-collecting ("exploitative") dimension of the gentry, and the Western historian the gentry's service functions (e.g., Chung-li Chang 1955, 1962). But they are alike in singling out the ruling elite and its distinctive characteristics in analyzing China's social system.

Of the two regions that I have studied, "gentry society" or "landlordism" seems more appropriate for the Yangzi delta, since this spotlights the great importance of landownership and land leasing for the ruling elites of the area, while "imperial China," which spotlights the imperial system and is the preferred category in current Western scholarship, seems more appropriate for North China, since tenancy was less highly developed and the state's presence loomed larger than the landlords or gentry. By the same token, the alternative Marxist category "Asiatic mode of production," which spotlights the centralized bureaucratic state, seems more appropriate for North China than the "feudal landlordism" of the official five-modes formula. But whether we choose to emphasize the gentry/landlord dimension or the state, or the Yangzi delta or North China, it should be clear that neither region can be adequately understood without reference to both sets of categories. The Yangzi delta's "gentry society" or "landlordism" is not comprehensible without taking into account the imperial state—indeed the very notion of a degree-holding gentry is predicated on the bureaucratic state and its examination system. North China, where the imperial state loomed so much larger than the gentry, similarly cannot be understood without attention to the special characteristics of the gentry elite that furnished the bureaucrats for the imperial state. The difference between the two regions is that each calls to mind more prominently a different mix of the two sets of categories; the commonality between them is that both regions need to be understood in terms of the interdependent combination of gentry society/landlordism with the imperial state.

Yet even if we combine the two sets of categories, we still cannot adequately capture the essentials of the two regional ecosystems. Whether for the Yangzi delta or for North China, we must attend also to the third major component: the high-density small-peasant economy that undergirded both the gentry/landlord system and the imperial state. That high-density peasant economy should be understood as the other side of the "landlordism" coin. And landlordism-cum-the high-density peasant economy was what made possible the centralized imperial state. This shared system of bureaucratic landlordism based on an involuted peasant economy was what knit the otherwise disparate regions of North China and the Yangzi delta together, making them the two key support bases for a unified China and a unified imperial state.

The system enjoyed remarkable longevity for a number of reasons. It was able to generate extraordinary military might for premodern warfare, with armies numbering in the hundreds of thousands already by the Han. Even a quite different social order, with a different military organization, like the Manchu Qing, adopted the same formula to perpetuate its power. Once in place, the system permitted a high degree of centralization, unchallenged by the "parcelized sovereignties" that the royal houses in medieval Europe had to contend with. The institution of the civil service examination, born of this system, was a singularly effective method of maintaining the structure. By opening elite status to talent rather than just birth, no matter how limited the extent in actual practice, the state was able to channel into official service the ambitions of the most talented and successful members of society. It thereby saw to the reproduction of the structure as well as to its continual reinvigoration by new blood.

The most crucial element, perhaps, was that the high-density peasant economy on which the entire system was based possessed a remarkable ability for involutionary growth, not merely through the intensification of agricultural production, but also through commercialization. As has been seen in this book, even after rice yields per unit land had topped out under "traditional" methods of cultivation, the Yangzi delta was able to involute further by turning to even more-labor-intensive cash crops, especially cotton and mulberries for silkworms. In so doing, the involuted peasant economy was able to sustain a landlordism that ultimately snuffed out alternative "capitalistic" organizations of farm production. Involuted small tenant farms were able to outcompete wage labor–based managerial farming by drawing on low-cost spare-time and auxiliary household labor. Even under the impact of international capitalism, that same involuted tenant farming was able to persist and prevail in the production of commercial crops for the same reason.

RURAL-URBAN RELATIONS IN CHINESE HISTORY

The involuted peasant economy was able to support very large and complex cities, and, by extension, also a highly advanced elite and urban culture, even if the surplus above subsistence produced by the average cultivator shrank from the diminished marginal returns that came with involution. This paradox is poorly understood. Large cities and advanced urban cultures are commonly associated with rural prosperity, but I would like to suggest that the opposite was actually the case in much of Chinese history.

Surplus above subsistence in preindustrial agriculture amounted at best to only a relatively small proportion of the peasant household's production. China's large cities, obviously, could only be supported by the surplus of large farm populations. At 10 percent of output, it would have required 1,000,000 peasants to support an urban population of 100,000. A city of 1,000,000 would have required a farming population of 10,000,000 for its support (see Boserup 1981: chap. 6 on this point).

The proportion that surplus above subsistence occupied in the total output of a peasant household, however, declined past a certain point of population density because of the diminished marginal returns to labor. Let us suppose that, as population density goes up tenfold, the surplus declines from, say, 30 percent of output to 10 percent. It should be obvious that the higher density peasant economy, even with a much lower surplus per household, would still be able to sustain a larger absolute surplus and hence a larger off-farm population: 10 percent of 10,000,000, or 1,000,000, is substantially more than 30 percent of 1,000,000, or 300,000. Herein lies what I see as the key to "medieval" China's ability to sustain larger and more-complex cities than medieval Europe.

One dynamic for the formation of those cities was of course the imperial bureaucratic administration. This is the aspect of Chinese cities that Max Weber highlighted. Yet as has been seen in this book, the involuted peasant economy gave rise in the late imperial era also to a complex system of peasant exchange, especially of grain for cotton products. That trade, "petty" in terms of individual peasant households but enormous in the aggregate, also promoted the formation of commercial towns and cities. This commercial dimension of Chinese urbanization is often overlooked, but it was surely as important as the administrative dimension, especially for late imperial China.

The conjunction of large cities with low rural per capita income, or urban "development" with rural involution, formed the basis for the conspicuous gap throughout so much of Chinese history between elite and peasant culture. The large and complex cities made possible the high level of development of urban elite culture, but they were built on the involutionary poverty of the countryside.

At the same time, the thin margins above subsistence that the state as well as the rural populations had to work with aggravated the tensions between the two, the more so with increased density and correspondingly diminished marginal returns to labor. The delicate balance between state extraction and peasant survival was threatened whenever man-made or natural disasters threatened peasant productivity. Any decline in the size of the surplus threatened both the survival of the state and the survival of its rural population, more so than in the case of the less-densely populated political economy in which the margin above subsistence was greater. Herein, I would speculate, lies one of the explanations for the frequency and intensity of state-peasant conflict in Chinese history.

The rural-urban gap of premodern China widened with the coming of the modern West, and the country's subsequent top-down industrialization and development. The coastal port cities and major metropolises began their "development" of modern industry, transport, and communications first, either under foreign ownership or Chinese state sponsorship, while the countryside continued to involute. The most vigorous industries in that development were precisely those that thrived on the involuted nature of the peasant economy and its enormous supply of cheap labor. The new cotton yarn mills drew on low-paid peasant labor for raw materials and cloth-weaving, while the filatures drew on the same kind of labor for mulberry-growing and silkworm-raising, and so on. The resulting interlinkage of accelerated urban development with continued rural involution widened the already large gap between city and countryside, and formed the empirical basis for an issue of major concern among twentieth-century Chinese intellectuals.

That gap, I would suggest, is critically important also for understanding China's "modern" urban history. Contrary to the classical Marxist image of the proletariat as the most downtrodden and exploited members of society, "with nothing to lose but their chains," the modern Chinese factory workers were a privileged group compared with the massive "semiproletariat" that lived between the countryside and the city, making their way as temporary workers, peddlers, itinerant artisans, and the like. Born of the vast impoverished countryside and forming something of a subproletariat, with incomes lower than the regular factory workers, these people were not the Marxists' "lumpen proletariat" or an underclass of unemployed drifters. They were people who straddled city and countryside, farming and urban work, rural and urban petty commodity production. Their massive and protracted presence is probably one important feature that distinguishes the modern Chinese city (and other high-density Third World cities) from the modern European city. Our field has yet to study systematically their influence on modern China's urban history.*

The Chinese government's current policy choices in the domestic realm need to be seen in the context of a long-standing pattern of urban extractions from the countryside, of urban development on the basis of rural involution. The secret was to enlarge the absolute size of the extractable total surplus by enlarging the population, without regard to the fact that incomes per workday diminished steadily at the margins. Now that that long-term trend is beginning to be reversed, and the surplus per household is beginning to increase with agricultural de-involution and rural industrialization, the big question is whether the state and the urban sector will allow the rural sector to retain that surplus for its own investment and development.

*Lu Hanchao is working on a Ph.D. dissertation at UCLA that will demonstrate how the industrial workers formed a relatively privileged group among the new "little urbanites" (xiaoshimin) of Shanghai.

APPENDIXES

Socioeconomic Profiles
of Eight
Yangzi Delta Villages

Basic features of the eight Yangzi delta villages for which we have detailed ethnographic data are presented overleaf. Given the limited size of the sample, I have not attempted to develop a village typology as I did for the 33 Mantetsu-surveyed villages in my North China book (1985). The best way to categorize these delta villages, as discussed in Chapter 2, is by their ecology and cropping patterns: whether on low-lying land, with embanked fields for wet-rice, or on high-lying land, with substantial proportions of dry-farmed cotton.

The data are drawn from the following sources: *Touzongmiao*, MT, Shanghai jimusho 1941b; *Xiaodingxiang et al.*, ibid. 1941a; *Yanjiashang*, ibid. 1939b; *Yaojing*, ibid. 1939c; *Dingjiacun*, ibid. 1939a; *Sunjiaxiang*, Hayashi Megumi 1943; *Kaixiangong*, Fei Hsiao-tung [Fei Xiaotong] 1939; *Huayangqiao*, MT, Shanghai jimusho 1940.

TABLE A.I

Eight Yangzi Delta Villages

Category	Touzongmiao, Nantong	Xiaodingxiang et al.,[a] Wuxi	Yanjiashang, Changshu
Main crops (pct. cropped area)	soybeans 49%, cotton 39% barley 73%, wheat 12%	rice 76%, mulberries 23% wheat 58%, broad beans 11%	rice 100% wheat 83%, alfalfa 16%
No. households	94	80	55
Pct. nonfarm households	10.6%	10.0%	30.9%
Total cultivated mu	283.6	190.3	200.7
No. cultivated mu per capita	0.7	0.6	0.9
Km from county seat	20	2	2.5
No. resident landlords	3	0	0
No. managerial farmers	0	0	0
Pct. cultivated land rented	33.5%	32.4%	82.4%[c]
Composition of farm households (pct.)			
Owners	46.4%	68.9%	8.1%
Tenants, part-tenants	50.0%	31.1%	91.9%
Year-laborers	3.6%	0	0
Pct. farm households hiring out by day	39.3%	27.0%	16.2%
Two-tiered land-ownership?	no	no	yes

[a] North of Zhenze zhen.
[b] There were a total of 17 year-laborers, but the pct. of farm households cannot be computed because the totals of non-farm and farm households are not given.
[c] The cultivators owned 1,212 mu of the topsoil in a total of 1,378.8 mu of rented land.

TABLE A.I *continued*

Yaojing, Taicang	Dingjiacun, Jiading	Sunjiaxiang, Wuxian	Kaixiangong, Wujiang	Huayangqiao, Songjiang
rice 60%, cotton 34% wheat 82%	rice 33%, cotton 50% broad beans 42%, rye 30%, wheat 22%	rice ?% wheat ?%	rice ca. 90% wheat ?%	rice 95% alfalfa 92%
52	53	209	360	63
9.6%	13.2%	10.1%	?	7.9%
398.9	512.4	1,556.3	3,000+	548.6
1.7	2.1	1.8	ca. 2.3	1.9
10	3	suburb	6 [a]	1
0	0	2	?	0
0	0	0	?	0
93.2%	40.3%	83.8%	ca. 66%	87.5%
4.3%	14.3%	0	?	0
93.6%	85.7%	97.3%	?	100%
2.1%	0	2.7%	? [b]	0
46.8%	28.6%	10.1%	?	46.7%
yes	no	yes [c]	yes	yes

APPENDIX B

Population and
Cultivated Acreage in the
Yangzi Delta, 1393–1932

The most credible of the available historical population data cluster around the early Ming, the mid-Qing, and 1932, when the governments made the most vigorous efforts to register and enumerate the population. The cultivated acreage data do not show the same degree of fluctuation over time as the population data.

The data for 1393 and 1816 seem to me credible and complete enough to be used for ballpark estimates of the order of the population increase relative to cultivated acreage in the intervening centuries. The 1932 data are only of limited comparability to the earlier numbers, mainly because of the redrawing of administrative boundaries in 1927, especially the establishment of the special administrative city of Shanghai, formed from portions of the earlier territory of five counties: Songjiang, Qingpu, Shanghai, Baoshan, and Nanhui. The discrepancies between the 1816 and 1932 numbers stem also from the seaward extension of the Shanghai land mass, affecting especially Nanhui county. The drastic decline in population for Suzhou reflects the decline of Suzhou city and the devastation wrought by the Taiping wars. Assuming the 1816 and 1932 totals are reasonably accurate, urbanization and wars together may have raised per capita acreage in these areas over the 116-year period.

All 1932 data in Table B.1 are from *Zhongguo shiyezhi: Jiangsu sheng* 1933, 1: 12–13, 2: 2–4, 3: 32–33.

The sources for the 1393 and 1816 population data are as follows: Songjiang prefecture: *Songjiang fu zhi* 1817, 28: 2b, 3a, 14a–b.

Taicang: *Taicang zhou zhi* 1919, 7: 1a–2a (for 1497 and 1797); *Zhenyang xianzhi* 1919, 4: 1a–b (for 1771); *Jiading xian zhi* 1605, 5: 1b–2b (for 1391); *Baoshan xian zhi* 1882, 3: 27a–28a (for 1795); *Chongming xian zhi* 1924, 6: 30a–32a (for 1753). 1816 department, Liang 1980: 273.

Suzhou prefecture: 1393 prefecture, all 1816 counties, and 1816 prefecture, *Suzhou fu zhi*, 1883, 13: 4a–6b, 9a, b; 1393 Wuxian,

Changzhou, *Wuxian zhi* 1933, 49: 1b–3a (for 1376); 1393 Kunshan, *Chongxiu Kunshan xian zhi* 1576, 2: 15b–16b; 1393 Changshu, *Chongxiu Chang Zhao hezhi* 1904, 7: 1b, 2a (for 1412); 1393 Wujiang, *Wujiang xian zhi* 1747, 5: 26b (for 1376).

Wuxi, Jiangyin: 1393 Wuxi, *Wuxi Jingui xian zhi* 1881, 8: 1b–3b, 1816 Wuxi, *Xi Jin shi xiaolu* 1752, 1: 5b (1752 estimate); Jiangyin, *Jiangyin xian zhi* 1840, 4: 1b–2b (for 1391), 4a (for 1839).

The 1393 and 1816 cultivated acreage data are from the following sources:

Songjiang: *Songjiang fu zhi* 1512, 7: 1a–2b (for 1391); ibid. 1817, 21: 52b–53a.

Taicang: *Taicang zhou zhi* 1919, 7: 32b–33b (for 1497), 35b (for 1810); Jiading, Chongming, ibid. 1883, 3: 8a (for 1883), *Suzhou fu zhi* 1379, 10: 6a–8b (for 1379); *Zhenyang xian zhi* 1919, 4: 36b (for 1810); *Baoshan xian zhi* 1882, 3: 25a–26a (for 1810).

Suzhou: 1393 prefecture, *Suzhou fu zhi* 1379, 10: 4a–4b; 1816 Wuxian, Changzhou, Yuanhe, *Wuxian zhi* 1933, 45: 30b, 46: 23a, 47: 17b (for 1818); Kunshan, Xinyang, Changshu, Zhaowen, Wujiang, Zhenze, Taihu ting, *Suzhou fu zhi* 1883, vol. 12 (for 1818).

Wuxi, Jiangyin: *Chongxiu Piling zhi* 1484, 7: 35a–36b (for 1391); *Wuxi Jingui xian zhi* 1881, 10: 3a (for 1865); *Jiangyin xian zhi* 1878, 4: 21b–22b (for 1875).

TABLE B.1

Population and Cultivated Acreage in Songjiang and Suzhou Prefectures, Taicang Department, and Wuxi and Jiangyin Counties, 1393–1932

(000 people; 000 mu)

Unit	1393		1816		1932	
	Pop.	Acreage	Pop.	Acreage	Pop.	Acreage
Songjiang pref.	1,220	4,760	2,484	4,011	[1,720]	[4,316]
Huating		2,554	303	521		
Songjiang					390	972
Louxian			261	450		
Shanghai		2,206	529	685	115	147
Fengxian			262	524	200	700
Nanhui			416	653	482	1,222
Chuansha			112	105	130	190
Jinshan			391	371	154	362
Qingpu			210	702	249	723
Shanghai City					3,112	1,236
Taicang dept.	[688]	[2,608]	1,772	[2,069]	[1,103]	[2,621]
Taicang	157	963	200	430	290	833
Zhenyang			165	425		
Jiading	444	1,419		644	245	647
Baoshan			376	570	162	341
Chongming	87	226	641		406	800

TABLE B.1 *continued*

Unit	1393 Pop.	1393 Acreage	1816 Pop.	1816 Acreage	1932 Pop.	1932 Acreage
Suzhou pref.	2,355	6,749	5,908	6,254[a]	[2,434]	[5,895]
Wuxian	285		2,110	646	908	1,815
Changzhou	381		479	712		
Yuanhe			386	604		
Kunshan	337		405	593	235	1,070
Xinyang			261	572		
Changshu	291		652	927	859	1,736
Zhaowen			462	799		
Wujiang	368		572	645	432	1,274
Zhenze			581	683		
Wuxi county	178	869	1,000	695	899	1,260
Jingui				739		
Jiangyin cty.	213	991	978	1,123	717	988
TOTAL	4,654	15,977	12,142	14,891	9,985	16,316

NOTE: Where the years for the data are not 1393 and 1816, the sources listed at the beginning of the appendix show the actual date. An indented county was established after the Ming. Bracketed prefecture totals are simply sums of the county figures. The combined totals are based on the source figure, not the summed county totals, in the case of Suzhou for 1393 and Taicang for 1816.
[a]Includes 73,000 mu for Taihu ting. *Suzhou fu zhi* 1883, 12: 44a, gives 6,223, but the individual county figures add up to 6,254.

TABLE B.2

Cultivated Acreage Per Capita in Songjiang and Suzhou Prefectures, Taicang Department, and Wuxi and Jiangyin Counties, 1393–1932

(mu)

Unit	1393	1816	1932
Songjiang prefecture	3.9	1.6	1.1[a]
Taicang department	3.8	1.9[b]	2.4
Suzhou prefecture	2.9	1.1	2.4
Wuxi county	4.9	1.4	1.4
Jiangyin county	4.7	1.1	1.4

SOURCE: Table B.1.
[a]Or 2.5 mu if Shanghai city is excluded.
[b]For Taicang, Zhenyang and Baoshan only.

Town Formation and Change in Shanghai Municipality During the Ming-Qing and the Republic

Table C.1 tallies 457 towns (*zhen*), market towns (*shi*), and markets (*cunji*) of (present-day) Shanghai municipality by the date of their first appearance in the gazetteers listed at the end of this appendix. Table C.2 lists 69 towns formed before 1851 by the basis given in the sources for their formation; Table C.3 lists 107 that were formed, or that disappeared, declined, or prospered in the period 1862–1937. The Xianfeng reign (1851–61) has been excluded because of extraordinary circumstances linked to the Taiping wars. Nine towns are identified in the sources as having suffered serious decline from the wars: *Nanhui*, Xinchang, Zhoupu, Datuan, Hengmian, Liuzao; *Qingpu*, Jinjiaqiao, Huangdu; *Baoshan*, Dachang; *Jiading*, Xianshi ximen. None is identified as having ceased to exist. Two new towns emerged as a result of in-migration from the Taiping areas: *Nanhui*, Nandaqiao; *Jiading*, Zhujiaqiao. No other new towns were formed during the period. (The information for the towns of [present-day] Suzhou district in the Ming and Qing are too fragmentary to tabulate.) Chongming island is not included in the tables.

Data for the Republican period are included in this appendix, but the reader should be cautioned that the gazetteers provide at best partial listings of the towns and markets that arose in that period. Also, there was no longer the consistent administrative practice of conferring zhen status on large or important market towns. These Republican data should not be used as any kind of an index of the actual extent of commercialization. They are included here only as one indication of a few of the dynamics of change in the period.

The periodization is by reigns, following the conventions of the Chinese gazetteers: 1662–1735, Kangxi and Yongzheng; 1736–95, Qianlong; 1796–1861, Jiaqing, Daoguang, Xianfeng; 1862–1911, Tongzhi, Guangxu, Xuantong; 1912–37, Republic down to the Sino-Japanese War.

Wang Wenchu (1983) tallies 146 towns down through 1850. My larger total of 193 (195 including the Xianfeng period, 1851–61) is due to the inclusion of market towns (shi) and markets (cunji) deemed significant enough by the gazetteer compilers for listing with the administratively designated towns (zhen), whereas Wang counts only the zhen. There is also some difference in the dating of times of establishment, stemming from my practice of dating a town back to its first mention as a market town or market.

Liu (1978e) tallies 354 towns and markets down to 1911, compared with my 457, but he does not consistently include (or exclude) market towns and markets.

SOURCES FOR APPENDIX C

Baoshan xian zhi, 1882; *Baoshan xian xuzhi*, 1921; *Baoshan xian zaixuzhi, xinzhi beigao*, 1931; *Chongxiu Huating xian zhi*, 1878; *Chuansha ting zhi*, 1879; *Chuansha xian zhi*, 1936; *Fengxian xian zhi*, 1878; *Huating xian zhi*, 1791; *Jiading xian zhi*, 1605; *Jiading xian xuzhi*, 1930; *Jiangsu sheng quansheng yutu*, 1895; *Jinshan xian zhi*, 1751, 1858, 1878; *Louxian zhi*, 1788; *Louxian xuzhi*, 1879; *Nanhui xian zhi*, 1879; *Nanhui xian xuzhi*, 1929; *Nanji zhi*, 1522–66; *Qingpu xian zhi*, 1879; *Qingpu xian xuzhi*, 1934; *Shanghai xian zhi*, 1872, 1935; *Shanghai xian xuzhi*, 1918; *Songjiang fu zhi*, 1512, 1817; *Songjiang fu xuzhi*, 1883.

TABLE C.1
The Development of Towns in Shanghai Municipality to 1911
and Under the Republic

County	Pre-Qing	1662–1735	1736–1795	1796–1861	1862–1911	Total	[1912–1937][a]
Songjiang pref.							
Huating	7	0	11	0	2	20	
Louxian	5	1	8	0	0	14	
Jinshan	5	0	9	0	72	86	
Fengxian	4	1	8	5	41	59	
Shanghai	10	3	8	2	51	74	[4]
Nanhui	8	10	8	3	27	56	[18]
Qingpu	30	1	2	3	10	46	[7]
Chuansha	1	0	1	10	6	18	[18]
Taicang dept.							
Baoshan	12	0	1	1	51	65	[28]
Jiading	13	0	2	2	2	19	[40]
TOTAL	95	16	58	26	262	457	[115]

NOTE: A total of 23 markets and towns fell into oblivion in this period: Louxian, 1 in Guangxu; Shanghai, 2 in Tongzhi; Nanhui, 1 in Jiaqing, 6 in Guangxu, 4 in Republic; Qingpu, 3 in Guangxu; Jiading, 2 in Republic; Baoshan, 4 in Republic. See Table C.3.
[a]Dubious figures. See the text of this Appendix.

TABLE C.2

Town Formation in Shanghai Municipality to 1850

(n = 69)

Basis of formation	No.	Town by county
Cotton goods	28	*Huating*: Shagang, Chedun. *Fengxian*: Jinhuiqiao. *Shanghai*: Longhua, Wenhang, Sanlintang, Donggou, Gaohang, Yangjing. *Nanhui*: Xiasha, Zhoupu, Jinjiahang. *Qingpu*: Chonggu. *Chuansha*: Caojialu. *Baoshan*: Luodian, Yangjiahang, Liuhang, Gaoqiao, Guijiaqiao. *Jiading*: Nanxiang, Jiwang, Loutang, Waigang, Gelong, Fangtai, Anting, Qianmentang, Lujiahang
Administrative/military	14	*Huating*: Zhang Jingyan. *Jinshan*: Zhujing. *Fengxian*: Taozhai, Nanqiao. *Shanghai*: Fahua, Wuhui, Wunijing. *Qingpu*: Tang Hang, Zhujiajiao, Zhangliantang, Zhaotun. *Baoshan*: Yuepu, Jiangwan. *Jiading*: Lianqi
Salt	8	*Jinshan*: Xicang, Beicang. *Fengxian*: Qingcun. *Nanhui*: Xinchang, Datuan, Hangtou, Situan. *Baoshan*: Dachang
Transport hub	6	*Fengxian*: Tairiqiao. *Nanhui*: Dujiahang, Zhagang. *Qingpu*: Shangta, Qibao, Qinglong
Aquatic products	4	*Louxian*: Tianmashan, Hengshan, Kunshan, Shenxiang
Silk	3	*Louxian*: Fengjing. *Nanhui*: Liudu. *Qingpu*: Panlong
Miscellaneous	6	*Nanhui*: Shenzhuang, Bocizhuang (sites of prominent estates), Sanzao (site of temple fair). *Qingpu*: Aiqi (sheep trade). *Jiading*: Xinjing, Xujiahang (straw sandals)

NOTE: The table includes all towns whose basis of formation is explicitly identified in the sources. Where more than one basis is given, I include the town only under the original or primary one given in the gazetteer. For example, though quite a number of administrative centers later took on commercial functions, they are shown here under the administrative/military category.

TABLE C.3

Town Formation and Change in Shanghai Municipality 1862–1937

(n = 107)

Basis of formation or change	No.	Town by county
Newly formed	40	
New factories	8	*Shanghai*: Zhoujiaqiao (textiles), Gaochangmiao (Jiangnan arsenal). *Nanhui*: Liuzaowan, Nicheng, Wanxiang (food processing), Qituanhang (towels). *Chuansha*: Qingdun (towels). *Baoshan*: Tanziwan
Adjacent to Shanghai city	6	*Shanghai*: Qujiaqiao, Tiantongan, Houjiamuqiao, Tanjiaqiao. *Baoshan*: Jiangwan, Shenjiahang
Handicraft cloth weaving and trade	8	*Shanghai*: Tangwan (later declined), Zhangjiaqiao. *Chuansha*: Batuan (towels). *Baoshan*: Guanjialong, Gucun (also cotton trade). *Jiading*: Jianbangqiao (also cotton trade), Shigangmen (declined in Republican times), Jinjiaxiang (declined shortly after)

TABLE C.3 *continued*

Basis of formation or change	No.	Town by county
Cotton trade	3	*Fengxian*: Yicunba, Liujiahang. *Jiading*: Luduqiao
Handicraft lacing	3	*Chuansha*: Gaohangnan zhen, Heqing, Xingang
Transport hub	2	*Nanhui*: Sujiaqiao. *Qingpu*: Zhaoxiang
Railroads	2	*Baoshan*: Zhanghuabang, Yangjiaqiao
Miscellaneous	8	*Fengxian*: Situan (fish). *Nanhui*: Laogang (reclaimed land). *Qingpu*: Xiaoping (fish), Shenxiang (fish). *Baoshan*: Shizilin (military garrison), Chenjiahang (cocoon trade), Wusongkou (maritime customs station). *Jiading*: Wangxianqiao (grain trade)
Ceased to exist for unspecified reasons	22	*Louxian*: Beiqian. *Shanghai*: Wunijing, Meiyuan. *Nanhui*: Ertuan, Erzao, Wangjiahang, Liqin, Waiqin, Xujialong, Shagang, Fanhang, Dongjiacun, Dongshengdian. *Qingpu*: Gutangqiao, Liuxia, Zhongde. *Baoshan*: Mushaozhen, Lijiajiao, Xishe, Zhaqiao. *Jiading*: Zhaqiao, Fengjiabang
Declined	17	
Decline of native cloth	14	*Shanghai*: Longhua, Minhang, Sanlintang, Tangwan. *Qingpu*: Qinglong. *Baoshan*: Gaoqiao. *Jiading*: Nanxiang, Jiwang, Loutang, Fangtai, Xianshi nanmen (but rose in Republican period with towel factory), Xianshi dongmen, Qianmentang, Jinjiaxiang
Miscellaneous	3	*Qingpu*: Fenghuangshan (removal of garrison). *Baoshan*: Xinxing (silting of river). *Jiading*: Xinjing (decline of straw shoes)
Prospered	28	
Sericulture	6	*Nanhui*: Xinchang, Zhoupu, Liuzao. *Qingpu*: Zhujiajiao, Chonggu. *Baoshan*: Guangfu
Handicraft lacing (Repub. period)	5	*Chuansha*: Gongjialu, Nan Xujialu, Caojialu (took over from hand-spinning and weaving), Gujialu, Bei Xujialu
Cotton	5	*Nanhui*: Shenzhuang, Datuan (cotton cultivation on reclaimed oceanfront). *Baoshan*: Guijiaqiao. *Jiading*: Gelong, Anting
Cloth weaving	3	*Nanhui*: Jinjiahang. *Baoshan*: Dachang, Zhenru
Manufacturing	3	*Qingpu*: Jinze (spinning wheels and spindles), Huangdu (looms). *Jiading*: Waigang (towels)
Miscellaneous	6	*Shanghai*: Zhudi (railroad). *Nanhui*: Zhagang (steamship transport), Sandun (in-migration of the rich). *Baoshan*: Pengpu (proximity to Shanghai city), Shengjiaqiao (price increases in farm produce). *Jiading*: Lujiahang (mechanized rice milling)

Off-Farm Employment
in Huayangqiao, 1950–1985

Tables D.1–D.3 show the record of off-farm employment for each of the three Huayangqiao production teams. Table D.4 tabulates the total number of off-farm jobs held by Huayangqiao villagers, grouped by state, commune, and brigade enterprises; Table D.5 shows the different avenues to off-farm employment, both regular and back door; and Table D.6 tallies off-farm employment by gender.

TABLE D.1
Off-Farm Workers, Xuejiada, 1950–85

Period/year	State	Commune	Brigade	Total
1950s	Xue Shoulin (1952) Wang Longde (1958; m. in)		Zhang Bingyu (1958)	3
1960s	[Xue Bulin] (1966) He Shutang (1968t, 1971–79)	He Juanhua (1965) Zhang Jufang (1965) He Huosheng (1966) Zhou Jianchu (1966)		6
1970s	[He Yunxian] (1971) Zhou Jianhua (1978) Xi Xiufang (1978; m. in) Xue Delin (1979t) Zhang Yongnian (1979t) He Shunyu (1979) He Meiying (1979) Zhang Zhengyun (1979t)	Zhou Niannian (1970t, 1983) Xue Baobao (1972) He Jinyu (1972) Xue Boquan (1973) Wu Qiufang (1974; m. in, 1974) Xue Huilin (1974t, 1980) Chen Xiufang[a] (1975) He Tujin (1976) He Delong (1978) He Maodi (1978t)	Zhang Caifa (1975) Zhang Yinlong (1978) Xue Zhilong (1978)	21

Period/year	State	Commune	Brigade	Total
1980	[Xue Chunhua] [Zhang Jinlong] [Zhang Meifang]	Zhong Linghua Zhang Bamei Xue Huiquan	Zhang Yongxing	7
1981	He Xiugen, t [Xue Qinfang]		Xue Minghui Shen Fenhua (m. in) [Xue Yuhua] (m. out, 1985) Xue Shunquan (1981–85) He Dexing (d. 1984) Xiao Mengjun (m. in)	8
1982		Zhou Simei Luo Mingxian Fan Taomei He Xiuzheng Xue Guibao Xue Fengfei Tang Quanzhen[a]	Xue Weilian Zhang Jinmen Ye Xiaomei (m. in) Xue Yuping Jin Minghua He Jinlong He Xiulong Xue Wenhua	15
1983		Xue Guoping Xue Yaolin Xue Zhichao Xue Guoming	Zhang Shunyun Xue Lianxiu Xue Yonglong	7
1984	[He Yonglong] (1984)	Xue Weiming Zhang Yongwei, t Xue Shunxing, t Xue Zhenghua, t He Yonglin, t He Guoxing	Zhang Renhua Zhang Jiudi Xue Buxing	10
1985		Zhang Guoquan Tang Meifang Xue Weifang Xue Ming Zhang Yonglin Xue Shunlong[a]	Yang Yinlong	7
1950–85	18	40	26	84

SOURCES: This list was first compiled by an interview with several informants from the village (H-III-21). The list of people employed in the brigade lock factory (21 for Xuejiada) was then checked against an official list supplied by the factory management. All the dates supplied by the informants checked out. In addition, the informants named three women who had married out and had slipped by the official list—Xue Jingxiu (m. out, 1967), Zhang Jinmei (m. out, 1970), and He Xueqin (m. out, 1971)—though they could not recall the years when they first began working. The three women in any case got their jobs after they had officially left Xuejiada; I have not included them on this list here. I suspect the records may also omit people who died some years ago, and these are likely to have escaped my informants' memories as well. This list is therefore probably not complete, but it suffices for the purposes here.

NOTE: Brackets indicate the person was no longer resident in the village. A "t" indicates the worker was on temporary status (*linshi gong*); a second date, if shown, is the year in which he or she changed to permanent status (*zhuanzheng*). On inclusive dates, the terminal date indicates the year of retirement, unless otherwise noted. "m. in" and "m. out" stand for married in and married out, and "d." means the person died that year. These same conventions are used in Tables D.2–D.3.

[a] Sanitation worker of Huayang town; not a commune unit.

TABLE D.2

Off-Farm Workers, Xubushanqiao, 1950–85

Period/year	State	Commune	Brigade	Total
1950s	Yang Xingcai (1958)	Wu Jinfa (1958; d. 1977) Wu Hugen (1958) Wu Xuelin (1958)		4
1960s		Zhang Genyun (1967) Yang Yue-e (1969)	Yang Chengzhang (1964)	3
1970s		He Yonggen (1970) Ding Xiyan[a] (1970) Fan Lindi (1974) He Haigen (1975)	Yang Xiquan (1976) Yang Shuxin (1978) He Jinlin (1979)	7
1980	Hu Guoliang	He Yuelong Wu Jiaquan Wu Yufang Wu Yuxiu	[Yang Qimei] (m. out, 1985)	6
1981		Li Jinlong	He Xiufang He Qiusheng	3
1982		Wu Yuming Wu Ruifang[a]	Yang Hongqiang Fan Genmei Wu Xiangjuan Yang Guilong [Wu Yinfang] (m. out, 1984) He Fujuan He Haijuan He Huotang Wu Achang He Xiaomao Wu Deyun He Guoping Geng Guizhen	15
1983		Yang Guiming Yang Meiqin	Li Bifang Shen Shunyu	4
1984		Wu Wenyun Yang Xizhong		2
1985		Wu Caijuan[a]	Yang Jufang	2
1950–85	2	21	23	46

SOURCES: H-III-5; otherwise same as Table D.1. In this case, the informants erred on the starting dates of five of the eighteen people employed by the lock factory. But they brought up three women who had married out and had slipped by the official list: Yang Qimei, who worked in the factory 1980–85, Wu Yinfang, 1982–84, and Yang Jinjuan, ?–1985 (who is not listed above).

[a]Member of the Huayang town Sewing Group, not a commune unit.

Off-Farm Workers, Xilihangbang, 1950–85

Period/year	State	Commune	Brigade	Total
1950s	Wu Jinbao (m. in, 1958)			1
1960s	Lu Bingxian (1968)			1
1970s	Lu Guiquan (1978t) Lu Mingqiang (1978t) Lu Haitang (1979t)	Lu Genshan (1970–8?) Lu Shudong (1972) Shi Jiaxian (1975t) Jin Zhifang (1975) Li Liuyu (1978) Lu Guiqiu (1978) Xie Zhenhua (1978t) Liu Laohu (1978–85t)	Gao Yonglin (1975–84) Lu Hailai (197?)	13
1980	[Zhang Shanping]		Lu Minghua	2
1981	[Wu Yongming] Gao Shunlong	Lu Xiulong Lu Huolin	Gao Jinjuan Gao Qinhua Gao Guiying [Lu Shuihua] (m. out, 1985)	8
1982	Ma Dalong (m. in, 1967) Gao Renyuan Lu Jinyu, t	Gao Weilin Lu Maosheng (1982?)	Gao Jinshu Gao Jinlong Gao Laigen Yang Jin-e Xie Meihua Zhang Xiuhua Lu Yulin Lu Huolong Li Fangzhen Lu Maoyuan Gao Biquan Zhang Xueying (m. in) Zhu Yanmin (m. in)	18
1983	Ma Yufeng, t Gao Zhengwen, t	Shi Jinhua Chen Xiu-e Zhang Taohua	Gao Xiaomei Jiang Xiulian Lu Mingyun	8
1984		Gao Buying		1
1985		Lu Huoyun Gao Jinfang Lu Shuifang		3
1950–85	13	19	23	55

SOURCES: H-III-21; otherwise same as Table D.1. In this case, the informants' list of people employed in the brigade lock factory included all but one of the nineteen workers shown on the official list and was accurate on all dates. The informants identified two other people—Ding Xiaodi, and Lu Xiaodi (b. 1955)—as being employed in commune units but could not supply their starting dates or other specifics.

TABLE D.4

Off-Farm Employment in Huayangqiao by Enterprise, 1950–85

Enterprise	Xuejiada	Xubushan-qiao	Xilihang-bang	Total
State				
Shanghai Municipal 703 Engineering Brigade	3t			3t
Songjiang Architectural Engineering Brigade		1	2	3
Supply and Marketing Coop	1		2	3
Shanghai Municipal Agricultural School		1	1t	1, 1t
Other	6, 7m, 1t		1, 2m, 5t	7, 9m, 6t
SUBTOTAL	7, 7m, 4t	2	5, 2m, 6t	14, 9m, 10t
Commune[a]				
Construction Station	9, 5t	7	2	18, 5t
Printing Factory	5		2	7
Sock Factory	4	1	2	7
Optical Parts Factory	1	2	2	5
"Welfare" Factory (clothing, umbrella, laundry)	2	1	3	6
Bricks and Tiles Factory	1		3t	1, 3t
Wool Yarn Factory	2		2	4
Town Neighborhood Sewing Group[b]		4		4
Town Sanitation Group[b]	3			3
Furniture Factory	2			2
Transport Station	1	1		2
Housing Office	1	1		2
Agricultural Implements (Repair) Factory		2		2
Culture Factory		1	1	2
Fertilizer Station (in Shanghai)	1			1
Grain Control Office			2	2
Other	3	1		4
SUBTOTAL	35, 5t	21	16, 3t	72, 8t
Brigade				
Mechanical Electrical Factory (lock factory)	20, 1m	16, 2m	18, 1m	54, 4m
Mill		1	2	3
Cadres	1	1		2
Fishery	2			2
Tractor driver	1	1		2
Barefoot doctor		1		1
Other	1	1	2	4
SUBTOTAL	25, 1m	21, 2m	22, 1m	68, 4m
TOTAL	67, 8m, 9t	44, 2m	43, 3m, 9t	154, 13m, 18t

SOURCES: Tables D.1–D.3; H-III-5.

NOTE: A "t" indicates a worker of temporary status, and an "m" one who has since moved away.

[a]A chicken-processing plant (Meat Products Company) was built in 1986, after this list was compiled.

[b]Town neighborhood organizations; not commune units; just one notch lower in status and desirability.

TABLE D.5
Avenues to Off-Farm Employment in Huayangqiao, 1950–85

Enterprise	Examination[a]	Objective assignment[b]	Hard ways:				Soft way[e]	Total
			Special skills	Veteran[c]	Succeed parent[d]	Former cadre[c]		
Xuejiada								
State	5m	1m	3t		2, 1m	2	3, 1t	7, 7m, 4t
Commune	5	15	3	1		1	10, 5t	35, 5t
Brigade		22, 1m	3					25, 1m
Xubushanqiao								
State	2	1		2				2
Commune	3	13, 2m	3	2	1		11	20, [1?]
Brigade			3					19, 2m, [2?]
Xilihangbang								
State	2, 1t	1m	2	1	1m	1t	2t	5, 2m, 4t, [2?]
Commune	6	2, 3t	2	2	1		3	16, 3t
Brigade		18, 1m	1			1	2	22, 1m
Brigade								
State	4, 5m, 1t	2m	2, 3t	1	2, 2m	2, 1t	2, 3t	14, 9m, 8t, [2?]
Commune	14	18, 3t	8	5	1	1	24, 5t	71, 8t, [1?]
Brigade		54, 4m	7	2	1	1	2	66, 4m, [2?]
TOTAL	18, 5m, 1t	72, 6m, 3t	17, 3t	8	4, 2m	4, 1t	28, 8t	151, 13m, 16t, [5?]

SOURCES: H-III-5; Tables D.1–D.3.

NOTE: A "t" indicates a worker of temporary status, an "m" one who has moved out of the village, and a bracketed "?" insufficient information.

[a] Academic examinations for entrance to technical schools (zhongzhuan) and colleges (dazhuan), as well as exams administered by factories.

[b] Assignments that peasants consider principled—e.g. every household with more than two members in farming gets one slot in the brigade factory, or the handicapped and households with special difficulties receive preferential consideration.

[c] Given priority in job assignments.

[d] Until 1986, a parent retiring from a state unit was permitted to name one child to succeed him or her. In the case of commune units, the same principle applied, but the parent then had to give up his retirement pay, usually pegged at 40% of salary.

[e] Entry to jobs via special connections with relatives or friends, a back-door avenue that peasants dub zuanchuqu ("boring one's way out," as opposed to yingchuqu, or "going out the legitimate [or hard] way").

TABLE D.6

Off-Farm Employment in Huayangqiao by Gender, 1950–85

Enterprise	Total	Male		Female	
		No.	Pct.	No.	Pct.
State	33	27	82%	6	18%
Xuejiada	18	12	67	6	33
Xubushanqiao	2	2	100	0	0
Xilihangbang	13	13	100	0	0
Commune	80	51	64	29	36
Xuejiada	40	25	63	15	37
Xubushanqiao	21	14	67	7	33
Xilihangbang	19	12	63	7	37
Brigade	72	42	58	30	42
Lock factory	58	28	48	30	52
Xuejiada	26	18	69	8	31
Lock factory	21	13	62	8	38
Xubushanqiao	23	13	57	10	43
Lock factory	18	8	44	10	56
Xilihangbang	23	11	48	12	52
Lock factory	19	7	37	12	63
TOTAL	185[a]	120	65%	65	35%

[a]Includes all categories of workers in the total column of Table D.5, including the five for whom there are insufficient data to class as temporary, permanent or moved.

The Changing Composition of Gross Output Value in Huayang and Rural China

Commune/township output in Chinese statistical usage approximates most closely "rural output" as defined in this study, since it includes the small-town industries and sidelines that have had such an impact on peasant employment. County output figures, by contrast, include urban industries that have little effect on rural employment.

There is no national statistical category exactly equal to "rural China" as defined in this book. I employ in Table E.1 the national category of "gross value of output of agriculture" (*nongye zongchanzhi*), which includes crops, forestry, animal husbandry, fishery, sidelines (including brigade industry, *dui/cun ban gongye*), and add to it the output of commune/township industry (*she/xiang ban gongye*). Although the national "agriculture" figure includes not just commune output but also the output of state units, the distortion is relatively minor: in 1980, for example, state units accounted for 3.9 percent of the gross value of output of crops and sidelines (*Zhongguo nongye nianjian*, 1981: 20).

The Chinese statistical category "gross value of output of rural society" (*nongcun shehui zongchanzhi*), instituted in 1985, closely approximates what this book means by rural output; it is shown in Table E.2.

Table E.3 gives the changing output of the Huayangqiao villages. These figures tell only part of the story, however, since they do not include the commune industries and sidelines that have played such a large role in village employment.

Composition of Gross Value of Output of Huayang Commune
Compared with Rural China, 1971–86

(percent)

Year	Crops Huayang	Crops China	Sidelines[a] Huayang	Sidelines[a] China	Industry[b] Huayang	Industry[b] China
1971	49.6%	72.5%	23.1%	20.5%	27.3%	6.9%
1972	53.5	70.2	15.3	21.5	31.2	8.3
1973	51.5	70.7	13.8	20.6	34.7	8.7
1974	45.9	69.9	19.0	20.1	35.1	10.0
1975	40.1	68.0	18.6	19.7	41.3	12.3
1976	42.1	63.4	14.9	19.7	43.0	16.9
1977	35.3	59.7	18.3	19.0	46.4	21.3
1978	37.2	59.2	15.8	18.0	47.0	22.8
1979	34.2	58.3	19.9	18.0	45.9	23.7
1980	24.2	54.7	18.3	18.3	57.5	27.0
1981	22.3	55.7	17.2	22.0	60.5	22.3
1982	23.0	55.3	15.7	22.6	61.3	22.1
1983	21.1	54.3	15.2	21.8	63.7	23.9
1984		50.1		21.6		28.3
1985		41.8		21.3		36.9
1986		37.1		20.3		42.6

SOURCES: *Zhongguo tongji nianjian* 1983: 215, 1984: 133; 1987: 157, 259.
[a]Includes forestry, animal husbandry, handicrafts, and fishery, as in local statistical usage in China.
[b]Includes commune/township industry (*she/xiang ban gongye*), as well as brigade-team/village industry (*dui/cun ban gongye*), but not individual/(private) group enterprises, which became increasingly more significant in the 1980s (see Table F.2).

TABLE E.2

Gross Value of Output in Rural China, 1985–86

(value in current prices)

Sector	1985 Billions of yuan	1985 Percent	1986 Billions of yuan	1986 Percent
Agriculture	361.9	57.1%	401.3	53.1%
Industry	175.0	27.6	238.1	31.5
Construction[a]	51.0	8.1	59.2	7.8
Transport[b]	19.0	3.0	24.6	3.3
Commerce, eateries[c]	27.0	4.2	32.3	4.3
TOTAL	633.9	100.0%	755.5	100.0%

SOURCE: *Zhongguo tongji nianjian* 1987: 156, 216–17.
NOTE: In the broad category "agriculture," crops are not distinguished from forestry, animal husbandry, fishery, and handicraft sidelines. In contrast to the State Statistical Bureau's usual usage of the term "value of output" (*chanzhi*), the new category here includes construction, transport, and commerce and eateries, which are not included in the output figures in Table E.1. It also explicitly includes not just commune/township and brigade-team/village enterprises, but also individual and (private) group enterprises.
[a]The value of structures built.
[b]The value of fees received.
[c]"Commerce" is the value of goods sold minus purchase cost and transport fees, and eateries (*yinshi ye*) the value of gross receipts.

TABLE E.3

Gross Value of Output in Huayangqiao Brigade, 1977–84

(value in current prices)

Year	Agriculture Yuan	Agriculture Pct.	Sideline Yuan	Sideline Pct.	Industry Yuan	Industry Pct.	Total value (yuan)
1977	112,608	85.2%	19,551	14.8%	0	0%	132,159
1978	152,545	84.5	27,931	15.5	0	0	180,476
1979	161,618	84.7	29,090	15.3	0	0	190,708
1980	152,495	77.8	25,335	12.9	18,298	9.3	196,128
1981	135,273	62.7	26,245	12.1	54,377	25.2	215,895
1982	161,001	54.4	32,399	10.9	102,874	34.7	296,274
1983	155,746	51.3	28,309	9.3	119,337	39.4	303,392
1984	209,258	55.6	31,005	8.3	135,791	36.1	376,154

SOURCE: Data furnished by brigade authorities.

Incomes of
Collective, Joint, and
Private Enterprises

Beginning in March 1984, the State Statistical Bureau included under the category "rural enterprises" figures for those owned by individuals, by households jointly, and by other kinds of groups. Earlier figures included only "commune enterprises/industry," published since 1960, and "brigade enterprises/industry," since 1971. Table F.1 shows the gross income of the various types of enterprises for selected areas in the year 1986. The data in Table F.2 are for rural China as a whole and cover the period 1984–86.

TABLE F.1
Gross Income of Rural Enterprises in Selected Areas,
by Organizational Type, 1986
(percent)

| | Collective | | | Joint | |
Locality	Township	Village	Group	household	Individual
China	37.4%	28.7%	1.7%	8.7%	23.5%
Shanghai	60.8	32.7	5.0	0.1	1.4
Beijing	41.8	48.7	—	1.1	8.4
Jiangsu	54.5	33.5	2.1	2.1	7.8
Zhejiang	54.2	29.3	0.1	8.0	8.4
Guangdong	39.3	24.1	5.0	7.4	24.2
Fujian	34.0	29.7	—	26.8	9.5
Sichuan	38.7	14.2	3.9	7.7	35.5
Hebei	19.4	25.9	—	23.3	31.4
Henan	14.5	20.4	3.7	18.1	43.3

SOURCE: *Zhongguo nongye nianjian*, 1987: 286.
NOTE: "Gross income" (*zongshouru*) differs from "gross value of output" (*zong chanzhi*) in several ways: (1) unlike the latter, "gross income" includes income from services; (2) it also includes only the income from that portion of output actually expended or distributed during the year, and excludes the increase in the accumulated value of the "output" (e.g. uncut lumber); and (3) "gross income" is computed in current prices, and the "gross value of output" normally in constant prices (*Zhongguo tongji nianjian*, 1984: 562).

TABLE F.2

Gross Income of Rural Enterprises in China by Organizational Type, 1984–86

(current yuan)

Year	Collective Township	Collective Village	Collective Group	Joint household	Individual	Total
1984						
Billions						
of yuan	70.97	55.85	3.07	11.98	11.84	153.71
Percent	46.2%	36.3%	2.0%	7.8%	7.7%	100.0%
1985						
Billions						
of yuan	103.90	78.84	5.79	23.07	44.96	256.56
Percent	40.5%	30.7%	2.3%	9.0%	17.5%	100.0%
1986						
Billions						
of yuan	125.95	96.41	5.84	29.24	78.99	336.43
Percent	37.4%	28.7%	1.7%	8.7%	23.5%	100.0%

SOURCE: *Zhongguo nongye niangjian*, 1985: 179, 1986: 226, 1987: 286.

REFERENCES

References

INTERVIEWS

I conducted 101 interview sessions, mainly with Huayangqiao villagers, in 1983, 1984, 1985, and 1988, totaling about 328 hours in all. References in the text to those interviews are headed first by "H," then the year of the project (1983 = I, 1984 = II, 1985 = III, 1988 = IV), and the interview session number for that year. The 1983 sessions took place between August 11 and August 24, the 1984 sessions between August 14 and August 31, the 1985 sessions between August 7 and September 3, and the 1988 sessions on May 29 and July 20 and 21. There was normally one interview in the morning, from 8:00 to 11:30, and another in the afternoon, from 2:00 to 5:00.

The session designations are followed by the names of the informants. Women are identified with an "(f)." The names and backgrounds of the village informants are listed in the following section. He Yonglong, brigade party branch secretary in 1983, was present at all the sessions with the Huayangqiao villagers and was a most helpful informant throughout. I list him only in those sessions in which he played an unusually large role. Interviewees other than Huayangqiao villagers are identified by their official positions.

Major subjects are listed for each session.

1983

H-I-1: Lu Longshun, Xue Jinlin, Yang Shougen, Yang Xiaofa. Nominal rent (xuzu) and actual rent (shizu); the rent agent (waizhang); rent reduction; soybean cake; Lu Longshun life history; boy-laborer; month-laborer (mangyue); buying and selling land; adopting a son-in-law.

H-I-2: Lu Longshun, Yang Xiaofa. Nominal and actual rent; short-term laborers' board; wages; fertilizer use; the "three plowings" (sangeng) of rice fields.

H-I-3: Gao Shitang, Lu Guantong, Lu Hailai, Lu Longshun. Redeeming pledged land; insects; soybean cake; hiring out as casual labor (sangong); subletting land; buying soybean cake on credit; the lineage orphanage (Yuying tang) and old folks' home (Laoren tang); hiring out.

H-I-4: He Kuifa, He Shutang, Wu Yucai, Xue Baoren. Short-term labor; rent rates; raising ducks; poor peasants; peddlers; subletting land; sharecropping; the Gus; the rent collection agent; clothing.

H-I-5: He Tugen, Wu Renyu. Buying and selling land; subletting; rent; reporting a poor harvest (*baohuang*); sitting-in to collect rent (*zuozhai*); short-term labor; buying on credit; village oral tradition (about the Xis); the "long-hairs"; the *baozheng* Yao; *baojia*; the notables.

H-I-6: Lu Haitang, Yang Xiaofa. The Han family canal; why wheat is not grown; comparison of four villages; the economics of the ox and water buffalo; the cattle broker.

H-I-7: Lu Haitang, Yang Xiaofa. Ox, pig, and sheep dung; raising pigs, sheep; numbers of households and day-laborers at time of land reform; transplanting; labor exchange (*peigong*).

H-I-8: He Chungen, Yang Xiaofa, Zhang Boren. Hejiada and Xuejiada; the different kinds of casual labor; wages; working in the beancurd shop; buying and selling rice; digging for loaches (*niqiu*); catching amphibious crabs (*pengqi*).

H-I-9: Gao Shigen, Wu Hugen, Yang Shougen. Yang Shougen life history; part-time carpenter; tax; marriage banquets.

H-I-10: Lu Guantong, Lu Hailai, Lu Longshun. Lujiada family trees; Qingming, funerals, weddings; burial ground; most respected person in the hamlet; the funeral of Lu Longshun's father.

H-I-11: Gao Laigen, Gao Shitang, Gao Yonglin. Gaojiada family trees; relations with Lujiada; Qingming; bandits.

H-I-12: He Kuifa, Wu Hugen, Yang Shougen. Xubushanqiao Yang and He family trees; Qingming, funerals, weddings; relations with other hamlets; labor exchange; newborn son banquet (*qing sanzhao*).

H-I-13: Xue Baoren, Xue Baoyi, Xue Jinlin. Xue family trees; household division; Qingming, funerals, weddings; newborn son banquet; most respected person in the village; taxes; military grain requisition (*junmi*) under the Japanese; *baozheng* and *baozhang*.

H-I-14: He Huosheng, He Shutang, Zhang Boren. Hejiada family trees; the credit association (*hehui*); newborn son banquet; Xuejiada Zhang family trees.

H-I-15: Wu Xiaomei (f), Yang Shougen. Xubushanqiao Wu family trees; Wu Xiaomei life history; mid-seventh month festival (*qiyueban jie*); control of purse strings in Xubushanqiao families; the henpecked of Xubushanqiao; the godfather and the adopted daughter.

H-I-16: Gao Dajie (f), Gao Buzhen (f), Lu Genshan. Nanda Lu family trees; social field of Gao Dajie and Gao Buzhen; birthplaces of Nanda wives; hamlet oral tradition; Gao Buzhen life history; the good-for-nothing husband (Lu Jintang).

H-I-17: Gao Shitang, Shen Yindi (f). Social relations among different Xilihangbang hamlets; social field of Shen Yindi; Shen Yindi life history; mid-seventh month festival; women and control of purse strings in Lujiada.

H-I-18: Gu Yindi (f), He Shutang, Xue Baoren. Birthplaces of Xuejiada wives; control of purse strings in Xuejiada; wives from the orphanage; social field of Gu Yindi and Xue Baoren; Xue Xiansheng and accounting; four villages compared; Gu lineage's three-date system for rent payments.

H-I-19: Lu Haitang, Yang Xiaofa. Cooperative rice husking; measures and weights (the big and small *huzi*); why more cotton is not grown; unirrigated odd patches of land (*xiangtou di*); Xi landlord of old; planting of early-rice; double-cropped rice.

H-I-20: He Shutang, Lu Longshun, Xue Baoren, Yang Xiaofa. Smuggling rice under Japanese occupation; best and worst farmers in each hamlet; spoken size (*koujiao di*) and actual size of plots: the big and small "plot mouth" (*tiankou*).

H-I-21–H-I-24: Xi Tianran (member of Communist Party underground during the Sino-Japanese War). Underground organizing in Huayangqiao, 1940–49; resisting military grain requisition, spring 1943; armed struggle, 1948; the landlords of Huayang; bandits; the peddlers and rice smuggling; smuggling routes; the teahouse as meeting place.

1984

H-II-1: Yang Xiaofa. The East and West drainage ditches; the Daming irrigation canal; checkerization of fields; double-cropped rice.

H-II-2: Xue Baoren, Yang Xiaofa. Subsoil ownership; landlord Xi; big official He; family history of the Xues; household-responsibility system; husking of rice; household division among the Xues.

H-II-3: He Jinlin, He Kuifa, Yang Shougen. Big official He; the stone path; Yang Shougen's household division; He Jinfa's and He Kuifa's household division; best and worst times; the "big mess hall" and the "small mess hall"; responsibility for land "at the mouth of the chickens"; exceeding quota under the responsibility system; loitering labor; the work recorder; the accountant's work; subsidies for cadres; the brigade brick factory; the small factory of the Seed Brigade; mushroom production under the responsibility system; the lock factory; contract work; working outside the village; connections; exiting the "hard way."

H-II-4: He Tugen, Wu Hugen, Yang Shougen. Buying and selling land; household division; machine yarn and cloth; prices of tobacco and liquor; "scientific wine"; the new Anhetou village; numbers of shoots transplanted; "busy month" worker; optimal size of farm.

H-II-5: Jiang Xiaochen (deputy party secretary, Huayang commune; chair, Committee for Economic Management). Labor power of the commune; household income; combining agriculture, commerce, and industry; economic benefit calculation; quota and above-quota prices in procurement (*pingjia* and *jiajia*); the planning process; Jiang's background.

H-II-6: He Jinlin, He Kuifa, Wu Genyu. Poor peasants' fertilizer use; raising pigs, chickens, ducks, and long-haired rabbits; cooking and washing; buying groceries; best times; He Kuifa's vegetable farming under the responsibility system.

H-II-7: Lu Longshun, Yang Xiaofa. Optimal size plot for rice; wheat cultivation; underground drainage for wheat; pooling oxen for wheat in 1953; checkerization of fields; poor peasants' fertilizer use; the Great Leap; 1978 adjustments; cotton cultivation and increases after 1978; comparing wheat and cotton returns; rape cultivation and raising yields; income.

H-II-8: Lu Guantong, Lu Hailai, Lu Longshun. Lu Guantong prosecuted and persecuted; location of farm plots before land reform; water use; raising pigs; best times.

364   REFERENCES

H-II-9: Gao Shigen, Gao Shitang, Gao Youfa. Household division; marriage; banquets; betrothal gift; best times; incomes over the years; cash value of a workpoint.

H-II-10: He Shutang, He Yonglong. Household division among the Hes; He Yonglong and his brother; gradations in ranks of cities; funerals.

H-II-11: Lu Genshan, Xue Baoyi, Xue Huilin, Xue Jinlin. The stone path; mouth of the Han family canal; buying and selling topsoil; cotton cultivation before the Revolution; yarn and cloth; Xue Jinlin life history; Xue Jinlin's income; the different hamlets of Xilihangbang; locations of different households' plots; betrothal gifts; dowries and banquets in Xue Jinlin's and Lu Genshan's marriages; adopted sons-in-law of the different hamlets.

H-II-12: Zhang Xiulong (deputy party secretary, Huayang commune, 1966–73). Land reform in Wujiaqiao village in Changlou brigade; collectivization; the Great Leap; checkerization of fields; learning from Dazhai; the five crafts.

H-II-13: Shen Baoshun (Shenjiacun administrative village head 1950–51; chair, Xinglong township peasant association, 1951–56; party branch secretary of Shenjiacun higher-stage collective 1956–60), Xue Shunquan (Xuejiada team leader, 1961–78). From land reform to the people's communes; Wang Deming; selecting and appointing team cadres; turnaround problems in double-cropping rice; population and the cash value of workpoints.

H-II-14: Deng Zhengfan (technician, Songjiang County Bureau of Agriculture). Yield data; crop yields during the Great Leap; climatic cycles; seed varieties and crop yields.

H-II-15: Chen Yucheng (high-level agricultural technician, Songjiang County). The Mingxing brigade; from triple-cropping to double; cultivating dry crops; cotton and wheat underground drainage; varieties of rice seed; hybrid rice; loosening control; the Great Leap; leftist thinking and triple-cropping.

H-II-16: Lu Longtan (member, Education Section, County Gazetteer Committee), Wu Xinquan (chief, Songjiang County Bureau of Education). Grammar and middle school; normal schools; technical schools.

H-II-17: Zhu Yaoliang (chief, Songjiang County Bureau of Water Control). Geographical environment; water control; economic benefits of water control.

H-II-18: He Jinlin, Yang Xiaofa. Land reform; early- and higher-stage collectives; the Great Leap; the "small four cleans" and the "big four cleans"; team cadres since 1978 reforms.

H-II-19: Lu Longshun, Lu Maoyuan. The cadres of Xilihangbang; playing chess and "poker"; watching television.

H-II-20: Gao Yonglin, Lu Haitang, Lu Maoyuan. Transfer of tractors from teams to brigade in 1982; changes in production costs after 1983; 1978 high yields in hybrid rice; problems in double-cropping rice; underground drainage for wheat; causes of low yields of different crops; early-rape; growing cotton in "nutrition bowls" (*yingyang bo*); the three-three cropping system.

H-II-21: Chen Donglin (brigade party branch secretary, 1978–81, 1982–84), Jiang Delong (brigade head, 1984–), Zhang Bingyu (brigade accountant, 1968–78, 1982–). Members of the party branch committee; first-, second-, and third-line cadres; the three rushes; production planning; pros and cons of single- and double-cropped rice.

H-II-22: Fu Jixin (secretary, Division of Agriculture and Industry, Songjiang County Party Committee). Income data for Songjiang county; distribution; composition of county income: agriculture, industry, sidelines.

H-II-23: Qian Yonglian (secretary, Songjiang County Supply and Marketing Cooperative). County's commercial network; socialist construction in commerce.

H-II-24: Chu Tongqing, Fang Rusheng (members of Songjiang County Gazetteer Office). The work of the County Gazetteer Office; Songjiang from the stone age to the Revolution; population and cultivated acreage data.

H-II-25: Gao Buzhen (f), He Huihua (f), Li Peihua (f). Mid-seventh month festival; women going to town; funerals in the hamlets of Xilihangbang; television; broadening of women's social fields; selling vegetables; social relations within the hamlet; Gao Buzhen's social field; young women going to Huayang town and to Songjiang; buying groceries; going to movies and department stores; returns of cotton cultivation by use of "nutrition bowls."

H-II-26: Gao Jinyun, Gao Yongnian, Gao Zonghan, Lu Xuefang (f), Yang Fengying (f). The different team leaders; Gao Jinyun's marriage; younger people going to Songjiang; playing "poker"; Lu Xuefang's grocery shopping; going to department stores in Songjiang; socializing; the Jin family hamlet (Jinjiada); knitting sweaters; crocheting; forms of mutual address.

H-II-27: Zhang [given name not recorded] (head of the township). Composition of commune income in 1983; the commune's pumping stations, tractors, threshing machines, factories, old folks' home; accumulation; plans for an electronic factory.

1985

H-III-1: He Jinlin, Yang Shougen, Yang Xiaofa. Raising rabbits; dried earthworms; traders in rabbit fur; different kinds of incomes; work benefits; quotas for pig raising; costs and returns of pig raising under the household-responsibility system.

H-III-2: Gao Youfa, He Jinlin, Lu Maoyuan. The workpoint system; standards of subsistence grain distribution; piecework; the three rushes; children and work; the big and small *huzi* measure in use before the Revolution.

H-III-3: Lu Guantong, Wu Renyu, Xue Baoren. Going to town; the teahouse; the "big average" and "small average" at the time of land reform; "struggling" landlords; dividing up the land; class classification; the Sanxing Coop; setting the subsistence grain standards; procurement; people's commune; private plots; the "small four cleans" and "big four cleans"; "struggling" Lu Guantong; ransacking homes in the Cultural Revolution.

H-III-4: He Yonglong, Yang Xiaofa, Zhang Bingyu. The brigade cadres; the "treasurer"; the work recorder; the work of the team leaders; settling disputes; mediating mother-in-law/daughter-in-law disputes; the team leaders; the brigade party branch secretary; authoritarianism in the team and the brigade; bureaucratism; superstition.

H-III-5: He Yonglong. Off-farm employment of the villagers; how jobs were obtained.

H-III-6: Gao Youfa, Wu Yucai. Prices; rabbit raising in the various hamlets; dried earthworms; vegetable price trends; what people want in getting married.

H-III-7: Dai Jincai (technician, Commune Drainage-Irrigation Station), Yang Gendi (head of Station). Organizational structure of water control; subsidies to "voluntary" labor service; canal digging and dredging in 1975–78; the different grades of rivers and canals; the embanked districts (*yu qu*); county and commune defense lines; irrigation; pumping stations; service teams; compensation for land used and housing torn down; construction of the Taipu River.

H-III-8: He Jinlin, Wu Renyu, Yang Xiaofa. Cash value of workpoints in Xubushanqiao; income from hiring out; computing the value of subsistence grain distributed in kind; labor for the housing office; temporary and long-term labor; decline in pig raising; Wu Renyu's secrets in pig raising.

H-III-9: Lu Maoyuan, Wu Mingchang, Zhang Bingyu. Income of Xue Baobao's family; sexual division of labor in Xilihangbang under the responsibility system; number of workers in the lock factory from the different hamlets; brigade cadres' and team leaders' contracted fields; Lu Maoyuan's wife's fear of outside world; barley as feed; proportion of chaff to grain in barley.

H-III-10: Chen Caifang (f), Guo Zhuying (f), He Huihua (f). Farmwork done by women; women who can transplant; who does more, male or female; straw shoes, cotton spinning, and cloth weaving; women had to do more after land reform; women's labor service during the Great Leap; Chen Shoulin's way of supervising work; men's incompetence in pulling up shoots; the women do more than men at planting time; rest period after giving birth; number of workdays; sexual division of labor in cotton cultivation; men digging the ditches for rape; men applying the chemical fertilizer; conflict between Lujiada and Nanda; Xue Shunquan as team leader; Li Peihua's difficulties as team leader; Wei Guoqian's problems; mother-in-law/daughter-in-law relations in Xilihangbang.

H-III-11: Zhu Wenjie (chief, Songjiang County Statistical Bureau). Prices; brigade industry accounting; 1979–84 per capita collective and private income; raising farm animals; hiring out.

H-III-12 and H-III-13: Cai Zuyun (Changlou administrative-village party branch secretary), Feng Senyun (deputy secretary), Gu Youcai (chair). Changlou brigade: overview, per capita income, brigade enterprises, factories; household sideline and labor selling income; standard of living; the horseshoe Metal and Sock factories; joint enterprise with a Shanghai casting factory.

H-III-14: Li Shunxiu (f), Wang Caiying (f), Yang Pinjuan (f), Yang Shougen. A village woman who does not pull up shoots; cotton work and women; a village woman with extraordinary farming abilities; women do more than men; women had to do more after land reform; men had to do more after the responsibility system; mother-in-law/daughter-in-law relationships in Xubushanqiao; cooking and washing; dumping chamber pots.

H-III-15: Shen Jinzhu (f), Chen Caifang (f), Xue Baoyi, Ye Yajuan (f). Kind of farmwork done by women in Xuejiada and Hejiada; mother-in-law/daughter-in-law relationships in Xuejiada and Hejiada; whom the old folks eat with.

H-III-16: Xue Baobao (f), Yang Jinxiu (f). Making straw baskets and ropes; raising rabbits; dried earthworms; crocheting; dowries; mother-in-law/daughter-in-law relationships; men carry out the shoots, women plant them; cooking and washing; emptying chamber pots; differences between the middle-aged and the young; general eagerness to get out of the village.

H-III-17: Gao Youfa, Lu Genshan. Villagers of Xilihangbang employed off-farm; Lu Genshan's relations with his third daughter-in-law; mother-in-law/daughter-in-law relationships in the village; taking over father's job; Gao Youfa's wife's relations with her mother-in-law.

H-III-18 and H-III-19: Cheng Mingqu (Xinqiao Township [commune] chair), Lu Shiming (foreign affairs officer), Song Mingjiang (head, Supply and Marketing Cooperative). Xinqiao commune: overview, 1978 and 1984 comparison; proportions of labor units at the team, brigade, and commune levels; specialized and mechanized wheat production in Chen Jiaxiang brigade; export of Christmas lights; specialized households for raising chickens and pigs; collective industrial enterprises.

H-III-20: Wu Renyu, Zhang Bingyu. Procurement; the three fixeds; subsistence grain allowances; changes in procurement prices; labor needed for different crops; bonuses; difference between *lianchan chengbao* and *dabaogan*; different collective sidelines.

H-III-21: He Deyu, Zhang Boren. Villagers of Xuejiada and Hejiada employed off-farm.

H-III-22: Yang Jinxiu (f), Yang Xiaofa. Insecticide application under the responsibility system; difference between *lianchan chengbao* and *dabaogan*; cropping choices; fertilizer purchase and distribution; price changes; prices of different grades of cotton.

H-III-23: Shen Shunchang (commune cadre concerned with sidelines since 1958). Collective pig raising, vegetable growing, straw-basket weaving, fish ponds, milk cows, rabbits; mushrooms; the Great Leap.

H-III-24: Zhu Yaoliang (chief, Songjiang County Water-Control Bureau). Organizational changes in water-control administration; water-control projects from 1950s to 1970s; subsidies; reducing the burden of the state; problem of remunerating labor for water-control projects in the future; use of labor from Zhejiang; the Taipu River.

H-III-25: Gao Yuchang (former Huayang commune head), Lu Defa (former Seed Brigade head), Zhang Xiulong (former Huayang commune head). The successive party secretaries and commune heads of Huayang; Wang Deming; the "small four cleans" and "big four cleans"; the Cultural Revolution; the Red Guards; armed struggle in Songjiang.

H-III-26: Lu Longshun, Wu Mingchang, Wu Renyu. Team collective sidelines: pig and rabbit raising, vegetables, mushrooms, nursery, fish pond; private sidelines: straw baskets, crocheting, pig and rabbit raising; Red Guards; ransacking homes

368   REFERENCES

during the Cultural Revolution; supervised labor of "struggle" targets; "struggling" Gao Yongnian.

H-III-27: Jiang Xiaochen (deputy party secretary, Huayang commune; chair, Committee for Economic Management). Waiving of procurement in 1985; state procurement prices of cotton and rapeseed in 1984 and 1985; procurement of all grain at above-quota prices; composition of labor force in 1976 and 1984; 1979 price adjustments; prices and peasant incomes; per capita distributed income among the agricultural population; loans at the brigade and commune levels; leading labor with capital investment (*yizi dailao*); sources of capital accumulation; changes in the relative proportions of industry, agriculture, and sidelines, 1977–84; sidelines, past and present.

H-III-28: Li Peihua (f), Xue Delong, Yang Xiaofa. The 13 party members of the Seed Brigade; "organized life" (*zuzhi shenghuo*) of the party; Shen Baoshun's expulsion from the party in the "small four cleans"; the poor peasant association of the Cultural Revolution; political study in 1968–71; Cultural Revolution's lack of impact on production; Red Guards; requirements for admission to the party; difference between *lianchan chengbao* and *dabaogan*.

H-III-29: Ding Yonglin (party branch secretary, Wuxing Brigade, Honghai Township, Fengxian County). Wuxing brigade: cotton cultivation, changes in yields and techniques; reforms and advances since 1978: composition of income, housing, factories.

H-III-30: Shen Fengying (f), Shen Songlin, Shen Youliang (villagers of Shenjiazhai hamlet/production team, Wuxing brigade, Honghai commune, Fengxian county). Shenjiazhai team: proportions of farmwork borne by women and men before the Revolution; yarn spinning and cloth weaving before and after the Revolution; distribution of housework; mother-in-law/daughter-in-law relationships; cotton cultivation labor needs.

H-III-31: Lu Maoyuan, Xue Minghui, Zhang Bingyu. History of lock factory; factory's income and expenditures; brigade cadres and the team for raising rice seeds.

H-III-32: He Deyu, Li Peihua (f), Zhang Bingyu. The evaluation system for brigade cadres; targets in house construction; the Three-Eight (March 8th, Women's Day) and Six-One (June 1st, Children's Day) teams for farming; helping relatives with farmwork under the responsibility system; maintenance of water control under the responsibility system.

H-III-33: Gao Jinying (f), Li Peihua (f), Zhao Yuxian (f). Responsibilities of the women's team leader: insecticide spraying, disinfecting the well water and the manure pool, child-care center, mediating mother-in-law/daughter-in-law conflicts, the childbirth program; changes in the childbirth program over time; Li Peihua's difficulties in serving as production team leader; Li Peihua's history.

H-III-34: Han [given name not recorded], Zhao [given name not recorded] (Wujiang County). Wujiang county: history of sericulture in the county; the rabbit-fur industry; milk cows; silk-reeling factories; the major towns; county archives.

H-III-35: Yin Fengsheng (leader, Miaogang Brigade, Miaogang commune,

Wujiang county), Zhou Zhenhua (Miaogang commune party secretary). Water control; the five sleeps of silkworms; the peach-raising specialty household.

H-III-36: Shen [given name not recorded] (Kaixiangong Brigade party branch secretary, Miaogang commune, Wujiang county). The sidelines of Kaixiangong: vegetables, fish, livestock, rabbits, silkworms; labor use in silkworms and in triple-cropping (early- and late-rice, wheat).

H-III-37: Tan Xirong (Kaixiangong brigade head), Zhou Fulin (former brigade head). Mulberry cultivation and labor use; the five sleeps of silkworms; silkworm raising and labor use; returns from rice, industry, rabbits.

H-III-38: Huang Maonan (chair, County Government Office, Fengqiao township, Wuxian county), Zhang Hongxing (head, Shenxianglang administrative village), Zhou Weimin (secretary, Township Government Office). Overview of Fengqiao township; commune industry: stone carving, bamboo products, electric fan parts, brick factory, Suzhou embroidery; brigade industry: plastic basins, paper boxes.

H-III-39: Shen Shuijin and Xu Niansheng (members of No. 3 team, Shenxianglang administrative village), Wang Penliang (chair, cooperative). Village industries: bamboo products and animal-feed processing; overview of No. 3 team; agriculture as a spare-time activity.

H-III-40: Huang Bingquan (deputy chair, Opening to Outside Office, Nantong city), Xu Jiabi (member, Planning Commission). Nantong city administrative history; composition of city's total output; opening to foreign investment since 1978; textile industry; composition of labor force; industries under command-type and guidance-type planning; industries regulated by market forces; controlled commodities and guided commodities.

H-III-41 and H-III-42: Huang Jinkun (chief, Bureau of Rural Enterprises, Nantong county), Lu Zhennian (County chief), Qian Weijun (chief, Planning Commission), Xu Qifan (chief, Bureau of Agriculture). Overview of county; river system; agricultural mechanization; cropping patterns; advances since 1978; collective enterprises; the construction brigade and its income; reasons for high degree of development of collective industry; domestic and foreign marketing; decline in cotton cultivation with coming of artificial fabrics; strengths and weaknesses of collective enterprises; lack of a "home" for rural industrial enterprises in the administrative structure; difference between the Bureau of Rural Enterprises and an industrial "company" of real substance.

H-III-43: Sun Zhongyue (chair, Manager's Office, Nantong Number One Cotton Textiles Factory [former Dasheng Yarn Factory]), Wang Xiang (member, Factory History Group). Record of development; productivity per spindle; the attached oil-pressing and paper factories; the land reclamation company; welfare activities; reasons for decline in the 1920s; revival under Li Shengbo; changes after 1949.

H-III-44: Zhang Dingxin (chief, Nantong city Bureau of Rural Enterprises). History of development since 1978; characteristics of scale, raw material use, and products; administrative structure; strategy; Wujin county; theory about commodities in a socialist economy; service to agriculture, large industries, and export sector.

H-III-45: Xiang Rong (secretary-general, Zhang Jian Research Center, Nantong city), Liu Daorong (head, Rare Books Section, Zhang Jian Research Center Library). The archival materials on Zhang Jian; Zhang Jian life history; the Dasheng combine; Zhang's philosophy and sources of weakness; the land reclamation company.

1988

H-IV-1 and H-IV-2: Xu Yaoqin (deputy head, Huayang township), He Yonglong, Wu Renyu, Yang Xiaofa. The township Clothing and Meat Products Factories; Xubushanqiao villagers employed off-farm since 1985; cotton cultivation, single-cropped rice, and wheat since 1985; saving labor with use of weed killers; procurement since 1985; pig and chicken raising since 1985; crisis in fertilizer use and water-control maintenance; household vs. collective vegetable growing; state vs. free-market vegetable prices; changes in township output; housing construction in Xubushanqiao; cost of a two-story house (*loufang*); changes in prices and wages.

H-IV-3: Xu Yaoqin (deputy head, Huayang township). Meat Products and "Welfare [Clothing] Factory"; tax benefits for a factory employing handicapped workers; lock factory's problems; the southern Jiangsu model.

H-IV-4: Xu Yaoqin (deputy head, Huayang township), He Deyu, He Yonglong, Wu Renyu. Plans for new factory; decline of the lock factory; labor input per mu; using weed killers; changes in wheat, single-cropped rice, rapeseed yields; appropriate-scale farming; costs and benefits of transplanter and harvester for rice.

H-IV-5: Yang Xiaofa, He Yonglong, Wu Renyu. Sideline employment and income of Xubushanqiao households.

THE VILLAGE INFORMANTS

All informants are identified by village/hamlet (Xuejiada = XJD; Hejiada = HJD; Xubushanqiao = XBSQ; Gaojiada = GJD; Lujiada = LJD; Nanda = ND) and year of birth. Female informants are identified by the name of the husband (in order to facilitate identification by household). Informants who have served as cadres are identified by the major positions held and terms of service. Team cadres are identified by their teams: No. 1 team (Xuejiada team) = XJD; No. 2 team (Xubushanqiao team) = XBSQ; No. 3 team (Xilihangbang team) = XLHB. Party members are shown with the designation "P," followed by the year of admission to the party.

Chen Caifang, wife of Zhang Boren; XJD, b. 1932
Gao Buzhen, wife of Lu Jintang; LJD, b. 1918
Gao Dajie, wife of Lu Jingen; ND, b. 1907
Gao Jinying, wife of Lu Huolong; ND, b. 1955
Gao Jinyun, GJD, b. 1954; deputy team head XLHB, 1977–81, team head XLHB, 1981–83

Gao Laigen, GJD, b. 1932; deputy team head XLHB, 1956–65
Gao Shigen, GJD, b. 1929
Gao Shitang, GJD, b. 1925
Gao Yonglin, LJD, b. 1924; deputy team head XLHB, 1965–69, team head XLHB, 1969–73
Gao Yongnian, GJD, b. 1917
Gao Youfa, GJD, b. 1937
Gao Zonghan, LJD, b. 1957
Gu Yindi, wife of He Shulin; HJD, b. 1911
Guo Zhuying, wife of Lu Hailai; LJD, b. 1924
He Chungen, HJD, b. 1917
He Deyu, HJD, b. 1951; team head XJD, 1978–79, 1984–85, brigade head, 1985–   ; P, 1984
He Huihua, wife of Lu Haitang; LJD, b. 1930
He Huosheng, HJD, b. 1923; team head XJD, 1959–61, brigade head, 1960–67; P, before 1956
He Jinlin, XBSQ, b. 1933; team accountant XBSQ, 1962–82
He Kuifa, XBSQ, b. 1926
He Shutang, HJD, b. 1917
He Tugen, XBSQ, b. 1903
He Yonglong, HJD, b. 1948; brigade accountant, 1978–81, brigade head, 1981–83, brigade party branch secretary, 1983–84; P, 1977
Li Peihua, wife of Lu Bingxian; ND, b. 1942; team head XLHB, 1975–77; brigade woman chair, 1978–   ; P, 1975
Li Shunxiu, wife of He Kuifa; XBSQ, b. 1925
Lu Genshan, ND, b. 1912
Lu Guantong, LJD, b. 1919
Lu Hailai, LJD, b. 1918; team accountant XLHB, 1956–65
Lu Haitang, LJD, b. 1926; team head XLHB, 1956–69; P, 1956
Lu Longshun, ND, b. 1926; team head XLHB, 1973; P, 1956
Lu Maoyuan, ND, b. 1951; team accountant XLHB, 1969–81
Lu Xuefang, wife of Lu Jinyu; ND, b. 1948
Shen Jinzhu, wife of Zhang Chunyu; XJD, b. 1907
Shen Yindi, wife of Lu Guantong; LJD, b. 1926
Wang Caiying, wife of Wu Renyu; XBSQ, b. 1934
Wu Genyu, XBSQ, b. 1917
Wu Hugen, XBSQ, b. 1917
Wu Mingchang, XBSQ, b. 1950; team leader XBSQ, 1978–80, 1982–83, brigade deputy leader for sidelines, 1984–
Wu Renyu, XBSQ, b. 1931; brigade deputy leader for sidelines, 1979–84, team leader XBSQ, 1984–   ; P, 1964
Wu Xiaomei, wife of Wu Jinfa; XBSQ, b. 1911
Wu Yucai, XBSQ, b. 1930
Xue Baobao, wife of Wang Longde; XJD, b. 1936
Xue Baoren, XJD, b. 1911

Xue Baoyi, XJD, b. 1915
Xue Delong, XJD, b. 1945; brigade head, 1983–84, brigade party branch secretary, 1985–   ; P, 1983
Xue Huilin, XJD, b. 1950
Xue Jinlin, XJD, b. 1928
Xue Minghui, XJD, b. 1953; brigade lock factory deputy manager, 1982–
Xue Shunquan, XJD, b. 1935; team head XJD, 1961–68, 1972–78, brigade deputy head for industry, 1979–85
Yang Fengying, wife of Lu Shudong; LJD, b. 1949
Yang Jinxiu, wife of Yang Chengzhang; XBSQ, b. 1934
Yang Pinjuan, wife of He Jinfa; XBSQ, b. 1927; P, 1974
Yang Shougen, XBSQ, b. 1910
Yang Xiaofa, XBSQ, b. 1931; team head XBSQ, 1958–78; P, 1956
Ye Yajuan, wife of Xue Shoulin; XJD, b. 1931
Zhang Boren, XJD, b. 1928; team head XJD, 1957
Zhang Bingyu, XJD, b. 1935; brigade accountant, 1968–78, 1982–   ; P, 1975
Zhao Yuxian, wife of He Xiaomao; XBSQ, b. 1942

SOURCES CITED

The following abbreviations are used in the citations: KC, *Chūgoku nōson kankō chōsa*; MT, *Minami Manshū tetsudō kabushiki kaisha*. Unless otherwise noted, local gazetteers are reprints published in Taibei by Chengwen Shuju.

Adachi Keiji 足立啓二. 1978. "Daizu kasu ryūtsū to Shindai no shōgyōteki nōgyō" 大豆粕流通と清代の商業的農業 (The circulation of soybean cake and commercial agriculture in the Qing period), *Tōyōshi kenkyū*, 37.3 (Dec.): 35–63.
Amano Motonosuke 天野元之助. 1962. *Chūgoku nōgyō shi kenkyū* 中國農業史研究 (Studies in the agricultural history of China). Tokyo: Ochanomizu shobō.
Arrigo, Linda. 1986. "Landownership Concentration in China: The Buck Survey Revisited," *Modern China*, 12.3: 259–360.
Baoshan xian zhi 寶山縣志 (Gazetteer of Baoshan county). 1882.
Baoshan xian xuzhi 寶山縣續志 (Continuation of the gazetteer of Baoshan county). 1921.
Baoshan xian zaixuzhi, xinzhi beigao 寶山縣再續志, 新志備稿 (Continuation of the continuation of the gazetteer of Baoshan county, and a draft of a new gazetteer). 1931.
Baran, Paul A. 1957. *The Political Economy of Growth*. New York: Monthly Review.
Beattie, Hilary J. 1979. *Land and Lineage in China: A Study of T'ung-ch'eng County, Anhwei, in the Ming and Ch'ing Dynasties*. Cambridge, Eng.: Cambridge University Press.
Beijing nongye daxue nongye jingji fa yanjiu zu 北京農業大學農業經濟法研究組, ed. 1981. *Nongye jingji fagui ziliao huibian* 農業經濟法規資料彙編 (Compendium of sources on laws and regulations governing agricultural economy). 8 vols. N.p.

Beijing zhengfa xueyuan 北京政法學院. 1957. *Zhonghua renmin gongheguo tudifa cankao ziliao huibian* 中華人民共和國土地法參考資料彙編 (Compendium of reference materials on the land reform laws of the People's Republic of China). Beijing: Falü chubanshe.

Bell, Lynda. 1988. "Redefining Rational Peasants: Sericulture and the Wuxi County Small-Peasant-Family Farm." Paper presented at the conference on "Economic Methods for Chinese Historical Research," Tucson, Ariz., January 1988.

———. 1985. "Merchants, Peasants, and the State: The Organization and Politics of Chinese Silk Production, Wuxi County, 1870–1937." Ph.D. dissertation, University of California, Los Angeles.

Bernhardt, Kathryn. 1987. "Elite and Peasant During the Taiping Occupation of the Jiangnan, 1860–1864," *Modern China* 13.4: 379–410.

———. 1986. "Peasants and the State: The Evolution of Tenant Rent Resistance in the Jiangnan Region, 1864–1937." Paper presented at the annual meeting of the American Historical Association, New York City.

Boserup, Ester. 1981. *Population and Technological Change: A Study of Long-Term Trends.* Chicago: University of Chicago Press.

———. 1965. *The Conditions of Agricultural Growth: The Economics of Agrarian Change Under Population Pressure.* Chicago: Aldine.

Bray, Francesca. 1986. *The Rice Economies: Technology and Development in Asian Societies.* Oxford: Basil Blackwell.

———. 1984. *Agriculture.* Vol. 6, part II, of Joseph Needham, ed., *Science and Civilization in China.* Cambridge, Eng.: Cambridge University Press.

Brenner, Robert. 1982. "The Agrarian Roots of European Capitalism," *Past and Present,* 97 (Nov.): 16–113.

Buck, John Lossing. 1937a. *Land Utilization in China.* Shanghai: University of Nanking.

———. 1937b. *Land Utilization in China: Statistics.* Shanghai: University of Nanking.

Byrd, William A., and Alan Gelb. 1988. "Why Industrialize? The Incentives for Local Community Governments." Chap. 16 of William A. Byrd and Qingsong Liu, eds., "China's Rural Industry: Structure, Development, and Reform." Unpublished manuscript.

Byrd, William A., and Qingsong Liu, eds. 1988. "China's Rural Industry: Structure, Development, and Reform." Unpublished manuscript.

Chan, Anita, Richard Madsen, and Jonathan Unger. 1984. *Chen Village: The Recent History of a Peasant Community in Mao's China.* Berkeley: University of California Press.

Chan, Sucheng. 1986. *This Bitter-Sweet Soil: The Chinese in California Agriculture, 1860–1910.* Berkeley: University of California Press.

Chang, Chung-li [Zhang Zhongli]. 1962. *The Income of the Chinese Gentry.* Seattle: University of Washington Press.

———. 1955. *The Chinese Gentry: Studies on Their Role in Nineteenth-Century Chinese Society.* Seattle: University of Washington Press.

Chayanov, A. V. 1986 [1925]. *The Theory of Peasant Economy*. Madison: University of Wisconsin Press.

Chen, Han-seng [Hansheng]. 1939. *Industrial Capital and the Chinese Peasants: A Study of the Livelihood of Chinese Tobacco Cultivators*. Shanghai: Kelly & Walsh.

Chen Hengli 陳恆力. 1963. *Bunongshu yanjiu* 補農書研究 (Study of the *Supplements to "Mr. Shen's Agricultural Treatise"*). Shanghai: Nongye chubanshe.

Chen Hengli and Wang Da 王達, eds. 1983. *"Bunongshu" jiaoshi* 補農書校釋 (Annotations on the *Supplements to "Mr. Shen's Agricultural Treatise"*). Beijing: Nongye chubanshe.

Chen Jiyu 陳吉餘. 1957. "Changjiang sanjiaozhou kouduan de dixing fayu" 長江三角洲口段的地形發育 (Development of the topography of the mouth of the Changjiang delta), *Dili xuebao*, 23.3: 241–53.

Chen Zhengmo 陳正謨. 1935. *Ge sheng nonggong guyong xiguan ji xugong zhuangkuang* 各省農工僱傭習慣及需供狀況 (Customary practices and supply and demand in agricultural labor hiring in the different provinces). Nanjing: Zhongshan wenhua jiaoyuguan.

Cheng Hong. 1988. "Rice Markets and Price Movements in the Prewar Shanghai Area." Unpublished manuscript.

Chongming xian zhi 崇明縣志 (Gazetteer of Chongming county). 1924.

Chongxiu Chang Zhao hezhi 重修常昭合志 (Recompiled combined gazetteer of Changshu and Zhaowen). 1904.

Chongxiu Fengxian xian zhi 重修奉賢縣志 (Recompiled gazetteer of Fengxian county). 1878.

Chongxiu Huating xian zhi 重修華亭縣志 (Recompiled gazetteer of Huating county). 1878.

Chongxiu Kunshan xian zhi 重修崑山縣志 (Recompiled gazetteer of Kunshan county). 1576.

Chongxiu Piling zhi 重修毘陵志 (Recompiled gazetteer of Piling (Changzhou). 1484.

Chuansha ting zhi 川沙廳志 (Gazetteer of Chuansha subprefecture). 1879.

Chuansha xian zhi 川沙縣志 (Gazetteer of Chuansha county). 1936.

Chūgoku nōson kankō chōsa kankōkai 中國農村慣行調查刊行會. 1952–58. *Chūgoku nōson kankō chōsa* (KC) 中國農村慣行調查 (Investigations of customary practices in rural China), ed. Niida Noboru 仁井田陞. 6 vols. Tokyo: Iwanami shoten.

The Civil Code of the Republic of China. 1930. Shanghai: Kelly & Walsh.

Coale, Ansley. 1984. "Rapid Population Change in China, 1952–1982." [National Academy of Sciences] Committee on Population and Demography report 27.

Da Qing lüli huitong xinzuan 大清律例會通新纂 (New compendium of the Qing Code). Taibei: Wenhai chubanshe.

Dai Yanhui 戴炎輝. 1966. *Zhongguo fazhi shi* 中國法制史 (History of Chinese legal institutions). Taibei: Sanmin shuju.

Dalton, George. 1969. "Theoretical Issues in Economic Anthropology," *Current Anthropology*, 10.1: 63–102.

De Vries, Jan. 1984. *European Urbanization, 1500–1800*. Cambridge, Mass.: Harvard University Press.

———. 1981. "Patterns of Urbanization in Pre-Industrial Europe, 1500–1800." In H. Schmal, ed., *Patterns of European Urbanization Since 1500*, pp. 77–109. London: Croom Helm.

Duara, Prasenjit. 1988. *Culture, Power, and the State: Rural North China, 1900–1942*. Stanford, Calif.: Stanford University Press.

Eberhard, Wolfram. 1965. *Conquerors and Rulers: Social Forces in Medieval China*. 2d rev. ed. Leiden: E. J. Brill.

Ebrey, Patricia Buckley, and James L. Watson, eds. 1986. *Kinship Organization in Late Imperial China, 1000–1940*. Berkeley: University of California Press.

Elvin, Mark. 1973. *The Pattern of the Chinese Past*. Stanford, Calif.: Stanford University Press.

Esherick, Joseph W. 1987. *The Origins of the Boxer Uprising*. Berkeley: University of California Press.

Fan Baichuan 樊百川. 1983. "Ershi shiji chuqi Zhongguo zibenzhuyi fazhan de gaikuang yu tedian" 二十世紀初期中國資本主義發展的概況與特點 (Development of Chinese capitalism in the early 20th century and its special characteristics), *Lishi yanjiu*, no. 4: 11–24.

Fan Shuzhi 樊樹志. 1983. "Shiyi zhi shiliu shiji Jiangnan nongye jingji de fazhan—chuantong jingji jiegou tupo de jubu kaocha" 十一至十六世紀江南農業經濟的發展—傳統經濟結構突破的局部考察 (Development of the agricultural economy of Jiangnan from the 11th to the 16th century—a partial study of the breakthrough of the traditional economic structure). Unpublished manuscript.

Fang Xing 方行. 1987. "Lun Qingdai qianqi mianfangzhi de shehui fengong" 論清代前期棉紡織的社會分工 (On the social division of labor in cotton spinning and weaving during the first half of the Qing period), *Zhongguo jingjishi yanjiu*, no. 1: 79–94.

———. 1986. "Lun Qingdai qianqi nongmin shangpin shengchan de fazhan" 論清代前期農民商品生產的發展 (On the development of peasant commodity production during the first half of the Qing period), *Zhongguo jingjishi yanjiu*, no. 1: 53–66.

———. 1984. "Qingdai qianqi xiaonong jingji de zai shengchan" 清代前期小農經濟的再生產 (On the reproduction of the peasant economy during the first half of the Qing period), *Lishi yanjiu*, no. 5: 129–41.

Faure, David. 1989. *The Rural Economy of Pre-Liberation China*. Hong Kong: Oxford University Press.

———. 1985. "The Plight of the Farmer: A Study of the Rural Economy of Jiangnan and the Pearl River Delta, 1870–1937," *Modern China*, 11.1: 3–37.

Fazhan yanjiusuo 發展研究所 (Guowuyuan nongcun fazhan yanjiu zhongxin 國務院農村發展研究中心). 1985. *Guomin jingji xin chengzhang jieduan he nongcun fazhan* 國民經濟新成長階段和農村發展 (Rural development and the new stage in the growth of the national economy). N.p.

Fazhan yanjiusuo zonghe keti zu 發展研究所綜合課題組. 1987. "Nongmin, shi-chang, he zhidu chuangxin" 農民, 市場, 和制度創新 (Peasants, the market, and institutional innovation), *Jingji yanjiu*, no. 1: 3–16.

Fei Xiaotong 費孝通. 1984. "Xiao chengzhen, da wenti" 小城鎮大問題 (Small towns, big problem), in Jiangsu sheng xiaochengzhen yanjiu keti zu, ed., 1984, listed below, pp. 1–40.

———— [Fei Hsiao-tung]. 1939. *Peasant Life in China: A Field Study of Country Life in the Yangtze Valley*. New York: Dutton.

Feinerman, James. 1989. "The *Dien* Transaction in China and Vietnam." Un-published manuscript.

Fengxian xian zhi 奉賢縣志 (Gazetteer of Fengxian county). 1878.

Feuerwerker, Albert. 1958. *China's Early Industrialization: Sheng Hsuan-huai (1844–1916) and Mandarin Enterprise*. Cambridge, Mass.: Harvard University Press.

Frank, André Gunder. 1978. "Development of Underdevelopment or Under-development of Development in China," *Modern China*, 4.3: 341–50.

————. 1967. *Capitalism and Underdevelopment in Latin America*. New York: Monthly Review.

Freedman, Maurice. 1966. *Chinese Lineage and Society: Fukien and Kwangtung*. London: Athlone Press.

Fu Yiling 傅衣凌. 1963. *Qingdai Jiangnan shimin jingji shitan* 清代江南市民經濟 試探 (Preliminary inquiry into the burgher economy of Jiangnan during the Qing). Shanghai: Shanghai renmin chubanshe.

Fudan daxue lishi dili yanjiu shi 復旦大學歷史地理研究室. 1981. "Taihu yidong ji Dong Taihu diqu lishi dili diaocha kaocha jianbao" 太湖以東及東太湖地區歷史 地理調查考察簡報 (Abbreviated report on the investigation of the historical geography of the Eastern Taihu and the [area] east of Taihu), *Lishi dili*, 1: 187–94.

Gamble, Sidney. 1963. *North China Villages: Social, Political and Economic Activi-ties Before 1933*. Berkeley: University of California Press.

Geertz, Clifford. 1963. *Agricultural Involution: The Process of Ecological Change in Indonesia*. Berkeley: University of California Press.

Georgescu-Roegen, N. 1960. "Economic Theory and Agrarian Economics," *Oxford Economic Papers*, 12.1: 1–40.

Goldstone, Jack. 1986. "The Demographic Revolution in England: A Reexamina-tion," *Population Studies*, 49: 5–33.

Gu Yanwu 顧炎武. 1962 [1695]. *Rizhi lu* 日知錄 (Notes of daily learning). 32 vols. Taibei: Shijie shuju.

————. 1662. *Tianxia junguo libing shu* 天下郡國利病書 (On the advantages and problems of the districts and states of the empire). 34 vols. In *Sibu congkan*. Shanghai: Shangwu yinshuguan.

Guangfu zhi 光福志 (Gazetteer of Guangfu [town]). 1900.

Guo Yuyang 郭浴陽. 1987. "Zhongguo xiangzhen gongyehua moshi bijiao he pingjia" 中國鄉鎮工業化模式比較和評價 (Comparative analysis and evaluation of the models in China's small-town industrialization), *Zhejiang xuekan*, no. 4: 82–89.

Gusu zhi 姑蘇志 (Gazetteer of the Suzhou area). 1506. Taibei: Xuesheng shuju.

Hamashima Atsutoshi 濱島敦俊. 1982. *Mindai kōnan nōson shakai no kenkyū* 明代江南農村社会の研究 (Study of rural society in Jiangnan during the Ming). Tokyo: Tōkyō daigaku shuppansha.

Hartwell, Robert M. 1982. "Demographic, Political, and Social Transformations of China, 750–1550," *Harvard Journal of Asiatic Studies*, 42.2: 365–442.

Hayashi Megumi 林惠海. 1943. *Chūshi Kōnan nōson shakai seido kenkyū* 中支江南農村社會制度研究 (Study of the social system of rural Jiangnan in Central China). Tokyo: Yūhikaku.

He Rongfei et al. 何榮飛. 1987. *Wenzhou jingji geju* 溫州經濟格局 (The structure of Wenzhou's economy). Wenzhou: Zhejiang renmin chubanshe.

Hinton, William. 1966. *Fanshen: A Documentary of Revolution in a Chinese Village*. New York: Random House.

Ho, Ping-ti [Bingdi] 何炳棣. 1985a,b. "Nan Song zhi jin tudi shuzi de kaoshi he pingjia" 南宋至今土地數字的考釋和評價 (Evaluation and analysis of the land data from the Southern Song to the present), *Zhongguo shehui kexue*, no. 2: 133–85; no. 3: 125–47.

———. 1959. *Studies in the Population of China*. Cambridge, Mass.: Harvard University Press.

Hou Chi-ming. 1963. "Economic Dualism: The Case of China, 1840–1937," *Journal of Economic History*, 23.3: 277–97.

Hsiao Kung-ch'üan. 1960. *Rural China: Imperial Control in the Nineteenth Century*. Seattle: University of Washington Press.

Hsü Cho-yun. 1980. *Han Agriculture: The Formation of Early Chinese Agrarian Economy, 206 B.C.–220 A.D.* Seattle: University of Washington Press.

Hu Rulei 胡如雷. 1979. *Zhongguo fengjian shehui xingtai yanjiu* 中國封建社會形態研究 (Study of China's feudal social formation). Beijing: Sanlian.

Huadong junzheng weiyuanhui 華東軍政委員會. 1952. *Jiangsu sheng nongcun diaocha* 江蘇省農村調查 (Investigation of the countryside of Jiangsu province). N.p.

Huang, Philip C. C. 1985. *The Peasant Economy and Social Change in North China*. Stanford, Calif.: Stanford University Press.

Huang, Philip C. C., and Lynda Schaeffer Bell and Kathy Lemons Walker. 1978. *Chinese Communists and Rural Society, 1927–1934*. Berkeley: Center for Chinese Studies, University of California.

Huating xian zhi 華亭縣志 (Gazetteer of Huating county). 1791.

Hucker, Charles O. 1985. *A Dictionary of Official Titles in Imperial China*. Stanford, Calif.: Stanford University Press.

Huzhou fu zhi 湖州府志 (Gazetteer of Huzhou prefecture). 1874.

Ishikawa, Shigeru. 1967. *Economic Development in Asian Perspective*. Tokyo: Kinokuniya.

Jia Dan 郟亶. 1067. "Wumen shuili shu" 吳門水利書 (Memorial on water control in the Wu area). In Fan Chengda 范成大, ed. *Wujun zhi* 吳郡志 (Gazetteer of the Wu region). In *Congshu jicheng*, no. 3149, vol. 19. Shanghai: Shangwu yinshuguan.

Jiading xian zhi 嘉定縣志 (Gazetteer of Jiading county). 1605.

Jiading xian xuzhi 嘉定縣續志 (Continuation of the gazetteer of Jiading county). 1930.

Jiang Gao 姜皋. 1963 [1834]. *Pu Mao nongzi* 浦泖農咨 (Report on agriculture in the [Huang]Pu River and Mao[hu] Lake area). Shanghai: Shanghai tushuguan.

Jiangsu dili 江蘇地理 (Geography of Jiangsu). 1980. Jiangsu: Jiangsu renmin chubanshe.

Jiangsu nongye dili 江蘇農業地理 (Agricultural geography of Jiangsu). 1979. Jiangsu: Jiangsu kexue jishu chubanshe.

Jiangsu sheng jin liangqian nian hong lao han chao zaihai nianbiao 江蘇省近兩千年洪澇旱潮災害年表 (Chronological table of flood, waterlogging, drought, and tidal floods in Jiangsu province during the last 2,000 years). 1976. N.p.

Jiangsu sheng quansheng yutu 江蘇省全省輿圖 (Map of all of Jiangsu province). 1895. Taibei: Chengwen shuju.

Jiangsu sheng xiaochengzhen yanjiu keti zu, ed. 江蘇省小城鎮研究課題組. 1987. *Xiaochengzhen quyu fenxi* 小城鎮區域分析 (Regional analysis of small towns). Jiangsu: Zhongguo tongji chubanshe.

———. 1984. *Xiaochengzhen da wenti: Jiangsu sheng xiao chengzhen yanjiu lunwen xuan* 小城鎮大問題:江蘇省小城鎮研究論文選 (Small towns, big problem: selected research articles on the small towns of Jiangsu province). N.p.: Jiangsu renmin chubanshe.

Jiangsu sheng Zhongguo xiandaishi xuehui, ed. 江蘇省中國現代史學會. 1983. *Jiangsu jin xiandai jingjishi wenji* 江蘇近現代經濟史文集 (Collected essays on the modern and contemporary economic history of Jiangsu). N.p.

Jiangyin xian zhi 江陰縣志 (Gazetteer of Jiangyin county). 1878, 1840.

Jiangyin xian xuzhi 江陰縣續志 (Continuation of the gazetteer of Jiangyin county). 1921.

Jiaxing fu zhi 嘉興府志 (Gazetteer of Jiaxing prefecture). 1878.

Jingji da cidian: nongye jingji juan. 經濟大辭典:農業經濟卷 (Dictionary of economics: agricultural economics volume). 1983. Shanghai: Shanghai cishu chubanshe.

Jinshan xian zhi 金山縣志 (Gazetteer of Jinshan county). 1878, 1858, 1751 (1929 reprint).

Kita Shina kaihatsu kabushiki kaisha chōsakyoku 北支那開發株式会社調查局. 1943. *Rōdōryoku shigen chōsa hōkoku* 勞働力資源調查報告 (Report on the investigation of labor resources). Beijing.

Kriedte, Peter, Hans Medick, and Jurgen Schlümbohm. 1981. *Industrialization Before Industrialization.* Cambridge, Mass.: Harvard University Press.

Kuhn, Thomas S. 1970 [1962]. *The Structure of Scientific Revolutions.* 2d ed. Chicago: University of Chicago Press.

Lardy, Nicholas. 1983. *Agriculture in China's Modern Economic Development.* Cambridge, Eng.: Cambridge University Press.

Lau Yee-fui, Ho Wan-yee, and Yeung Sai-cheung. 1977. *Glossary of Chinese Political Phrases.* Hong Kong: Union Research Institute.

Lenin, V. I. 1956 [1907]. *The Development of Capitalism in Russia.* Moscow: Foreign Languages Press.

Levine, David. 1977. *Family Formation in an Age of Nascent Capitalism*. New York: Academic Press.

Li Bozhong 李伯重. 1985a. "'Sang zheng daotian' yu Ming-Qing Jiangnan nongye shengchan jiyue chengdu de tigao" '桑爭稻田' 與明清江南農業生產集約程度的 提高 ("Mulberries take over rice fields" and the intensification of agricultural production in Jiangnan during the Ming and Qing), *Zhongguo nongshi*, no. 1: 1–12.

———. 1985b. "Ming Qing Jiangnan nongye ziyuan de heli liyong" 明清江南農業 資源的合理利用 (The rational use of agricultural resources in Jiangnan during the Ming and Qing), *Nongye kaogu*, no. 2: 150–63.

———. 1984. "Ming Qing shiqi Jiangnan shuidao shengchan jiyue chengdu de tigao" 明清時期江南水稻生產集約程度的提高 (The intensifying of wet-rice production in Jiangnan during the Ming and Qing period), *Zhongguo nongshi*, no. 1: 24–37.

Li, Lillian M. 1981. *China's Silk Trade: Traditional Industry in the Modern World, 1842–1937*. Cambridge, Mass.: Council on East Asian Relations, Harvard University.

Li Rongchang. 1989. "Labor Markets in China." Unpublished manuscript.

Li Wenzhi 李文治. 1981. "Lun Zhongguo dizhu jingji zhi yu nongye zibenzhuyi mengya" 論中國地主經濟制與農業資本主義萌芽 (China's landlord economy and the sprouts of capitalism in agriculture), *Zhongguo shehui kexue*, no. 1: 143–60.

———, ed. 1957. *Zhongguo jindai nongyeshi ziliao* 中國近代農業史資料 (Source materials on the agricultural history of modern China), vol. 1: *1840–1911*. Beijing: Sanlian shudian.

Li Wenzhi, Wei Jinyu 魏金玉, and Jing Junjian 經君健. 1983. *Ming Qing shidai de nongye zibenzhuyi mengya wenti* 明清時代的農業資本主義萌芽問題 (The problem of the sprouts of capitalism in agriculture during the Ming-Qing period). Beijing: Zhongguo shehui kexue chubanshe.

Li Zailun 李再倫. 1982. "Woguo mafang shi shang ji ge wenti de tantao" 我國 麻紡史上幾個問題的探討 (Inquiry into several problems in the history of our nation's hemp, flax, and ramie spinning). Unpublished manuscript.

Liang Fangzhong 梁方仲. 1980. *Zhongguo lidai hukou tiandi tianfu tongji* 中國歷代 戶口、田地、田賦統計 (Statistics on population, cultivated area, and land taxes during China's successive dynasties). Shanghai: Renmin chubanshe.

Lippit, Victor. 1974. *Land Reform and Economic Development in China*. White Plains, N.Y.: International Arts and Sciences Press.

Liu Dunyuan 劉敦愿 and Zhang Zhongge 張仲葛. 1981. "Woguo yangzhu shihua" 我國養豬史話 (Informal comments on the history of hog raising in our country), *Nongye kaogu*, no. 1: 103–5.

Liu Shiji 劉石吉. 1978a,b,c. "Ming-Qing shidai Jiangnan shizhen zhi yanjiu" 明清 時代江南市鎮之研究 (Study of the towns of Jiangnan in the Ming-Qing period), *Shihuo yuekan*, 8.6: 27–43; 8.7: 30–41; 8.8: 15–30.

———. 1978d. "Taiping tianguo luan hou Jiangnan shizhen de fazhan" 太平天國 亂後江南市鎮的發展 (Development of towns in Jiangnan after the Taiping Rebellion), *Shihuo yuekan*, 7.11: 19–48.

———. 1978e. "Ming Qing shidai Jiangnan shizhen zhi shuliang fenxi" 明清時代 江南市鎮之數量分析 (Quantitative analysis of the towns of Jiangnan during the Ming-Qing period), *Si yu yan*, 16.2: 26–47.

Louxian zhi 婁縣志 (Gazetteer of Lou county). 1788.

Louxian xuzhi 婁縣續志 (Continuation of the gazetteer of Lou county). 1879.

Ma Zhenglin 馬正林. 1981. "Zhongguo lishi dili xue sanshi nian" 中國歷史地理學 三十年 (Thirty years of historical geography in China). In *Zhongguo lishi dili luncong* 中國歷史地理論叢 (Essays on China's historical geography), vol. 1, pp. 196–230. Xi'an: Shaanxi renmin chubanshe.

MacKinnon, Stephen R. 1980. *Power and Politics in Late Imperial China: Yuan Shi-kai in Beijing and Tianjin, 1901–1908.* Berkeley: University of California Press.

Mandel, Ernest. 1970 [1968]. *Marxist Economic Theory.* 2 vols. New York: Monthly Review Press.

Mann, Michael. 1984. "The Autonomous Power of the State: Its Origins, Mechanisms and Results," *Archives européennes de sociologie*, 25: 185–213.

Mao Tun [Dun]. 1979 [1956]. *Spring Silkworms and Other Stories.* Beijing: Foreign Languages Press.

Mao Zedong 毛澤東. 1977a [1955]. "Guanyu nongye hezuohua wenti" 關於農業 合作化問題 (On the problem of agricultural collectivization). In *Mao Zedong xuanji* 毛澤東選集 (Selected works of Mao Zedong), vol. 5, pp. 168–91. Beijing: Renmin chubanshe.

———. 1977b [1955]. "Nongye hezuohua de yichang bianlun he dangqian de jieji douzheng" 農業合作化的一場辯論和當前的階級鬥爭 (Debates over agricultural collectivization and the present class struggle). In *Mao Zedong xuanji*, vol. 5, pp. 195–217.

———. 1972 [1939]. "Zhongguo geming yu Zhongguo gongchandang" 中國革命與 中國共產黨 (The Chinese revolution and the Chinese Communist Party). In *Mao Zedong ji* 毛澤東集 (Works of Mao Zedong), vol. 1, pp. 207–49. Tokyo: Hokubōsha.

———. 1964 [1942]. "Zai Yan'an wenyi zuotan hui shang de jianghua" 在延安文藝 座談會上的講話 (Speech at the Yan'an Conference on Literature). In *Mao Zedong xuanji*, pp. 849–80. Shanghai: Renmin chubanshe.

Marx, Karl. 1967 [1867]. *Capital.* 3 vols. New York: International Publishers.

Medick, Hans. 1976. "The Proto-Industrial Family Economy: The Structural Function of Household and Family During the Transition from Peasant Society to Industrial Capitalism," *Social History*, 1.3: 291–315.

Mendels, Franklin F. 1972. "Proto-Industrialization: The First Phase of the Industrialization Process," *Journal of Economic History*, 32.1: 241–61.

Min Zongdian 閔宗殿. 1984. "Song Ming Qing shiqi Taihu diqu shuidao mu chanliang de tantao" 宋明清時期太湖地區水稻畝產量的探討 (Study of the per-*mu* yields of rice in the Lake Tai area during the Song, Ming, and Qing). *Zhongguo nongshi*, no. 3: 37–52.

Minami Manshū tetsudō kabushiki kaisha (MT) 南滿洲鐵道株式会社, Hokushi jimukyoku chōsabu 北支事務局調査部. 1938–41. *Nōka keizai chōsa hōkoku:*

Hōjun ken 農家經濟調查報告：豐潤縣 (Report on the investigation of peasant household economy: Fengrun county), vol. 1: *1937*; vol. 2: *1938*; vol. 3: *1939*. Dalian.

———, Kitō nōson jittai chōsahan 冀東農村實態調查班. 1937a,b,c. *Dainiji kitō nōson jittai chōsa hōkokusho: tōkeihen*, 1: *Heikoku ken*, 3: *Hōjun ken*, 4: *Shōrei ken* 第二次冀東農村實態調查報告書：統計篇, 1: 平谷縣, 3: 豐潤縣, 4: 昌黎縣 (Report on the second investigation of actual conditions of northeastern Hebei villages: statistical volume, 1: Pinggu county, 3: Fengrun county, 4: Changli county). Dalian.

———, Shanhai jimusho 上海事務所. 1941a. *Kōso-shō Mushaku ken nōson jittai chōsa hōkokusho* 江蘇省無錫縣農村實態調查報告書 (Report on the investigation of actual conditions in the countryside of Wuxi county, Jiangsu province). N.p.

———, ———. 1941b. *Kōso-shō Nantsū ken nōson jittai chōsa hōkokusho* 江蘇省南通縣農村實態調查報告書. (Report on the investigation of actual conditions in the countryside of Nantong county, Jiangsu province). N.p.

———, ———. 1940. *Kōso-shō Shōkō ken nōson jittai chōsa hōkokusho* 江蘇省松江縣農村實態調查報告書 (Report on the investigation of actual conditions in the countryside of Songjiang county, Jiangsu province). N.p.

———, ———. 1939a. *Shanhai tokubetsushi Kateiku nōson jittai chōsa hōkokusho* 上海特別市嘉定區農村實態調查報告書 (Report on the investigation of actual conditions in the countryside of Jiading district in the special municipality of Shanghai). N.p.

———, ———. 1939b. *Kōso-shō Jōjuku ken nōson jittai chōsa hōkokusho* 江蘇省常熟縣農村實態調查報告書 (Report on the investigation of actual conditions in the countryside of Changhsu county, Jiangsu province). N.p.

———, ———. 1939c. *Kōso-shō Taisō ken nōson jittai chōsa hōkokusho* 江蘇省太倉縣農村實態調查報告書 (Report on the investigation of actual conditions in the countryside of Taicang county, Jiangsu province). N.p.

Miu Qiyu 繆啓愉. 1982. "Taihu diqu tangpu yutian de xingcheng he fazhan" 太湖地區塘浦圩田的形成和發展 (Formation and development of Lake Tai's canals and embanked fields), *Zhongguo nongshi*, no. 1: 12–32.

———. 1959. "Wuyue Qianshi zai Taihu diqu de yutian zhidu he shuili xitong" 吳越錢氏在太湖地區的圩田制度和水利系統 (The embanked fields and water-control system of the Qians of Wuyue in the Lake Tai area), *Nongshi yanjiu jikan*, 2: 139–53.

Morita Akira 森田明. 1967. *Shindai kōnan ni okeru uden suiri no ichi kōsatsu* 清代江南における圩田水利の一考察 (Study of yutian water control in Jiangnan during the Qing), *Shakai keizai shi gaku*, 33.5: 485–505.

Murphey, Rhoads. 1977. *The Outsiders*. Ann Arbor: University of Michigan Press.

Nanhui xian zhi 南滙縣志 (Gazetteer of Nanhui county). 1879.

Nanhui xian xuzhi 南滙縣續志 (Continuation of the gazetteer of Nanhui county). 1929.

Nanji zhi 南畿志 (Gazetteer of the southern capital). 1522–66 (Ming Jiajing).

Nanjing daxue lishi xi, Ming-Qing shi yanjiu shi 南京大學歷史系明清史研究室, ed. 1981. *Ming Qing zibenzhuyi mengya yanjiu lunwen ji* 明清資本主義萌芽研究

論文集 (Research articles on the sprouting of capitalism in the Ming and Qing). Shanghai: Renmin chubanshe.

Niida Noboru 仁井田陞. 1964 [1933]. *Tōryō shūi* 唐令拾遺 (Forgotten fragments of the Tang code). Tokyo: Tōkyō daigaku shuppansha.

Ning Ke 寧可. 1980a. "You guan Handai nongye shengchan de jige shuzi" 有關漢代農業生產的幾個數字 (Some figures on agricultural production in Han times), *Beijing shiyuan xuebao*, no. 3: 76–90.

———. 1980b. "Shilun Zhongguo fengjian shehui de renkou wenti" 試論中國封建社會的人口問題 (A tentative discussion of the population problem in China's feudal society), *Zhongguo shi yanjiu*, no. 1: 3–19.

Oi, Jean C. n.d. *State and Peasant in Contemporary China*. Berkeley: University of California Press. Forthcoming.

Ogilvie, Sheilagh C. 1985. "Corporatism and Regulation in Rural Industry: Woollen Weaving in Württemberg, 1690–1740." Ph.D. dissertation, Cambridge University.

Pan, Min-te 潘敏德. 1985. *Zhongguo jindai diandangye zhi yanjiu* 中國近代典當業之研究 (Study of pawnshops in modern China). Taibei: Shifan daxue lishi yanjiusuo (zhuankan, 13).

Parish, William L., and Martin King Whyte. 1978. *Village and Family in Contemporary China*. Chicago: University of Chicago Press.

Perkins, Dwight. 1969. *Agricultural Development in China, 1368–1968*. Chicago: Aldine.

Perry, Elizabeth J. 1980. *Rebels and Revolutionaries in North China, 1845–1945*. Stanford, Calif.: Stanford University Press.

Polanyi, Karl, Conrad M. Arensberg, and Harry W. Pearson, eds. 1957. *Trade and Market in the Early Empires: Economies in History and Theory*. Glencoe, Ill.: Free Press.

Potter, Jack, and Sulamith Potter. n.d. *China's Peasants: The Anthropology of a Revolution*. Forthcoming.

Potter, Sulamith Heins. 1983. "The Position of Peasants in Modern China's Social Order," *Modern China*, 9.4: 465–99.

Putterman, Louis. 1989. "Entering the Post-Collective Era in North China: Dahe Township," *Modern China*, 15.3: 275–320.

Qinchuan sanzhi buji 琴川三志補記 (Supplement to the three gazetteers of Changshu). 1831.

Qinchuan sanzhi buji xubian 琴川三志補記續編 (Continuation of the supplement to the three gazetteers of Changshu). 1835.

Qingpu xian zhi 青浦縣志 (Gazetteer of Qingpu county). 1879.

Qingpu xian xuzhi 青浦縣續志 (Continuation of the gazetteer of Qingpu county). 1934.

Rawski, Thomas G. 1989. *Economic Growth in Prewar China*. Berkeley: University of California Press.

Rowe, William T. 1984. *Hankow: Commerce and Society in a Chinese City, 1796–1889*. Stanford, Calif.: Stanford University Press.

Schultz, Theodore W. 1964. *Transforming Traditional Agriculture*. New Haven, Conn.: Yale University Press.

Schurmann, Franz. 1968. *Ideology and Organization in Communist China*. 2d ed. Berkeley: University of California Press.

Scott, James C. 1976. *The Moral Economy of the Peasant: Rebellion and Subsistence in Southeast Asia*. New Haven, Conn.: Yale University Press.

Selden, Mark. 1971. *The Yenan Way in Revolutionary China*. Cambridge, Mass.: Harvard University Press.

Shanghai nongye dili 上海農業地理 (Agricultural geography of Shanghai). 1978. Shanghai: Shanghai kexue jishu chubanshe.

Shanghai shehui kexueyuan jingji yanjiu suo 上海社會科學院經濟研究所. 1958. *Shanghai jiefang qianhou wujia ziliao huibian, 1921–1957* 上海解放前後物價資料滙編 (Compendium of materials on the price of goods in Shanghai before and after liberation). Shanghai: Renmin chubanshe.

Shanghai tongji nianjian 上海統計年鑑 (Statistical yearbook of Shanghai). 1987. Shanghai: Shanghai renmin chubanshe.

Shanghai xian zhi 上海縣志 (Gazetteer of Shanghai county). 1935, 1872.

Shanghai xian xuzhi 上海縣續志 (Continuation of the gazetteer of Shanghai county). 1918.

Shanin, Teodor. 1986. "Introduction" to A. V. Chayanov, *The Theory of Peasant Economy*. Madison: University of Wisconsin Press.

———. 1972. *The Awkward Class: Political Sociology of Peasantry in a Developing Society: Russia 1910–1925*. London: Oxford University Press.

Shenshi nongshu 沈氏農書 (Mr. Shen's agricultural treatise), 1936 [ca. 1640]. In *Congshu jicheng*, no. 1468. Shanghai: Shangwu yinshuguan.

Shue, Vivienne. 1988. *The Reach of the State: Sketches of the Chinese Body Politic*. Stanford, Calif.: Stanford University Press.

———. 1980. *Peasant China in Transition: The Dynamics of Development Toward Socialism, 1949–1956*. Berkeley: University of California Press.

———. 1976. "Reorganizing Rural Trade: Unified Purchase and Socialist Transformation," *Modern China*, 2.1: 104–34.

Shunyi xian dang'an guan 順義縣檔案館. Shunyi xian dang'an 順義縣檔案 (Shunyi county archives). [Classified by category, *juan* no., and date.]

Sicular, Terry, 1986. "Recent Agricultural Price Policies and Their Effects: The case of Shandong." In Joint Economic Committee of the U.S. Congress, ed., *China's Economy Looks Toward the Year 2000*, vol. 1, pp. 407–30. Washington, D.C.: U.S. Government Printing Office.

Skinner, G. William. 1977. "Regional Urbanization in Nineteenth-Century China." In G. William Skinner, ed., *The City in Late Imperial China*, pp. 211–52. Stanford, Calif.: Stanford University Press.

———. 1964–65. "Marketing and Social Structure in Rural China," 3 parts, *Journal of Asian Studies*, 24.1: 3–44; 24.2: 195–228; 24.3: 363–99.

Smith, Adam. 1976 [1775–76]. *An Inquiry into the Nature and Causes of the Wealth of Nations*. 4th ed. 3 vols. London: n.p.

Solomon, Susan Gross. 1977. *The Soviet Agrarian Debate: A Controversy in Social Science, 1923-1929.* Boulder, Col.: Westview Press.

Songjiang fu zhi 松江府志 (Gazetteer of Songjiang prefecture). 1817, 1512.

Songjiang fu xuzhi 松江府續志 (Continuation of the gazetteer of Songjiang prefecture). 1883.

Suzhou fu zhi 蘇州府志 (Gazetteer of Suzhou prefecture). 1883, 1379.

Taicang zhou zhi 太倉州志 (Gazetteer of Taicang Department). 1919.

Takikawa Kitarō 滝川亀太郎. 1960. *Shiji huizhu kaozheng* 史記会注考證 (Compendium of commentaries on the *Shiji*). Tokyo: Tōkyō daigaku Tōyō bunka kenkyūjo.

Tan Qixiang 譚其驤. 1982. "Shanghai shi dalu bufen de hailu bianqian he kaifa guocheng" 上海市大陸部分的海陸變遷和開發過程 (The process of change in ocean and land and in the development of the continental portion of Shanghai municipality) [with postscript added]. In *Shanghai difang shi ziliao* 上海地方史資料 (Source materials on Shanghai local history). Shanghai: Shanghai shehui kexue chubanshe.

———. 1973. "Shanghai shi dalu bufen de hailu bianqian he kaifa guocheng" [see preceding entry], *Kaogu*, no. 1.

Tao Xu 陶煦. 1884. *Zuhe* 租覈 (The truth about rents). In Suzuki Tomō 鈴木智夫, ed., *Kindai Chūgoku nōson shakaishi kenkyū* 近代中國農村社会史研究 (Study of modern China's rural social history). Tokyo: Daian, 1967.

Tao Youzhi 陶友之, ed. 1988. *Sunan moshi yu zhifu zhi dao* 蘇南模式與致富之道 (The southern Jiangsu model and path to prosperity). Shanghai: Shanghai shehui kexue chubanshe.

Tilly, Charles, ed. 1978. *Historical Studies of Changing Fertility.* Princeton, N.J.: Princeton University Press.

Tudiweiyuanhui 土地委員會 (Land Commission). 1937. *Quanguo tudi diaocha baogao gangyao* 全國土地調查報告綱要 (Abstract of the report on the nationwide investigation of land). Nanjing.

Walder, Andrew. 1986. *Communist Neo-Traditionalism: Work and Authority in Chinese Industry.* Berkeley: University of California Press.

Walker, Kenneth. 1984. *Food Grain Procurement and Consumption in China.* Cambridge, Eng.: Cambridge University Press.

Walker, Kathy. 1986. "Merchants, Peasants and Industry: The Political Economy of the Cotton Textile Industry, Nantong County, 1895-1935." Ph.D. dissertation, University of California, Los Angeles.

Wallerstein, Immanuel. 1979. *The Capitalist World Economy.* Cambridge, Eng.: Cambridge University Press.

———. 1974. *The Modern World-System: Capitalist Agriculture and the Origins of the European World-Economy in the Sixteenth Century.* New York: Academic Press.

Wang Wenchu 王文楚. 1983. "Shanghai shi dalu diqu chengzhen de xingcheng yu fazhan" 上海市大陸地區城鎮的形成與發展 (The formation and development of cities and towns in the mainland area of Shanghai municipality), *Lishi dili*, 3: 98-114.

Wang Yeh-chien. 1973. *Land Taxation in Imperial China, 1750–1911*. Cambridge, Mass.: Harvard University Press.

Wang Yuru 王玉茹. 1987. "Lun liangci shijie dazhan zhi jian Zhongguo jingji de fazhan" 論兩次世界大戰之間中國經濟的發展 (On the development of the Chinese economy between the two world wars), *Zhongguo jingjishi yanjiu*, no. 2: 97–109.

Wei Songshan 魏嵩山. 1979. "Taihu shuixi de lishi bianqian" 太湖水系的歷史變遷 (Historical changes in the Lake Tai river system), *Fudan xuebao*, no. 2: 58–64.

Weir, David. 1984. "Rather Never Than Late: Celibacy and Age at Marriage in English Cohort Fertility, 1541–1871," *Journal of Family History*, no. 9: 340–54.

Wittfogel, Karl August. 1957. *Oriental Despotism: A Comparative Study of Total Power*. New Haven, Conn.: Yale University Press.

Wolf, Margery. 1985. *Revolution Postponed: Women in Contemporary China*. Stanford, Calif.: Stanford University Press.

Wong, Christine. 1988. "Interpreting Rural Industrial Growth in the Post-Mao Period," *Modern China*, 14.1: 3–30.

Wong, R. Bin, Pierre-Etienne Will, and James Lee, with the assistance of Peter C. Perdue and Jean Oi. 1987. *Nourish the People: The State Granary System in China, 1650–1850*. Ann Arbor: Center for Chinese Studies, University of Michigan.

Wright, Mary Clabaugh. 1957. *The Last Stand of Chinese Conservatism: The T'ung-Chih Restoration, 1862–1874*. Stanford, Calif.: Stanford University Press.

Wrigley, E. Anthony. 1985. "Urban Growth and Agricultural Change: England and the Continent in the Early Modern Period," *Journal of Interdisciplinary History*, 15.4: 683–728.

Wu Chengming 吳承明. 1985. *Zhongguo zibenzhuyi de mengya* 中國資本主義的萌芽 (The sprouting of capitalism in China), vol. 1 of *Zhongguo zibenzhuyi fazhan shi* 中國資本主義發展史 (History of the development of capitalism in China). Beijing: Xinhua shudian.

———. 1984. "Woguo ban zhimindi ban fengjian guonei shichang" 我國半殖民地半封建國內市場 (The semicolonial and semifeudal domestic market in our country), *Lishi yanjiu*, no. 2: 110–21.

Wu Hui 吳慧. 1985. *Zhongguo lidai liangshi muchan yanjiu* 中國歷代糧食畝產研究 (Study of per-*mu* grain yields during China's successive dynasties). Beijing: Nongye chubanshe.

Wu Shenyuan 吳申元. 1986. *Zhongguo renkou sixiangshi gao* 中國人口思想史稿 (Draft history of China's demographic thought). Chongqing: Zhongguo shehui kexue chubanshe.

Wujiang xian zhi 吳江縣志 (Gazetteer of Wujiang county). 1747.

Wujiang zhi 吳江志 (Gazetteer of Wujiang). 1488.

Wuxi Jingui xian zhi 無錫金匱縣志 (Gazetteer of Wuxi and Jingui counties). 1881.

Wuxian zhi 吳縣志 (Gazetteer of Wuxian county). 1933.

Wuxing beizhi 吳興備志 (Draft gazetteer of Wuxing [Huzhou]). 1642. In *Siku quanshu zhenben*, vol. 9. Taibei: Shangwu yinshuguan.

Wuxing zhanggu ji 吳興掌故集 (Compendium of anecdotes about Wuxing [Huzhou]). 1560. 17 vols. Taibei: Chengwen shuju.

Xi Jin shi xiaolu 錫金識小錄 (Wuxi Jingui gazetteer, miscellaneous items). 1752.

Xia Lingen 夏林根. 1984. "Lun jindai Shanghai diqu mian fangzhi shougongye de bianhua" 論近代上海地區棉紡織手工業的變化 (On changes in the cotton handicraft spinning and weaving industry in the Shanghai area during modern times), *Zhongguo jingjishi yanjiu*, no. 3: 24–31.

Xiushui xian zhi 秀水縣志 (Gazetteer of Xiushui [Jiaxing] county). 1596.

Xu Daofu 許道夫. 1983. *Zhongguo jindai nongye shengchan ji maoyi tongji ziliao* 中國近代農業生產及貿易統計資料 (Statistical materials on agricultural production and trade in modern China). Shanghai: Renmin chubanshe.

Xu Guangqi 徐光啓. 1956 [1639]. *Nongzheng quanshu* 農政全書 (Complete treatise on farm administration). Shanghai: Zhonghua shuju.

Xu Jinzhi 徐近之. 1981. "Woguo lishi qihou xue gaishu" 我國歷史氣候學概述 (General account of historical climatology in our country). In *Zhongguo lishi dili luncong* 中國歷史地理論叢 (Essays on China's historical geography), vol. 1, pp. 176–95. Xi'an: Shaanxi renmin chubanshe.

Xu Xinwu 徐新吾. n.d. "Zhongguo tubu chanxiao guji, 1840–1936" 中國土布產銷估計 (Estimate of the production and sale of native cloth in China). In *Zhongguo zibenzhuyi fazhan shi* 中國資本主義發展史 (History of the development of capitalism in China), vol. 2. Forthcoming.

———. 1981a. *Yapian zhanzheng qian Zhongguo mianfangzhi shougongye de shangpin shengchan yu zibenzhuyi mengya wenti* 鴉片戰爭前中國棉紡織手工業的商品生產與資本主義萌芽問題 (Commodity production in the cotton handicraft spinning and weaving industry in China before the Opium War and the issue of the sprouts of capitalism). N.p.: Jiangsu renmin chubanshe.

———. 1981b. "Zhongguo he Riben mianfangzhi ye: zibenzhuyi mengya de bijiao yanjiu" 中國和日本棉紡織業:資本主義萌芽的比較研究 (The cotton spinning and weaving industries of China and Japan: a comparative study of the sprouting of capitalism), *Lishi yanjiu*, no. 6: 69–80.

Xue Muqiao, ed. 1982. *Almanac of China's Economy, 1981, with Economic Statistics for 1949–1980*. Hong Kong: Modern Cultural Company.

Yan Zhongping 嚴中平 et al., eds. 1955. *Zhongguo jindai jingjishi tongji ziliao xuanji* 中國近代經濟史統計資料選輯 (Selected statistical materials on modern Chinese economic history). Beijing: Kexue chubanshe.

Yang, C. K. 1959. *Chinese Communist Society: The Family and the Village*. Cambridge, Mass.: M.I.T. Press.

Ye Mengzhu 葉夢珠. 1935 [ca. 1693]. *Yue shi bian* 閱世編. In *Shanghai Zhanggu congshu* 上海掌故叢書 (Compendium of anecdotes about Shanghai). N.p.

Yeh, Kung-chia, and Ta-chung Liu. 1965. *The Economy of the Chinese Mainland: National Income and Economic Development, 1933–1959*. Princeton, N.J.: Princeton University Press.

Yip, Honming. 1988. "The Political Economy of Tobacco and Textiles, Weixian, Shandong." Ph.D. dissertation, University of California, Los Angeles.

Zhang Lüxiang 張履祥. 1658. *Bunongshu* 補農書 (Supplements to the [*Mr. Shen's*] *Agricultural Treatise*). In Chen Hengli and Wang Da, eds., listed above.

Zhang Xinyi 張心一. 1931. "Shandong sheng nongye gaikuang guji baogao"

山東省農業概況估計報告 (Report on the estimating of the general agricultural situation in Shandong province), *Tongji yuebao*, 3.1: 20–45.

———. 1930a. "Jiangsu sheng nongye gaikuang guji baogao" 江蘇省農業概況估計報告 (Report on the estimating of the general agricultural situation in Jiangsu province), *Tongji yuebao*, 2.7: 23–51.

———. 1930b. "Hebei sheng nongye gaikuang guji baogao" 河北省農業概況估計報告 (Report on the estimating of the general agricultural situation in Hebei province), *Tongji yuebao*, 2.11: 1–56.

Zhang Youyi 章有義, ed. 1957. *Zhongguo jindai nongyeshi ziliao* 中國近代農業史資料 (Source materials on the agricultural history of modern China). Vols. 2 and 3: *1912–1927, 1927–1937*. Beijing: Sanlian shudian.

Zhang Yulin 張雨林. 1984. "Nongye shengyu laodongli de fenceng zhuanyi—Wujiang xian sige xingzhengcun de diaocha" 農業剩余勞動力的分層轉移—吳江縣四個行政村的調查 (The stratified transfer of surplus labor in agriculture—an investigation of four administrative villages in Wujiang county). In Jiangsu sheng xiao chengzhen yanjiu keti zu, ed. 1984, listed above, pp. 266–85.

Zhang Yulin and Shen Guanbao 沈關寶. 1984. "Yige nongcun quyuxing shangpin liutong zhongxin de xingcheng he fazhan" 一個農村區域性商品流通中心的形成和發展 (Formation and development of a rural regional commodity circulation center). In ibid., pp. 107–25.

Zhenyang xian zhi 鎮洋縣志 (Gazetteer of Zhenyang county). 1919.

Zhongguo nongcun fazhan wenti yanjiuzu 中國農村發展問題研究組. 1985–86. *Nongcun, jingji, shehui* 農村, 經濟, 社會 (Villages, economy, and society). Vols. 1–4. Beijing.

Zhongguo nongye nianjian 中國農業年鑑 (Statistical yearbook of Chinese agriculture). Vols. for 1981, 1985–87. Beijing: Nongye chubanshe.

Zhongguo nongye yichan yanjiushi 中國農業遺產研究室. 1984. *Zhongguo nongxueshi* 中國農學史 (History of agronomy in China). 3 vols. Beijing: Kexue chubanshe.

Zhongguo renmin daxue Zhongguo lishi jiaoyanshi 中國人民大學中國歷史教研室, ed. 1957. *Zhongguo zibenzhuyi mengya wenti taolunji* 中國資本主義萌芽問題討論集 (Essays on the question of the sprouts of capitalism in China). 2 vols. Beijing: Sanlian shudian.

Zhongguo shiye zhi: Jiangsu sheng 中國實業誌:江蘇省, (Gazetteer of China's industry and commerce: Jiangsu province). 1933. Shanghai: Shiyebu guoji maoyi ju.

Zhongguo tongji nianjian 中國統計年鑑 (Statistical yearbook of China). Vols. for 1983–84, 1986–88. Beijing: Zhongguo tongji chubanshe.

Zhonghua renmin gongheguo gong'an fagui xuanbian 中華人民共和國公安法規選編 (Selected public security laws and regulations of the People's Republic of China). 1982. Beijing: Falü chubanshe.

Zhonghua renmin gongheguo quanguo renmin daibiao dahui changwu weiyuanhui gongbao 中華人民共和國全國人民代表大會常務委員會公報 (Bulletin of the Standing Committee of the National People's Congress of the People's Republic of China). 1986. No. 6.

Zhongyang renmin zhengfu nongyebu 中央人民政府農業部. 1950. *Huabei dianxing cun diaocha* 華北典型村調查 (Investigations of representative villages in North China). N.p.

Zhu Zongzhou 朱宗宙. 1981. "Ming mo Qing chu Taihu diqu de nongye guyong laodong" 明末清初太湖地區的農業僱佣勞動 (Agricultural wage labor in the Taihu area during the Ming-Qing transition). In Nanjing daxue lishi xi, ed., listed above, pp. 571–601.

CHARACTER LIST

Character List

Very well-known place-names (e.g., Beijing, Tianjin) and personal names appearing only in the Appendix D tables are not included. See the Sources Cited section of the References for the characters on Chinese and Japanese works cited.

a-ge 阿哥
a-jie 阿姐
a-shu 阿叔
Ai nan zao yihao 矮南早一號
Aijiao nan tehao 矮腳南特號
Aiqi 艾祁
Amano Motonosuke 天野元之助
Anhetou 庵河頭
Anting 安亭
Bai Chengzhi 柏成志
Baihejiang 白鶴江
bangong bannong 半工半農
bao 保
bao 包
Bao Shichen 包世臣
Bao'an *xiang* 保安鄉
Baodi *xian* 寶坻縣
baogan daohu 包幹到戶
baohuang 報荒
baojia 保甲
Baoshan *xian* 寶山縣
baozhang 保長
baozheng 保正
Batuan 八團
bayang 拔秧

Beicang 北倉
Beiqian 北錢
Bei Xujialu 北徐家路
Beiyan *zhen* 北延鎮
Beiyutang 北俞塘
Bencao gangmu 本草綱目
biaobu 標布
Bocizhuang 撥賜莊
Bu nongshu 補農書
buban 不辦
buhao 不好
Cai Zuyun 蔡祖雲
caibing 茱餅
Canye gaijin weiyuanhui
  蠶業改進委員會
Cao Xuanwei 曹宣慰
Caojialu 曹家路
Caojing *gongshe* 漕涇公社
caomi 漕米
chaguan 茶館
changgong 長工
Changjing *zhen* 長涇鎮
Changli *xian* 昌黎縣
Changlou *dadui* 長漊大隊
Changshu *xian* 常熟縣

changzhang 場長
changzhang 廠長
Changzhou *fu* 常州府
Changzhou *xian* 長洲縣
chanzhi 產值
Chedun *gongshe* 車墩公社
Chefang *gongshe* 車坊公社
Chelu *cun* 車路村
chen 沉
Chen Caifang 陳彩芳
Chen Donglin 陳冬林
Chen Mingqu 陳明渠
Chen Shoulin 陳壽林
Chen Yongkang 陳永康
Chen Yucheng 陳玉成
Chengbei *xiang* 城北鄉
Chengdong *gongshe* 城東公社
Chenghu 澄湖
Chenjiahang 陳家行
Chenjiaxiang *dadui* 陳家巷大隊
chi 尺
chi guojia fan 吃國家飯
chi jiti fan 吃集體飯
Chongde *xian* 崇德縣
Chonggu 重固
Chongming *xian* 崇明縣
Chu Tongqing 褚同慶
Chuansha *xian* 川沙縣
chuji hezuo she 初級合作社
Chunxi 淳熙
chuzhong 初中
cu siliao 粗飼料
culiang 粗糧
cun 村
cunfu 村副
cunji 村集
Cunqian *cun* 村前村
cunzhang 村長
cunzheng 村正
cunzuo 村佐
da [*dai*] 埭

Da Ajie 大阿姐
da pingjun 大平均
dashitang 大食堂
da siqing 大四清
daban 大辦
dabaogan 大包幹
dabaoji 踏包機
Dabeiguan 大北關
Dachang 大場
dadui guanli weiyuanhui
　大隊管理委員會
dahua 大花
Dai Jincai 戴進才
Dajiang *gongsi* 大江公司
daminggou 大明溝
dan 擔
dang zhibu 黨支部
dang zhibu shuji 黨支部書記
Daoguang 道光
Dasheng shachang 大生紗廠
Datuan 大團
dayu bang xiaoyu,
　xiaoyu bang xiami
　大魚幫小魚,
　小魚幫蝦米
dayu chi xiaoyu, xiaoyu chi xiami
　大魚吃小魚, 小魚吃蝦米
Dazhai *dadui* 大寨大隊
dazhuan 大專
Deng Zhengfan 鄧正凡
di 地
dian 典
dianmai 典賣
Dianshanhu 澱山湖
ding 丁
Ding Wenjiang 丁文江
Ding Yonglin 丁永林
dingchan 定產
dinggou 定購
Dingjia *cun* 丁家村
dingti 頂替

dingxiao 定銷
Dongbang dadui 東浜大隊
dou 斗
dui/cun ban gongye 隊/村辦工業
Fangtai 方泰
Fanhang 范行
fanxiaoliang 返銷糧
Fei Xiaotong 費孝通
Feng Senyun 鳳森雲
Fenghuangshan 鳳凰山
Fengjiabang 封家浜
Fengjing *zhen* 楓涇鎮
Fengqiao 楓橋
Fengrun *xian* 豐潤縣
fengsu 風俗
Fengwei *gongshe* 楓圍公社
Fengxian *xian* 奉賢縣
Fengyang *xian* 鳳陽縣
Foshan 佛山
fu cunzhang 副村長
Fu Jixin 傅紀新
Fu ju 傅菊
fukua zhi feng 浮誇之風
funü duizhang 婦女隊長
funü zhuren 婦女主任
fushi 副食
fushi butie 副食補貼
fuwu dui 服務隊
fuye 副業
gailiang tubu 改良土布
ganqing 感情
Gao Agen 高阿根
Gao Botang 高伯堂
Gao Buzhen 高補珍
Gao Changsheng 高長生
Gao Dajie 高大姐
Gao Huojin 高火金
Gao Jindi 高金弟
Gao Jinying 高金英
Gao Jinyun 高金雲
Gao Laigen 高來根

Gao Liangsheng 高良生
Gao Meiying 高美英
Gao Quansheng 高全生
Gao Shigen 高世根
Gao Shitang 高世堂
Gao Yindi 高引娣
Gao Yonglin 高永林
Gao Yongnian 高永年
Gao Youfa 高友發
Gao Yuchang 高裕昌
Gao Zonghan 高宗漢
Gaochangmiao 高昌廟
Gaohang 高行
Gaohangnan *zhen* 高行南鎮
gaoji hezuo she 高級合作社
Gaojiachang 高家場
Gaojiada 高家埭
Gaoqiao 高橋
Gaoyang *xian* 高陽縣
Gelong 葛隆
geti qiye 個體企業
gezihua 格子化
gong 工
gongfen zhi 工分值
Gongjialu 龔家路
gongliang 公糧
gongtong zhifu 共同致富
gongye 工業
Goujian, Yue wang 勾踐, 越王
gu gongren 僱工人
Gu Mingzhi 顧銘芝
Gu Yanwu 顧炎武
Gu Yindi 顧引娣
Gu Youcai 顧友才
guangtu zhongmin 廣土衆民
Guangxu 光緒
Guangxue lingjian chang
　　光學零件廠
Guanjialong 管家衖
guanli 官利
guanliao zhuyi 官僚主義

guantian 官田
guanxi 關係
Guanzhong 關中
Guanzi 管子
Gucun 顧村
guding zichan yuanzhi 固定資產原值
Gui'an xian 歸安縣
Guijiaqiao 桂家橋
Gujialu 顧家路
Guo Zhuying 郭竹英
guojia 國家
guojia ganbu 國家幹部
Guomindang 國民黨
Gutangqiao 古塘橋
Hai'an xian 海安縣
haiguan dan 海關担
Haimen ting 海門廳
handi 旱地
Hangzhouwan 杭州灣
Hanhaitang 捍海塘
hantian 旱田
He Chungen 何春根
He Dexing 何德興
He Deyu 何德餘
He Guohua 何國華
He Huihua 何會花
He Huosheng 何火生
He Huoyun 何火雲
He Jinlin 何金林
He Kuifa 何奎發
He Shulin 何書林
He Shunyu 何順餘
He Shutang 何書堂
He Tugen 何土根
He Xiaomao 何小毛
He Xiudi 何秀弟
He Xiugen 何秀根
He Yonggen 何永根
He Yonglong 何勇龍
Hejiada 何家埭

Hejin cun 鶴金村
Hengmian 橫沔
Hengshan 橫山
hengtang 橫塘
heping tugai 和平土改
Heqing 合慶
hetonggong 合同工
hezuo qiye 合作企業
Hangtou 航頭
Hongdong xian 洪洞縣
Honghai xiang 紅海鄉
Hongzhi 弘治
Houjiamuqiao 侯家木橋
Houjiaying 侯家營
Houxiazhai 后夏寨
Huaihe 淮河
Huailu xian 獲鹿縣
Huan [gong], (Qi) 齊桓公
Huang Bingquan 黃冰泉
Huang Daopo 黃道婆
Huang Jinkun 黃金坤
Huang Maonan 黃毛南
Huang Xiyu 黃錫餘
Huangdu 黃渡
Huangpujiang 黃浦江
Huating xian 華亭縣
Huayang zhen 華陽鎮
Huayang xiang 華陽鄉
Huayangqiao 華陽橋
huiguan jin 會館斤
huishou 會首
hukoujuan 戶口捐
hunzhong 混種
huojiandui 火箭隊
huomai 活賣
Huoxian zhihuibu 火綫指揮部
Huzhou fu 湖州府
ji 續
ji 集
jia 甲

Jia Dan 郏亶
Jiading *xian* 嘉定縣
Jiajing 嘉靖
Jiaju chang 傢俱廠
Jianbangqiao 戗浜橋
Jiancha weiyuanhui 監察委員會
jiandu laodong 監督勞動
Jiang Delong 蔣德龍
Jiang Gao 姜皋
Jiang Xiaochen 蔣曉晨
Jiangnan tubu shi 江南土布史
Jiangnan (zhizaoju) 江南製造局
Jiangning 江寧
Jiangwan 江灣
Jiangyin *xian* 江陰縣
jianian 加拈
Jiaqing 嘉慶
jiating fuye 家庭副業
Jiaxing *diqu* (*fu*) 嘉興地區(府)
Jidian chang 機電廠
jiegao 桔槔
jieji ganqing 階級感情
jieshangren 街上人
jigongyuan 記工員
jihu 機戶
Jin 金
jin 斤
jin 堁
Jin Tangmei 金堂梅
Jin Yongqiang 金勇強
Jin Zhitang 金志堂
Jinan 濟南
Jing Defu 景德福
jingji xiaoyi 經濟效益
jingji baoguanyuan 經濟保管員
Jingjiang *xian* 靖江縣
jingkuan 警款
Jingui *xian* 金匱縣
Jingxi 荊溪
Jinhuiqiao 金滙橋

Jinjiada 金家埭
Jinjiahang 金家行
Jinjiaxiang 金家巷
Jinshan *xian* 金山縣
jinshi 進士
Jinze 金澤
jishi 集市
jiti qiye 集體企業
Jiwang 紀王
juan 卷
juemai 絕賣
junmi 軍米
Kaifeng 開封
Kailuan 開灤
Kaixiangong 開弦弓
Kangxi 康熙
keyi 可以
koujiao di 口叫地
kouliang di 口糧地
kouliang tian 口糧田
Kuang Zhong 況鐘
kuang 筐
Kunshan *xian* 崑山縣
Kunshan 崑山
kyōdōtai 共同體
la guanxi 拉關係
langdang gong 浪蕩工
Lao lai qing 老來青
laodong shengchan lü 勞動生產率
Laogang 老港
Laoren tang 老人堂
Lengshuigou 冷水溝
li 里
Li Peihua 李佩華
Li Shengbo 李昇伯
Li Shizhen 李時珍
Li Shunxiu 李順秀
Li Xianglin 李祥林
lianchan chengbao 聯產承包
lianchan daohu 聯產到戶

lianchan jichou 聯產計酬
liangshi baoguanyuan 糧食保管員
liangshi sanding 糧食三定
liangtou cu, zhongjian xi
　兩頭粗，中間細
Liangxiang *xian* 艮鄉縣
Lianqi 練祁
Lianxing *she* 聯星社
Liaoqianjun 撩淺軍
Lihutang 里護塘
lijia 里甲
Lijiajiao 李家角
lijin 釐金
Linqing 臨清
linshi gong 臨時工
Liqin 里秦
Lishui *xian* 溧水縣
Litai shachang 利泰紗廠
litu bulixiang 離土不離鄉
Liu Daorong 劉道榮
Liu'an *xian* 六安縣
Liuhang 劉行
Liuhe 瀏河
Liujiahang 劉家行
Liuxia 劉夏
Liuzao 六竈
Liuzaowan 六竈灣
Lixiahe 里下河
Longhua 龍華
Louxian 婁縣
loufang 樓房
Loujiang 婁江
Loutang 婁塘
Lu Bingxian 陸秉咸
Lu Danan 陸大囡
Lu Defa 陸德法
Lu Desheng 陸德生
Lu Dirong 陸迪榮
Lu Genshan 陸根山
Lu Gensheng 陸根生
Lu Guiquan 陸桂泉

Lu Guantong 陸關通
Lu Hailai 陸海來
Lu Haitang 陸海堂
Lu Jintang 陸金堂
Lu Jinyu 陸金餘
Lu Longshun 陸龍順
Lu Longtan 陸龍潭
Lu Maosheng 陸茂生
Lu Maoyuan 陸茂園
Lu Mingqiang 陸明强
Lu Minghua 陸明華
Lu Shiming 陸侍明
Lu Shoutang 陸壽堂
Lu Shudong 陸樹東
Lu Shuifang 陸水芳
Lu Xuefang 陸雪芳
Lu Yongzhou 陸永舟
Lu Yulian 陸玉蓮
Lu Zicai 陸子才
Luancheng *xian* 欒城縣
Luduqiao 陸渡橋
Lujiada 陸家埭
Lujiahang 陸家行
Luo Dian 羅點
Luodian 羅店
luoxuan ganbu 落選幹部
Ma Dalong 馬大龍
madoubing 蔴豆餅
Maihuaqiao 賣花橋
Majishan 馬跡山
Mancheng *xian* 滿城縣
manggong 忙工
mangyue 忙月
Mao Dun 茅盾
Mao Gen 茅艮
Maogang *gongshe* 泖港公社
Maojinggang 泖涇港
Maotiao chang 毛條廠
meidoubing 梅豆餅
Meigang *xiang* 梅港鄉
Meiyuan 梅源

Mengjiashang 孟家上
mianbing 棉餅
Miaogang *dadui* 廟港大隊
Miaogang *gongshe* 廟港公社
Michang *cun* 米廠村
mihang 米行
minbing lianzhang 民兵連長
minbing paizhang 民兵排長
Mingxing *dadui* 明星大隊
Minhang 閔行
mintian 民田
mu 畝
Mushao *zhen* 木杓鎮
Nanda 南埭
Nandaqiao 南大橋
Nanhui *xian* 南滙縣
Nanmen 南門
nannü wenti 男女問題
Nanqiao 南橋
Nantong *diqu* 南通地區
Nantong *shi* (*xian*) 南通市（縣）
Nanxiang 南翔
Nanxujialu 南徐家路
Nanxun *zhen* 南潯鎮
niaosu 尿素
Nicheng 泥城
niqiu 泥鰍
nongcun shehui zongchanzhi
　農村社會總產值
nongchang 農場
Nongji chang 農機場
Nongken 58 hao 農墾58號
nongye 農業
nongye shouru 農業收入
nongye shui 農業稅
Old Tung Pao [Tongbao] 老通寶
Panlong 盤龍
Panlonghui 盤龍滙
peigong 陪工
Peixian 沛縣
peiyang duixiang 培養對象

Peng Dehuai 彭德懷
Pengpu 彭浦
pengqi 蟛蜞
pi 匹
Pin xiazhong nong zaofan dui
　貧下中農造反隊
Ping Yajuan 平亞娟
Pinggu *xian* 平谷縣
pingjia 平價
Pingwang 平望
Qian Pu 錢樸
Qian Yonglian 錢永連
qiangshou 搶收
qiangzhong 搶種
Qianliangge *zhuang* 前梁各莊
Qianlong 乾隆
Qianmentang 錢門塘
Qiantangjiang 錢塘江
qianzhuang 錢莊
Qibao 七寶
Qimin yaoshu 齊民要術
qing sanzhao 請三朝
Qingchun 青村
Qingdao 青島
Qingdun 青墩
Qinglong 青龍
qingming 清明
Qingpu *xian* 青浦縣
Qituanhang 七團行
qiushou 秋收
qiuyin 蚯蚓
qiuzheng 秋徵
qiuzhong 秋種
qiyueban jie 七月半節
qu 區
quanmian fazhan 全面發展
quanmian laping 全面拉平
quanmian tuiguang 全面推廣
Qujiaqiao 屈家橋
Qunxing *she* 群星社
quzhang 區長

Ren Zhengang 任振綱
renzheng 仁政
Roushipin chang 肉食品廠
san san zhi 三三制
sanba duiwu 三八隊伍
Sandun 三墩
sange yiqian 三个一千
sangeng 三耕
sangong 散工
sanjiang 三江
Sanlintang 三林塘
sanliu 三留
Sanmenliu 三門溜
sanqiu 三秋
sanxia 三夏
Sanxing *she* 三星社
Sanzao 三竈
Shaan-Gan-Ning 陝甘寧
shachuan 沙船
Shagang 沙岡
Shajing *cun* 沙井村
Shang Yang 商鞅
shang zhongnong 上中農
Shanghai *xian* 上海縣
shangmian xialai zuo gongzuo
　　上面下來做工作
shangnong 上農
shangpinliang 商品糧
Shangta 商榻
Shanyin *gongshe* 山陰公社
Shazhou *xian* 沙洲縣
she/xiang ban gongye 社/鄉辦工業
shehui xingtai 社會形態
Shen Baoshun 沈寶順
Shen Fengying 沈鳳英
Shen Huaming 沈華明
Shen Jinzhu 沈金珠
Shen Shuijin 沈水金
Shen Shunchang 沈順昌
Shen Songlin 沈松林
Shen Xuetang 沈雪堂

Shen Yindi 沈引娣
Shen Youliang 沈友良
sheng 升
shengchandui duizhang 生產隊隊長
Shengjiaqiao 盛家橋
Shenjia *cun* 沈家村
Shenjiada 沈家埭
Shenjiahang 沈家行
Shenjiazhai 沈家宅
Shenshi nongshu 沈氏農書
Shenxiang 沈巷
Shenxianglang *cun* 沈巷郎村
Shenxin shachang 申新紗廠
Shenzhuang 沈莊
shi 市
shi 石
shidian 試點
shidu guimo 適度規模
Shigangmen 石岡門
shijin 市斤
shijing 市井
Shimen *cun* 石門村
shizhen 市鎮
Shizilin 獅子林
shizu 實租
shoushi 首事
shuangqiang 雙搶
Shunde *xian* 順德縣
Shunyi *xian* 順義縣
shuoshu 說書
Sibeichai *cun* 寺北柴村
sihang 絲行
Situan 四團
Song Mingjiang 宋明江
songbang 鬆綁
Songjiang fangta xiaoxue
　　松江方塔小學
Songjiang *fu* (*xian*) 松江府 (縣)
Songling *zhen* 松陵鎮
sui 歲
Sujiaqiao 蘇家橋

Sun Zhongyue 孫中岳
Sunan moshi 蘇南模式
Sunjia xiang 孫家鄉
Sunjiada 孫家埭
Sunjiaqiao 孫家橋
Suo chang 鎖廠
Suqian *xian* 宿遷縣
Suzhou *diqu* (*fu*) 蘇州地區(府)
Tai-pu 太浦
Taicang *xian* (*zhou*) 太倉縣(州)
Taihu 太湖
Taihu *ting* 太湖廳
Taiping *xiang* 太平鄉
Tairiqiao 泰日橋
Taizhou 泰州
Tan Meijuan 談美娟
Tan Xirong 譚錫榮
tanding rudi 攤丁入地
Tanghang 唐行
Tangwan 塘灣
Tangxi *xiang* 塘西鄉
Tanjiaqiao 譚家橋
Tanziwan 潭子灣
Tao Xu 陶煦
Tao Zongyi 陶宗儀
Taozhai 陶宅
Tian Junchuan 田俊川
tiankou 田口
Tianmashan 天馬山
Tiantong'an 天通庵
tiantou zhi 田頭制
tiaodao 挑稻
Tiaoshanying 眺山營
tiaoxian gongzuo 條綫工作
tiaoxie 挑[塝]
tiaoyang 挑秧
tielunji 鐵輪機
Tinglin *zhen* 亭林鎮
Tingxin *gongshe* 亭新公社
Tong Jiahong 童家洪
tonggou 統購

tongxiao 統銷
Tongzhi 同治
Tongzhou 通州
touxian 投獻
Touzongmiao 頭總廟
tu 圖
Tu Pinshan 屠品山
tubu 土布
Wa chang 襪廠
wahe shuhe 挖河, 疏河
Waigang 外岡
Waiqin 外秦
waizhang 外帳
Wang Caiying 王彩英
Wang Deming 王德明
Wang Penliang 王盆良
Wang Shunzhong 王順中
Wang Yongquan 王永全
Wang Zanzhou 王贊周
Wang(ting)-Yu(shan)he
  望(亭)—虞(山)河
Wangjiahang 王家行
Wangquan *cun* 望泉村
Wangxianqiao 望仙橋
Wanli 萬歷
Wanxiang 萬祥
Weixian 濰縣
Wei Guoqian 魏國簽
Weihe 渭河
weitian 圍田
weituo jiagong 委託加工
weixingdi 衛星地
wen 文
Wenzhou 溫州
Wu Achang 吳阿昌
Wu Genyu 吳根餘
Wu Hugen 吳虎根
Wu Jinfa 吳金發
Wu Kuan 吳寬
Wu Mingchang 吳明昌
Wu Renyu 吳仁餘

Wu Shunyu 吳順餘
Wu Xiaomei 吳小妹
Wu Xinquan 吳信全
Wu Yucai 吳雨才
Wu Yungang 吳雲剛
wuda caichan 五大財產
Wudian *cun* 吳店村
Wuhui 吳會
Wujiang *xian* 吳江縣
Wujin *xian* 武進縣
Wukong *xiang* 悟空鄉
Wunijing 烏泥涇
Wuquangang 吳泉港
Wusongjiang 吳淞江
Wusongkou 吳淞口
Wuxi *xian* 無錫縣
Wuxian 吳縣
Wuxing *dadui* 五星大隊
Wuyishan 武夷山
Wuyue 吳越
Xi Tianran 奚天然
Xi Xiufang 奚秀芳
xiabu 夏布
xiafang zhishi qingnian 下放知識青年
Xianfeng 咸豐
xiang 鄉
Xiang Rong 向榮
xiangbao 鄉保
Xiangcheng *xian* 項城縣
xiangtou di 項頭地
xiangyue 鄉約
xianong 下農
Xianshi 縣市
xiao changnian 小長年
xiao pingjun 小平均
xiao shitang 小食堂
xiao siqing 小四清
xiaoban 小辦
Xiaochanggang 小長港
Xiaodingxiang 小丁巷
Xiaoguanpu 小官浦

xiaomie danjidao 消滅單季稻
xiaonong jingji 小農經濟
Xiaoping 小坪
xiaoshimin 小市民
Xiaoyu *xiang* 小漠鄉
Xiaozong 孝宗
Xiasha 下沙
xiashou 夏收
xiazheng 夏徵
xiazhihui 瞎指揮
xiazhong 夏種
xibo 錫箔
Xicang 西倉
Xida 西埭
Xie Xuefang 謝雪芳
xiexia 歇夏
xiliang 細糧
Xilihangbang 西里行浜
Ximen 西門
Xin Tongyang yunhe 新通揚運河
Xinchang 新場
Xindu *zhen* 新瀆鎮
Xingang 新港
Xingguo *xian* 興國縣
Xinjing 新涇
Xinglong *dadui* 興隆大隊
xingzhengzu 行政組
Xinmin *cun* 新民村
Xinnong *dadui* 新農大隊
Xinnong *xiang* 新農鄉
Xinxing 新興
Xinyang *xian* 新陽縣
Xinyu *dadui* 新餘大隊
Xishe 西庫
Xiushui *xian* 秀水縣
Xu Gongji 許公記
Xu Jiabi 徐家碧
Xu Liang 徐艮
Xu Mujin 徐木金
Xu Niansheng 許年生
Xu Qifan 徐起凡

Xu Yaoqin 許耀勤
Xuantong 宣統
Xubushanqiao 許步山橋
Xue Baobao 薛寶寶
Xue Baoren 薛寶仁
Xue Baoyi 薛寶義
Xue Bingrong 薛炳榮
Xue Bulin 薛補林
Xue Chunhua 薛春華
Xue Delong 薛德龍
Xue Gentao 薛根桃
Xue Huilin 薛會林
Xue Minghui 薛明輝
Xue Peigen 薛培根
Xue Shunquan 薛順泉
Xue Renxing 薛仁興
Xue Xiansheng 薛咸生
Xuedian *zhen* 薛典鎮
Xuejiada 薛家垛
Xuejian *xiang* 薛間鄉
xuekuan 學款
Xujiahang 徐家行
Xujialong 徐家衖
xumu 畜牧
Xuzhou 徐州
xuzu 虛租
Yancheng *xian* 鹽城縣
Yang Chengzhang 楊成長
Yang Fengying 楊鳳英
Yang Gendi 楊根棣
Yang Guiming 楊桂明
Yang Hongqiang 楊洪強
Yang Ji 楊計
Yang Jinxiu 楊金秀
Yang Pinjuan 楊品娟
Yang Shougen 楊壽根
Yang Tusheng 楊土生
Yang Weisheng 楊味生
Yang Xiaofa 楊小發
Yang Xingcai 楊杏財
Yang Xiutang 楊秀堂

Yang Yinlong 楊銀龍
Yang Yuan 楊源
Yangjiahang 楊家行
Yangjiaqiao 楊家橋
Yangjing 洋涇
Yangjinggang 洋涇港
Yangmuqiao 楊木橋
Yangzhou 揚州
Yanjiashang 嚴家上
Yanli *xiang* 堰里鄉
Yanqiao *xiang* 堰橋鄉
Yantietang 鹽鐵塘
Yaojing 遙涇
yaoshengji 搖繩機
Ye Shilin 葉士林
Ye Yajuan 葉亞娟
yeshi dianli 業食佃力
yi da er gong 一大二公
Yicunba 益村壩
yijia 議價
yiliang weigang 以糧為綱
Yin Fengsheng 尹鳳生
ying chuqu 硬出去
ying gutou 硬骨頭
yingyang bo 營養鉢
yinshi ye 飲食業
Yinshua jijie chang 印刷機械廠
Yishan 宜山
yiwu gong 義務工
yizi dailao 以資代勞
Yongzheng 雍正
youmian xianzhi 優免限制
yu 圩
yuan 元
Yuan 元
Yuan Shikai 袁世凱
Yuanhe *xian* 元和縣
yue da yue hao 越大越好
Yuepu 月浦
Yunlin *xiang* 雲林鄉
Yuqi *zhen* 玉祁鎮

yuqu 圩區
yutian 圩田
Yuying tang 育嬰堂
zeren tian 責任田
Zhagang 閘港
Zhang Bamei 張八妹
Zhang Bingyu 張炳餘
Zhang Boren 張伯仁
Zhang Chonglou 張重樓
Zhang Chunyu 張春餘
Zhang Dingxin 張鼎新
Zhang Hongxing 張洪興
Zhang Houxin 張厚昕
Zhang Huosheng 張火生
Zhang Jian 張謇
Zhang Jinlong 張金龍
Zhang Lüxiang 張履祥
Zhang Rui 張瑞
Zhang Shousheng 張壽生
Zhang Shunyong 張順勇
Zhang Xiulong 張秀龍
Zhang Yinlong 張銀龍
Zhang Zhenyun 張正雲
zhangfang 帳房
Zhanghuabang 張華浜
Zhangjiaqiao 張家橋
Zhangliantang 章練塘
Zhao Limin 趙立民
Zhao Lin 趙霖
Zhao Ren 趙仁
Zhao Shaoting 趙紹廷
Zhao Yuxian 趙玉仙
Zhao Ziyang 趙子揚
zhaotian paiyi 照田派役
zhaotie 找貼
Zhaotun 趙囤
Zhaowen *xian* 昭文縣
Zhaoxi 苕溪
Zhaoxiang 趙巷
Zhaqiao 柵橋

zhen 鎮
Zhengda *gongsi* 正大公司
Zhengde 正德
Zhengding *xian* 正定縣
Zhengxiang 鄭巷
Zhenjiang 鎮江
Zhenru 眞如
Zhenyang *xian* 鎮洋縣
Zhenze *xian* 震澤縣
Zhenzong 眞宗
Zhexi 浙西
zhigong 職工
Zhihetang 至和塘
Zhili 直隸
zhishi fenzi 知識分子
zhishu 支書
zhizaoju 織造局
zhizhong kouliangdi
   de wugong renkou
   只種口糧地
   的務工人口
Zhongda 中埭
Zhongde 種德
zhongji 中機
Zhongxing meikuang 中興煤礦
zhongzhuan 中專
Zhongzi *dui* 種籽隊
Zhongzichang *dadui* 種籽場大隊
Zhou Chen 周忱
Zhou Fulin 周復林
Zhou Jianhua 周建華
Zhou Kongjiao 周孔教
Zhou Weimin 周偉芪
Zhou Zhenhua 周振華
Zhoujiaqiao 周家橋
Zhoupu 周浦
Zhouxiangshang 周巷上
Zhouxin *zhen* 周新鎮
Zhu Guozhen 朱國禎
Zhu Wenjie 朱文傑

Zhu Yaoliang 朱耀民
Zhua geming cu shengchan lingdao
 xiaozu
 抓革命促生產領導
 小組
Zhuang Yougong 莊有恭
zhuanyehu 專業戶
zhuanzheng 轉正
Zhudi 諸翟
Zhujiajiao 朱家角
Zhujiaqiao 朱家橋
Zhujing 朱涇
zhupai 竹牌
zhutang xiuyu 築塘修圩

Zhuxing gongshe 朱行公社
zibao gongping 自報公評
ziran cun 自然村
zong chanzhi 總產值
zong shouru 總收入
zonglingdao 總領導
zongpu 縱浦
zoutou wulu 走投無路
zuan chuqu 鑽出去
zuozhai 坐債
zuzhang 組長
zuzhi shenghuo 組織生活
zuzhi anpai 組織安排

INDEX

Index

In this index an "f" after a number indicates a separate reference on the next page, and an "ff" indicates separate references on the next two pages. A continuous discussion over two or more pages is indicated by a span of page numbers, e.g., "57–59." *Passim* is used for a cluster of references in close but not consecutive sequence.

Adachi Keiji, 89n, 131
Administrative village, 176f, 193
Agricultural Implements Factory (Huayang commune), 253f, 272, 279
Agricultural tools: and rural industry, 253
Agriculture, 2–5, 332; dry vs. wet, 31, 41, 43; history, in China, 77–78; growth in output, early 20th century, 137; PRC's state control over, 180–86, 194; 1980s reforms in, 195–96; as sideline activity, 213–14, 215, 218–19, 289; feminization of, 213f; growth vs. development in, in PRC, 222–51 *passim*; and rural industries, 253, 265; and family farming, 307f, 320–21; technology, 327. *See also* Cash crops; Cropping patterns; Crop production; Crop yields; Family farming/production; Farm size; Labor; Managerial agriculture/farms; Modernization, agricultural; Technology; *and specific crops by name*
Alfalfa, 99, 131, 228
Amano Motonosuke, 49f, 157
Anhui, 48, 123
Appropriate scale economies, 247–48, 321
Army: and peasantry, 325f, 331
Arrigo, Linda, 42n
Asiatic mode of production, 330

Bai Chengzhi, 159
Baihejiang (river), 34
Banks, 110
Bao Shichen, 89

Baodi county (Hebei), 36, 128n, 152, 175
Baojia system, 38, 155, 192. *See also* Li-jia system
Baoshan county (Jiangsu), 22n, 48n, 87
Baozheng system, 155, 175
Barley, 50, 53, 99, 125, 241; under collectivization, 225, 228–30, 231, 240, 243, 271, 280f, 316
Batuan (Chuansha county), 119
Beancake fertilizer, 88–90, 101, 130–32, 139f, 222–23
Beattie, Hilary, 107n
Beijing, 45
Bell, Lynda, 126, 127n, 134
Biaobu cloth, 45
"Big four cleans" movement, 276
Boserup, Ester, 11, 332
Boxer Rebellion, 43
Bray, Francesca, 327
Brenner, Robert, 306
Bricks and Tiles Factory (Huayang commune), 257
Brigade industries, 252f, 258, 265, 283, 291, 293f, 318. *See also* Industrialization, rural
Brigades, *see* Production brigades
Broad beans, 99
Buck, John Lossing, 42n, 49, 51, 57, 126, 138f; on agricultural labor, 59, 65f, 84, 127n
Bureaucracy (imperial), 330f, 333
Bureaucratism, 185
Byrd, William, 261

Cadres, 271–78 *passim*, 292–93, 321f
California: agricultural labor in, 66

Library of Congress Cataloging-in-Publication Data

Huang, Philip C., 1940–
The peasant family and rural development in the Yangzi Delta,
1350–1988/Philip C. C. Huang.
    p. cm.
Includes bibliographical references.
ISBN 0-8047-1787-7 (alk. paper)—ISBN 0-8047-1788-5
(pbk. : alk. paper)
    1. Rural development—China—Yangzi River—Delta. 2. Rural families—
China—Yangzi River—Delta. 3. Yangzi River (China)—Delta—Economic
conditions. I. Title.
HN740. Y36H83   1990
307.1'412'09512—DC20   89-49546
                                                          CIP

⊗ This book is printed on acid-free paper